THE

A HABITAT FOR

SILICON

INNOVATION AND

VALLEY

ENTREPRENEURSHIP

EDGE

THE
SILICON
VALLEY
EDGE

A HABITAT FOR

INNOVATION AND

ENTREPRENEURSHIP

EDITED BY

CHONG-MOON LEE

WILLIAM F. MILLER

MARGUERITE GONG HANCOCK

AND HENRY S. ROWEN

STANFORD UNIVERSITY PRESS · STANFORD, CALIFORNIA

Stanford University Press
Stanford, California

Library of Congress Cataloging-in-Publication Data

The Silicon Valley Edge : a habitat for innovation
and entrepreneurship / edited by Chong-Moon
Lee . . . [et al.].
   p. cm.
Includes bibliographical references and index.
ISBN 0-8047-4062-3 (alk paper) —
ISBN 0-8047-4063-1 (paper : alk. paper)
   1. High technology industries — California —
Santa Clara County.   2. New business
enterprises — California — Santa Clara County.
3. Entrepreneurship — California — Santa Clara
County.   4. Santa Clara County (Calif.) —
Economic conditions.   5. Santa Clara County
(Calif.) — Social conditions.   I. Lee, Chong-Moon.
HC107.c22 s3965 2000
330.9794'73 — dc21   00-056340

⊖ This book is printed on acid-free, recycled paper.

Original printing 2000
Last figure below indicates year of this printing:
09 08 07 06 05 04 03 02 01 00

Printed in the United States of America

PREFACE

Most contemporary societies are interested in economic growth as a path to a higher standard of living and a better quality of life. There are essentially three ways to achieve economic growth: 1) by increasing and improving the factor inputs of labor and capital, 2) through trade and comparative advantage (specialization), and 3) through innovation and entrepreneurship. Of course, these three approaches are not mutually exclusive and may reinforce each other. The third approach, however—the pursuit of innovation and entrepreneurship—has recently attracted particular interest worldwide, as countries recognize that it is through entrepreneurship, especially high-tech entrepreneurship, that they can participate in the development of new products, new markets, and new industries, and thereby enter the high-growth sectors of the world economy. Special attention has been focused on the United States, where exceptional job growth and wealth creation have been driven by an entrepreneurial information economy composed of the information industries and "informationalized" older industries.

The authors and editors of this book, the first in a series on entrepreneurship worldwide, believe that it is important to study the experiences of entrepreneurial regions so that entrepreneurs and policy makers may select the best features of different regions to advance entrepreneurship in their own regions. We have chosen to focus on Silicon Valley in this first book for two reasons. First, Silicon Valley is considered by many outside the United States, as well as within it, to be the quintessential example of an entrepreneurial region. Second, as Valley residents, we receive hundreds, perhaps thousands, of visitors each year who ask questions about how Silicon Valley works. We expect this book to contribute to their understanding of the unique qualities of this region.

In particular, we focus not just on the entrepreneurs themselves, but on the business environment or "habitat" for high-tech entrepreneurship in Silicon Valley, a habitat geared toward the creation of new firms and new industries. This approach emphasizes the importance of start-ups to the Valley economy. Although large, established companies play an essential role in the economy and develop many advances in technology, as well as new products, it is generally recognized that they are less likely to develop radical or disruptive technologies that create sea changes in industries or create whole new industries. The history of two of the fastest-moving technologies, biotechnology and information technologies, bear witness to this.

The book and series editors are also involved in studying and working with entrepreneurial regions in other parts of the world. We believe that it is equally important to explore their experiences for the betterment of all, and future books will feature entrepreneurial regions worldwide.

Chong-Moon Lee
William F. Miller
Series Editors

ACKNOWLEDGMENTS

Our story of Silcon Valley is the result of our partnership with many people here. We feel fortunate to have collaborated with 25 academic and industry leaders who shared a wealth of experience and insight. We also thank the many colleagues, students, and business practitioners who contributed ideas and lively debate to our Silicon Valley seminars throughout 1998 and 1999.

Special gratitude goes to the current and former staff of the Asia/Pacific Research Center, including Waka Takahashi Brown, Sue Hayashi, and Rafael Ulate, for their steadfast administrative support, and to Victoria Tomkinson for expert publication assistance.

Far from least, we express appreciation to Laura Comay of Stanford University Press, whose vision and steady editorial hand made this a much better book.

Finally, we thank the Chong-Moon Lee Foundation for the generous support that made this whole venture possible.

Chong-Moon Lee
William F. Miller
Marguerite Gong Hancock
Henry S. Rowen

CONTENTS

FIGURES, TABLES, AND MAP

FIGURES

xiii

TABLES

MAP

CONTRIBUTOR BIOGRAPHIES

JAMES D. ATWELL is a partner at Summit Partners in Palo Alto. Prior to joining Summit, he held a number of leadership positions at Pricewaterhouse-Coopers LLP, most recently as Global Managing Partner of Private Equities. He was also a member of the firm's board of directors and Managing Partner of the San Jose/Menlo Park offices from 1994 to 1998. With twenty years of experience in public accounting, the last seventeen years at Pricewaterhouse-Coopers, he has served numerous companies and assisted in more than twenty initial public offerings. His first-hand experience with emerging technology companies and his accounting expertise have made him a regular speaker at conferences, at training courses, and on television. He is also on the executive board of Santa Clara University's Board of Fellows, and the Economic Development Impact Board at Stanford. He received his bachelor of science and commerce degree from Santa Clara University.

DADO P. BANATAO is a venture partner at the Mayfield Fund. A successful Silicon Valley entrepreneur, he specializes in identifying investment opportunities involving semiconductor and software solutions for telecommunications, client-server computing, and consumer electronics. He currently serves as chairman of Cyras Systems, Inc., Marvell Semiconductor, Inc., New-Moon.com, NewPort Communications, Inc., Silicon Access Technology Inc., SiRF Technology, Inc., Stream Machine, and Sandcraft, Inc. Before joining the Mayfield Fund, he founded three Silicon Valley semiconductor companies, and is credited with developing several key semiconductor technologies during a career that has included positions at National Semiconductor, Seeq Technologies, Intersil, and Commodore International.

JOHN SEELY BROWN is Chief Scientist of Xerox Corporation and director of its Palo Alto Research Center (PARC). At Xerox, he has expanded the role of corporate research to include organizational learning, ethnographies of the workplace, complex adaptive systems, and techniques for unfreezing the corporate mind. A member of the National Academy of Education and Fellow of the American Association for Artificial Intelligence, he also serves on numerous advisory boards and boards of directors. His books include *Seeing Differently: Insights on Innovation* and *The Social Life of Information* (co-authored with Paul Duguid), and in 1999 he received the Holland Award for the best paper published in *Research Technology Management Magazine.*

EMILIO J. CASTILLA is a doctoral candidate in the Department of Sociology at Stanford University, specializing in economic sociology, organizations, and comparative sociology. He received his master's degrees in sociology from Stanford University and business analysis from Lancaster University, and also holds bachelor's and master's degrees in economics from the University of Barcelona. His most recent book examines advanced quantitative methodologies for the analysis of longitudinal data in the social sciences. An active researcher and teacher, he received the Cilker Teaching Award in 1999 and the Stanford Centennial Teaching Award in 1998. Currently, he studies the influence of social networks on intra-organizational career paths and employee performance. He is also working on a comparative network analysis of venture capital firms in Silicon Valley and Route 128.

JOHN C. DEAN is President and CEO of Silicon Valley Bancshares and Chairman of Silicon Valley Bank, its wholly owned subsidiary, the only national provider of banking services to emerging stage technology and life science companies. In the course of his twenty-year banking career, he has held president and CEO positions at several other major financial institutions, including Pacific First Bank in Seattle, First Interstate Bank of Washington, and First Interstate Bank of Oklahoma. A former Peace Corps volunteer in Western Samoa, he earned a bachelor's degree in economics from Holy Cross College and an MBA from the Wharton School at the University of Pennsylvania.

PAUL DUGUID, a historian and social theorist affiliated with the University of California, Berkeley, and the Xerox Palo Alto Research Center (PARC), is co-author of *The Social Life of Information*. His commitment to multidisciplinary work has led him to collaborate throughout his career with social and computer scientists, economists, linguists, management theorists, and social psychologists. His articles and reviews have been published in the *Times Literary Supplement*, the *Nation*, and the *Threepenny Review*, as well as in a broad array of scholarly journals in fields including anthropology, business and business history, cognitive science, computer science, design, education, economic history, human-computer interaction, management, organization theory, and wine history.

KEVIN A. FONG is a Managing Partner of the Mayfield Fund. An entrepreneur and venture capital leader in the communications industry, he directs Mayfield's communications group, which invests in wireless, broadband equipment and communications services, optical communications, and digital television. He serves on the boards of a number of companies, including Geocast Networks, Legato Systems, Burst Networks, and InterWave. A nationally recognized philanthropist, he co-founded Silicon Valley Social Ventures (SV2), and is an invited member of the American Leadership Forum. He holds MBA and master of science degrees in electrical engineering from Stanford University, and a bachelor's in electrical engineering from the University of California, Berkeley.

THOMAS J. FRIEL, President of Heidrick & Struggles's Global Practices Division, directs the worldwide industry, functional, and leadership practices of this internationally recognized recruitment firm. He also serves as a member of the firm's board of directors. Since joining in 1979, he has established the firm's Silicon Valley presence; co-founded its International Technology Practice, serving clients in computer, software, telecommunications, instrumentation, defense electronics, and related high-technology industries; and launched its Asia Pacific offices. Listed among the top 200 executive recruiters in the world by *The Global 200 Executive Recruiters*, he also received in 1998 the John Struggles Partnership Award, the firm's most significant honor. An honors graduate of Purdue University, where he majored in industrial engineering and operations research, he also holds an MBA from Stanford University.

JAMES F. GIBBONS received his bachelor of science degree from Northwestern University, and his Ph.D. from Stanford, where he subsequently joined the faculty. In 1964, he was appointed professor of Electrical Engineering, and named Reid Weaver Dennis Professor of Electrical Engineering in 1983. From 1984 to 1996, he served as Dean of the School of Engineering. His principal research and teaching interests focus on semiconductor device analysis, process physics, and technology. In 1957, he began working at the Shockley Semiconductor Laboratories, where silicon processing was initiated in Silicon Valley, and he has consulted widely in the semiconductor electronics industry for the past 40 years. He sits on the boards of Lockheed Martin Corporation, El Paso Natural Gas, and Cisco Systems, as well as several start-up ventures.

ELLEN GRANOVETTER received her master's degree in urban planning from Johns Hopkins University. She has served as project director, research analyst, and proposal/report writer on a variety of research projects, ranging from the causes of homelessness to the demand for continuing education from industry. She currently works as a freelance writer and researcher.

MARK GRANOVETTER is Joan Butler Ford Professor in the Department of Sociology at Stanford University. He received a Ph.D. from Harvard University, and an honorary doctorate from Stockholm University. He has published many articles in professional journals on social networks, inequality, and economic sociology. Currently, he directs a research project funded by Stanford's Bechtel Initiative, on the "Networks of Silicon Valley." He is also working on two book manuscripts: *Society and Economy: The Social Construction of Economic Institutions*, forthcoming from Harvard University Press, and, in collaboration with Patrick McGuire and Michael Schwartz, *The Social Construction of Industry: Electricity in the United States, 1880–1925*, forthcoming from Cambridge University Press.

MARGUERITE GONG HANCOCK manages the Silicon Valley Networks Project at the Asia/Pacific Research Center at Stanford University. A specialist on government-business relations in information technology development, she has served as Director of Network Research for the Computer Industry Project at Stanford's Graduate School of Business, and Research Associate at the East Asia Business Program of the University of Michigan. She received a B.A. in humanities and East Asian studies from Brigham Young University and an M.A. from Harvard University in East Asian studies. Her Ph.D. work at Tufts University's The Fletcher School of Law and Diplomacy focused on computer industry development in China. Her current research centers on Silicon Valley and regions of innovation and entrepreneurship in Asia.

THOMAS F. HELLMANN is Assistant Professor of Strategic Management at Stanford University's Graduate School of Business. His research and teaching focus on strategic management, and entrepreneurship and venture capital, examining both the theoretical foundations of the industry and its empirical regularities. He obtained his Ph.D. from Stanford's Department of Economics, where he worked and co-authored with Professor Joseph Stiglitz, former head of the Council of Economic Advisors under President Clinton and subsequently chief economist of the World Bank. He obtained his bachelor's degree in economics at the London School of Economics. He has lectured and consulted extensively on entrepreneurship and venture capital across the United States, Europe, Asia, and Latin America.

DOUG HENTON is the founder and President of Collaborative Economics in Palo Alto, specializing in collaborative projects to improve regional competitiveness and economic development. Previously, he spent a decade as Assistant Director of SRI International's Center for Economic Competitiveness, where he directed local strategy projects in diverse regions, including Florida, California, Texas, Hong Kong, Japan, and China. He has provided consulting assistance to many organizations, including the President's Commission on Industrial Competitiveness, the U.S. Department of Commerce, the James Irvine Foundation, and the Heinz Endowments. An active speaker at interactive "Civic Entrepreneur Workshops," he has also co-authored a book, *Grassroots Leaders for the New Economy*, with Kim Walesh and John Melville. He holds a bachelor's degree in political science and economics from Yale University and a master's degree in public policy from the University of California, Berkeley.

HOKYU HWANG is a doctoral candidate in the Department of Sociology at Stanford University, specializing in comparative, economic, and political sociology, organizations, and development. He received his master's degree in sociology from Stanford and his bachelor's from the University of California, Berkeley. He is currently a teaching fellow at Stanford, and his recent research covers social networks in Silicon Valley, university collaboration with industry, and commerce in legal services. For his dissertation, he is studying changes in international development practices by focusing on national development planning. In 2000, he was honored with Stanford's Littlefield International Graduate Fellowship.

CRAIG W. JOHNSON is Chairman of Venture Law Group. A graduate of Yale University and a former Peace Corps volunteer in Ethiopia, he worked with Burroughs as a systems computer programmer, and subsequently received his law degree from Stanford University. He joined the Palo Alto law firm of Wilson, Mosher & Sonsini (now Wilson Sonsini Goodrich & Rosati), and in 1993 co-founded Venture Law Group. Among the companies his firm has helped to start are Yahoo!, eToys, Cerent, Foundry Networks, Garage.com, Phone.com, Chemdex, Hotmail, Drugstore.com, and Netcentives. In 1997, he was recognized by *Business Week* as one of Silicon Valley's top 25 "movers and shakers," and in 1999 by *Red Herring* as one of the Valley's nine "top power brokers."

STEVE JURVETSON is a managing director of Draper Fisher Jurvetson. He served on the board of directors of Hotmail from its inception through its acquisition by Microsoft, and was the founding venture investor in Kana, Interwoven, and Lightwave Microsystems. Formerly an R&D engineer at Hewlett-Packard, he has also worked at the Center for Materials Research, Mostek, Apple, NeXT, and Bain & Co. At Stanford University, he finished his bachelor's degree in 2½ years, graduating first in his class, and subsequently earned a master's in electrical engineering and an MBA. Recently named "The Valley's Sharpest VC" on the cover of *Business 2.0*, he was also chosen by the *San Francisco Chronicle* and *San Francisco Examiner* as one of "the ten people expected to have the greatest impact on the Bay Area in the early part of the 21st Century."

E. FLOYD KVAMME is a partner at Kleiner Perkins Caufield & Byers, a high-technology venture capital firm, and currently sits on the boards of Brio Technology, Gemfire, Harmonic, National Semiconductor, Photon Dynamics, Power Integrations, and Silicon Genesis. He is chairman of Empower America and is a director of the Technology Network and National Venture Capital Association. One of five members who began National Semiconductor in 1967, he helped to build it into a billion-dollar company, first as General Manager of Semiconductor Operations, and later as President of the National Advanced Systems computer subsidiary. He has also served as Executive Vice President of Sales and Marketing for Apple Computer. He holds two degrees in electrical engineering, a bachelor's from the University of California, Berkeley and a master's from Syracuse University.

CHRISTOPHE LÉCUYER, a graduate of the Ecole Normale Supérieure in Paris, received his Ph.D. in history from Stanford University. He is currently a postdoctoral fellow at the Dibner Institute for the History of Science and Technology at the Massachusetts Institute of Technology, and is preparing a book on the history of Silicon Valley. He has written extensively on university-industry relations and the history of medical and scientific instrumentation. Among his publications are "MIT, Progressive Reform, and 'Industrial Service,' 1890–1920" (*HSPS*, 1995) and, in collaboration with Timothy Lenoir, "Instrument Makers and Discipline Builders: The Case of Nuclear Magnetic Resonance" (*Perspectives on Science*, 1995).

CHONG-MOON LEE serves as a consulting professor at the Asia/Pacific Research Center at Stanford University, as well as Chairman and CEO of AmBex Venture Group, and Chairman Emeritus of S3, Inc. Previously, he founded Diamond Multimedia Systems, an internationally successful producer of PC graphics accelerator products. As Vice Chairman of the United States National Committee for Pacific Economic Cooperation Council (US-PECC), he chaired the Organizing Committee for the inaugural U.S. and Asia/Pacific Information Technology Summit. A native of Seoul and a naturalized U.S. citizen, he has a diverse background in education, cultural exchange, business, and philanthropy. His current research interests include Korean entrepreneurship and the networks of Silicon Valley. In 1993 and 1994, he was a finalist for *Inc.* magazine's Entrepreneur of the Year in the Northern California region.

REGIS M^cKENNA is chairman of The McKenna Group, an international consulting firm specializing in the application of information and telecommunications technologies to business strategies. He is also a venture partner of the venture capital firm Kleiner Perkins Caufield & Byers. Over the past 30 years, he has worked with a number of entrepreneurial start-ups, including AOL, Apple, Compaq, Electronic Arts, Genentech, Intel, Linear Technology, Lotus, Microsoft, National Semiconductor, Silicon Graphics, and 3Com. In the last decade, he has consulted on strategic marketing and business issues to firms in the United States, Japan, and Europe. The author of four books— *The Regis Touch, Who's Afraid of Big Blue, Relationship Marketing,* and *Real Time: Preparing for the Age of the Never Satisfied Customer*—he lectures extensively on the social and market effects of technological change. He attended Saint Vincent College and Duquesne University.

WILLIAM F. MILLER is Herbert Hoover Professor of Public and Private Management emeritus at Stanford University's Graduate School of Business, where he also co-directs two executive education programs on strategy and entrepreneurship in the high-technology sector. Formerly Stanford's Vice President and Provost, he also served as President and CEO of SRI International, as well as Chairman of the Board, CEO, and a founder of the David Sarnoff Research Center (now the Sarnoff Corporation). He has served on many government commissions, directed several nonprofit organizations, and is currently actively involved, through speaking engagements and research, in developing new information infrastructures, both in Silicon Valley and internationally. He serves on several boards of directors of Silicon Valley companies. He studied at Purdue University, where he received a B.S., M.S., Ph.D., and D.Sc., *honoris causa.*

T. MICHAEL NEVENS is a director in McKinsey & Company's Silicon Valley office, and Managing Partner of the firm's Global High Tech Industry Practice. Working primarily with international clients in the computer, software, networking, semiconductor, and telecommunications industries, he focuses on revitalizing core businesses, creating new business, market entry, acquisitions, mergers, and alliances. He has written on these issues in the *Wall Street Journal, Financial Times*, and *Harvard Business Review*, and speaks regularly to industry groups. Prior to joining McKinsey, he held several staff positions with the U.S. House of Representatives, and also worked as a consultant with Arthur Andersen & Company's computer systems practice. A graduate of the University of Notre Dame, he also received a master's degree in industrial administration from the Krannert School of Purdue University.

HENRY S. ROWEN is Director of the Asia/Pacific Research Center at Stanford University. He is also Senior Fellow at the Hoover Institution, and Professor of Public Policy and Management emeritus at Stanford's Graduate School of Business. An expert on international security, economic development, and Asian economics and politics, he served as Assistant Secretary of Defense for International Security Affairs in the U.S. Department of Defense from 1989 to 1991. He was Chairman of the National Intelligence Council from 1981 to 1983; president of the RAND Corporation from 1968 to 1972; and Assistant Director, U.S. Bureau of the Budget, from 1965 to 1966. He is a widely published author, whose current research focuses on centers of innovation and entrepreneurship around the world, economic growth prospects for the developing world, and political and economic change in East Asia.

ANNALEE SAXENIAN is Professor of Regional Development in the Department of City and Regional Planning at the University of California, Berkeley. She is internationally recognized for her research on technology regions in the United States and Europe, and has written extensively about innovation and regional development, urbanization and the technology industry, and the organization of labor markets in Silicon Valley. Her book *Regional Advantage: Culture and Competition in Silicon Valley and Route 128* received the Association of American Publishers award for the best professional and scholarly book of 1994. She holds a B.A. in economics from Williams College, an M.C.P. in city and regional planning from the University of California, Berkeley, and a Ph.D. in political science from the Massachusetts Institute of Technology.

THE SILICON VALLEY EDGE

A HABITAT FOR INNOVATION AND ENTREPRENEURSHIP

1

The Silicon Valley Habitat

CHONG-MOON LEE, WILLIAM F. MILLER,

MARGUERITE GONG HANCOCK,

AND HENRY S. ROWEN

Silicon Valley has many stories—true tales of brilliant (and often lucky) entrepreneurs turned billionaires, epics of the rise (and sometimes fall) of new companies. On January 1, 1939, two classmates at Stanford University launched from a one-car garage in Palo Alto an electronic measuring device company. Six decades later their company, Hewlett-Packard, led the Valley in revenues, with $47.1 billion in 1999. In April 1994, another pair of Stanford students worked during their spare time to build "Yet Another Hierarchical Officious Oracle." Today their firm is called simply Yahoo! and is the first and leading web search engine, with a market capitalization of $70 billion.

These now legendary examples are only two episodes in Silicon Valley's rise during the last half of the twentieth century. Indeed, for every significant advancement in information technology, a company born and grown in Silicon Valley is a leader: integrated circuits (National Semiconductor, Intel, Advanced Micro Devices), personal computers (Apple), workstations (HP, Sun Microsystems), 3D graphics (Silicon Graphics), database software (Oracle), and network computing (3Com, Cisco Systems). And, in the recent Internet boom, the Valley's preeminence has only been extended. Think of Netscape, Excite@Home, and eBay. This, then, is the Valley's strength: despite rising costs in land and labor, increasing global competition, and periodic downturns in the business environment, Silicon Valley has sustained its leading edge in

1

wave after wave of information technologies by consistently fostering entrepreneurship.[1]

Benchmarks summarize the Valley's current position. During the 1990s, the portion of the Valley's workforce in R&D-related jobs hovered around 10 percent, a full 2½ times the national average. In 1999, overall value added per employee in the Valley reached $115,000, compared to the U.S. average of $78,000. That year, the region's number of initial public offerings (IPOs) surged to a record of 72. Also in 1999, the Valley attracted $13 billion in venture capital, a full third of the U.S. total (Joint Venture: Silicon Valley 2000). In contrast, other regions, though armed with strong intellectual or capital assets, have not (yet) been as prolific or as enduring (DeVol 1999). Pressing questions face the would-be Silicon Valleys popping up all over the globe. In the United States, for example, why has the information technology industry never flourished in Pittsburgh, despite the presence of Carnegie Mellon, which possesses one of the foremost American computer science departments (Collaborative Economics 1999)? How can Cambridge, England, where the electron was discovered, the atom split, and the first successful digital computer built, achieve its entrepreneurial aspirations (Garnsey and Smith 1998)?

Virtually every government seems to want to create its own Silicon Valley–like region. Their easiest step is to adopt the word "Silicon"—hence "Bog" (Ireland), "Glen" (Scotland), "Fen" (England), "Beach" (Vietnam), "Wadi" (Israel), and scores of others. But taking on a name, and perhaps establishing some business incubators or building a few semiconductor firms, PC factories, or software houses, is not enough.

How does Silicon Valley work? Why here and not somewhere else? Although many accounts chronicle the story of Silicon Valley through the lives of important entrepreneurs or companies, these are insufficient to answer the compelling questions of how and why the Valley works. This book argues that the Valley's sustaining edge arises from factors that go beyond any individual or single company. Rather, the Silicon Valley edge stems from an entire environment, or habitat, honed for innovation and entrepreneurship.[2] This habitat has developed endogenously over time, co-evolving with generation after generation of new firms and new technologies.

NEW TECHNOLOGIES, NEW FIRMS, NEW WEALTH

Silicon Valley's habitat specializes in breeding companies. In other words, the region's story is not primarily about advances in science or breakthroughs in technology, although some important ones have occurred here. An incomplete list includes, in electronics, the invention of the klystron vacuum tube by the Varian brothers; in silicon, the invention of the planar method of making transistors and the co-invention of the integrated circuit at Fairchild Semiconductor, as well as the invention of the microprocessor by Intel engineers. In computers, Douglas Engelbart proposed the concept of the computer for personal productivity in 1968 at SRI International; Xerox PARC has a stellar record of breakthroughs, including the graphical user interface; Apple produced the first successful microcomputer; IBM's Almaden laboratory invented the random-access method of magnetic disk storage and relational databases; and researchers at Stanford and the University of California at Berkeley made important advances in RISC architecture and relational databases.

The Valley's competencies are built on such noteworthy foundations. But many fundamental technological advances, including the transistor, packet switching, the world wide web, and browser technology, occurred elsewhere. Information technology breakthroughs have been widely distributed geographically, around the United States and the world.

What sets Silicon Valley apart are not the technologies discovered here, but the companies created in the region that develop, market, and exploit these technologies. In other words, the Silicon Valley story is predominantly one of the *development* of technology and its *market applications* by firms—especially by start-ups.[3] The result: new companies focused on new technologies for new wealth creation.

SILICON VALLEY'S HABITAT

Like a natural habitat for flora and fauna, the habitat of Silicon Valley is one in which all the resources high-tech entrepreneurial firms need to survive and thrive have grown organically over time. Silicon Valley's habitat includes people, firms, and institutions—their networks and modes of interaction. And like a natural habitat, it is marked by complex, dynamic, interdependent relationships.

Although some refer to Silicon Valley as a mindset, it is first and foremost a geographic region. A sliver of land covering 1,500 square miles in Northern California, Silicon Valley spreads from its heart in Palo Alto to San Mateo County in the north and Santa Clara County in the south (Joint Venture: Silicon Valley 2000). Within this region, 2.5 million people live in close proximity.

This region is an "industrial district," a concept formulated by the economist Alfred Marshall more than a century ago (Marshall 1890). His idea was that local technological spillovers cause companies in the same line of work to cluster. Reinforcing this localizing effect are similar demands for specialized labor and specialized intermediate goods. There are many clusters in the world, such as those for watches in Switzerland, machine tools in Germany, the design of clothing and furniture in Milan, wood furniture in North Carolina, knives in Sheffield, drugs in Basle, superior beers in Bavaria, and many more (Porter 1990).

Many things can start an agglomeration process: a source of raw materials (coal), a logistic advantage (port, rivers), a source of power (waterpower in nineteenth-century New England), or the migration of skilled workers (Huguenots driven from France developed Switzerland's watch industry—an instance of a chance event helping to launch a national industry). Once an industry is started, technical (idea) spillovers, the accumulation of skills, the availability of complementary inputs to production, and a wide variety of feedback can sustain a competitive advantage. Silicon Valley has experienced such a process, one that began with electronics firms, then continued with each wave of information technology.[4]

These clusters underscore the importance of proximity, of things local. As Michael Porter puts it, "enduring competitive advantages in a global economy lie increasingly in local things—knowledge, relationships, motivation—that distant rivals cannot match" (Porter 1998). Silicon Valley is a prime example of a region leveraging the advantages accrued from local clusters of knowledge and relationships.

The Valley, like other industrial districts, is fundamentally shaped by centripetal and centrifugal forces in tension. As Paul Krugman suggests, forces that promote concentration include market size effects (linkages that lower costs for suppliers and customers), thick labor markets (especially for specialized skills), and pure external economies (e.g., spillovers of ideas). As transaction costs fall, the density of activities increases, which, if other things are equal, lowers costs further. Forces that encourage dispersal of activities include immobile factors (land, distant markets, foreign labor forces), high land rents (increased by high localized productivity), and pure external diseconomies (e.g., congestion) (Krugman 1996).

In some industries, however, even developments that may seem like forces for dispersal, such as reductions in the cost of moving information and goods (including reduced barriers to trade), are fostering greater local concentrations. It may seem paradoxical, but lower costs of moving information and goods—that is, "globalism"—lead companies to seek out regions of specialization where they can gain spillover benefits by virtue of their location and so improve their competitive position. The disk drive industry's radical change in structure and organization between 1980 and 1999 supplies a good illustration (McKendrick, Doner, and Haggard 2000). In 1980, much design and manufacturing was being done throughout the United States and Japan, but by the late 1990s, almost all design work was being done in Silicon Valley and most production had migrated to Southeast Asia. Design is being done in Silicon Valley because of the need for continuous innovation in this highly competitive industry, while Southeast Asia's initial strength, cheap labor, is increasingly being replaced by the higher value-added advantage of learned production skills. As a result of the disk drive industry's evolution, the two regions' strengths are distinct yet complementary.

Like Hollywood and Detroit, Silicon Valley is marked by a distinctive collection of people, firms, and institutions dedicated to the region's particular industrial activities. The Valley's focus on the intersection of innovation and entrepreneurship is evidenced by the many specialized institutions and individuals dedicated to helping start-ups bring new products to market. These include universities and research centers, specialist suppliers, and local services—from chip designers to software writers; from angel investors and venture capitalists to commercial banks; from patent and venture lawyers to marketers, headhunters, accountants, and more.

These people have many overlapping kinds of associations. They may have been colleagues at an established firm, such as Intel or HP, or share university ties, having been fellow classmates at Stanford. They may share an ethnic identity and belong to a group such as The Indus Entrepreneurs or Monte Jade, or they may share a professional identity as microprocessor designers, financial specialists, or lawyers. Or having the same investors, such as the Band of Angels, may link them. Some associations are formal (a university, a law firm); some are informal and have short lives (famously, in the mid-1970s, the Homebrew Computing Club, a collection of mavericks including Steve Jobs and Steve Wozniak, co-founders of Apple Computer, with an interest in making more user-friendly, cheaper computers).

The sum of these associations is a vast network composed of many smaller networks of contributors to the Valley's process for innovation and entrepreneurship; it is remarkable for its scope as well as for its dense concentration. Tight links built over time by the rich accumulation of shared conversations, projects, and deals have yielded a treasure trove of rich and productive relationships. Interactions are marked by collaboration, competition, and mutual feedback, which facilitate the critical flow of knowledge and ideas, people, and capital.

The prevailing business philosophy of Silicon Valley promotes openness, learning, sharing of information, the co-evolution of ideas, flexibility, mutual feedback, and fast responses to opportunities and challenges. AnnaLee Saxenian, in her book *Regional Advantage*, described the Valley as a "regional network-based industrial system that promotes collective learning and flexible adjustment among specialist producers of a complex of related technologies. . . . The functional boundaries within firms are porous in a network system, as are the boundaries between firms themselves and between firms and local institutions such as trade associations and universities" (Saxenian 1996, 2). As demonstrated following a substantial downturn in the late 1980s and early 1990s, it is this overall environment that has enabled Silicon Valley to re-invent itself and thrive.

TEN FEATURES OF THE VALLEY'S HABITAT

Within this overall framework, we find ten features to be crucial to the habitat of Silicon Valley. We suggest that this set of features is necessary, but not necessarily sufficient, for understanding—and possibly emulating—the Valley's model for innovation and entrepreneurship. This list is intended as a portfolio, not a ranking in order of importance, especially given the dynamic nature of the habitat, in which different features have been crucial at different times and in various industries. We begin with the macrolevel environment of national laws and regulations and end with the region's distinctive specialized business infrastructure. To be sure, other innovative and entrepreneurial communities worldwide have developed these characteristics to varying degrees. But they are particularly well developed here. Marc Andreessen, founder of Netscape, summed it up this way: "Silicon Valley has the people, the venture capital, the infrastructure, and the creative energy to turn ideas into successful businesses. Many places try to imitate the Valley, but none of them comes close" (Joint Venture: Silicon Valley 1998a).

Favorable rules of the game. Silicon Valley operates within the distinctive American system of innovation and entrepreneurship. As described in Chapter 9 by Henry Rowen, this national system is composed of laws, regulations, and conventions for securities, taxes, accounting, corporate governance, bankruptcy, immigration, research and development, and more. This system is decentralized and fragmented—but it has more coherence than is evident at first glance. The American system is more favorable to new business ventures than are the systems of virtually all other countries. Because these governing rules are generally uniform throughout the country, they do not explain Silicon Valley's unique position within the United States, but they have played a large role in American firms' leadership of the world IT industry.[5] These governing rules have been a necessary condition for Silicon Valley's preeminence.

Knowledge intensity. The Valley is a cauldron of ideas for new products, services, markets, and business models. They come from entrepreneurs, people in established firms, faculty and students at universities, venture capitalists, and people elsewhere in the world who move here. This region arguably generates the highest flow rate of ideas about information technologies of any place in the world.

In this book, several chapters discuss the origins and circulation of new ideas and practices in the Valley. Using Jerry Yang and David Filo, John Chambers,

Scott McNealy, and Jim Clark as examples, Chong-Moon Lee lays out four distinct styles of Valley entrepreneurship in Chapter 6. In Chapter 8, Christophe Lécuyer describes how the seminal advances in silicon were made at Fairchild Semiconductor; Michael Nevens (Chapter 5) treats the development of new business models; and, with a broader eye to the region as a whole, John Seely Brown and Paul Duguid (Chapter 2) show how collaborative practices give participants working closely together an edge in creating new products—and also cause knowledge to spread widely.

A high-quality and mobile work force. The Valley is a magnet for talent. Many engineers, scientists, and entrepreneurs have been educated in Silicon Valley, and skills are continuously advanced in doing demanding work. The region's major universities play a critical teaching and training role; in this book, James Gibbons (in Chapter 10) and Emilio Castilla et al. (in Chapter 11) describe the contributions of Stanford University.[6] In addition, because merit is rewarded—and the rewards can be large indeed—many talented people come here from around the world, as exemplified by the immigrant entrepreneurs discussed by AnnaLee Saxenian in Chapter 12.

The Valley's labor force is also unusually mobile, resulting in a market that matches the needs of individuals and firms in a rapid, continual recycling of people.[7] A highly mobile work force contributes to collective learning, as tacit knowledge is conveyed and shared when professional employees move from one company to another. The whole region gains, as knowledge is spread throughout the community, and professional employees find positions that maximize their contributions.

Results-oriented meritocracy. In the Valley, talent and ability are king. In today's Silicon Valley, ethnicity, age, seniority, and experience are not what dictate opportunity or responsibility. As illustrated by Chong-Moon Lee in Chapter 6, successful entrepreneurs in the Valley vary widely in age and style, but they share a common feature of raw ability. The region's merit-based system removes obstacles for immigrant entrepreneurs, as demonstrated by the founding members of Intel (Andrew Grove from Hungary), Sun (Vinod Khosla from India), Yahoo! (Jerry Yang from Taiwan), and many other pillar Valley firms. Intel CEO Craig Barrett says, "every doctorate should come with a green card attached to it" (Takahashi 1998).

In addition to their impressive contributions here, large groups of immigrant entrepreneurs from around the world build connections to high-tech centers in their home countries (see Chapter 12). These networks give Valley firms access to skills, technologies, and markets in other regions. Two-way flows of capital lead to outsourcing, co-investments, technology exchanges, and network-based innovations across countries, an important source of Silicon Valley's vitality.

A climate that rewards risk-taking and tolerates failure. Certainly a distinctive—and to many observers, unique—feature of Silicon Valley in comparison with other regions, especially non-U.S. ones, is the degree to which its business climate encourages risk-taking and tolerates failure. In pursuit of opportunities created by the most advanced new technologies and markets, most high-tech ventures fail. So a climate in which the stigma of failure hangs over the unsuccessful entrepreneur is a powerful deterrent to starting, especially if the rewards for risk-taking are not high.

As discussed by Floyd Kvamme in Chapter 4, calculated risk-taking and an optimistic entrepreneurial spirit are part of the fabric of the Valley. In Silicon Valley, there are many examples of entrepreneurs who have failed and successfully started over. These entrepreneurs (and their financiers) usually view failure as a learning experience, and they are rarely punished for it in subsequent ventures. This toleration of failure (up to a point) is reinforced by bankruptcy laws that provide for limited liability for entrepreneurs (e.g., laws that limit liability to invested capital and do not permit creditors to reach beyond the company). Similarly, limited partnerships for venture capital firms remove important liability barriers for them to participate in risky high-tech ventures.

On the reward side, laws that permit entrepreneurs to receive stock in a company for the ideas, organization, and hard work they put into it reinforce the taking of bold initiatives. Regis McKenna, in Chapter 19, attributes "the culture of independence, egalitarian management, and networking and the introduction of venture capital" to the eight rebels who left Shockley Transistor to form Fairchild Semiconductor. That model established the pattern for a host of spin-offs over the years—more than twenty semiconductor firms came from Fairchild alone.

Open business environment. Although companies in Silicon Valley fiercely compete, there is also an attitude that all can gain from sharing knowledge that is not company-secret. Ed McCracken, former CEO of Silicon Graphics, once said that some secrets are more valuable when shared, meaning that all parties in a community, including the holder of the secret, can gain from the wide propagation of certain knowledge. This is the philosophy behind open standards, which permit developers to produce many applications or products using others' platforms or products, thereby providing a wider audience for the original platform.

During the 1980s, Silicon Valley firms moved toward alliances and joint ventures for technology and marketing. Reduced communications and transaction costs due to lower costs of equipment and the adoption of open standards led to the dismantling of vertically integrated companies. This was the beginning of the era of virtual companies with the outsourcing of many functions. Companies learned how to deal with many partners so that all parties gained.

Within this open environment, individuals are open to win-win exchanges of knowledge. Whether in formal or informal settings, interactions among people with overlapping networks of relations are continuous and intense. Chapter 2, by Brown and Duguid, and Chapter 11, by Emilio Castilla, Hokyu Hwang, Ellen Granovetter, and Mark Granovetter, detail these interactions.

Universities and research institutes that interact with industry. Research institutions and universities are such rich sources of advanced research, and of well-trained and often experienced scientists and engineers, that locating near them is now widely recognized as a powerful advantage for high-tech companies. What has been especially important for Silicon Valley, however, is that people from these institutions have interacted effectively with industry. For such interaction to work well, ideas and knowledge—best embodied in people—need to pass in two directions between universities and industry.

In the information technologies, Stanford has been a major source of ideas and people that have led to the creation of many Silicon Valley firms. (Gibbons, in Chapter 10, and Castilla et al., in Chapter 11, address Stanford's roles.) The universities foster these exchanges by allowing faculty to participate in industry as consultants and advisors to companies, to be on their boards of directors, and, if it is consistent with the universities' needs, to take short-term leaves of absence. The companies, in turn, further exchanges by sponsoring research at universities. At both Stanford and Berkeley, lively exchanges regularly occur among industry professionals, faculty, and students at seminars and conferences.

Collaborations among business, government, and nonprofit organizations. In addition to collaborations between universities and industry, those among companies and trade associations, labor councils, and service organizations have built a coherence of purpose in Silicon Valley's community. As discussed by Doug Henton in Chapter 3, these organizations, including such nonprofits as Joint Venture: Silicon Valley Network, are financed and largely led by those in the private sector, along with public-sector and community leaders. Initially aimed at mitigating the Valley's economic downturn in the late 1980s, these organizations worked at improving education, building the information infrastructure, reducing traffic congestion through telecommuting, and improving government operations. More recently, Joint Venture: Silicon Valley has focused on producing an annual "Index of Silicon Valley" that benchmarks the region's status on economic, educational, health, and quality of life factors and links it to a forward-looking policy agenda for long-term sustainability of the region.

High quality of life. The beauty of the Bay Area, its proximity to open spaces and the urban amenities of San Francisco, and the intellectual qualities of its leading universities historically have been major attractions. Recently, however, frustrating highway congestion, soaring housing prices, and a relentless, "24/7" pace of work have led some people to a less enthusiastic view of life in the Valley. Nevertheless, opportunities for innovation and entrepreneurship, as reflected in new job growth and higher wages, have (so far) continued to draw people to the Valley. As discussed by Henton in Chapter 3, these factors are in a delicate balance, with major initiatives underway to address growing concerns about the Valley's quality of life.

A specialized business infrastructure. Perhaps the most distinctive feature of Silicon Valley's habitat is its array of support services for new high-tech businesses. These include venture capitalists and bankers, lawyers, headhunters, accountants, consultants, and a host of other specialists.

FINANCE. Individuals ("angels"), venture capital limited partnerships, commercial banks, and investment banks are some of the channels though which businesses receive financing. The risk profile for high-tech ventures, for which the principal assets are ideas, human resources, and knowledge of technology and markets, is very different from the risk profile of leveraged buyouts and other enterprises involving many real assets. A failed high-tech venture has virtually no residual assets, in contrast to a real estate venture or a manufacturing venture, where there may be a considerable amount, albeit at reduced value. On the other hand, the rewards for success are very great in high-tech ventures. Thus an important requisite of the region's success is a venture capital industry that understands high tech and knows how to structure deals and portfolios so that successes more than make up for failures.

Venture capitalists and angel investors often do much more than simply supply funds for new firms, however. These backers, many of whom have experience in running high-tech firms, often coach founders who lack important kinds of know-how and need advice. Thomas Hellmann in Chapter 13 promotes a view of venture capitalists as coaches to start-ups.[8] Steve Jurvetson, and Dado Banatao and Kevin Fong, offer the perspective of experienced venture capitalists in Chapters 7 and 14. John Dean (Chapter 15) describes how the Valley's leading commercial bank adapted to serve start-up firms.

LAWYERS. In conjunction with the American system of laws, which is especially suited to fostering entrepreneurship (as noted above), Silicon Valley's lawyers themselves have become important assets for local start-ups. Lawyers are not only expert at handling the legal procedures involved in putting together and running new firms but, more importantly, in counseling inexperienced entrepreneurs; they, too, act as coaches. Craig Johnson, in Chapter 16, offers the perspective of a long-time Valley counselor.

HEADHUNTERS. Headhunters make the market matching people with jobs more efficient, especially by recruiting people for CEO and other senior positions. This is a crucial service in Silicon Valley, where leadership is key, speed is all-important, and a critically short supply of people endangers both. As discussed by Thomas Friel in Chapter 17, Valley executive search firms have played a key role through rapid, effective targeting and recruitment of top company leaders, especially through aggressive compensation and equity packages.

ACCOUNTING FIRMS. Accountants in Silicon Valley serve firms whose needs and practices often do not fit with generally recognized accounting rules and standards. Typical Valley start-ups are young firms with few tangible assets, highly uncertain revenue streams, no profits, and stock options outstanding. James Atwell, in Chapter 18, discusses how Valley accountants provide value far beyond their traditional roles as auditors and tax advisers, acting as innovative interpreters of accounting practices and valued guides for structuring new venture deals.

CONSULTANTS. Consultants—in public relations, marketing, strategic management, and other areas—provide specialized services for firms that need targeted expertise outside the boundaries of their company. As Silicon Valley, with its dynamic business environment and advancing technologies, has evolved, so have the roles of the growing array of consultants. In Chapter 19, pioneering marketing consultant Regis McKenna gives his perspective on consulting the Silicon Valley way.

THE HABITAT'S CONTRIBUTIONS TO THE VALLEY'S EDGE

As these elements of Silicon Valley's habitat have co-evolved with the region's industries, they have facilitated a cycle of endogenous growth. The result is a whole that is more than the sum of its parts, which yields at least two critical advantages. One is speed. Money can be supplied quickly. Personnel search firms can recruit CEOs fast because they are in continuous contact with executives and professional staff in the region and elsewhere. Lawyers can help negotiate, develop, and review legal documents with great speed because they are so familiar with the issues for venture businesses and they are close at hand.

Being first to market has always been an important, although not always decisive, advantage. There are especially large advantages to first movers in communications services and the Internet, as well as in the software sector. New
subscribers to a telephone company or an Internet company benefit the old
subscribers because they provide more people to connect to. And the more
people to connect to, the more valuable the network. For this reason, Internet companies work hard and fast to increase their numbers of subscribers or
visitors to their sites. In software, the marginal cost of producing and distributing an additional copy is extremely low compared with the front-end cost
of development. The more users of the software, the more individuals with
whom each user is compatible, the more individuals who can share knowledge
about it, and the more the software can become a dominant platform. Because
software distribution can be rapid, this, too, provides great advantages to the
first mover. Silicon Valley helps companies gain this advantage by enabling
them to get started quickly and to grow fast.

A second critical advantage enabled by Silicon Valley's habitat is in the advancement of knowledge in the nexus of innovation and entrepreneurship. In
Chapter 2, Brown and Duguid offer an important insight into how Silicon
Valley's industrial system gives it an edge in sensing and pursuing new ideas.
Their argument is that geographic proximity enables specialists to form "practices," a word that denotes the activities of skilled craftsmen, much of whose
expertise is tacit, not reducible to explicit programs. Small groups working together sharing insights and judgments develop and circulate the most fruitful
and focused forms of knowledge. As the authors observe, "New ideas and inventions are spun out of practice and circulate most readily among people who
share practice." In some ways this scene today, especially in the software sector, is similar to Britain's in the industrial revolution. Its advances were based
in large part on many skilled artisans who learned on the job. Then, as now,
there was much circulation of ideas through copying and improving existing
technologies (Mokyr 1990).

Knowledge about what others are up to, at least in general, motivates everyone to keep innovating, because even a small lead can be decisive and a small
lag fatal. This produces what Brown and Duguid call a "collective bootstrapping" in all the different specialties in the Valley. This localized ability to sense
new ideas and directions causes many firms, from around the United States

and around the world, to set up research and development operations here. Communities of practice within which repeated and satisfactory interactions occur build trust, which lowers transaction costs. In this way, this second advantage reinforces speed, the first major advantage.

These mutually reinforcing factors are critical to understanding the Valley as an industrial system that reinvents itself by creating new companies in successive waves of technology. This book tells the story of Silicon Valley as a practiced and creative process among people networked within a habitat, the cumulative product of much trial and error and learning over time. Widely acclaimed for its unprecedented technological and entrepreneurial achievements, Silicon Valley today deserves recognition, and perhaps emulation, for another major contribution: the model it provides of an industrial system, a vibrant habitat for sustaining innovation and entrepreneurship.

2

Mysteries of the Region

Knowledge Dynamics in Silicon Valley

JOHN SEELY BROWN AND PAUL DUGUID

The mysteries of the trade become no mysteries;
but are as it were in the air.
—ALFRED MARSHALL, *Principles of Economics*

BEEN THERE, DONE THAT?

Despite all the recent insightful writings on "clusters" (Porter 1998), "technopoles" and "innovative milieux" (Castells and Hall 1994), and "regional advantage" (Saxenian 1996), it can feel as though researchers are only adding footnotes to Alfred Marshall's magisterial economic exploration of "localization," written more than a century ago.

For example, Saxenian's study importantly shifts attention from economic issues to social and cultural ones. That shift recalls Marshall's insight that in localization "social forces co-operate with economic ones." For their part, Castells and Hall, reflecting Sturgeon's work (1992, 2000), throw light on the historical determinants of regions. Silicon Valley, they note, goes back much further than the silicon chip or even the fabled garage of Hewlett and Packard. Its roots extend at least to the development of radio technologies before the First World War. Marshall would no doubt have approved of such historicizing. He traced the roots of the south Lancashire steel industry in the nineteenth century, for example, to the settlement of smiths after the Norman conquest in the eleventh century.

Again, recent analyses have noted the importance of the lawyers, venture capitalists, marketing firms, and the like that have grown to support the core firms of Silicon Valley. Kenney and von Burg (2000) insightfully refer to this as the "second economy," Lynn et al. (1996) as the "superstructure." Both these approaches call to mind Marshall's account of the "subsidiary" trades that develop around the primary firms of an industrial localization.

Finally, analysts increasingly argue that the conventional dichotomy of firm and market inherent in the "transaction cost" view of business organization is too stark to explain something like Silicon Valley. With its complex array of subcontracts, cross-licenses, joint ventures, and so on, much of Silicon Valley falls organizationally into what Hennart (1993) calls the "swollen middle" between firm and market. Indeed, Gilson (1996) provocatively asks, "Is Silicon Valley—a complex network of shifting alliances, relationships, intermediaries, firms and investors—in fact a firm?" The heart of Marshall's analysis, of course, concerns the way that industrial localization has collective, systemic properties that fall somewhere between market and firm.[1]

LIMITS TO PROPHECY

In all, Marshall was remarkably insightful and "foresightful," presenting and predicting at the end of the nineteenth century many of the characteristics now associated with Silicon Valley at the end of the twentieth. Given his prescience, and given how hard prediction of any sort is, it will seem churlish to concentrate on one point where he seems less clear and accurate about future trends. Great thinkers, however, are often as interesting when they get things wrong as when they get them right. Moreover, Marshall treads with uncharacteristic timidity in exactly the spot where many people since (most of whom have probably never heard of Marshall) rush in with confident predictions. Marshall's hesitancy and the limitations of these predictions, we suggest, should prompt us all to rethink many of the explanations of, to put it briefly, why clusters cluster.

Standing on his robust analysis of localization and looking to the future, a future in which we now live, Marshall notes, "Every cheapening of the means of communication alters the action of the forces that tend to localize industries" (1916, 273). The phrase suggests that clusters are held together by the limits of communications technologies. As these technologies develop, Marshall seems to believe, the need for clusters should fall away. Yet contemplating better communications (and lower tariffs), Marshall seems unable to discern, path dependency aside, any future logic to the distribution of industry. On the one hand, he suggests, some industries may continue to cluster. On the other, they may spread apart. He points to "two opposing tendencies," but offers no clear idea of what drives either. What Marshall seems to lack, and what we want to offer here, is a diagnostic tool for understanding how these opposing forces, one centripetal, the other centrifugal, will resolve themselves.

More recently, theorists have been far less hesitant than Marshall. They speak clearly and confidently of, for instance, the "death of distance" (Cairncross 1997), or what Castells (1996) calls the "space of flows." A society "organized around flows of information," Castells argues, will create a "new spatial logic." Arguments like these tend to focus on Marshall's centrifugal forces and to assume, as he did, that with the improvement of communications, the centripetal forces of localization will wither away.

But before we accept the compelling logic of such theoretical arguments, it's important not to ignore the stubbornness of history. For since Marshall wrote, the technological means of communication have cheapened and changed beyond wildest expectations. In 1890, when the first edition of *The Principles of Economics* appeared, the telephone was a fledgling technology. Radio was barely a dream, television unthought of. Computers and the Internet were almost completely unthinkable. Since Marshall's prediction, all these and more means of communication, from the fax to Federal Express, have fallen into place and fallen in price. Yet clusters continue to exist as robust and important social and economic entities. So while "disagglomeration" is undoubtedly an industrial reality, in some industries and some regions dramatic cheapening does not appear to have significantly altered "the action of the forces" that keep competitors geographically local. Hence "regional advantage" and "clustering" are still salient issues, politically and economically, today.

Of course, it may seem reasonable to argue that what clustering exists today is no more than a path-dependent legacy of old industrial organization. Yet that argument must confront the evidence that the cluster that is probably the best known and economically most significant, the one societies around the world most want to imitate, actually lies not in the remnants of the industrial age but on the cutting edge of the information age and communication technologies. Not only did Silicon Valley initially develop around early work in radio technology, but in the last decade it has reinvented itself around the technologies of networking and the Internet. In so doing, the region seems only to have reinforced its centripetal attraction. And although it inevitably spawns imitators around the world, it makes the formation of rival regions difficult by continuing to draw the best scientists and engineers from across the globe, with what Marshall called its "constant market for skill" (1916, 271). Even organizations at the heart of other clusters succumb to its magnetism. Thus in 1998, Microsoft, though itself a pole for localization in Washington state and committed to the distal power of the Internet, moved part of its research arm to the Valley to take advantage of Marshall's mysteries in the air. It would seem that as Silicon Valley has cheapened the "means of communication" and improved its capacity to disaggregate, the "forces that tend to localize industries" have, in its case, paradoxically only intensified.

The critical questions, then, are *why* and *where*. Why, despite a century of predictions to the contrary, and the development of technologies for overcoming distance, does localization remain and even thrive? And where, given the significant forces of disagglomeration, might we expect localization to continue? Exploring these questions throws light on a number of critical issues, as we try to show in this chapter. Overall, the tenacity of Marshall's localization suggests how little is still understood about the character of the local and the importance of direct human interaction. Particularly where knowledge is a critical factor, these need to be taken seriously. Usually, they are taken for granted.

So, taking Marshall's quotation about mysteries in the air as our starting point, we argue first for the importance of proximity and, in particular, of collaborative practices to the flows and dynamics of knowledge. Next, we suggest that the challenge of moving knowledge helps explain the function and internal structure of the firm. Economics and sociology often turn the inside of the firm into an almost magical "black box" where communication is "costless" or otherwise unproblematic. Only by understanding the difficulty of moving knowledge can we really understand the challenge of innovation and the contribution of the firm to the innovative process. We then go on to claim that the same explanation that accounts for the internal relations of the firm in terms of knowledge dynamics also explains many of its external relations to other firms.

Explaining internal and external relations in terms of knowledge leads us to lay out the region schematically as a matrix structure made up of knowledge flows, some that run within firms, some that run between them. Conceptually, this matrix appears to extend indefinitely into a national or even global network. It soon becomes clear, however, that the overall network has a topography that can vary significantly. Here, the simple lines of the matrix give way to multidirectional flows, complex feedback loops, structural forms of amplification, and intricate relations of interdependence. At this point in our argument, despite the ease and elegance of matrix or network models, it seems more useful to think in terms of ecologies. And the ecological model of regions then answers the question that seems always to be in the air when people talk about regions: Why are regions so hard to replicate?

MYSTERIES IN THE AIR

In the Air

The idea that critical organizational knowledge that would usually be secret and hard to find is widely known in clusters is familiar to almost anyone who has lived or worked in Silicon Valley. (Indeed, Marshall's phrase about mysteries in the air turns up repeatedly in articles about the Valley.) As Saxenian (1996) has shown, there is an extraordinary level of knowledge available to all who work in the Valley.

To understand exactly what this means, let us make a distinction. Undoubtedly there is a high level of knowledge *in* firms in the Valley. These firms thrive on their proprietary knowledge. But so do all high-tech firms, whether in clusters or in isolation. In the Valley, however, there's also a very high level of knowledge *about* the firms. People are remarkably well informed about what their competitors are up to. It's not hard to find out who's good at a particular task (and who's not), who's reliable (and who's not), and so forth. This ambient knowledge helps people understand almost implicitly what's old and so not worth pursuing, and what's new and worth a second look. Inevitably, much of this knowledge is also evident from outside the Valley. What seems to be less evident from outside is any idea of what's missing or what's coming: where the new opportunities, the "next new thing," is likely to come from.

As an example, consider 3Com, which through its work on Ethernet technologies developed as a networking firm. Initially, its obvious market was minicomputers. These, several firms realized, badly needed good networking capabilities. But, as Kenney and von Burg (1999) argue, 3Com's position in the Valley allowed the firm to see a little further. Its managers understood that however lucrative they might appear in the short term, minicomputers formed a soon-to-be-dying market. Thus the company bypassed this obvious market, while its competitors continued to battle for it. Instead, 3Com positioned itself for a barely visible but ultimately far more lucrative and enduring PC market that was developing in the Valley. Such foresight, we believe, is principally available to those who very literally are *in* the know—in the heart of a cluster, breathing the air in which its mysteries spread.

More generally, the level of knowledge about firms leads to a great deal of collective benchmarking. Ambient awareness of what its close competitors are up to drives a firm to innovate to stay ahead. And the "tipping" effect in high technology, which quickly turns small leads into insurmountable ones, is such that no one can let a rival increase market share uncontested. If one firm seems to be getting ahead, its competitors in the Valley will be among the first to know and thus the first to respond. Consequently, the almost-public knowledge that comes from constantly looking over each other's shoulder leads to collective bootstrapping in all the different specialties of the Valley.

This sort of benchmarking develops around both formal and informal components. Formal components include such things as announcements of future products (vaporware aside) or the registration of patents. Of course, such public declarations are open to all, whether inside or outside the Valley. But close competitors working on similar issues within the zeitgeist of the Valley understand more quickly and better than others what the implications of a product or a patent might be, and can, as a result, make well-informed anticipatory moves. This process of action and reaction drives close competitors through rapid cycles in a spiral of innovation. Hence the Valley is currently watching a struggle between digital and optical network switches as proponents of each try to prove that they have the key advantages for next-generation networking.[2]

But the Valley is rich in informal sources of benchmarking, too. Within its narrow confines, competitors shop in the same stores, eat in the same restaurants, send their kids to the same schools, travel in the same car pools, work with the same suppliers, even smoke in the same groups outside the smoke-free office buildings. And, of course, many shuffle between firms, changing jobs with relative ease. All this intermingling makes it almost impossible for people not to know what others are up to. And it gives participants the extra insight to interpret a product announcement, read a patent, understand the significance of a product, or use a new tool. Critically, then, the level of shared informal knowledge "in the air" within a locality provides an unrivaled key for interpreting the formal knowledge produced there.

Mysteries

This interplay between the informal and the formal suggests to us why Marshall doesn't simply say that in a cluster there's a lot of information in the air. Instead, he uses this curious word "mysteries." By it, he no doubt means that what would be secret elsewhere is public knowledge within these clusters. But to anyone who was a student of English manufacturing, as Marshall was, the word means a good deal more. Historically, "mystery" was a term for the old guilds, associations or networks of craftsmen. Marshall seems to suggest that in clusters, these networks are no longer formal organizations, but come with the territory. This is an important idea that we shall return to a little later. For the moment, we want to turn to yet another meaning of the word. "Mystery" also denoted skills, crafts, and the sort of embodied, implicit knowledge that they represent. Thus Marshall puts in the air the sort of knowledge that comes from learning in situ, from being where the knowledge is used and getting the opportunity to use it.

This sense of "mystery" takes us beyond ideas of information and starts to put some limits on where knowledge will flow and where it won't. Knowledge of the sort that is valuable in the Valley doesn't spread easily unless people are engaged in the skill, craft, or practices to which the knowledge applies (Brown and Duguid 2000). Without a shared practice, it's hard to get knowledge to move. This sort of "stickiness" helps to explain the confidence of Gordon For-ward, CEO of the innovative steel manufacturer Chaparral Steel. He told Dorothy Leonard-Barton (1995) that his firm has no problem with giving plant tours. "We will be giving away nothing," he argued, "because they can't take it home with them." They can't because they don't share the underlying practice that makes what they see usable.

Knowledge, then, is hard to acquire in a usable form unless the people who acquire it engage in the actual activity or practices of which the knowledge is a part. Consequently, it doesn't travel indifferently over digital networks, local or wide-area, as information does. As Jeff Papows, president of Lotus, whose Notes is a widely used tool for knowledge management, acknowledges, for all the power to communicate that Notes and similar groupware provide, "spread-ing the practice has not been easy." And spreading practices is the key to spreading actionable knowledge.

Actionable Knowledge and Collective Practice

The difference between knowledge that is actionable and knowledge that is sterile builds on a well-known distinction made by the philosopher Gilbert Ryle (1949). Ryle argued that actionable knowledge has two components, know *how* and know *that*. Know *how* is akin to practical experience, know *that* to abstract information. Without the requisite know *how*, know *that* has lim-ited usefulness. With only know *that*, you might talk a good game, but you would never be able to play one. To play you need know *how*. And we learn know *how*, Ryle argues, through engaging in the relevant practices.

This argument suggests that knowledge you can put into practice curiously comes out of practice. New ideas and inventions are spun out of a practice and circulate most readily among people who share that practice. These claims may appear to violate several almost sacred tenets about human knowledge. For ex-ample, on their face they seem to deny the importance of theory. In fact, they do not. Theorizing is important. But it is also, as Ryle argues, just another form of practice—the practice of theorizing. Here, as anywhere else, practical ex-perience counts for a good deal.

The importance of a *shared* practice to the creation and circulation of knowledge also seems to deny the primacy of the individual in the creation of knowledge. The individual genius and lone inventor is a cherished figure. Yet it does not detract from geniuses to note the ways in which they drew on (and inspired) collaborators and competitors. Shakespeare, for example, worked at the center of a group of quite exceptional London dramatists. At different times, members of this group collaborated. They also all stole willfully from one another. (Consequently, there is a great deal of work that cannot easily be attributed to an individual author.) Simultaneously, they all competed, driving each other to greater and greater heights. None of this limits Shakespeare's towering genius. Similarly, the early impressionists as a group experimented with radical innovations in the world of painting, working together, driving each other, and providing a sympathetic audience for each other while the public at large could make no sense of what each was up to. None of this lessens Monet's achievements.

Nor will such arguments offend those familiar with modern scientific or high-tech innovation, who have long associated major breakthroughs with clusters of names: Watson and Crick; Shockley, Bardeen, and Brattain; Gates and Allen; or Jobs and Wozniak, for example. Moreover, in almost all of these cases, the known names in fact stand for much larger groups of unacknowledged collaborators.

Communities of Practice

The way small, tight-knit groups of people working together develop and spread knowledge helps explain the power of what are known as "communities of practice." Lave and Wenger (1991) showed how these groups of interdependent members circulate and reproduce a corpus of actionable, community-based knowledge. Such groups are also critical to the creation and development of new knowledge (Constant 1987; Brown and Duguid 1991). Furthermore, as we might expect from Ryle's refusal to separate theory and practice, the community of practice explains knowledge dynamics for groups regardless of whether they are predominantly practical or theoretical. Studies have used the concept to examine data entry processors (Wenger 1998), service technicians (Brown and Duguid 1991; Orr 1996), engineers (Constant 1989), research scientists (Brown and Duguid 2000), and top management (Spender and Kessler 1995). At whatever level or task, small groups working closely together, sharing insights and judgment, both develop and circulate knowledge inevitably as part of their practice.

Practice, however, is not a knowledge panacea. The strength of these groups is simultaneously their weakness. Shared practice makes it easy to circulate new ideas within such groups. But the absence of shared practice beyond a group's boundaries can make it difficult to get these ideas out of the community. Consequently, nascent artistic movements, for example, can seem absurd to their contemporaries who don't share the practice (as was the case for the impressionists). And new scientific discoveries can seem unintelligible to the scientist's contemporaries. As in the arts and the sciences, so in all regions of life and work, knowledge tends to stick where shared practice ends. The practice has to spread before the ideas can. "Practice," as Ryle notes, "precedes the theory." When they come in this order, once unfathomable ideas can quickly become familiar. Now that people are used to viewing and assessing impressionist art, it no longer seems exceptional at all. Now that working with the ideas of relativity or quantum mechanics has become commonplace, the underlying theory is no longer unfathomable. Thus anyone interested in spreading new knowledge—in the workplace, in the marketplace, through the organization, or wherever, must attend not simply to the relevant know *that* but to the practice of which it is a part. Failure to attend to the practice involved in knowledge dissemination may not only lead to failed dissemination. It may also lead to the inability to understand (and so remedy) the causes of failed dissemination.

High-tech history is littered with accounts of now-familiar ideas that initially "stuck" at the boundary of the local community and its practices. The transistor stuck among a group of core researchers in Bell Labs. The graphical user interface (the GUI, which lies behind—or rather, in front of—both the Macintosh and Windows operating systems) stuck at Xerox PARC. It's easy to tell these stories as simple cases of inept management. But that doesn't do justice to the difficulty of spreading new knowledge. Though the value of new technologies may seem obvious in hindsight, their implications are very hard to see as they emerge and before the relevant practices are established. Alexander Graham Bell misunderstood the potential of his own telephone, Thomas Edison, his gramophone. Tim Berners-Lee underestimated the potential of the world wide web. Gordon Moore, co-founder of Intel and writer of Moore's

Law, which reveals a great deal of foresight, candidly admitted that when he first contemplated the PC, he "didn't see anything useful in it, so [Intel] never gave it another thought" (Lester 1998, 120). The difference between hindsight and foresight is that hindsight can take advantage of the diffusion of practice. Now that everyone depends on transistors, uses personal computers with graphical user interfaces, and spends time on the web, the application of the theories behind them is much easier to understand.

Inside Out

This view of the relationship between knowledge and practice throws new light on the firm. Economists tend to describe the firm as a region of costless information. And sociological views, too, tend to render firms as internally unitary "interpretive systems." But firms built around an internal division of labor are inevitably made up of diverse communities, with different practices and, as a result, different interpretive systems. Moving knowledge in these conditions is a profound challenge. Indeed, from the perspective of knowledge dissemination (the critical perspective for the knowledge economy), the firm's strength lies not in its ability to render knowledge flows costless or to amortize transaction costs, but rather in its willingness to take on the high initial costs of getting knowledge to flow between groups with minimal shared practice. From this perspective, the costless view of the firm obscures the firm's core function of generating and disseminating knowledge.

Once the internal barriers to knowledge flow become visible, it is possible to understand the essential role firms play in innovation. For, as is now well recognized (see Rosenberg 1994; Teece 1986), innovation is usually a systemic process that involves linking the inventive knowledge of diverse communities into something robust and rounded enough to enter the marketplace. Many of the systemic components may be technological. So, for example, a new printing process may require new kinds of ink, new ways of drying, new paper paths, and the like. But, as often as not, innovation requires other types of organizational coordination. Thus xerography required not only new technologies, but also new kinds of marketing and new kinds of leasing to succeed. Single communities, then, may be less well equipped than multicommunity firms to make the journey from invention to innovation. Innovative firms succeed by bringing together different communities—scientists and engineers, engineers and designers, designers and marketing, and so forth—and coordinating their different practices and belief systems.

So innovative firms might be said to exist to drive knowledge across the gulfs between the different practices necessary to build a path from invention to innovation. It is a difficult process that must always do battle with the diversity it seeks to unify and the risk involved in making everyone adapt to a new idea that may or may not succeed. Given that people's livelihoods are at stake when such risks are taken, resistance can be intense. Corporate antibodies will regularly swarm to keep out a new idea. Inevitably, the challenges of innovation grow dramatically when the invention is disruptive and the attendant risk involves completely letting go of the old—old technologies, old ways of doing things, old organizational forms, and old income streams—despite its proven potential, before the new can prove its worth.

While managing the difficulties and resistance inherent in coordinating new knowledge this way, firms also face the problem that what sticks hard within them may, paradoxically, leak out easily. For example, the knowledge of the transistor left Bell Labs and ended up on the West Coast in a series of firms that began with Shockley, then went from there to Fairchild and the "Fairchildren," which are dominated at the moment by Intel. And the knowledge of the GUI left Xerox and ended up first at Apple and later at Microsoft. Now that venture capitalists stand at the door offering knowledge a ready route out, firms must apply their coordination skills much more quickly and effectively or risk losing the knowledge altogether. The conventional decision of "make or buy" may be becoming less significant for innovative firms than the decision to "make or sell"—take productive advantage of the knowledge they have developed, that is, before they simply lose it.

Back in the Air

But if knowledge sticks within firms, why should it not be just as sticky on the outside? To explain this leakiness, let us first turn back to Marshall's comments about mysteries in the air. We noted that the term "mysteries" could encompass secrets and skills, both of which pervade a cluster. But we also noted that it could refer to guilds or other types of professional or craft associations that extended across employers, linking people who do similar jobs for different firms. These sorts of networks are very much in the air in Silicon Valley, where researchers, programmers, engineers, and managers from all the different firms regularly rub shoulders with their counterparts in rival firms.

We think of these networks as "networks of practice" to suggest that they are related to, but distinct from, communities of practice. Networks of practice are made up of people that engage in the same or very similar practice, but unlike in a community of practice, these people don't necessarily work together. So, for example, there is a network of hematologists that runs across hospitals, research labs, and medical schools. All members of the network have a lot in common by virtue of the work they do.[3] Though the people in such networks do not all work directly with one another, such a network shares a great deal of common practice. Consequently, its members share a great deal of insight and implicit understanding. And in these conditions, new ideas can circulate. These do not circulate as in a community of practice, through collaborative, coordinated practice and direct communication. Instead, they circulate on the back of similar practice (people doing similar things but independently) and indirect communications (professional newsletters, listservs, journals, and conferences, for example).

Because such a network is not completely uniform, however, knowledge within it does not necessarily circulate uniformly. Hematologists working on leukemia will be able to share some specialized knowledge with other such specialists outside their immediate community, but what they share may not be intelligible to everyone else in the broader hematology network. Furthermore, those doing specialized leukemia research in experimental centers will form a yet tighter circle, again larger than a community of practice but significantly smaller than the network of practicing hematologists. Finally, cutting-edge researchers working directly together on unprecedented work will form the tightest subset of the network, which is the community of practice. Much of their work may be unintelligible beyond that immediate circle.

Take as another example of network and community members a local group of photocopier repair technicians. They generate a great deal of local knowledge, which they share, often through shared practice, with one another (Brown and Duguid 1991; Orr 1996). But the group of ten or so who work closely with one another, forming as they do a community of practice, are only part of a much larger network of Xerox technicians, amounting to some 25,000 technicians around the world. In such a large network, only certain very general ideas will make it across the network as a whole. Some will only make sense to the subset that works on similar machines or for similar customers, or in similar geographical regions. So although the community is more or less uniform within, the network is not. Its density (and ability to circulate knowledge) will depend on the extent of shared practice.

These sorts of networks help explain how ideas sticking within a firm may leak outside it. The GUI, for example, wouldn't pass readily to the Xerox engineers, with their distinct practice and lack of any experience with personal computers. It leaked, however, to like-minded researchers engaged in similar practices—and hence part of an implicit network—within Apple. Thwarted within, knowledge leaked along a path of lesser resistance to other groups who stood a better chance of overcoming stickiness. Again the mystery, this time in the sense of a virtual guild, was in the air, determining where this knowledge could and would flow.

Mysteries of the Matrix

We have thus far described formal and informal links that connect communities and allow them to share knowledge. The firm provides formal links, joining diverse communities into a coupled system for getting work done and, in particular, for promoting new ideas into marketable products or services. Highly schematically, we could represent it as in Figure 2.1. Each of the small blobs represents a different community of (a different) practice linked together in the firm. (We need to emphasize that this is highly schematic. It is not meant to preclude "U" shaped, "M" shaped, matrix, or other organizational forms. Equally, there usually is some overlap between communities within an organization, though we have not dealt with this important issue here.) The solid vertical line represents the connections established by business processes within the firm. The open lateral lines, in contrast, represent the network-of-practice connections that link each of those communities to other communities of similar practices in different firms. Accountants in one firm,

Figure 2.1   **Figure 2.2**

for example, have implicit, practice-based links—through their professional newsletters and journals, though informal contacts, and so forth—to accountants in another.

Consequently, a similar but orthogonal diagram can represent a network, as in Figure 2.2. In this figure the broken solid lines running vertically represent the links within the different firms to which these communities belong, while the horizontal line represents the networks of practice running between them and along which knowledge about that practice will more easily flow. Professional associations, which lie along these lines, have often been important routes for the spread of new knowledge (Constant 1987).[4]

The links across such a network may be fairly distant. Most people in a large professional association, for example, are unknown to one another. Even those from different firms that do know one another may meet only sporadically at national conferences. This sort of distance puts significant limits on the amount of knowledge that can be shared. But such links can also be fairly close—as they are, of course, in clusters. Here, people in similar jobs who see each other every day in a car pool, who once worked together and have kept in touch because they are still neighbors, or whose kids are on the same team will tend to intensify the relations within a network of practice. (Indeed, connections can become so dense that interfirm communities of practice may form de facto. This can happen in joint ventures when engineers from different partners, for example, work closely together across firm boundaries.) Clusters provide the sort of density that allows for proximity and interaction like

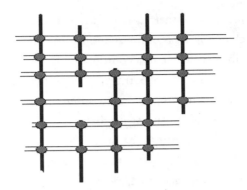

Figure 2.3

this. Consequently, in clusters, knowledge, supported on the rails of practice but accelerated by interpersonal relations, can travel particularly easily between different organizations.

The relations of the region, then, comprising both network and organizational links, can be represented as in Figure 2.3. Again, the vertical lines represent organizations vertically integrating diverse practices, while, conversely, the horizontal lines are networks linking similar practitioners in diverse organizations.

The organizations, of course, are not all the same. Some may be universities, some government agencies (the military, after all, was long one of the most important organizations in Silicon Valley), and many will be private firms. Depending on their constitution, these different organizations will integrate different practices in different ways. In the Valley, for example, some firms internalize almost all functions in a sweep from finance to fulfillment. Some are only Marshall's "subsidiary" trades—venture capitalists, marketing firms, fabricators, and the like. And others are stripped down to a few basic functions—research and engineering but not manufacturing, for example. Hence, in Figure 2.3 some of the firms represented intersect many of the networks of practice that run throughout the region, others only a few. The latter may then integrate complementary functions not under the hierarchical order of a firm, but through market relations of subcontracting or through some of the other hybrid arrangements that, as we mentioned, fall somewhere between market and firm. These hybrid links are most easily formed where interfirm relations are close, the links between them dense. This sort of density is particularly important in fast-changing areas of the economy, in which all partners to a venture need to be able to change in a coordinated fashion.

Such density not only allows partners to coordinate closely, but it also allows people to differentiate finely between different firms, finding the most apt for a particular task or idea. And again this discrimination tends to promote leakiness. Because of the density a regional cluster creates, the horizontal links of a network will be more like those found in a community of practice than like the distant sort found across a large professional association. Here, as we have argued, knowledge can leak more readily and successfully. Moreover, as Arrow (1984) has argued, classic knowledge workers—scientists, academic researchers, and the like—are often as loyal to the knowledge they work with as to the organizations they work for. Consequently, new ideas that are going nowhere across the gulfs within an organization may not just leak but get a significant push toward fellow practitioners who, those pushing know, can give the idea a better home.

In all, as a consequence of the density and differentiation within a cluster, localization can make efficient use of people and ideas. In an account of labor movements in Silicon Valley, Angel (2000) notes that "the decisions of individual workers, whether to stay within an existing employer or to change jobs, would appear to be a highly efficient means through which to deploy labor skills and experience within the local labor market." These fluid movements are most likely, Angel suggests, when likely employers are clustered together, when there's a great deal of knowledge "in the air" about who can do what, when the costs of moving are low (no need to sell your house or move the kids to a new school), and when, in Marshall's (1916) words, there's a "constant market for skill."

Similarly, localization promotes fluidity of ideas (what we are calling leakiness), by lowering the cost (in terms of knowledge dissemination) of moving them. If a firm fails to use them effectively, ideas, like people, are unlikely to stick around for long. And where informal connections are dense and the mysteries of practice are in the air, the inefficiencies that keep ideas within isolated firms, hedged in by intellectual property strategies and ignorance, are less of a constraint on mobility. People in closely situated and closely related organizations will not be ignorant of what the ideas might signify and how to use them. So ideas will travel (or be pushed or pulled) along networks of practice until they are used. One of the great motivating forces here, as we have noted, is venture capital (see Kenney and Florida 2000), which tempts both people and ideas to move out of existing firms into start-ups. (That people and ideas move in similar directions is not surprising, given our argument that ideas cling very closely to people and travel along rails built by practice.)

Structure and Spontaneity

As ideas and people move rapidly, driven by venture capital, it's easy to believe that a cluster like Silicon Valley conforms to the "Law of the Microcosm" (Gilder 1989) or the "Law of Diminishing Firms" (Downes and Mui 1998). Such laws predict that ultimately there is no place for the vertical integration of communities, which we have suggested is the essence of the firm. All such relations will dissolve in the marketplace. Arguments of this sort, we believe, misunderstand Marshall and misread Silicon Valley. Marshall's localizations, though populated with small, specialist firms, do not represent a shift from firm to market. Rather they lie adeptly between firm and market, drawing on both.

Similarly, Silicon Valley does not represent a relentless progress from large firm to small so much as a symbiotic relationship between the two. Small firms, after all, are often the products of large ones. As Kogut, Walker, and Kim (1995) show, large firms sometimes spin off the small to test markets, explore niches, or develop networks of users committed to a particular standard. Certainly, this is not always the case. Often start-ups are the result of a competitive departure, when disappointed employees leave to form a rival, much as the founders of Intel left Fairchild. Nonetheless, whether the spin-out was friendly or hostile, it is important not to overlook "spin-ins," which move in the opposite directions as large firms take small firms in. Some firms in the Valley, like Cisco Systems, seem masterful at spinning in smaller firms and remaining coherent.[5] Indeed, just as many spin-outs are deliberate, so many apparently independent start-ups are really designed to be spun in. And, of course, some that are not taken in grow instead to be even bigger than their forebears, as Intel did.

Indeed, the reciprocating movements of the Valley need to be read as an elaborate balance between stabilizing structure, on the one hand, and dynamic spontaneity, on the other. Venture capitalists, as we have suggested, play an important role in pulling ideas and people out of large firms and into start-ups. Playing this role, they usefully destabilize the "core rigidities" (Leonard-Barton 1995) of established firms, the "tradition" of long-term networks (Constant 1987), or the simple reproduction (Lave and Wenger 1991) of communities of practice. In so doing they are playing a vital part in Schumpeter's idea of creative destruction.

But venture capital thrives on capital gains, which in turn rely on the explosive growth of new firms. By its very nature, venture capital doesn't hang around for profits that come from steady income streams. For these a different process takes over, one that is less spectacular and gets less attention. Now the firms to which the venture capitalists played destructive midwife must develop a structure capable of continuous innovation. They must establish practices, build traditions, and establish core competencies. At this stage, the creative abrasion that comes from holding things together, rather than the creative destruction that comes from pulling them apart, becomes important. The destruction and the construction are obviously two quite different processes calling for quite different skills. (Jim Clark of Silicon Graphics and Netscape, as the *Economist* pointed out in 1999, has proven himself very good at starting businesses but poor at running them.) But each depends on the other. For, ultimately, if there is no promise of long-term profitability, there will be no short-term explosive growth. Without a stable future for the firms at issue, IPOs are no more than Ponzi schemes.[6]

So, undoubtedly, small firms will continue to emerge. And certainly large ones will come under repeated attack. But large ones will continue to grow as well and small ones will continue to turn into large ones. Although many firms will undoubtedly shrink in regions like Silicon Valley, others will undoubtedly grow.

Reach and Reciprocity

As we try to understand the complexities of the regional matrix in terms of structure and spontaneity, it's important to see that such a matrix also balances reach and reciprocity. Market structures, as Hayek (1945) famously showed, achieve remarkable reach through the information available in the price system. In working markets, price signals the state of supply and demand over global distances. And, in a sense, it is this sort of reach that Marshall seems to believe will come with cheaper communications technology. Firms will be free to locate "near to the consumers who will purchase their wares" (Marshall 1916, 274) without losing what, with less efficient communication, localization provided.

But Hayek's market works by obliterating the details of local knowledge and the minutiae of practice. Reducing all these to price, it makes such knowledge and practice (which are hard to fathom from a distance) superfluous for the purpose of exchange. But as we have been arguing, such things are not superfluous for the purposes of learning, innovating, sharing practice, circulating new, actionable knowledge, and the like. (Markets, as Arrow [1984] convincingly argued, are not well adapted for knowledge.) For these, extensive reach, whether offered by markets or by technology, can be highly problematic, as the survival of Marshall's localizations, particularly in knowledge-dense industries and despite the cheapening of the "means of communication," argues. More than reach, learning, innovating, sharing practices, and circulating inchoate knowledge all require reciprocity—close interaction and mutual exchanges among the people involved. The links between communities of practice within our matrix (both horizontal and vertical) are two-way links that reflect dense, interpersonal, and often face-to-face interactions. Hence, they are not indifferent to distance.

The necessary reciprocity might be seen, for example, in the workings of the universities within the region. While canonically these are assumed to generate knowledge that passes out into the region, in fact the flow goes both ways. All the schools and departments closely connected to firms in the region—computer science, engineering, and business, for example—live by two-way traffic. Faculty and students carry ideas to the firms, helping the firms to develop their knowledge. But the schools reciprocally develop their knowledge through visits—for talks, seminars, tutorials, and so on—from people who work in the region's firms. Similarly, faculty consulting in the region and students engaged in internships carry knowledge both ways.

The reciprocity is also evident in much of the subcontracting and joint venturing of the region. As Saxenian (2000) shows, firms like Sun and Apple insist on having their most important suppliers close by. Distant connections, she suggests, are inadequate for the constant cycle of ideas back and forth needed to make subcontracting in dynamic knowledge industries work. No contracts can be written to deal with the contingencies involved when specifications must change at the pace of change in the Valley. And even if they could, they could never be enforced. Instead, these agreements must rely on personal connections and trust.

Again, reciprocity seems to be needed to develop the grounds for trust. Cohen and Fields (1999) argue persuasively that the Valley is not a site of the sort of long-term social capital and trust that Putnam (1993) describes based in part on his experiences in the "Third Italy." The networks of family relations Putnam relies on do not exist in Santa Clara County, where almost everyone seems to have come from somewhere else. Instead, the Valley seems to give rise to what Meyerson, Weick, and Kramer (1996) call "swift trust," a trust that can develop over short, intense periods of interaction. Again, for this sort of trust, close interdependent interaction and reciprocity, and not distal communications, seem particularly important, as indeed do durable networks of practice. Arguing against Putnam, Cohen and Fields conclude by arguing "the sequence runs from performance to trust, not from community" (1999, 126). We suspect that they oversimplify the question a little. As we have been arguing, reliable performance (or practice) builds communities and networks, and out of this can come trust. But these are not the familial communities of Northern Italy. They are the workplace communities developed as people work together.

From Matrix to Ecology

We have been trying to explain the complexities of the region in terms of a simple two-dimensional matrix. With each line we write it becomes more difficult. It's hard to see structure and spontaneity in a matrix. You might see reach and reciprocity, but not the complex feedback loops that develop as a result of reciprocity; nor the symbiosis that leads to swift trust; nor the way communities seem to spill over the borders marked by firms and networks; nor the constantly changing relations (firm, market, hybrid) that ripple across the region; nor the spaces that new firms occupy.[7]

In all, it seems more useful to switch, as others have, to an ecological metaphor for the region. Seeing the region as an ecology that is home to multiple species but whose growth is ultimately a collective process does much more justice both to Marshall's insight and the richness of regions like Silicon Valley. For the ecological view provides a systemic perspective. What is good for the ecosystem as a whole is not necessarily good for individual species or firms. Indeed, some of these may have to die for the region as a whole to survive. (Deaths in Silicon Valley get much less attention than births—though see Freeman [1990]). Conversely, protecting individual species, as many working to build a region try to do, may be counterproductive.

The leaking of proprietary knowledge may represent a significant loss to the firm that loses it. If it flows to where it will be more effectively used, the region as a whole, by contrast, gains. A firm faced with such a loss may try to seal itself off from the system. But such isolation, as Saxenian (1996) and Mounier-Khun (1994) indicate, can be quite damaging. Firms that feed into the ecology will, by the same routes (in particular, networks of practice), feed off it. Closing off these routes isolates a firm, and isolation often means death.

The ecological view helps explain why Marshall's focus on the means of communication limited his otherwise expansive view of localization. From the ecological perspective, the means of communication are only a small part of the overall complexity of the knowledge dynamics of the region. Ecological robustness is built—mysteries are put in the air—through shared practice, face-to-face contacts, reciprocity, and swift trust, all generated within networks of practice and communities of practice. New communications technologies can certainly reinforce these. It is more doubtful that they can readily replace them.

An ecological perspective also addresses the burning question of replication. Throughout the world, people are trying to imitate Silicon Valley by creating what Castells and Hall (1994) call "technopoles." Politicians and business groups are seeking to "bootstrap" new high-tech clusters in their regions so that they can compete with the established ones and propel themselves from the periphery to the center of the knowledge economy. Such ventures, Castells and Hall argue, would "have to be launched on a huge scale" (1994, 221), setting in place a large number of interdependent organizations, institutions, and networks simultaneously. But the problem is probably not simply one of scale and cost. Even if these costs, which could clearly be enormous, could be met (replicating even part of such institutions as Stanford University, the University of California at Berkeley, San Jose State University, and Santa Clara University along with the infrastructure of the Valley would be prohibitive), that is surely not enough. For the Valley and its residents embody a situated, shared experience that has been developed over time and in practice. Both Marshall's history and Silicon Valley's present suggest that knowledge ecosystems develop over time, building connections between participants until they reach a critical mass and take on a collective dynamic all their own. By this time, the units in the whole are not only heavily interdependent, but also path dependent, reflecting the cumulative, participatory practices that have brought them to this point. In all, when regions have reached a point where the mysteries are in the air, if these are mysteries of any great worth, it has probably taken a great deal of time, effort, experience, and trial and error to get them up there.

Our argument is not intended to dismiss attempts to develop strong regional competencies. Quite the reverse. Unlike those who assume the death of distance, we believe "regional advantage" will play a significant economic role well into the future, and that those who do not want to be marginalized must try to develop their own regional strengths. Our point, rather, is that these collective competencies are grown organically, not simply implemented mechanically. Aspiring regions can clearly learn from established ones, but because local factors (of culture, institutional forms, and so forth) contribute critically to localization, it would be a mistake (and probably an expensive one) for aspirants simply to imitate the established.

CONCLUSION

At the outset, we suggested that, given the persistence of clusters despite the cheapening of the means of communication, the two critical questions to address were *why* and *where*. Why do clusters persist? And, given that the modern economy has seen plenty of disagglomeration, where might we expect to find them? Our answer to *why* is that clusters persist despite advances in communications technologies because, marvelous though many of these technologies are and extensive though their reach is, they do not have the necessary reciprocity to spread fast-breaking knowledge. In championing the distal powers of new communications technologies to spread information, prognostications easily underestimate the richness of face-to-face interactions and local communications to spreading knowledge.

The answer to *why* then provides the answer to *where*. Though he hints that clusters might continue to exist, Marshall, as we argued, offers no clear idea of where they will continue to exist. We, in contrast, have tried to show that localization meets the demands of knowledge. At least with the current generation of communications technologies, clusters will continue to exist in exactly those industries where fast-breaking knowledge is at a premium. Consequently, as we have suggested, those wanting to develop a robust knowledge economy need to learn how to develop (and not simply imitate) a robust knowledge ecology.

Silicon Valley Today

A View from the Inside

INTRODUCTION

Steve Jurvetson says that today "a good idea can take off like wildfire and spread more quickly across the planet than was ever possible before." That is an exceptional claim, but it is hard to deny it. Ideas have no more weight than the electrons or photons that convey them across computer networks, and they are being conveyed today in unprecedented numbers. Of course, there are significant inertial tendencies in human habits and institutions, but the new Valley mantra Jurvetson proclaims, "The Internet changes everything," has much to be said for it.

The Valley today is caught up in a frenzy of Internet-related activity. In many ways the scene is not very different from those of the past. People come up with ideas, build teams, seek financing, develop products, try to sell them, succeed, fail, merge, have an IPO, grow. But the speed and intensity of all this is without precedent. Not least, the amounts of money available for risk investment have become enormous. In 1999, a reported $13 billion in risk capital was raised in the Valley, about 40 percent of the U.S. total. Floyd Kvamme, senior partner at Kleiner Perkins Caufield & Byers, reports that the first Kleiner Perkins fund in 1972 consisted of $4 million, while today's KPCB IX fund totals more than $350 million. Even allowing for inflation, that is an extraordinary increase. And there has been a parallel growth in angel finance, which is often estimated at about twice the size of organized venture funding. At this writing in early 2000, which may be the peak of the frenzy to occupy Internet space, the deal flow has become a veritable torrent. Associated with this flood of money are wild swings in the market valuation of new Internet companies.

In this section, some of the Valley's key players give the flavor of life at ground zero of this revolution, while attempting to put today's frenzy in the context of the region's longer-term development. The rise of the software sector, especially Internet firms, is changing the region's economy. Doug Henton, president of Collaborative Economics, presents data not only on growth in jobs, but also on the shifting composition of employment in the Valley. He shows that the share of software jobs grew from 7 percent to 14 percent of the Valley's high-tech economy between 1992 and 1998; it must have grown substantially more since then with the acceleration of the Internet boom. Despite this shift, his data show that hardware remains the Valley's dominant product category. After all, Intel, Cisco Systems, Hewlett-Packard, Sun Microsystems, Advanced Micro Devices, Seagate, and many other large companies that design and manufacture things thrive here (even though much manufacturing is outsourced to other firms in the region and elsewhere). The financial returns support this observation: Kvamme observes that, despite his firm's big Internet winners such as Amazon.com, the largest returns for Kleiner Perkins have come from hardware firms.

Another change in the regional economy is indicated by Henton's data on the slowdown in job growth in the late 1990s. Some of this reflects the effects of the Asian financial crisis of 1997–98, but the high and still growing price of housing and increasing congestion in Silicon Valley are more fundamental reasons for the slowdown. These forces continue to cause lower value added activities to be moved away. As Henton observes, the Valley "will continue to shift from commodity products to highly customized, flexible services." This shift is similar to the one that happened on Wall Street when back-office functions were moved across the river to New Jersey, to North Dakota, and out of the country altogether. Michael Nevens, director of McKinsey and Company's Palo Alto practice, says that he suspects one-third to one-half of software firms in the Valley have moved some development offshore, and nearly all labor-intensive assembly manufacturing has been moved.

One consequence of this sectoral shift is that the roles played by physicists, electrical engineers, and even computer scientists are less dominant than before, although they remain very important. Kvamme himself started as a technologist before working in sales and marketing and then becoming a venture capitalist, following a path similar to those of other prominent people in the Valley. But new career patterns have emerged; he describes the rise of MBAs in the 1980s and of professional managers turned entrepreneurs. Especially in the Internet space, there are many opportunities for people in fields other than physical sciences and engineering; people of all backgrounds and ages are starting Internet companies.

This is evident in the chapter on the Internet by Jurvetson, managing director of Draper Fisher Jurvetson, which strikingly displays the proliferation—one might call it a veritable zoo—of new business models in an industry that is, as he observes, "barely five years old." Michael Nevens, writing about Silicon Valley business models more generally, observes that only recently has there been wide recognition that inventing business models is a major creative activity. Improvements in computing and telecommunications offer opportunities for invention to people everywhere, but, he says, Valley entrepreneurs and managers are on the leading edge in exploiting these possibilities—for example, developing no-bricks-and-mortar manufacturing and fabless semiconductor companies, integrating information into supply chains, and exploiting increasing returns from network effects. A series of court decisions enabling broad patent claims for business models have resulted in a torrent of such claims: 2,500 in the past year. This form of business protection is stimulating business model inventions and attracting large amounts of capital. (Whether such broad patent protection for business models is good for the country is more doubtful.)

At the heart of this entire process is the individual entrepreneur. Chong-Moon Lee, successful entrepreneur and Chairman and CEO of AmBex Ventures, sees most Silicon Valley entrepreneurs as more intense, passionate, and revolutionary than those elsewhere: these are people who expect to change the world, and who communicate their visions to wide audiences. Within these common characteristics, he identifies different personality types as illustrated by four leading Valley entrepreneurs: the long term "visioneer," the acquisition entrepreneur, the transformational entrepreneur, and the serial entrepreneur.

Lee sees downsides in the rise of entrepreneurs who merely want to get rich and not build businesses; the torrent of money that has recently arrived has led to an increase in what he describes as "unhealthy, speculative deals." The market sorts these deals out in due course, but at a cost in wasted resources and reputations. Lee also has a mixed view of his fellow entrepreneurs from a social standpoint, seeing some highly successful ones as lagging in philanthropy, but also admiring the generosity of many others with their time and money.

Whatever the social ramifications of the recent flood of money, it is clear that the Valley today is on a roll. The world watches, invests, and tries to uncover the region's mysteries so that they can be emulated in the crucible of practice.

3

A Profile of the Valley's Evolving Structure

DOUG HENTON

If you were to name it today, it would probably be called "Innovation Valley." The one constant in the economic evolution of this region has been continuous innovation, as the economy has reinvented itself on a regular basis. This chapter takes a closer look at how successive waves of innovation have shaped Silicon Valley, offering a statistical picture of the region's economic evolution and considering the implications of this evolution for the future. In doing so, it highlights the factors that have made this a truly innovative region.

AN INNOVATION FRAMEWORK

The economist Joseph Schumpeter, best known for coining the phrase "creative destruction" to describe the process of economic innovation, outlined a dynamic framework for understanding innovation: Economies are driven by successive waves of innovation, during which entrepreneurs take advantage of opportunities, and then "swarms" of new firms cluster around talent and technology. The evolution of Silicon Valley can be viewed in a Schumpeterian perspective of technology waves (see Figure 3.1).

There have been at least four major technology waves that have shaped Silicon Valley since World War II. Each wave has built innovation networks of talent, suppliers, and financial service providers that have helped make the next technology wave possible.

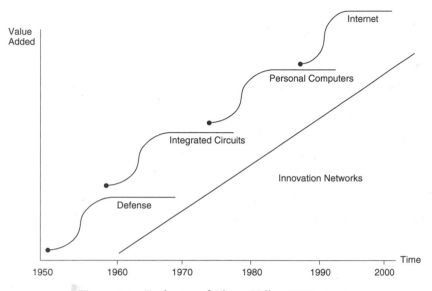

Figure 3.1. Evolution of Silicon Valley, 1950–2000.

Defense. World War II and especially the Korean War had a dramatic impact on the Valley by increasing demand for electronics products from Valley firms such as Hewlett-Packard and Varian Associates. Defense spending helped to build the technology infrastructure of firms and support institutions during the 1950s.

Integrated circuits. The invention of the integrated circuit in 1959 led to the explosive growth of the semiconductor industry in the 1960s and 1970s. Starting with Shockley Semiconductor—which begot Fairchild and its many offspring, including Intel, Advanced Micro Devices, and National Semiconductor—more than 30 semiconductor firms were started in the Valley during the 1960s. This is the period when Silicon Valley got its name from Don Hoefler, a reporter from *Electronics News.*

Personal computers. The technology foundation established by the defense and integrated circuit waves created a rich environment for launching this next wave. Young talent meeting at the Homebrew Computer Club eventually gave birth to more than twenty computer companies, including Apple.

The initial focus on personal computers quickly led to the development of more sophisticated workstations led by firms such as Sun Microsystems.

Internet. After a period of slow economic growth in the early 1990s, caused by the defense cutbacks at the end of the Cold War and growing global competition in both the semiconductor and computer hardware industries, the question arose about what would be Silicon Valley's next act. Could the Valley reinvent itself once again? The answer became clear with the commercial development of the Internet in 1993 and the creation of the world wide web. Building on its technology strengths, the region became a leader in the Internet revolution. The result was the explosive growth of Internet-related firms. At the forefront were Netscape, Cisco Systems, and 3Com.

THE VALLEY'S EVOLVING CLUSTERS

Silicon Valley's successive waves of innovation have stimulated the rapid evolution of industry clusters. Industry clusters are concentrations of competing, complementary, and interdependent firms and industries that create wealth in regions through export to other regions. Proximity is important to clusters because of what firms and people gain from being in the same area: the ease and speed of sharing a specialized workforce, suppliers, and networks. Proximity helps to reduce transaction costs, which is critical to the success of fast-moving firms.

Silicon Valley is a prototypical cluster-based economy. Building on formal and informal networks, industry clusters in the Valley grow because they benefit from sharing talent, technology, and financial resources based in the region. Because of this clustering, Valley firms exhibit high productivity, measured by value added per worker (see Figure 3.2).

This high productivity is a major reason why the average wages in the Valley are more than 50 percent higher than the national average (see Figure 3.3). It also explains how Valley firms can prosper in an environment of high labor and land costs. With high productivity and low transaction costs due to cluster economies, Valley firms can pay higher wages and still be profitable. This result turns traditional economic development theory on its head. The model

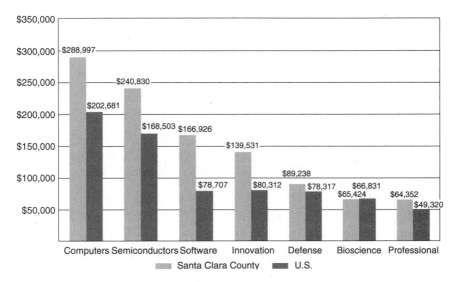

Figure 3.2. Value added per employee by industry cluster in the 1990s.

SOURCES: Index of Silicon Valley, Regional Financial Associates.

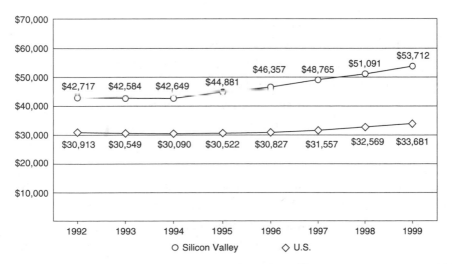

Figure 3.3. Average wage per employee for Silicon Valley and the United States, 1992–99 (1999 dollars).

SOURCES: Index of Silicon Valley, Current Population Survey.

Table 3.1 Changing Employment Profile of Silicon Valley

Number of jobs by cluster

	1959	1975	1990	1996
Computing and office equipment	3,611	25,837	57,143	31,133
Communications equipment	2,532	17,270	18,239	26,863
Electronic components	10,241	33,109	73,446	75,301
Guided missiles, space vehicles	n/a	17,850	37,675	17,560
Instruments	992	17,218	39,459	36,930
Software and data processing	n/a	5,387	41,569	71,851

SOURCES: U.S. County Business Patterns and Saxenian 1994

that suggests firms will seek the lowest cost environment no longer works in the high-value new economy in which a premium is placed on access to skills and technology. A location near talent and other firms matters.

The growing Internet economy in Silicon Valley is built on this new value-added development model. A survey of Internet firms in Silicon Valley found that Internet companies gravitate to locations with "access to a talented pool of employees, proximity to core (non-Internet) businesses, established infrastructure, access to capital and the presence of quality educational and research institutions." In that survey, talent and proximity to core businesses ranked as the highest factors in the choice of location for growing Internet businesses (Joint Venture: Silicon Valley 1999a).

Silicon Valley's clusters have evolved through the region's successive waves of innovation. A snapshot of the region's economic profile (using County Business Patterns from the U.S. census for Santa Clara County) in 1959, 1975, 1990, and 1996 shows very different pictures (Table 3.1). The evolution of the Valley's clusters has followed a path from early defense technology through semiconductors to hardware and finally software. Today, the region is more diversified than it was two decades ago.

It is important to note, however, that the firms in Silicon Valley's current innovation wave have successfully built on the technology of prior generations. Probably the clearest example of this evolution is the path of digital communications and networking technologies from the defense and space industry into computing and then Internet firms.

Although the defense cluster that grew from 1950 to 1969 (the end of the

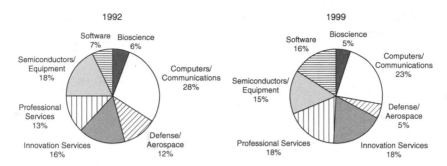

Figure 3.4. Changing employment structure of Silicon Valley.

SOURCES: Index of Silicon Valley, ES202

Vietnam War build-up) and then grew again in the 1980s now accounts for only 5 percent of the region's employment, down from 12 percent at the beginning of the 1990s (see Figure 3.4), the technology base created by defense spending has helped create the semiconductor, computer, software, and Internet industries. ARPA spending helped fund the development of both UNIX and the Internet, while driving much of the computer and networking applications behind Silicon Valley firms.

The computer hardware cluster, which grew rapidly in the 1970s and 1980s after the birth of the personal computer, slowed in the 1990s, due to both increasing competition and productivity growth (which meant more output per job). The percentage of hardware jobs in the Silicon Valley economy declined from 28 percent to 23 percent of total jobs. At the same time, software grew rapidly, increasing from 7 percent of the region's economy to 16 percent. The Internet boom stimulated this rapid growth in software as well as explosive growth in the number of new firms. The average size software firm is 27 people. This is a very different picture from the traditional hardware firm, which averages more than 200.

SILICON VALLEY TODAY

Following the recession of the early 1990s, Silicon Valley grew by 250,000 jobs between 1992 and 1999, with most of the growth in the software and computers/communications clusters (based on cluster employment data for the

Table 3.2 Number of Jobs in Silicon Valley by Industry Cluster, 1992–1999

Industry	1992	1993	1994	1995	1996	1997	1998	1999
Bioscience	21,886	21,593	22,411	21,528	20,194	21,445	25,287	24,033
Computers/ Communications	92,384	95,278	89,278	90,388	100,539	108,016	114,230	114,399
Defense/Aerospace	40,948	34,223	31,211	28,021	25,988	25,052	27,096	21,805
Innovation Services	55,737	58,148	62,241	67,026	74,607	80,692	80,051	87,417
Professional Services	44,723	47,058	53,022	60,788	81,328	84,991	88,680	91,740
Semiconductors/ Equipment	59,974	56,560	58,409	64,323	73,961	76,906	83,614	70,181
Software	25,467	32,314	35,020	43,700	52,722	61,003	67,972	80,558
Cluster Total	341,119	345,174	351,592	375,774	429,339	458,105	486,930	490,133
All Industry Total	1,029,114	1,031,146	1,049,341	1,088,360	1,153,558	1,212,281	1,258,654	1,286,797

SOURCES: Index of Silicon Valley, ES202

four-county region tracked by Joint Venture: Silicon Valley; see Table 3.2). After rapid growth since 1992, however, the Silicon Valley job machine slowed in 1998 and 1999. The annual job growth of 5.2 percent in 1997 fell to 2.9 percent in 1998 and to 1.7 percent in 1999. Figure 3.5 illustrates the slow-down in job growth.

The primary reason for the slower growth was the decline in Silicon Valley exports to Asia. Exports had risen rapidly during the 1992 growth period, especially in semiconductors and computer hardware. More than 60 percent of Silicon Valley total manufacturing exports have been to Asia. The Asian crisis resulted in a slowdown of exports beginning in 1998 (Figure 3.6), although exports appear to have rebounded quite recently.

In addition, both the semiconductor and computer clusters were affected by overcapacity and price cutting that squeezed profit margins. Both industries have begun to take on the character of more mature industries, with competition waged increasingly on price as products become more likely cost-driven commodities. This has clearly been the case in both memory chips and personal computers.

These pressures resulted in lower profits for major Silicon Valley firms in 1998. In particular, the semiconductor industry experienced a 21 percent decline in profits, and disk drive firms suffered losses of nearly $1 billion. Overall profits of the 150 largest firms were $14.2 billion in 1998, a decline of 8 percent from 1997. This was the first decline in profit by Valley firms since 1991.

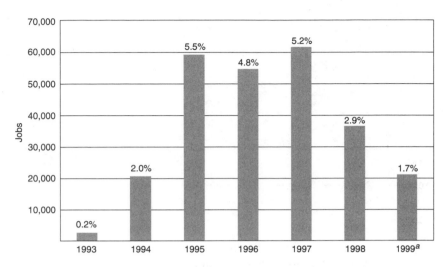

Figure 3.5. Absolute and percentage change in the number of
Silicon Valley jobs from the year prior, 1993–99.

SOURCES: Index of Silicon Valley, ES202.

aEstimate

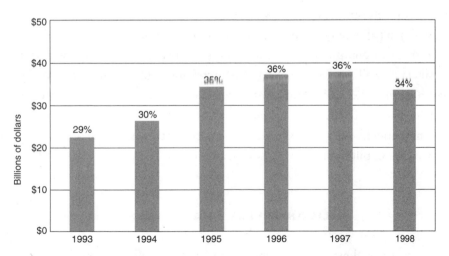

Figure 3.6. Silicon Valley's manufacturing export sales,
and share of California's export sales (1998 dollars).

SOURCES: Index of Silicon Valley, U.S. Commerce Department.

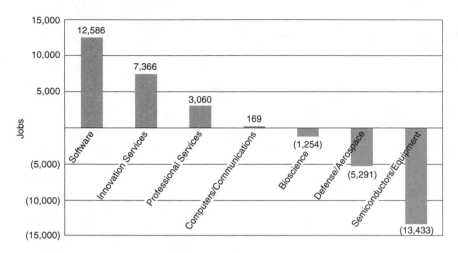

Figure 3.7. Silicon Valley industry cluster job growth,
second quarter 1998 to second quarter 1999.
SOURCES: Index of Silicon Valley, ES202a.

The structural shift in the Valley economy from hardware to software is dramatically illustrated when looking at job growth by cluster (Figure 3.7). Almost all job gains came from software, with job losses in semiconductors and no growth in computers/communications hardware. We see in the profit numbers as well as the job growth an increasing bifurcation of the Valley economy into the older companies that make hardware and the newer ones that focus on software, content, and the Internet. This reflects the current Internet surge in the Valley, shown most clearly by the rise of the networking firms, with $2 billion in profits in 1998, an increase of 73 percent from 1997.

SILICON VALLEY CHALLENGES

The recent slowdown in employment growth and profits, especially among semiconductor and computer hardware firms, raises some questions about Silicon Valley's next phase.

The continuing shift to high-value, high-productivity work suggests that Silicon Valley's economic role will remain that of an "incubator," where networks of talented people, venture capitalists, university researchers, and suppliers invent new products and market new ideas. An incubator can create high-wage jobs and create prosperity for the Valley even as growing firms decide to locate some less innovative activities in other regions. This creates a "win-win" situation: Silicon Valley continues to prosper, along with other regions that are adopting its waves of technology. The Internet is the latest case in point. Although the Internet was pioneered in the Valley, many other regions are growing Internet firms today.

Silicon Valley faces several major challenges as it reshapes itself while continuing to preserve the critical ingredients of a creative incubator. These challenges were identified in the vision statement "Silicon Valley 2010," prepared by Joint Venture: Silicon Valley Network.

Qualitative growth. Future economic growth in the Valley may be driven more by productivity increase than adding more jobs as the region shifts into its next phase of high-value growth. Simply put, the Valley will continue to shift from commodity products to highly customized, flexible services. Job growth in the future will raise wages based on productivity but is likely to be slower than in the recent past.

Skills imbalance. The high-value businesses of the Valley demand highly skilled workers. A survey of the fastest growing firms in the Valley found that 84 percent of the jobs required at least two years of college. Just as skill requirements are rising, however, the skills of the local residents are not measuring up. Only 57 percent of Latinos, the fastest-growing population in Silicon Valley, are graduating from high school, and only 23 percent of Latinos complete basic courses needed to get into college. There are economic consequences of this skills gap for businesses. A recent survey of Silicon Valley high-tech firms found that it cost businesses $3–$4 billion in incremental hiring costs in recruiting for unfilled positions. The challenge for Silicon Valley will be to cross the "digital divide" by making sure that the new economy and new demographics match.

Livable communities. One of the major challenges facing the Valley is creating livable communities with affordable housing, good schools, and adequate transportation and open space. Today, the declining quality of life in the region makes it difficult to attract and retain the talent essential for the new economy. Efforts to promote quality growth that will create livable communities will be required to ensure that the region continues to prosper.

Leaders in the Valley are learning that it is as important to be innovative in the design of communities as it is in the design of new technologies. A high quality of life is essential to attract the best talent.

SOCIAL INNOVATION IN SILICON VALLEY: FORGING A NEW PUBLIC-PRIVATE COLLABORATION

Not all of the innovations in Silicon Valley have been in technology and business. In recent years, Silicon Valley has been creating new mechanisms for addressing its economic and community challenges. One such mechanism is Joint Venture: Silicon Valley Network, created by business, government, and civic leaders in 1992 in response to the economic slowdown resulting from the end of the Cold War as well as the global competitive pressures on both the semiconductor and computer industries. Joint Venture has joined top level business, government, and community leaders in an unprecedented regional network that promotes innovative solutions to the region's economic and community issues, such as preparing the workforce for the new economy and developing strategies for quality growth.

Three examples of Joint Venture's accomplishments illustrate both the new model of regional collaboration and the importance of this new approach to sustaining Silicon Valley's continuous innovation. In 1993, Joint Venture created Smart Valley, a nonprofit organization led by technology business leaders that acted as a catalyst in connecting the region's schools, local government, and community groups to the Internet. At a critical time in Silicon Valley's transition to the Internet era, Smart Valley helped to stimulate the adoption of the Internet by making the Valley a "test bed" for innovative solutions to connecting the region in such areas as e-commerce, schools, libraries, and government. Second, Joint Venture worked with 27 local governments in the region to streamline the local permit process, create a unified building code, and establish a "smart permitting" system using the Internet. These innovations have helped to reduce the transaction costs for businesses and made it easier for industry clusters to continue to grow in this region. In short, Joint Venture helped bring government into the Internet age. Finally, Joint Venture stimulated a renaissance in education by bringing technology, businesses, and schools together in Challenge 2000, an innovative social venture capital fund that has sparked changes in local schools that have resulted in improved student performance. Business leaders identified education as a top priority for the region because of the need for a quality workforce. Joint Venture applied a new economy approach to addressing that challenge.

Local government's role in supporting regional innovation has been changing as well. Several cities, including San Jose, Sunnyvale, Mountain View, Fremont, and Milpitas, have designed economic development strategies to help meet the needs of technology firms. Each has developed innovative ways to become "total quality" providers of government services and ensure that their regulatory processes are responsive. Mayors and local government officials in the Valley meet with technology firms on a regular basis and have reshaped local government services to meet industry cluster needs.

SILICON VALLEY'S NEXT ACT

What is the next act for Silicon Valley, the innovation region? Although it is clearly not possible to predict the future, it is possible to make a few educated guesses about what might be next. The innovation relationships of the Valley have created a strong foundation for Silicon Valley to capture the next event and move along a new wave.

E-business. The area of greatest opportunity in the immediate future will be the continued expansion of e-business across all industries. Forrester Research estimates that Internet commerce between businesses in the United States could reach $327 billion by 2002, while retail Internet commerce could reach $168 billion. To date, Silicon Valley's Internet employment growth has been concentrated primarily on building the e-commerce infrastructure. The question is what will happen to all the Internet start-ups in Silicon Valley as this industry becomes more mature. How will Silicon Valley take the Internet and e-commerce to the next level of innovation?

Creative content. In the Internet economy, content rules. It is not enough to be a master at making the tools for connectivity—the future will belong to the talent that can create interesting content for the Internet. In this regard, the future of Silicon Valley may see a marriage between the toolmakers of the Valley and the creative content providers of San Francisco's Multimedia Gulch and the digital producers of Hollywood. This marriage of art and technology is likely to be the next wave of the Internet. Other regions such as New York, Los Angeles, and the Washington, D.C., area have strengths in content as well. Can Silicon Valley move beyond toolmaking to content?

Bioinformatics. Although the bioscience cluster has grown slowly in the Valley, the Bay Area is the nation's leader in bioscience, with more than 500 companies and 60,000 jobs. Silicon Valley's strength is primarily in medical devices, while the East Bay and San Francisco and San Mateo counties have greater strength in pharmaceuticals. The twenty-first century is likely to be a biotech era with revolutionary applications of DNA research in health care, agriculture, and new materials. The next wave for the Valley might be the marriage of information and health care technologies in the field of bioinformatics, the use of information tools in health care.

The lesson to be learned about Silicon Valley, the innovation region, is that new events will drive entrepreneurs toward opportunities in a ceaseless cycle of Schumpeterian creative destruction. In this model of discontinuous economic development, it is difficult to predict the future based on current trends. Innovation is driven by new breakthroughs and entrepreneurs who drive dynamic change resulting from those breakthroughs. What we do know is that the innovation region will continue to discover the new opportunity and take advantage of it. Innovation and entrepreneurship built on a strong foundation of regional networks is the right model for the future of Silicon Valley.

4

Life in Silicon Valley

A First-Hand View of the Region's Growth

E. FLOYD KVAMME

Silicon Valley has come to mean many things: technological innovation, entrepreneurship, the "New Economy," and cultural diversity, among others. In this chapter, I will attempt to trace many of the roots of Valley trends by recounting my personal experience. Having worked in the Valley in the semiconductor, computer, and venture capital fields for more than 35 years, I've had the pleasure of working with some of the most inventive people of the latter part of the twentieth century. The explosive growth that is associated with Silicon Valley, now recognized around the globe, is, in my view, the result of innovation, risk taking, and entrepreneurial fervor at a level not previously seen in any other place or at any other time. This chapter will use a chronological approach to describe the development of the Valley.

THE 1960s

Since I started work at Fairchild Semiconductor in April 1963, I have had the good fortune of seeing Silicon Valley grow from the seeds that were planted in the early 1960s. Having graduated from the University of California at Berkeley in 1959, I had completed one year of engineering work at a Southern California military systems company when it became clear that there was a big future in semiconductors. Letters to more than 30 colleges and universities revealed that only two offered a masters program in semiconductors—

Purdue University in Indiana and Syracuse University in New York. Purdue's program was started as a result of the work at the Naval Air Development Center in Crane, Indiana. NAD, Crane (as it was known) had reportedly discovered the transistor effect within a few weeks of the team led by William Shockley at Bell Labs, but, as it was second, it was not given any credit for the discovery. General Electric's Semiconductor Products Department, which was located in North Syracuse, supported Syracuse University's program. I chose to attend Syracuse because I needed to work, and GE gave me a job in the semiconductor division working on transistor and early integrated circuit applications. In two years I completed my master's degree (mostly through night courses) and left GE and Syracuse.

After spending a year at Space Technology Laboratory (a division of TRW) in Southern California as a circuit designer, I joined Fairchild at its headquarters facility on Whisman Road in Mountain View, California. Fairchild was one of a dozen or so high-technology firms located in the area. Hewlett-Packard had been founded in Palo Alto twenty or so years earlier; Lockheed had established an aerospace division in the early 1950s; and several military and aerospace firms and some telecommunications equipment companies such as Lenkurt were located in the region around Stanford University. But it would have been an exaggeration to suggest that the area was the technology center of California. That title would have been given to the Los Angeles/Orange County area, where many more technology companies existed.

Nevertheless, I was attracted to Fairchild because of its strong links between technology and business. At the personnel level, stock options were standard at Fairchild, tying us young engineers to the company. When I graduated from Berkeley and worked in a privately held small company in Los Angeles, I didn't even know who owned the company. Similarly, at GE and Space Technology Labs, I did not worry about stock or ownership. But when I was offered stock options at Fairchild, it caused me to be sensitive about where the company's shares were. The tie between your job and the financial community was closer, because everyone had options in the company. In my experience, owning a piece of the pie goes back to the very beginning of the Valley.

At the company level, Fairchild committed its business to the cutting-edge technology of silicon. Eight scientists who had worked with William Shockley in Palo Alto, where he had founded Shockley Semiconductor near the Stanford campus, had founded Fairchild in the late 1950s. By 1963, Fairchild was the darling of the semiconductor business. From its very beginning, Fairchild had chosen to work only in silicon. In those days, most companies made semiconductor devices in both germanium and silicon. Germanium transistors were commonly used in commercial and consumer applications such as computers and radios, whereas silicon devices were more common in military and aerospace applications, for which their extended operating temperature range was considered more suitable. Fairchild had elected to forgo work in germanium in the hopes that silicon would be capable of meeting all needs—a decision that proved very successful.

The 1963 Fairchild silicon product line was made up of a wide array of transistors for many computer and military applications, a simple line of integrated circuits known as RTL (resistor transistor logic) circuits, and a growing number of custom circuits designed for large customers. I was hired to fill a new product marketing position created to garner more of this custom integrated circuit business for Fairchild. The business was very technical in nature. All members of the marketing and sales staffs had engineering degrees; I don't recall anyone on the staff who had a business degree.

In my role as custom circuits marketing engineer, I was in constant contact with the R&D facility located in the Stanford Industrial Park in Palo Alto. Gordon Moore, one of the founders of Fairchild, headed R&D. Many of the engineers at R&D were foreign born. Engineers graduating from America's universities were usually attracted to military and aerospace companies, but U.S. citizenship was a requirement for those jobs.

To advance in marketing at Fairchild required spending time as a sales engineer. As a result, I accepted a sales position in 1964 calling on accounts in the Boston area. At that time, the Apollo computer was being designed at the Massachusetts Institute of Technology (MIT). MIT was also responsible for designing the computers for use in the Polaris and Poseidon missile systems. After completing the designs, aerospace firms built the end products for use by the government programs. Raytheon Semiconductor, also located in the Boston area, had the contract for building the Apollo computer in its Waltham plant. In addition, new companies such as Digital Equipment Corporation (DEC) and Data General were being formed in the Boston area to provide computers for use by technologists. Competition to win the supply contracts at these Boston-based accounts was intense. Fairchild had six full-time sales engineers in Boston, but was matched by sales forces from Motorola, Texas Instruments, Raytheon, Harris, and a host of others. The Santa Clara Valley was not the only place semiconductors were built; many other regions had developed similar expertise.

After I had spent a year in Boston, Fairchild management asked me to return to manage all of the integrated circuit product marketing as microcircuit marketing manager. Having fulfilled the requirement to have some field sales experience, I gladly returned with my family to California. The method of integrated circuit design was changing. Until the mid-1960s, except for simple families of logic circuits such as RTLs, end user engineers designed new circuits. But, by 1965, circuit design was becoming a function of the integrated circuit companies themselves. Fairchild decided to change its marketing organization to match this opportunity, so the sales force was divided into four groups: Military/Aerospace (Mil/Aero), Computer, Consumer, and Industrial.

The largest opportunities were still in Mil/Aero and Computer. The product marketers reported to the head of Mil/Aero, Jerry Sanders (later one of the founders of Advanced Micro Devices). These were heady days of good growth and very good profits, but the staff was growing restless with the fact that the profits of Fairchild Semiconductor were only part of the consolidated results reported by the parent corporation, Fairchild Camera and Instrument Corporation. The semiconductor division was reporting better profits than the whole of the corporation.

At this time, Charles Sporck was heading the semiconductor division. He decided to lead a team to leave Fairchild and establish his own semiconductor company. Since venture capital was not an established source of financing in late 1966, Sporck talked to a number of other corporations to seek backing. Plessey, the English telecommunications company, came close to making a deal to back Sporck and his team, but they could not agree on terms. Sporck was then contacted by members of the board of fledgling National Semiconductor, then a Danbury, Connecticut, company, and asked to become its president and move its headquarters to Santa Clara, California. Sporck accepted the offer, and I was one of the five to leave Fairchild with Sporck to start up the National operations in California.

National was established on the premise that semiconductor devices were now capable of fulfilling many of the functions necessary for industrial applications, not just for traditional military/aerospace and computer applications. The departure of Sporck from Fairchild stimulated others to try their hand at establishing independent semiconductor companies and, within about one year, Intel was formed by Robert Noyce and Gordon Moore, and Advanced Micro Devices was founded by a team headed by Jerry Sanders and John Carey. The establishment of Intel and AMD differed from that of National, however, in that they were backed by venture investors and were not part of an East Coast firm. There were others who left Fairchild at this time as well to start down their own entrepreneurial path.

As the 1960s came to a close, Santa Clara County was definitely becoming Silicon Valley. The innovation that had characterized Fairchild was now also practiced at the upstarts National, Intel, and AMD, as well as the other companies that had ties with eastern firms such as Signetics and Raytheon Semiconductor. Competition to create the best new products was intense. Mobility of the work force meant that management had to be vigilant to ensure that the best and brightest of their employees were adequately compensated in terms of both salary and ownership through stock options in the company. Valley companies became wedded to the notion that all employees should have some ownership of the company through stock options. Also, importantly, the management of the leading firms—National, Intel, and AMD—were engineers and technologically savvy individuals practicing their own new brand of entrepreneurialism, an entrepreneurialism that involved intimate contact with customers, close attention to product development schedules, and a focus on product excellence. These management teams had, a few years earlier, all worked together at Fairchild; now they were competing and enjoying the challenge of calling the shots at their own companies.

THE 1970s

During the 1960s, most semiconductor companies competed on the basis of the performance of their components: the part with the fastest switching speed, the lowest power, or some other specification won the business. In the

1970s, with the ability to place more transistors on a chip of silicon, competing on the basis of function became more important. Keyboard interface integrated circuits (ICs) that interpreted the strokes on a keyboard for use by a computer and chips that arranged data for video display were introduced. The market began to seek applications for which the full function was placed on a single silicon chip. At National, timing devices and calculators were targeted.

By the early 1970s, single-chip calculators and ICs performing all of the functions of a calculator or a watch were built. These chips were not exactly embraced by the calculator and watch industries. Their tradition of building all of the parts within their products would have to change dramatically if all of the springs, levers, stepping motors, and gears that had been part of the calculator or watch manufacturing process were to disappear. The rate of market acceptance of these innovative chips was so disappointing to the chip suppliers that some of them decided to enter these end product markets on their own. National started a consumer products division to supply calculators and watches; Intel entered the watch business; Hewlett-Packard started a calculator operation to serve its engineering clientele. Outside Silicon Valley, Texas Instruments similarly entered both the watch and the calculator markets. Although virtually all of these end product efforts of the semiconductor vendors were to end within a decade, they set the stage for Silicon Valley to transition from supplying components and test equipment exclusively to building consumer products as well.

It was during this time that the Valley built its foundation on what Steve Jobs would call making "insanely great products." Everyone really believed that people would beat a path to your door if you could design a great product. And that's why people questioned the value of consumer marketing here. Instead, product marketing, which depends upon a close relationship with the engineers in product development, was important. A certain style of product marketing was invented here. During this time it was apparent that if we went to the marketplace and asked people what they wanted, they would give a very complete list of our competitor's parameters. But a company would never get into the passing lane with that information. All great products arose not from customer research, but from product marketing and a full understanding of what customers were really trying to do.

One example of this early Valley-style product marketing was a concept called tri-state logic. Tri-state logic represented the notion that output drivers could be in some interim state, so that on or off need not be the only options. The tri state is how all bus structures work and gave rise to the early days of microprocessors. No one asked us as engineers to build a microprocessor. Instead, microprocessors came out of a development for the calculator industry. We were trying to integrate more and more elements to come up with a simpler, single-chip calculator. Integration of components on a single chip was progressing as predicted by Moore's Law, Gordon Moore's prediction in the mid-1960s that ICs would increase in complexity by a factor of two every eighteen months or so. Ted Hoff, at Intel, who had a computer programming background, was trying to build a computer on a chip. By 1972, Intel had put all of the functions of a computer on a single chip: the microprocessor was born. Then the 8008—the first microprocessor with any following—was invented. The key was that somebody saw beyond what the customers were asking for.

Young engineers were meeting in clubs to discuss and compare their latest systems. Speculation was rampant as to what new functions would be integrated next to form new products. Out of one of these clubs came the relationship between Steve Wozniak and Steve Jobs, which led to the formation of Apple Computer (using a processor chip that wasn't even from the Valley).

The success of the investment in Intel by Arthur Rock, an early venture capitalist, started another important trend in the Valley—the professional venture capital market was starting to form. In the early 1960s financing had come from existing corporations; in the late 1960s, from angel investors, many from the East Coast. Then, Eugene Kleiner, who had been one of the founders of Fairchild Semiconductor, and Tom Perkins, an inventor who had been instrumental in starting the computer division at Hewlett-Packard, were introduced to Henry Hillman, a wealthy Pittsburgh financier, by Sandy Robertson, an investment banker. The venture firm of Kleiner Perkins Caufield & Byers was born. It was 1972. A fund of $8 million was raised, and the rules by which venture capitalists would be compensated and judged were established. Many of the angel investors of the 1960s formed similar firms and also raised funds, primarily from eastern capital sources.

These early funds did not invest exclusively in the technology field, but after a few years the investors found that technology investments were far more profitable than other types. Early venture-backed technology companies were primarily in the systems field. Companies such as Tandem Computers and Amdahl were started in the early 1970s. Tandem's goal was to set new standards in computer reliability by using more circuitry than would normally be required to achieve the performance needed. Amdahl was started as a direct competitor to IBM's mainframes. But venture capitalists did not only invest in computer technology companies; Genentech was also started at this time to begin work in the new biotechnology field.

Funding for these new start-ups was limited, however, because the size of the venture backer's bank account was limited. In the case of Tandem, getting its product to market so that its return on investment could help fund operations was essential. In the case of Genentech, however, there was no hope of reaching the market on the meager funds available from the venture backers. New funding vehicles had to found. Again, the ingenuity of the venture backers came into play with the invention of such new financing vehicles as the R&D partnership, which was to play a critical role in so many of the early biotechnology start-ups.

During the 1970s the semiconductor companies diversified their activities. They continued their forward integration into equipment enterprises. The consumer efforts at both Intel and National had become important contributors to corporate growth. And some semiconductor memory component suppliers, such as National, had entered the market for IBM add-on memory systems. National had even entered the market for checkout systems in grocery stores as well as the market for mainframe computers compatible with IBM large-scale computers. Part of the appeal of this diversification was that these products had a cost structure driven principally by their semiconductor content.

The Valley had had almost no contact with Washington or with California state governmental authorities during its first fifteen years. The industry supplied its silicon components to government contractors with only the requirement for government inspection on some occasions before shipments could be made to mil/aero customers. Most semiconductor companies assembled their products in factories established in East Asia. Negotiations with U.S. authorities regarding duty payments and tax matters of these offshore operations were largely of a bureaucratic nature and certainly never involved any contact with politicians.

As the mid-1970s approached, however, California was swept up in the nationwide oil crisis. Since fossil fuels were a major factor in the supply of electricity, the semiconductor makers had to ensure that any rationing of power would not impact their operations. At that time, a power failure of as little as an hour was very disruptive to the semiconductor fabrication process. The furnaces in which semiconductor diffusion took place contained glass tubes that held the silicon wafers; these tubes would shatter if not removed from the furnace in a prescribed manner. A sustained loss of power was catastrophic. A proposed solution to the energy crisis, imposing roving blackouts on all communities on a regular schedule, would have been very costly to the industry. Trips to the state capitol in Sacramento resolved the issue—the first time the industry acted in consort to resolve a common problem using the political process.

Later in the decade, a more ominous business/political problem arose for the Valley semiconductor companies. They had grown dramatically during most of the decade, despite a recession in the mid-1970s. But the nature of the business was changing. Previously, the operational side of the business had been very labor intensive, which led to the establishment of factories to assemble the silicon chips into their packages in Hong Kong, Singapore, Thailand, Malaysia, the Philippines, and other places where labor was plentiful. But, increasingly, the business was becoming capital intensive. Wafer fabrication lines that had cost only a million or so dollars in the late 1960s now required hundreds of millions to be competitive. Capital and the cost of capital were becoming important factors, particularly in light of the ballooning interest rates of the period. Silicon Valley, by the late 1970s, was clearly viewed as the home of innovation in integrated circuits, but competition that had previously come almost exclusively from within the United States—principally Texas Instruments and Motorola—was now arriving from Japan. Japanese suppliers were competing primarily on the basis of price and reliability. Experts disputed the reliability claims made by Japanese suppliers, but there could be no disputing the fact they offered lower prices. U.S. semiconductor manufacturers felt that Japan was dumping its products on the U.S. market.

Many of the U.S. semiconductor companies had been members of the American Electronics Association (formerly the Western Electronic Manufacturers Association, and just recently transformed into a national organization). These semiconductor companies now decided that the industry needed its own agency and formed the Semiconductor Industry Association (SIA). The SIA immediately went to work to emphasize to government that their vital industry was under attack and needed trade protection from Japanese dumping.

As the 1970s came to an end, the semiconductor companies could look back on a very successful period of fast growth, but they also looked forward to a much more competitive world based on Silicon Valley–style product marketing. The venture capital industry had given birth to an increasing number of technology-based start-ups, was starting to raise larger funds, and was expanding its ranks with the addition of young engineers who were close to leading-edge developments. At Kleiner Perkins, two such young engineers to join the firm were John Doerr and Jim Lally—both experienced technologists from Intel. While the semiconductor companies and Hewlett-Packard were still the largest of the Silicon Valley companies, new firms such as Tandem Computers, Amdahl, and Apple Computer were growing and showing very good signs of expansive growth ahead. For the first time, Valley companies had perceived and collectively acted on joint interests in the political arena, a precedent that would be expanded on in the following decade.

THE 1980s

As the 1980s began, there was a general concern about the economics of the semiconductor business, driven mostly by the growing competition with Japanese suppliers. The cost of new wafer fabrication facilities had increased steadily until it was now in the range of hundreds of millions of dollars. While the demand for semiconductors had risen steadily during the previous two decades, the industry was now a capital-intensive industry, and the cost of capital in the United States was not competitive with that of foreign suppliers—especially the Japanese.

Members of the SIA began to consider steps to address what they perceived as the unfair trade practices of Japanese suppliers. After considerable study, the SIA was able to gain congressional support in Washington for the formation of SEMATECH, a joint industry/government consortium chartered to perform research in semiconductor manufacturing technology. Sematech was established in Austin, Texas, with the goal of developing equipment and process technology that would make U.S. manufacturers more competitive by sharing the cost of early development phase research. Sematech was a dramatic departure for the semiconductor industry. Until this time, the industry had had virtually no dealings with the federal government, except as they pertained to the trade rules for exporting and importing products from their foreign assembly plants. Now, the industry found itself a partner with the government in product research. Sematech was also a departure for the government in certain ways. Previously, industries that were granted such support were those in decline; with Sematech a vibrant, growing industry was gaining support to maintain its presence in the United States.

At the time, comparisons were made to the steel and automobile industries, which many felt were also hurt by foreign (again, mostly Japanese) competition, but which did not receive similar support. Sematech was intended to head off the loss of the semiconductor industry in the United States and the jobs and technology that it represented.

In addition to the formation of Sematech, the semiconductor industry gained, as a result of negotiations between the U.S. government's Special Trade Representative and the Japanese Ministry of International Trade and Industry (MITI), a legislated commitment from its Japanese competitors that U.S. suppliers would enjoy 20 percent of the Japanese market for semiconductors later in the 1980s. This agreement was negotiated as U.S. semiconductor shipments to Japan were falling well below the 15 percent level, and Japanese manufacturers were winning an increasing number of the local designs. The merits of this type of legislation can be disputed, but the trade pact illustrated that the industry had clearly gained recognition as a vital part of the economy in the eyes of Washington politicians and bureaucrats. Yet, even with this involvement of the federal government in the affairs of the Valley, visits from Washington political figures were not a common occurrence in Silicon Valley.

Within the industry, semiconductor memory products were the fastest-growing market segment, as mainframe computer manufacturers and add-on memory suppliers had largely abandoned the use of magnetic core memory in favor of semiconductor devices. The mainframe computer industry—then known as IBM and the BUNCH, referring to Burroughs, Univac, NCR, CDC, and Honeywell—was the largest buyer of memory chips. IBM's installed base of computers represented the largest market share, estimated by some to be over 60 percent of the total computer market. Several systems manufacturers marketed products that directly competed with IBM's offerings; among these were add-on memory products based on semiconductors supplied by Silicon Valley companies Intel, National, and AMS, as well as other, non-Valley companies.

These memory systems represented another advance in Silicon's Valley's capabilities—the capability to sell and service systems for the largest users of computers, such as the large insurance, banking, and airline companies. These large users started to visit the Valley to become more familiar with these products, as well as the full mainframe computers supplied by Amdahl, Tandem, and National Advanced Systems, the computer division of National Semiconductor. These customers would become more frequent visitors in the following years as the Valley gained a reputation as the technological hub of the country.

The microprocessor that had been first introduced in 1972 had still not found a very large market at the beginning of decade, but that was to change in 1982, when Intel won the design for the IBM Personal Computer. Apple Computer had chosen the 6502 microprocessor product built by MOS Technology for its early Apple II and Apple III products and was working with Motorola microprocessors for its soon-to-be announced Lisa and Macintosh products. Thus IBM's choice of Intel was a critical win for Silicon Valley, but the shipment of microprocessors themselves would not become an important component of Valley semiconductor revenue until very much later in the decade.

Even though Apple had not chosen a local microprocessor product, its rapid revenue ramp during the early 1980s (reaching $1 billion in annual sales by its September 1984 reporting period) attracted considerable national attention and entrepreneurial support. Steve Jobs and Steve Wozniak were feted on numerous magazine covers as the heroes of a new age. Indeed, in many respects they were.

Early adopters of the Apple were using their machines for hundreds of applications, much to the amazement of the less computer literate. Local schools were offering night courses in computer programming to full classes. In marketing and engineering departments across the country, Apples were finding their way into sales tracking and forecasting applications, engineering design applications, and a host of other uses. But the IT departments in these companies were not buying them; instead, they were being carried in by individual users. Working at Apple was a goal of many—particularly younger engineers and marketing people. Even though the Valley had many systems houses by the early 1980s, Apple was to change the perception of the Valley in the minds of many. It would no longer be a semiconductor component supplier but a systems supplier, and more specifically a personal computer systems supplier. Not only was Apple providing systems, but it was selling systems that were being marketed to consumers through a whole new retail channel—the computer retail store. Valley residents flocked to these establishments not only to consider the purchase of a computer, but also to learn about computing through courses offered at virtually every retail outlet.

Until the rise of Apple, most of the professional jobs in the Valley were very technical in nature. Engineering degrees were a requirement not only for the design, manufacturing, test, and support phases of most company products, but also for the selling and marketing phases. The products were technical products sold to technical buyers. As a result, there were very few persons whose college degrees were not in the technical fields.

With Apple, consumer marketing became a necessity. Customers were not technologists; they were professionals, students, retailers, and ordinary citizens who didn't want to know the inner workings of the machine, but only wished to use it to make their jobs more efficient. Although engineering know-how was still treasured, business and marketing know-how became important, too, and people with MBA degrees in addition to their engineering degrees or with no technical degree at all started to fill key roles.

The Apple phenomenon created opportunities for others to start companies that would supply the support products that were required to make a full computer system. Disk drive manufacturers such as Seagate and Quantum were founded to serve the storage requirements; printers to attach to microcomputers were being designed by Qume and others; and software companies were proliferating. Designing products to plug into or attach to an Apple computer was very popular with Valley engineers—many of whom had dreams of building a company that could be as large as Apple and as popular. The announcement of the IBM PC had legitimized the microcomputer in the minds of many, and also created a larger market for these add-on equipment suppliers to serve.

Starting a company was becoming very fashionable; any lingering doubts that being part of a start-up was as desirable as being employed by one of the Valley's larger companies was disappearing. These new ventures would require financing, investment banking, corporate banking, legal services, accounting, employment agencies, and the other support services of a growing economy. With few exceptions, until the early 1980s most of these services had been based in San Francisco rather than Silicon Valley.

Here in Silicon Valley, up until the mid-1980s, the law firm of Wilson Sonsini Goodrich & Rosati represented all the start-ups, and Brobeck, Phleger & Harrison represented all the venture capitalists. Suddenly the latter firm started representing companies when they realized that more money could be made. Entrepreneurs moved into service businesses, carving out certain areas of expertise. As the 1980s progressed, more and more service firms established Valley offices and finally, by the end of the decade, many moved the bulk of their operations to Silicon Valley to better serve the growing complex of Valley companies. Although no reliable count of the number of technology companies in the Valley has ever been produced, it seems that during the 1980s the number grew from a few hundred to several thousand.

With the rise of specialists in various business services came the development of networks within the Valley. For example, a venture capitalist would say, "Once you have a good law firm at company X, you should introduce them to company Y." The flow also went the other way: an entrepreneur who had a new idea and wanted to protect that idea would go to Sonsini first, and Sonsini would then approach Kleiner Perkins.

The professional venture capital industry, which by this time had been in existence for about ten years, had seen some success from its funding of start-ups. Early funds, although small, had seen reasonable returns, and the new age of microcomputer companies was looking like a lucrative investment opportunity. Outside the Valley, early 1980s venture investing successes such as Lotus and Compaq had convinced funding sources that it was reasonable to put more money into venture funds.

Technology company initial public offerings (IPOs) had a banner year in 1983. Not only had the first wave of microcomputer companies, such as Apple, gone public, but a new group of semiconductor companies such as LSI Logic and a number of biotechnology companies had raised public funds. Interest in technology investing was rapidly rising. The first venture capital megafund (at its inception a $150 million fund) closed in 1983. Many more large funds were to follow. In the first decade of technology investing most start-ups were aimed at markets that had either not previously existed or markets that were dominated by larger companies that were considered too large to respond to a more adroit entrepreneurial firm. With the influx of larger funds, the venture investing business became more competitive, as fund managers would back entrepreneurs building virtually the same product as another start-up.

Disk drive companies, printer companies, microcomputer software companies, and a new category—workstation companies such as Sun Microsystems and Apollo Computer—enjoyed considerable venture investing support. By the middle of the decade, the acronym JAWS was used to signify an investment in Just Another Work Station, but such terminology could easily have been applied to other product areas as well. With the large funds and the rush to invest in technology, many ideas were funded that would fail. In fact, according to data from Venture Economics, a leading venture investing scorekeeper, the average venture fund started during the latter half of the 1980s had a return of 0 percent—they were just able to return the original invested capital.

Semiconductor firms were not doing very well in the middle part of the decade, either. A recession caused by an inflated estimation of the usage rates of semiconductors by emerging companies coupled with a slowdown in the demands of the mainframe computer users and Japanese competition created the first loss quarters in years for most of the semiconductor companies. Intel sought investment from IBM, which came forward because they were experiencing incredible success with their PC product and needed Intel's microprocessors. National suffered its first losses since arriving in the Valley. Other semiconductor suppliers had similar hard times, with the exception of the newer ASIC (Application Specific Integrated Circuit) companies. The recovery in the semiconductor market would only occur as the demand for personal computers increased later in the decade. From that time through the 1990s, the personal computer was the driver for the semiconductor industry.

In October 1987, Wall Street suffered a dramatic loss that influenced technology stocks. So, as the decade ended, the venture capital industry was suffering from a lack of public market support for its companies, and the amount of money coming to the venture capitalists was shrinking from its 1986 highs. Apple Computer was suffering from growing competition from the IBM-type PC being produced not only by IBM and Compaq but also by a host of other "clone" manufacturers. Sun Microsystems was in a battle to outdistance Apollo Computer, now part of Hewlett-Packard. The legions of software companies that were vying for shelf space at the retailers were struggling to differentiate themselves. The Valley was clearly in need of another blockbuster product like the PC had been. Efforts at the end of the decade centered on smaller, more portable machines, but there were also the seeds of the coming decade's communications explosion. Quantum Computer Services, which later changed its name to America Online, had been formed in the 1980s to promote e-mail and user communities. Similarly, new and existing companies such as 3Com were making better modems and network products for use in making communications between computers easier.

Against the backdrop of these developments of the mid-1980s, the arrival of the MBAs was also of great importance. Up until then engineers had dominated the Valley, but MBAs brought a different focus and expertise, helping push the Valley toward marketing directly to consumers. The 1980s were the days of packaged software and channels. Kleiner Perkins had never invested before in companies like Business Land and Computer Land; we had never invested in chains. Previously, people were afraid of going after consumer-oriented business. But the cumulative effect of these developments laid the groundwork for explosive changes in the 1990s.

THE 1990s

During the 1990s the Valley cemented its role as the center of entrepreneurship, attracting unprecedented capital and people. It also extended its reach into state and national politics and set new precedents for technology standards and business models.

One significant development for the Valley in the 1990s was its coming of age in the world of politics. In the early 1990s, the Valley's high-technology business leaders were not focused on politics and certainly not politically active. Even Sematech, which was actually based in Texas, not in Silicon Valley, was viewed as controversial. The arrival of presidential candidate Bill Clinton changed all that. When he first came to court voters in the Valley, he convinced twenty or so people from the region to endorse him. It was a first and brilliant act. Every previous presidential candidate had come to the Bay Area and headed straight for San Francisco. Clinton, on the other hand, invested in developing a relationship with the Valley.

From that turning point, people in the Valley saw the benefits of active political involvement. I became involved by organizing in August 1996 the endorsement of Bob Dole and Jack Kemp by 245 Silicon Valley CEOs. The Valley now had the seeds of political organizations for both parties. At the end of 1996, the groups supporting both parties formed Technology Network, TECHNET, a bipartisan political action group headed by leaders from around the Valley. Our first event featured former secretaries of education Lamar Alexander and Bill Bennett to address what could be done about problems in education. That first meeting was packed with key people from the Valley. We realized we were on to something.

During its first year, TECHNET won two big successes with the Uniform National Standards and a charter school initiative for K–12 education. In 1998, work continued on the education side, and TECHNET sponsored bills related to H1B visas and Y2K that passed. For the first time the Valley was successful in mobilizing support for specific candidates, getting legislation passed, and significantly impacting policies. By the end of the decade, the Valley was ensconced in politics. As evidence, between December 1 and 15, 1999, alone, 23 U.S. senators visited the Valley.

Another dramatic change of the decade took place in the world of venture capital. New venture capital raised had reached its lowest point in more than a decade in 1991, when only $1.3 billion in new capital was raised. Clearly the bloom was off investing in new start-ups, but that was about to change dramatically. By the end of the decade, the situation was totally different: in 1999, venture capital invested reached $40 billion. What made the difference? The Internet.

I remember when it dawned on me that the Internet was going to be huge.

It was 1994, and I was driving down the street when a bus passed me. The ad on the bus had a dot-com address, and I thought to myself, "Wow, that's interesting." That early awareness of the Internet's potential to reach large numbers of people was followed quickly by opportunities to fund companies.

Personally, I first learned of a better way to communicate from a friend in the federal government who described the product Mosaic, developed at the University of Illinois. A few months later, John Doerr introduced to our partnership an investment in a new company that came to be called Netscape. There were other browsers (including Mosaic) on the market, but Netscape took the market by storm almost immediately by giving the software away to new users in order to establish a commanding lead in market share for this new category of product. Netscape was soon to become the next in a long string of Valley successes. Everyone wanted to be on the Internet.

Jim Barksdale, who had been attracted to run Netscape, used management skills honed at Federal Express and McCaw to build a product and marketing company. Virtually all top management personnel before Netscape had been from a technical background, or at least were focused on the product. Barksdale, however, was an experienced manager, the first of many that would soon come to the Valley to lead raw start-up companies. Netscape's meteoric rise led to a host of new venture ideas that would ease or facilitate the use of computer access to the Internet.

The gold rush was on to make computers into communications devices using existing telephone facilities and routers supplied by such new companies as Cisco Systems and Ascend Communications (of San Francisco). The number of companies founded to take advantage of these new communications opportunities was expanding rapidly when a new idea was launched.

With the Internet well established as a communications tool, Jeff Bezos visited Silicon Valley to describe his idea of how commerce could be conducted over the Internet. Bezos represented a new kind of entrepreneur for the Valley. The all-engineer work force characteristic of Fairchild in the 1960s had given way to an influx of marketing and nontechnical people at Apple at the beginning of the 1980s. During that period, however, people starting companies, such as Scott McNealy and Jim Clark, still had very technical backgrounds. But there was a change with the rise of MBAs in the later 1980s, and the phenomenon of the professional manager–turned–entrepreneur, exemplified by Jim Barksdale, in the early 1990s. By the time Bezos, formerly an analyst on Wall Street, came along later in 1990s, he was part of a generation of new entrepreneurs with very different backgrounds. Bezos had studied several different commodities and concluded that an initial effort to sell books over the Internet could grow rapidly. Once Amazon.com began to sell books, every product from loans to automobiles to groceries was fair game. The venture industry began investing in a wide array of e-commerce companies that were planning to sell virtually anything over the Internet. Wall Street bought into this flood of new companies not only by taking them public at large valuations, but also by investing dollar amounts that exceeded anything the Valley had ever previously seen.

What impact has the Internet had on venture capital in the Valley? It has changed both the amount of money invested per company and the type of risk encountered by new firms. In 1972 the first Kleiner Perkins fund raised $8 million, investing $4 million in a few companies that fortunately included Tandem and Genentech. Over time, the size of the funds increased, with Kleiner Perkins raising $20 million, then $55 million, then $150 million, and so on, until today's fund of more than $350 million. What is interesting is that even though there has been an enormous increase in capital invested, every fund still has had approximately 40 companies. The number of companies has not increased; the monitoring by the VC team has not been diluted. Rather, the amount of capital invested per company has increased significantly.

The main reason for this change is that money is now directed toward different kinds of risk, with varying capital requirements. As a venture capitalist, I encounter three kinds of risk: 1) technical risk, such as developing a cure for cancer, for which the market is assured if the solution is achieved; 2) market risk, such as for the PC or Amazon.com, for which the technology is within reach but there is uncertainty whether there is a viable market; and 3) sales risk, such as for a better restaurant, for which neither technology nor market presents risks or growth opportunities, but the challenge is simply attracting sales. Dollar requirements for new firms increase as you move from technical to market to sales risk. No VC firms invest in sales risk.

In the early days, about 80 percent of investments were made on technical risks and only 20 percent on market risks. In the 1990s the thrust toward e-commerce reversed the proportions, with 80 percent of capital going toward market risk deals. The huge amount of capital that dot-com companies require to establish their brand to attract people to their site is a whole new thing for the venture world. Amazon.com and Drugstore.com have been huge winners for our firm.

In addition to investing in firms with market risk, we have also balanced our portfolio of companies with firms facing technical risks, such as those in optics, optical switching, photonics, and wireless communications. It is critical not to lose sight of the fact that, in spite of all of the hype, Kleiner Perkins has still made more money in technical risks. So, even though Amazon.com and Drugstore.com have been winners, our two biggest winners on the books are still technical risks: the $4 million we invested in Cerent suddenly became worth $2.5 billion when Cisco acquired it, and our approximately $4 million investment in Juniper Networks is now worth $3 billion dollars.

What will the next chapter in the Internet story be? So far stocks have gone very well, but sooner or later these companies are going to need to make some money. Companies that have no earnings are valued at many times their sales volumes because it has become clear that the Internet is creating a whole new way for businesses to communicate and do business with their customers, whether they are consumers or other businesses. There is no doubt that the second half of the 1990s will stand out in history as a time when communications between individuals, commerce between consumer and supplier, and interaction between government and governed changed in a fundamental way— never to return to its earlier one-to-one or broadcast models.

There is no question that although the Valley was born as a technology product center in the late 1950s, it has become the heart and soul of the New Economy centered on information technology. One source of the Valley's success has been its ability to take what already exists and continuously build on it. With generation after generation of building blocks, the Valley went from gate circuits to medium-scale integration to large-scale integration to microprocessors. Now, with the existence of the microprocessor, networks, and telecommunication, there are opportunities for the next building block to be a marketing-oriented one, as e-mail moves into e-commerce, which leads to commerce in a particular area . . . and so on in an exciting evolution.

The phenomenal opportunities ushered in by the Internet have brought commensurate challenges. The current environment for venture capitalists is shaped by larger sums of money, great market-oriented risk, and a gold rush mentality. I see the National Venture Capitalist Association's recent data as a cause for caution: the amount of money that flowed into venture businesses in 1999 was triple that of 1998. And the overall total of $49 billion dwarfed the figures at the beginning of the decade—$1.3 billion in 1991. A serious challenge now for the Valley is to maintain returns on the enormously increasing influx of money. We faced that challenge in 1986 and we failed—and that was only $8 billion. The investments and the stakes are much higher now.

Fortunately, however, I see the process of innovation and entrepreneurship continuing, not only here in the Valley but in other regions as well. When I look back at my experiences here during the almost four decades since I first joined Fairchild, I see how much fruit can come from a single seed. I see a similar process happening in Northern Virginia with its four hundred companies, following the success of AOL. And where would the Seattle software business be had Microsoft not succeeded? Those regions are very much like the Valley in its early days. It is as if an apple tree shoots up, and the apples that fall off that tree plant more seeds, causing new saplings to begin to grow on their own.

I have felt fortunate to be a partner in that process. I have seen that there will be failures, but there will also be great successes. To quote an old saying of Tom Perkins's, "the nice thing about venture investment is you can only lose one times your money, but you can make many times your money." The key has been to seize the opportunity to partner with a promising entrepreneur. To return to the story of Amazon.com, I remember the day when Jeff Bezos introduced the new model for a business that we had no specific experience with. All the partners here at Kleiner Perkins went home that night and bought books. I was on my way to the Galapagos Islands, and I knew that most bookstores in the area carried only one or two books on the area. That night I looked at Amazon.com and found eleven books to choose from. It was amazing. We invested $5 million dollars in the company (a large amount to invest in those days).

In a very real sense, my job is to help people's dreams flourish. I don't think you can be successful in the venture capital business if you say, "You've got to be kidding, you're crazy, that's never going to happen, get real." Those are expressions that just don't exist here in Silicon Valley. You have to be realistic about certain things (like running out of money), but it's important to say

"Terrific idea. How can we implement this?" You might come to the conclusion that the idea isn't practical, but at least you're not pouring sand and water on a spark. Enthusiasm is a very, very big part of what makes Silicon Valley work. And in my life here in Silicon Valley, believing in the unbelievable has worked out pretty well.

5

Innovation in Business Models

T. MICHAEL NEVENS

On December 31, 1998, Silicon Valley was the most valuable "company town" in the United States. Publicly held companies headquartered in Silicon Valley had a market capitalization of $743 billion. Wall Street firms had a market capitalization of $514 billion, Detroit's auto industry $136 billion, and Hollywood's entertainment firms $76 billion. Silicon Valley firms had achieved a value added per employee of $115,000 versus a $78,000 average across the United States. Further, value added per employee has been increasing at 6 percent per annum in Silicon Valley, significantly faster than U.S. productivity growth overall. Two in five Silicon Valley companies had achieved an annual growth rate greater than 20 percent, versus one in thirty-five across the United States.

Although Silicon Valley is justly famous for technological innovation, innovations in management approaches, policies, and investment strategies—in short, business models—are equally responsible for the Valley's extraordinary economic performance. These innovations are relevant well beyond the confines of Silicon Valley. Valley executives are leading the way in developing new business models, much as did Sloan, Morgan, and Zanuck earlier in this century in Detroit, on Wall Street, and in Hollywood.

Silicon Valley business models have several notable attributes. These companies are flexible. They move quickly. Many are highly focused, not only on a particular product set and customer segment, but also on one part of the value chain. As a result, most Silicon Valley companies are tightly networked to outsourcers and complementing suppliers. Silicon Valley business models are talent-driven. Technical, marketing, and managerial talent is in short supply, and Silicon Valley firms have devised ways to leverage other people's talent as well as develop their own. Finally, Silicon Valley business models are open and fluid. Open to new ideas and new people as well as to new technical standards, the winning companies in Silicon Valley are constantly inventing new ways of doing business.

Managers have developed innovative business models in response to changes in the microeconomics of the high-tech industries based in Silicon Valley. As I will describe, these changes are large in scale and broad in their reach. As a result, managers who have understood and acted on these changes have created enormous value for themselves and for their shareholders. Further, these changes are spreading to the rest of the economy at a rapid pace. Managers elsewhere can learn from the successes and failures of Silicon Valley managers in coping with these shifts in the economy.

DECLINE IN INTERACTION COSTS

Silicon Valley managers have taken advantage of a precipitous decline in interaction costs. Studies by McKinsey & Company's Global Institute show that interaction costs account for roughly half of all labor costs in most developed economies. Even in less developed economies, such as India, interaction costs account for 35 to 40 percent of labor costs. Because labor costs are typically in the range of 75 percent of total costs in the economy, interaction costs—not manufacturing or transporting goods—are the dominant factor in economic life. Interaction costs include searching, monitoring, and coordinating: searching for needed products or services, or for better prices or for new customers; monitoring the performance of employees, vendors, partners or customers, and market trends; and coordinating the activities of business units, business functions, and outsourcers.

These activities are important in all industries. In some service industries interaction costs constitute as much as 75 percent of total costs. In most high-tech industries they are as much as 50 to 60 percent of total costs.

Advances in computing and telecommunications, culminating in the world wide web, have slashed these costs by a factor of five to a factor of twenty. The output of Silicon Valley companies has enabled this reduction in transaction costs, which in turn has enabled significant innovation in Silicon Valley business models. Relational databases, enterprise resource planning software packages, TCP/IP networks, pervasive use of PCs, and the explosive growth of business-to-business electronic commerce have all played a role. Research by the McKinsey Global Institute has shown that leading companies have achieved an 85 to 95 percent reduction in interaction costs for tasks such as placing an order with an outside supplier and monitoring its execution.

Silicon Valley managers have aggressively exploited falling interaction costs because they have had easy, "down the street" access to outsourcers for many business functions. The rise of standards of many kinds in high-tech industries, the open culture of Silicon Valley industry, and the great number of specialized local companies have enabled Silicon Valley managers to be on the leading edge in exploiting this economic trend. They have pioneered several innovative business models, including the creation of "no bricks and mortar manufacturing" companies, "reverse" markets, and the increased integration of services and information into supply chains.

No Bricks and Mortar Manufacturing

"No bricks and mortar manufacturing" (i.e., contracting out all manufacturing to third parties) manifests itself in the rapid growth of both fabless semiconductor companies and contract manufacturers. Fabless semiconductor companies have grown from a minuscule portion of the industry to nearly 15 percent in 1998. These firms design products, coordinate the launch of new products, manage production schedules, and monitor production volumes, but contract out chip fabrication. Silicon Valley firms such as S3, Altera, and FdX have taken advantage of the digital platform that has dramatically lowered the costs of these sorts of interactions with manufacturers and foundries in Silicon Valley and around the world.

Similarly, firms such as Hewlett-Packard and Cisco rely on contract manufacturers to produce quality products and deliver them on time. Cisco, perhaps the pioneer and leading example of this trend, has invested almost nothing in its own manufacturing facilities while growing to $8.5 billion in revenue and a $146 billion market capitalization at the end of 1999. Cisco has contracted out nearly all of its manufacturing. To manage this network of third parties, Cisco invested in information technology and networks that allow Cisco and its contractors to operate from a single "digital image" of the business.

Reverse Markets

Reverse markets allow buyers to "advertise" their needs to many suppliers rather than suppliers advertising their wares to buyers. While this has long been possible, only recently has the Internet made it cost-effective for a single buyer to reach a large number of sellers. Ariba's purchasing software, Commerce One, and scores of other entrepreneurial ventures are enabling small and large companies to search for the best supplier at a fraction of the cost that would have been required before the advent of the web. This has enabled manufacturers and service providers to continually lower costs while creating a wholly new business model around market making.

Silicon Valley executives have exploited this trend, both as buyers and as sellers. More broadly, they have led the way in innovative integration of information and services into their supply chains. Firms as diverse as Intel, Oracle, and Sun Microsystems have used these technologies to create more supplier options for themselves (getting lower costs and better service); build tighter relationships with their customers by exploiting real time, rich customer data; and make better supply chain decisions by using more current, more complete data on suppliers and customers. The pressure of short product life cycles, the need to retool core IT systems to cope with growth, and the proximity of suppliers and customers, enabling rapid deployment across multiple firms, are three primary reasons why Silicon Valley firms have been quick to jump into the lead in this area.

EXPONENTIAL RETURNS TO SCALE

Scale has long been an important factor in the electronics industry. Silicon Valley firms invest heavily in research and development, manufacturing facilities, building brands, and creating worldwide sales, support, and distribution channels. Then, the costs of these facilities are spread over, hopefully, a large volume of sales. Each unit of incremental sales typically adds the same amount to covering the fixed costs or growing profits—a linear effect. Firms such as Intel and Oracle have made these traditional sorts of scale advantages an important part of their competitive and value-creation strategies.

Exponential scale advantages arise from so-called network effects that produce increasing returns. The more customers who buy a particular application package, the more service firms that will invest in learning how to install and support the package, and the more software developers that will invest in developing additional features to increase the utility of the product. So the more customers for the product, the more valuable the product becomes—a network effect. At the same time, the developer of the original application package can sell it at a progressively lower average cost. Thus, the profits or returns from each additional sale are higher than from the previous sale—an example of increasing returns.

Taken together, network effects resulting in increasing returns create nonlinear or exponential scale advantages. Many Silicon Valley businesses have adapted their business models to seize these opportunities. They defer profitability to invest more heavily in gaining customers. Or, they spend heavily on encouraging third parties to support their products—willingly yielding profitable portions of the business to these third parties in order to increase the value for customers and increase profits for their firm over the medium to long term.

For example, Intel has invested heavily and consistently in building the peripherals and software businesses that add value to the "Intel Inside" PC business. They spend money on developer programs to attract more companies and engineers to create products and services around the Intel architecture. Intel also invests a meaningful amount of its prodigious cash flow in start-ups pursuing these opportunities. Although Intel has earned attractive returns on these investments, the more important benefit is the accelerated growth of revenue and profits in the core business.

Well-known Internet companies such as Yahoo! have developed business models that have been highly valued by the stock market while still unprofitable, or at least not as profitable as they could be. The lack of profits has largely been due to a high and growing investment in attracting customers. Slower growth would allow greater profits. However, the markets seem to recognize the potential payoff in the longer term—exponential returns to scale. Less visibly, other Silicon Valley companies have adopted this model. Hewlett-Packard and Sun have both spent heavily on third-party software and service providers to support their Unix systems businesses. As important as the competition for price and performance leadership is, the executives leading these businesses understand and invest in the exponential scale advantages of network effects and increasing returns.

EMERGENCE OF ECONOMIC MULTIPLIERS

Over the last five years, companies around the world have invested $6 to $7 trillion in information technology and digital communications. In the United States, this investment in a digital technology platform has accounted for roughly 50 percent of capital spending. Importantly, the uses of this technology are heavily dependent on standards. The Internet protocols (FTP, HTTP, TCP/IP, XML) are well known. Equally important is the emergence of the "Wintel" standard for personal computers, SQL, ODBC, and other standards that allow enterprises to manage software, data, and communications across products from a variety of vendors. Similarly, the leading enterprise resource planning (ERP) software vendors that control most of the applications market have created a de facto standardization of some important business processes. Multiprotocol routers have enabled the interoperation of diverse data networks.

In an important sense, new products and services that comply with these standards can "assume the platform" and leverage a large chunk of the $7 trillion investment in digital technology. The rapid growth of companies such as Netscape, Ariba, and E*Trade depends on their being able to leverage the platforms customers already have to add value disproportionate to the cost of their products. Despite the hype about Netscape's competition with Microsoft, the rapid growth of Netscape's browser business depended on (1) the existence of a pervasive, modem-equipped Windows platform, (2) the emergence of Internet service providers (ISPs) willing to provide Internet access at low cost, and (3) the investment of thousands of web site operators who gave Netscape customers something interesting and valuable to browse. Similarly, Netscape's server business grew rapidly on Sun's Solaris server-installed base. E*Trade was one of the pioneers in delivering a sophisticated service and distinctive customer experience via a simple desk-top machine. E*Trade could presume that customers had a browser, a modem, and an Internet connection provided by an ISP that had installed modem banks across the country.

Silicon Valley companies such as Oracle have been more aggressive than most in taking advantage of the capital deployed by others. Oracle worked closely with Hewlett-Packard and Sun Microsystems to ensure that Oracle's database software was available and performed well on the standard Unix platforms sold by these market leaders. This gave Oracle access to a large and growing installed base. Oracle also quickly adopted and influenced standards for accessing and connecting databases—including Internet access. Thus, Oracle's customers were able to be early users of the growing Internet and world wide web infrastructures. Finally, Oracle's customers and other software developers invested billions of dollars to build applications and business processes around Oracle software. The open culture of Silicon Valley companies and the proximity to so many other players gives Oracle and other Silicon Valley companies an edge in exploiting this global platform.

IBM was the most impressive growth company of the 1960s. IBM had a compound growth of 21.3 percent from 1965 to 1970. From 1990 to 1998 Dell grew at a compound growth rate of 92.5 percent, Cisco at 90.9 percent, Sun at 42.4 percent, and Intel at 33.2 percent. By innovating while embracing standards, these companies, like Oracle, created business models with stunning levels of growth and value creation.

THE CHANGING ECONOMICS OF SCARCITY

No longer are capital, labor, and land the factors that determine which companies win and lose. Rather, the scarce commodities are billion-dollar investment opportunities, management talent, and the attention of customers and sales channels.

Readily Available Capital

The globalization of capital markets and the increase in the value of the equity markets over the past decade have provided relatively easy and low-cost access to capital for most companies and entrepreneurs. Venture capital funds have been raising and investing record amounts of money each quarter for the last few years. Similarly, private equity or buy-out funds have been raising and deploying record amounts of capital. With the addition of substantial amounts of seed funding from so-called angel investors and a relatively robust market for initial public offerings, few good ideas or businesses lack for funds. In particular, Silicon Valley companies have little or no trouble attracting funding. Surveys typically show Silicon Valley receiving 30 to 40 percent of all U.S. venture capital investment and the lion's share of IPO proceeds.

In fact, the opposite problem is beginning to present itself. Investors are seeking larger investment opportunities. Venture funds are moving toward later rounds and larger stakes in individual companies. Equity funds are seeking larger companies and business units to acquire. Ideas requiring deployment of large amounts of capital are, in fact, in short supply. Many start-ups target niche markets. These companies can develop a narrowly focused product, build sales and service networks, operate globally, and still consume less than $100 million in invested capital.

One successful software start-up illustrates this phenomenon. The founders raised roughly $5 million to build a prototype product that demonstrated the commercial feasibility of a technology developed as part of a postdoctoral research project. They then raised $15 million that was spent over 11 months as they built and tested a ready-to-ship version of the product, hired the first sales and service people, and got a few customers up and running. Their final round of private fundraising was for $40 million. By the time they consumed this—14 months later—their annual revenue run rate was around $20 million per year. They had positive cash flow. They went public about this time with a nearly $400 million valuation. The cash proceeds from the IPO were modest—roughly $80 million—and largely served as a buffer against unexpected difficulties. The IPO was driven mainly by the founders' and investors' desire for liquidity.

By contrast, new companies seeking to provide high-speed local access to telecommunications networks, or applications "over the wire" to medium and small businesses, often require several hundred million dollars in capital to launch. Similarly, venture capitalists are now receiving plans to invest as much as $200 to $250 million to launch web businesses. These plans factor in the up-front marketing costs to build a large customer base to benefit from scale and network effects.

Abundant Labor, Scarce Talent

The globalization of the economy, combined with digital communications technologies and increased automation of nearly all manufacturing processes, has largely alleviated labor shortages. Can't hire enough software engineers in Silicon Valley? Open a development center in Bangalore, India, and build a network link to the rest of your design teams around the world. Similarly, labor-intensive assembly operations in the semiconductor industry can easily be located in Penang, Malaysia. As Cisco has demonstrated with its "no bricks and mortar philosophy," production planning, quality control, and inventory management can be done over networks as easily as if the plant were down the road. Although there have been no comprehensive surveys, it is reasonable to suspect that one-third to one-half of software companies have moved some development offshore and that nearly all labor-intensive assembly manufacturing has been moved as well.

What remains in short supply is the technical management and leadership talent to run development, manufacturing, marketing, and sales. McKinsey's internal research project "War for Technical Talent" estimates a worldwide shortage of roughly 650,000 skilled engineers in 1999. A recent survey conducted by A. T. Kearney for Joint Venture: Silicon Valley estimated that it took an average of 3.7 months to fill a variety of senior technical and managerial positions in Silicon Valley. For some skills, the survey reported an average search time of six months. Search firms anecdotally report literally scores of open searches for CEOs, senior sales and marketing executives, and CFOs.

In response, managers are outsourcing functions to leverage the abilities of accounting firms, IT consultants, marketing service firms, and others to aggregate talent. Similarly, venture capitalists and private equity firms are investing as much time in nurturing a network of executives they can deploy as they do raising money.

Many executives cite the availability of talent as one of the reasons they locate their firm in Silicon Valley. Not only is there a large career-mobile technical and managerial workforce, but a large contingent workforce is available as well. There is a small, but important, pool of "temporary CEOs." The venture community calls on one of these "temps" for a few months to help a company over a rough patch, often on a part-time basis, while a search is conducted. In addition, Silicon Valley firms can outsource information technology, marketing, internal audit, purchasing, and even sales (to so-called manufacturers reps). This allows management to spend little or no time on recruiting and managing people in functions that are not critical to their success.

Although this process is seen in many parts of the world, it is more extensively used in Silicon Valley because of the open culture of Valley firms and the availability of a wide range of alternative providers just down the road. The demand for these services has also attracted people drawn to contingent employment. Many former employees of technology companies have started their own service businesses around this demand for high-level contingent labor. In addition to the usual business services, they offer "CFOs for rent," temporary manufacturing managers, and the occasional CEO "temp."

Similarly, savvy CEOs are spending a significant part of their time attracting and retaining talented managers. Often they hire people without a specific position in mind, deploy them on a special project, and then put them into a management slot a few months later. These same firms spend time sharpening their business strategies to attract senior technical and managerial talent and depart from classic organizational design rules (e.g., spans of control, size of organizational units to justify high salaries) in order to "overstock" with talent. In some markets, cornering the best of the available talent has become an explicit and likely successful competitive strategy. It is widely acknowledged that two specialized semiconductor firms, Linear and Maxim, have used these approaches to corner the market as analog designers. As a result, they have been very successful in establishing a leadership position in several product areas in this fast-growing segment of the semiconductor market.

The Geography of Mind Share

Although real estate values are soaring in Silicon Valley, the location independence offered by networking has taken some pressure off land as a scarce resource. At the same time, the plethora of new products and services has made it harder to capture the attention of customers, distributors, and retailers. Silicon Valley managers are developing innovative business models to overcome this problem.

One obvious solution is the symbiotic relationship developing between companies such as Cisco and Microsoft and the venture capital community. These companies have mind share with the channel and customers. By buying the best of breed of the new venture-funded start-ups, the large companies can leverage the value of their intangible asset, mind share, leaving the risk of early stage research to the venture capitalists, who are arguably better suited to manage that risk. At the same time, the venture firms and their entrepreneurs avoid the cost, time, and risk of developing brands, channels, and support operations, a risk they are often ill suited to manage. This sophisticated form of risk sharing is becoming an increasingly common business model.

At the same time, smaller companies with new products and services are resorting to innovative techniques to gain mind share. One increasingly common, if controversial, model is to promote the CEO as a personality. CEOs such as Scott McNealy at Sun and Larry Ellison at Oracle, and venture capitalists such as John Doerr at Kleiner Perkins, have all used this technique with varying results. Although these approaches can be powerful in helping companies break through the competition for mind share in the short run, the long-term viability of this sort of business model is not yet proven.

WHAT'S NEXT FOR SILICON VALLEY

Flexible, fast, focused, open, tightly networked, and talent-driven are apt descriptions of Silicon Valley business models. While these labels are generally used to point out positive attributes of Silicon Valley businesses, they point to challenges as well. Meeting these challenges will, in part, lead to the next wave of innovations in Silicon Valley business models.

For example, the generous use of stock grants and stock options has overwhelmed cash as the favored form of compensation. Many talented executives and senior technical managers move from company to company and start-up to start-up. They receive even more generous grants of stock and options with each move. Many established companies now have a hard time keeping their best executives from being lured away into these sorts of arrangements. These companies cannot offer similarly valued equity currency as start-ups and they cannot afford to make up the difference in cash. In some extreme cases, the future prospects of important companies have been diminished by this sort of talent loss.

This sophisticated, highly compensated contingent workforce is not what most people think of when they think of contingent workers. The common perception is of a laborer who is struggling to support a family on less than a full-time income and who often works without medical or retirement benefits. Sadly, this latter type of contingent work is growing in Silicon Valley as well. The presence of contingent workers at both the top and the bottom of the income spectrum is contributing to the growing wage disparity in Silicon Valley, at the same time that it creates the flexibility that helps the industry innovate and grow.

Besides the social issues raised by the growing wage disparity, there are important questions about the effect of workforce instability on the long-term health of the industry. If fewer institutions are built to last, the industry will have to find other structures to create stability. For example, some venture capitalists talk about the Keiretsu (a network of noncompeting companies linked via investors, cross-board memberships, and the like that do business with each other on favorable terms to help all of the members prosper) they are forming among their investors, large company "strategic partners," and their cadre of executives and entrepreneurs.

Whether this Keiretsu form endures or not remains to be seen. It is likely that alternatives to the enduring, publicly traded, limited liability company will emerge from the ongoing innovations in Silicon Valley business models. The recent successes of the Internet Capital Group and CMGI may point the way. These firms act as VCs but continue to hold important, often controlling stakes in the companies they found. They then shuffle companies, assets, and talent back and forth to maximize the performance of the whole portfolio. The next generation of Silicon Valley business model innovations will likely occur in this area.

So, what innovations are we likely to see in business models in Silicon Valley in the next few years? Many businesses are likely to become much more focused on either turning out innovative products, or building large-scale infrastructures, or managing customer relationships in particular segments—but not all three. Today, many if not most companies are aggregations of these three types of businesses. Divestitures to create focused firms and re-aggregations to create scale are necessary and likely steps down this path. This would be one logical outcome of the trends we have already seen in response to lower interaction costs enabling outsourcing and other new forms of business organization. The semiconductor industry offers one illustration of this emerging model. Fabless design companies are developing new products to be manufactured by foundries and taken to market, ultimately by equipment vendors that sell and service to end customers.

We will see the inevitable emergence of dominant or monopoly competitors in markets that exhibit network effects and increasing returns to scale. Other competitors will have to innovate to find niche businesses that can co-exist with these giants or sell out to the eventual winners in a timely way. Antitrust regulators will also have to innovate to respond quickly to abuses while not fighting the microeconomics driving these trends. Similarly, there should be increasing innovation in the competition around standard setting and around the exploitation of standards in ways that allow firms to assume the platform and accelerate their growth.

We are nearly certain to see innovative arrangements that allow companies to draw on talent via mechanisms other than full-time, permanent employment. Finally, both executives and political leaders will need to find innovative ways to deal with the growing income disparity that could undermine the social cohesion of the Valley. At the same time, these changes need to be crafted so as not to interfere with the ability of Valley firms to innovate and compete in the global market. Without these innovations, the future of the Valley is unlikely to be as bright.

6

Four Styles of Valley Entrepreneurship

CHONG-MOON LEE

Entrepreneurship is the ability to create and build a vision from
practically nothing: fundamentally it is a human, creative act.
— JEFFRY TIMMONS, *New Venture Creation*

Silicon Valley entrepreneurs are different from traditional entrepreneurs and small business founders. The rapid pace and "invent-the-future" orientation of Silicon Valley corresponds to a unique way of thinking about business management and about the world. In this chapter, I explore a dozen aspects of business that illustrate the unique mindset of the Silicon Valley entrepreneur. This unique perspective shapes and is shaped by the Silicon Valley habitat. I also discuss four approaches to entrepreneurship, using a famous Silicon Valley example of each.

Most discussions about Silicon Valley entrepreneurs focus on their brilliant ideas and insights, their decisive actions, and the special know-how and talents that have made them so successful in business. Few authors have anything to say about the personal qualities of entrepreneurs that might also contribute to success. I would therefore like to begin this chapter with some comments about the personality and emotional makeup of the entrepreneur. These qualities seem to hold true regardless of the entrepreneur's business style.

First, entrepreneurs need to create rich connections to other people. They must build a substantial network of people: a management team and employees, investors, suppliers, customers. They share their vision with this extended group, and they solicit feedback to assess their progress. In Silicon Valley, entrepreneurs tend to share their idea with a broader group, including potential competitors. They are willing to share valuable business expertise. Satisfaction comes from the act of sharing knowledge, promoting a personal business vision, and creating win-win situations.

This need to create and maintain close connections with many people persists throughout the entrepreneur's professional life. An enduring need to connect with people may be the reason that so many successful entrepreneurs become angel investors and advisors to entrepreneurs, or start another company themselves. In spite of the superstar quality that seems to set some successful entrepreneurs apart from everyone else, they are not loners. They can't build a business alone. They share their vision, their work, and their risks. They are an integral part of the team they create.

A second general observation about entrepreneurs has to do with the high level of intensity that they bring to their business activities. There are many personality traits that an executive might possess, such as persistence, motivation to excel, and optimism. It is the emotional intensity of these and other personal qualities, however, that is the compelling feature of entrepreneurs. All successful businesspeople have to be highly motivated during the course of their careers, but entrepreneurs appear to have a depth of passion that brings them extraordinary emotional strength. This strength helps them withstand the stress of taking business risks as they create their companies. In the words of Steve Jobs, CEO of Apple Computer, "You need to have passion about your idea and you need to feel so strongly about it that you're willing to risk a lot. Starting a company is so hard that if you're not passionate about it, you will give up" (Jager and Ortiz 1997). Venture capitalists often emphasize that they are looking for passion in the entrepreneur because they understand the need for that dedication and intensity.

Finally, I would like to point out that in Silicon Valley connectedness is a way of life, and passion is understood and supported. Silicon Valley's encouragement of entrepreneurs is embedded deeply both in the business support infrastructure (for example, venture capitalists, attorneys, and consultants), and in the attitudes of the general population. Local government, schools, and civic associations facilitate communication and connection through every means, from the installation of high-speed city networks to sponsorship of business gatherings. Far more importantly, area residents, whether part of the high-tech community or not, fundamentally approve of entrepreneurial endeavors. They support entrepreneurs in the pursuit of their passions. In particular, people understand and accept the high-risk nature of business creation, and they respect the efforts of the entrepreneurs whether they succeed or fail.

SILICON VALLEY ENTREPRENEURS

In this section I discuss some of the differences in perspectives and approaches among small business owners, traditional entrepreneurs, and entrepreneurs in Silicon Valley. By "traditional entrepreneurs" I mean founders of traditional businesses such as Sam Walton of Wal-Mart and Ken Olsen of Digital Equipment Corp. This type of entrepreneur builds big companies with stable management hierarchies, formal processes, and a collective will to win by dominating all competitors. The importance of the "team" is paramount, and employee loyalty is highly valued. Business secrets are closely guarded, risks are tightly controlled, and cooperation with competitors is rare.

In contrast, Silicon Valley entrepreneurs have created a business culture in which the rapid pace of technological change compels a higher level of risk-taking; an unusual degree of connection and cooperation with competitors, investors, suppliers, outsourcers, and customers; and a stronger orientation toward the value of individual employees rather than the team. The dynamic environment also engenders more acceptance of business failure as an integral part of the business creation process, and produces highly flexible professionals that can move easily from failed companies to new opportunities.

I acknowledge that there is far more diversity among these three types of entrepreneurs than I will describe in this chapter. My primary goal, however, is to point out some of the fundamental differences in perspective that characterize these three groups. I also want to focus particularly on the thinking of Silicon Valley entrepreneurs, and observe how the habitat may have shaped their ideas. I summarize the points in Table 6.1.

Motivation for Venture Creation

The possible motivations for starting a business are many. Small business owners most often express a desire to control their own destiny and obtain some measure of financial security. Minimizing risk is central to their interest in being self-employed. In contrast, traditional entrepreneurs think about creating a new product or service, or finding a niche in a large market and competing in that niche. They are willing to take risks and are highly motivated to succeed. They focus on one big idea, one vision, and they follow it through to its logical end.

In Silicon Valley the motivation that many entrepreneurs describe for starting a business is often considerably more extreme, demonstrating the intensity and passion that I described earlier. These entrepreneurs are revolutionary. They say that they want to change the world. More importantly, they actually *expect* to change the world. Their location in the Silicon Valley habitat—where the infrastructure is seemingly optimized for creating global business revolutions—gives these already passionate entrepreneurs the additional confidence and resources to do the nearly impossible (i.e., change the world) on a regular basis. Jim Clark, for example, decided to change the way the entire healthcare industry did business after a prolonged illness provided him with an opportunity to experience first-hand the frustrating administrative process. In 1996 he started Healtheon, now a $4 billion company, and he is well under way in his bid to use technology to change entirely the world of healthcare services.

Leadership

For the small business owner, the company is a way of life, an extension of the family. Leading the company consists primarily of providing management decision-making and an appropriate work environment for a small number of employees. The traditional entrepreneur has a more difficult leadership task. His company may have more employees and a considerably more complex set of business challenges. The entrepreneur must provide strong leadership within his organization to keep employees motivated to innovate and compete, and to ensure the long-term stability and success of his company. Strong internal leadership includes such formidable, but less entrepreneurial, tasks as building an effective management hierarchy to offer a reasonable career path to employees; creating salary-based performance incentives; instituting supportive

Table 6.1 Silicon Valley Entrepreneurs Compared to Small Business Owners and Traditional Entrepreneurs

	Small Business Owner	Traditional Entrepreneur	Silicon Valley Entrepreneur
Motivation for Venture Creation	Make daily living and hope for financial success. Achieve social and economic security. Work for oneself, not for others. Commercialize a particular idea, technology, or skill. Business style reflects owner's personality traits.	High motivation for success; willingness to compete. Innovative ideas and concept. Commercialization of highly sophisticated technology or patent. Accumulation of wealth, resources, influence, fame, and respect.	Revolutionary mindset; wants to change the world with brilliant ideas. Willingness to compete and take risk. Aiming for global level of success with entirely new technology. Seeks financial reward, increasing sphere of influence, respect, and name recognition.
Ownership	Privately owned by founders or partners.	Founders or management want to own controlling interest, or at least a majority for management control. Focused on maximizing return by leveraging ownership position.	Try to control market rather than company. Founders settle for a smaller piece of a very big pie. Try to maximize return by dominating market and therefore increasing the net value of the enterprise.
Management Team	Any age level. Business sense or experience a plus. Professional background not required, unless the specific business model demands it.	More middle aged, with years of industry experience. Professional experience or track record valued. Highly specialized concept or technical knowledge required. Academics sometimes on board or advise management	Management often divided into two distinctly different groups: young engineering team, including founders; and board of directors, consisting of venture capitalists, industry experts, and advisors, as well as founders. Board often brings in professional management team, CEO or COO, controller/CFO, etc., and works with team to build the business. Highly strategic and globally oriented.
Managerial Style	Trial and error, learns through experience. More personal than organizational; professional managerial skill not a priority. Local or community orientation, rather than national or global. Cautious, avoids risk as much as possible.	Organized according to management team's previous experience. Greater emphasis on professionalism than in Silicon Valley's management style.	Young founders with little managerial experience. Flat and flexible work environment, on-the-spot decision making, globally targeted strategy. Emphasis on continuous product innovation dictates high R&D investment.

Managerial Style (continued)	Steady cash flow and steady growth most important.	Risk taking weighs heavily on management, because in many cases founders serve as CEO/CTO, or senior managers of marketing, sales, and/or finance.	Risk shared among founders, investors/board members, and other business partners. Concept and technology may lie with founders, but strategy for success rests on management team and board of directors. Board serves as risk minimizer or risk sharer. Refusal to accept number two position in the market; wants to stay ahead because of "winner take all" or "fast eat slower" nature of the industry.
Leadership	Focus is on the business as a "way of life." Emphasis on maintaining strong relationships. Leads by example. Encourages collaboration. Anticipates small but solid wins.	Focus is on envisioning future success. Searches for challenging ideas and opportunities: new technology, products, and markets. Recognizes and rewards contributions. Creates new management leadership.	Focus is on collective effort and struggle, collective sharing of results. Envisions the future success, inspiring a shared vision. Encourages team effort by sharing the progress of business development. Recognizes contributions and celebrates accomplishment.
Employees	Employees trade off high stress, high risk, high pay for job security, reasonable hours, intimate atmosphere. Emphasis on team rather than reliance on individual talent. Recruitment from local area.	Prospective technologists recruited on national or even global level. Employees highly motivated and goal oriented because of superior compensation packages. Less mobility in the workforce than in Silicon Valley.	Extremely motivated, multicultural, competitive, and highly skilled technologists. Steady flow of engineers from over 20 colleges and universities in the region, coupled with high-quality immigrants. Young engineers inspired by local stories of mergers, acquisitions, and IPOs. Employees know their goal and expect to be amply rewarded when they achieve it. High mobility in the workforce. Three OK's—OK to talk to competitors, OK to move to another company, and OK to fail.
R&D and Innovation	Constant struggle to maintain business, stay competitive, and improve products/services.	R&D and innovation are top priorities. However, may not be able to find the experts	Global IT industry leadership in R&D and innovation.

Table 6.1 (*continued*) Silicon Valley Entrepreneurs Compared to Small Business Owners and Traditional Entrepreneurs

	Small Business Owner	Traditional Entrepreneur	Silicon Valley Entrepreneur
R&D and Innovation (*continued*)	Owner is responsible for enhancing product offering and creating new business. Long product development cycles with limited resources for innovation. Few accumulated technological assets.	needed locally and on time; sometimes have to outsource to a national base. May achieve highly creative ideas for new products and markets, as with 7-Eleven, FedEx, UPS, Compaq, and MCI.	Excellent access to new technology within the region. Specialized engineering resources available locally in conjunction with universities, including Stanford and U.C. Berkeley. Highly talented, tightly integrated, multilevel and multicultural project teams. Speed is everything; intense push to reduce time to market.
Outsourcing and Networking	Some outsourcing relationships developed in the normal course of business, but often not a central strategy. Aggressive business owners will try to expand their growth network by attending local and national events.	Very important to find high-quality engineering capability, consultants, advisers in the local area, but talent may be difficult to find, or unavailable. Often local talent is general, rather than highly specialized in the area the business needs. Global-level networking may not be there when it is needed.	Molding new ideas, defining technology, and developing products together with an outsourced team is common practice. Many world-class options available for any service in the IT area. Networking activities concentrate locally, offering many opportunities for information exchange, knowledge creation, and mobilizing resources.
Target Market	Local at first stage; may hope to expand to regional or even national level. Competition with existing products in an established market. Concerns mostly revolve around cost and service in the particular industry.	National immediately, and then global in most cases; in some cases simultaneous reach for national and global market. In many cases, collection of market information as well as connection and penetration into foreign markets takes longer than in Silicon Valley. Focus on winning new customers through technologically innovative products, building partnerships with customers in product design and support markets.	Often global from the start. Global customer information and networks available through local channels. Emphasis on speed in marketing, presale, and postsale activities through business partners locally as well as globally. Aim to be alert and competitive with respect to global markets: specialize in niche, but look for high-growth-potential markets; maintain technological superiority and strategy that can defend global markets; aim not just to meet customer need, but to exceed expectations and educate customer.

Growth Potential	Influenced by economic cycles.	Seeks fastest global penetration, strategic partnerships, and build-up of service networks in major countries and markets.	Growth is dependent on ability to stay agile in a constantly changing marketplace, in which new technology evolves every day, existing technology renews every 3–6 months, market changes every 6 months. In most cases, business model will change every year or two.
	Aggressive growth is not the first priority; steady growth preferred.	May achieve extremely aggressive revenue and market-share growth.	Company may grow quickly by acquiring technology, if that is faster than research and development.
		Goal is to become the leader in the market in the shortest possible time.	Strong emphasis on global alliances, partnerships, and leadership in order to maintain growth momentum.

business processes; and developing programs to train and retrain employees throughout their careers with the company.

The Silicon Valley venture business founder may have some different challenges. He hires entrepreneurial-minded employees who participate in the ownership of the company. Not only must he inspire these employees to work within a common vision, but he must also convince them that his vision will be a successful one. As Andy Grove of Intel puts it, a leader "needs to have the goodwill and intellectual investment of the employees that he or she leads."[1] In the highly mobile and talent-focused labor environment of Silicon Valley, a leader's failure to make a convincing case for the ultimate success of his vision will result in his inability to get and keep the best people, and may well lead to failure for his company.

A Silicon Valley entrepreneur often finds that it is not enough to provide strong internal leadership and vision. He must also effectively communicate his passion and vision to a broader community. Unlike the founders of Wal-Mart and Starbucks, the Valley entrepreneur is often creating a brand-new industry based on an unfamiliar new technology or business model. He must explain and promote not just his company, but also his vision for the new market or industry he is creating. He must undertake this larger leadership role with regard to investors, suppliers, customers, and, frequently, to the public at large as well. For example, six years ago, Netscape's Marc Andreessen traveled and spoke widely, not just about his company, but to explain what the Internet was and how it could benefit both businesses and individuals in their daily lives.

Ownership

A small business owner typically retains 100 percent ownership in his company. Since the primary motivation in founding a company is financial independence and control, there are usually no outside investors. He may, however, take on some relatively small amount of debt financing. Traditional entrepreneurs must balance the desire for full ownership of their companies with the need to develop their ideas and operations quickly enough to compete. By the time that their companies have reached maturity, they may still retain a significant ownership position, but have probably become answerable to one or more outside shareholders. In sharp contrast, the Silicon Valley entrepreneur may end up with only a very small share of his own company by the time it is sold or goes public. The founder accepts this dilution because taking significant outside investment allows him to create a big company with a big market opportunity very quickly. In the end he can make more money by accepting a small piece of a much larger pie, and his company can achieve greater success.

Entrepreneurs that accept money from outside investors always consider the issue of company control. Can they run their companies effectively if others have a say in the management? These entrepreneurs, especially entrepreneurs in Silicon Valley, have come to recognize that having control of their companies is not the essential point at all. What's important is the influence that they have on the outside world. As Professor William F. Miller, of Stanford's Graduate School of Business, points out: "Successful high-tech entrepreneurs recognize that you can not control your fate by controlling your company. You control your fate by controlling your market. Once an entrepreneur focuses on gaining control of his or her market, all other desired outcomes follow."[2]

Risk Taking

Steady cash flow and steady growth are of key importance to the small business owner. While there are different levels of risks for small manufacturing companies and small service providers, both prefer to avoid risk as much as possible. On the other hand, traditional entrepreneurs recognize that accepting risk is an integral part of starting a venture business, but they may not have the financial resources or external support infrastructure to undertake significant risk. Alternatively, they may have sufficient resources, but prefer to assume less risk by choosing a more moderate growth path or a narrower business focus.

Silicon Valley entrepreneurs take enormous risk in order to create new technologies, new products, new markets, and sometimes entire new industries. Gunjan Sinha, a young Silicon Valley entrepreneur and co-founder of WhoWhere? Inc. and eGain Communications Corp., has said that he raises his goals and expectations until he feels scared: "If I don't feel scared, the bar isn't high enough." He does not mean to say that he takes foolish risks. Rather, he sets challenging goals and works hard to reduce the risks in pursuing those goals.[3]

Sinha and other local entrepreneurs have learned to use the Silicon Valley habitat to manage risk. First, they share the risk broadly through distribution of equity. Start-ups offer equity not only to investors but also to employees, suppliers, and every type of service provider, from attorneys to incubators. All players now have more to gain if the start-up succeeds, and of course more to lose if they fail. Everyone associated with the company is therefore motivated to see it succeed. Thus the second way that Silicon Valley entrepreneurs reduce risk is to actively seek advice and help from everyone motivated to see their company succeed. Members of the board of directors and advisory boards provide networking opportunities, and employees actively recruit more people. Both angel investors and venture capitalists will spend significant amounts of time to guide new entrepreneurs and help them with everything from informal brainstorming to putting together the management team. Some angels include themselves on the management team.

Managerial Style

Small businesses with few employees often have informal management practices. Their management style is focused on managing personal relationships with employees. New business owners may have to learn how to run a successful business by trial and error, since they don't often find mentors or more experienced advisors. Founders of traditional venture firms may have more managerial experience by the time they start their ventures. They are more likely to institute a formal management infrastructure from day one, and to practice a management style with a high level of process, well suited to a company with significant growth potential. A great many Silicon Valley entrepreneurs, however, are without previous managerial experience. They tend to create flat and flexible work environments that encourage managerial flexibility, creativity, and on-the-spot decision-making. This informal managerial style turns out to be especially effective when starting up a business in a globally competitive, rapidly changing industry like high tech, where time-to-market with the first product may determine success. There is time later to develop a management hierarchy and business processes as the company succeeds and grows.

Management Team

Individuals of every age, experience level, and background start small businesses. Tenacity, hard work, and a few other key character traits can often compensate for a lack of specific experience or education. In traditional venture businesses, where there are outside investors, a solid management team is usually required. Often the management team has relevant professional background that investors rely on, as well as a good track record in the industry. Substantial experience implies a middle-aged management team.

Silicon Valley management teams may be younger and have less experience. Fortunately, young engineers and newly minted MBA's can get substantial support from more experienced investors, advisors, and outsourcing firms. Their venture capitalists may bring in more seasoned management or help the entrepreneurs recruit experienced people to serve on the boards of directors. The Silicon Valley habitat has in effect created a way to combine the creativity and energy of youthful entrepreneurs with the experience necessary to succeed in a competitive global environment.

Employees

Small business owners, traditional entrepreneurs, and Silicon Valley entrepreneurs each offer a very different work environment to their employees. They each tend to attract, therefore, job candidates with different interests and priorities. Employees use a number of criteria in their selection decisions, including the number of likely overtime hours, the compensation structure, and the company's perceived stability. Potential employees may also consider other, more subjective factors. For example, in high-tech start-ups the charisma of the CEO and the perceived competence of the existing technical team can often influence the entrepreneur's ability to recruit new technical talent.

As a practical matter, small business owners cannot recruit beyond their local or regional boundaries. Moreover, the compensation and challenges offered to potential employees are likely to be comparatively modest. On the other hand, owners may be able to offer other attractive job features, such as personal mentoring or no overtime.

Traditional entrepreneurs can and do recruit nationally, and more often in recent years, they recruit internationally as well. They typically offer superior compensation packages, including stock options, to attract high-quality employees. They take pains to retain these high-quality employees to help build a stable and successful company. In contrast to traditional entrepreneurs, who want good people aspiring to make a long-term contribution to the company's success, Silicon Valley entrepreneurs are focused squarely on recruiting the best employees for the present. They know they must pay extraordinary premiums for the right people—people with exactly the right expertise who can come on board immediately and make a significant contribution in the short term.

This short-term, merit-based hiring philosophy, combined with the Valley's unusually diverse demographics, tends to produce a highly multicultural mix of employees in most Silicon Valley companies. These heterogeneous groups of employees share a common outlook, however: they are all entrepreneurial in their attitudes about their jobs. They are extremely mobile workers who "vote with their feet" for the companies that they believe have high potential for success. They are highly competitive, they work the same long hours as the founders, and they understand the risk of business failure just as the founders do. This type of top team is vital to help the entrepreneurs create extraordinary value quickly in the globally competitive and rapidly changing high-tech marketplace.

Creativity and Innovation

All companies need to be creative in their business strategies. Creativity in small businesses is often tempered, however, by limited resources and by a desire to avoid undue risks. By their very nature, traditional venture companies come into being and grow successfully by being creative, not just once, but repeatedly. Not only does a successful venture need *sustained* creativity, but it needs creativity in all aspects of the business. It is obvious to most entrepreneurs, for example, that a brilliant technology cannot succeed on its own; it must be coupled with creative strategies in marketing, distribution, finance, sales, and every other function in the company.

The Silicon Valley habitat gives its entrepreneurs a special edge in creativity. Entrepreneurs aggressively seek out advantageous partnerships and alliances with complementary area firms to help distribute the responsibility for massive and rapid innovation. More interestingly, the habitat's support firms also play an important role in the invention process. Entrepreneurs can outsource not just routine tasks, but creativity and innovation, to a huge infrastructure of support firms experienced in helping start-ups succeed. These support firms, offering every service from advertising to web site architecture, have first-hand experience in many more start-ups than any individual Silicon Valley entrepreneur. As a group repository for the knowledge of the Valley, they allow the entrepreneur and his small team to be as continually innovative and globally competitive as a company with far more people.

R&D

All companies need to innovate in order to survive. In the smallest firms, it is the owner-manager who must observe the changes in the marketplace and respond to them. In traditional entrepreneurial firms, there are usually mechanisms in place to address the design and development of new product and service offerings. Often, the biggest problem is finding enough appropriate expertise locally to do timely R&D. In Silicon Valley, almost every conceivable expertise is available locally, with service offerings tuned to fast-moving start-ups. Valley entrepreneurs can successfully outsource complex engineering and business tasks to globally competitive support firms, or collaborate with professors or students at one of many local universities. The entrepreneur must ensure that vital R&D is done timely and well, but he does not have to build a sophisticated R&D capability internally. His role is primarily to drive the product development process toward competitive innovation in the midst of rapid change.

John Chambers, CEO of Cisco Systems, has taken the outsourcing of R&D to the extreme. Cisco acquires entire small companies that have already completed the new product development that Cisco needs. They call this strategy "acquisition and development." In 1993, he and former CEO John Morgridge recognized that Cisco would not be able to develop new technologies in-house at the pace that the swiftly moving networking market required. While the company offered a growing array of hubs, switches, and routers, it was not able to develop timely offerings to address customer demands for complete networking solutions. They therefore embarked upon a strategy of rapid acquisition and assimilation of "small local companies with market-proven technologies that complemented Cisco's own ever-broadening line" (LaPlante 1997). In the past seven years, Chambers has overseen the acquisition of more than 50 companies to acquire the technology and technical talent that his company needs to stay competitive.

Outsourcing and Networking

My preceding comments about R&D might give readers the impression that outsourcing new product development or other services is purely a business transaction. In reality, outsourcing relationships are often extensions of networked personal relationships, similar to partnerships. In Silicon Valley, the idea of outsourcers as partners is particularly relevant, since the level of trust needed to outsource key strategic components of the business, and the heavy reliance on those outsourcers to perform, is extreme.

Networking, whether for the purpose of finding outsourcing partners or not, is a universal activity of all business leaders. Small business owners may confine their networking to local or regional organizations, while venture leaders may network nationally or even globally. Silicon Valley entrepreneurs have some networking advantages, since many of the people they need to know—investors, potential employees, service providers—are local. Moreover, the entrepreneur's location in Silicon Valley often opens doors to companies elsewhere in the world that want to establish closer connections with companies in the region. While this global network of entrepreneurs grows stronger every year, the local personal network in Silicon Valley remains uniquely powerful and productive.

Networking may lead to formal business alliances, such as co-marketing agreements and joint ventures. The openness of the entrepreneur to seek out and make these alliances is often indicative of his eventual success. A 1997 joint study of Andersen Consulting and Stanford University found that high-performing entrepreneurial companies had three times as many market alliances and collaborative investment initiatives as low performers.[4]

Target Market and Market Size

While the market aspirations of small business owners and entrepreneurs are unbounded, the practical reality is dictated by both the nature of the business idea and the company's access to funds. Local or perhaps regional plays are all that most small business owners can do, or even want to do. Loans or investments for small businesses typically come from non–venture capital sources that are risk-averse and limited in amount. These conservative funding sources make it difficult for small business owners to target a national market, even if their ideas are suitable for a national or international market.

Traditional entrepreneurs, especially if they have venture capital funding, typically target a national market immediately, and perhaps have a timetable for international activities. If these entrepreneurs are not located in a business cluster like Silicon Valley, penetrating foreign markets may be a difficult undertaking, because it requires detailed market information and connections that may be hard to come by. In contrast, Silicon Valley entrepreneurs are well positioned to exploit the expatriate network for all of the key foreign markets, since the Valley is home to such a diversity of businesspeople from all over the world.

Because of Silicon Valley's high level of technical and business innovation, entrepreneurs can often create a new global market and achieve a notable market share with their cutting-edge ideas before other companies are able to catch up. Moreover, Valley entrepreneurs recognize that speed is everything. The ability to effectively address the challenge of rapid change is an additional competitive advantage in entering any global high-tech market.

Customers

Small businesses attract customers through location, as well as through transaction-based differentiators such as lower-cost products or better customer service. In contrast, the traditional venture firm attracts customers with innovation. Like Federal Express, which first offered overnight delivery in a three-day delivery world, these companies present compelling new products or services, reaching customers through a variety of established marketing and distribution channels.

The Silicon Valley approach to customers is based on a third model that focuses on partnerships. As with alliance partners and outsourcers, customers are often intimately involved in the innovation process. Entrepreneurs often go through a period of co-invention of their products with their strategic customers. These customers are very often located in Silicon Valley, where entrepreneurs can work closely with them. The customers act as beta testing sites for new products, and offer vital feedback for the creation of a successful product that best suits their needs. Customers want to cooperate with entrepreneurs because it provides an opportunity to experiment with cutting-edge products ahead of their competitors. Customers appreciate that their ideas can also influence pricing and marketing strategies as well as later product versions. Valley customers have one additional advantage for new start-ups: they are willing to invest time in co-inventing with the entrepreneur, even though they know that the product might ultimately fail.

Even though partnership-based customer relationships are harder for the entrepreneur to manage, they are very valuable. Start-ups without enough internal expertise can complement outsourcers' assistance with practical advice from customers in such areas as quality assurance, usability analysis, market research, and business strategy. For example, Silicon Valley entrepreneur Peter Friedland, of Intraspect Software, was able to recruit both Hewlett-Packard and Cisco Systems as beta sites to help his small start-up refine and reorient its original enterprise groupware product marketing strategy toward business-to-business collaboration.[5] Both of the latter companies recognize their important role in promoting innovation in the habitat and welcome a wide range of relationships with start-ups like Intraspect.

Growth Potential and Ambition to Grow

Small business owners tend to concentrate on steady growth and strive to moderate the effects of economic cycles. Aggressive growth strategies bring on unwanted additional risk. Entrepreneurs in traditional venture businesses aim aggressively for high growth and market penetration as fast as possible. Capturing market share has a higher priority in the short term than achieving steady profits.

Silicon Valley entrepreneurs have the funding and support, as well as the passion, for even bolder growth ambitions; they seek to capture the global mind share. Within months, these entrepreneurs create a substantial company with global capabilities. They hire employees, often at rates of two or more a day, sign on perhaps dozens of alliance partners, and spend millions of dollars (sometimes all the money they have) on high-profile marketing campaigns. The goal of their efforts is to capture the world's mind share, that is, the special attention and esteem of a global market that has bought into the company's vision. Mind share coupled with market share can make their companies far more valuable than a traditional venture business. Yahoo! is a good example of a Silicon Valley business that enjoys a significant global mind share as well as a substantial share of the Internet portal market.

FOUR STYLES OF SILICON VALLEY ENTREPRENEURSHIP

In the previous section, I discussed some of the perspectives, attitudes, and approaches of three different types of entrepreneurs in a number of different business contexts. I pointed out how Silicon Valley entrepreneurs are playing a different game. Now I will focus particularly on four well-known start-up entrepreneurs and their companies to further illustrate the Silicon Valley perspective. Although each of these individuals has a very different entrepreneurial style, they all were shaped by the forces I described in the previous section. I will discuss their styles in more depth, looking at how they perceive their worlds, and how they think about their business missions. I will look particularly at the approaches that often distinguish them from their more traditional entrepreneurial counterparts.

The four entrepreneurs I discuss below have different, sometimes extreme, attitudes towards risk-taking with regard to both their businesses and their careers. Some forgo personal financial security in pursuit of a vision; others put corporate profits on the line by adopting especially high-risk business strategies. Each is passionate about his ideas. Each has taken on a broader leadership role in the business community in order to communicate and sell his vision for how his technology will transform the world. Finally, in each case the entrepreneur understands and uses the Silicon Valley habitat to improve his chances of success through such approaches as distributing risk, outsourcing innovation, and networking. I have named the four styles I examine (1) long-term vision entrepreneur (visioneer); (2) acquisition entrepreneur; (3) transformational entrepreneur; and (4) serial entrepreneur.

Long-Term Vision Entrepreneur (Visioneer)

> *If I had finished my thesis, what impact would I*
> *have had? Maybe 100 in the world would have*
> *read it. . . . Whereas the attraction of Yahoo! was*
> *that millions of people were going to read what*
> *we produced. And that, to me, is like a drug.*
>
> —JERRY YANG, in *Forbes*[6]

Most entrepreneurs found their companies with the idea that they will continue to manage the company as it grows. Their idea of success has as much to do with their role as a leader as it does with the success of the company itself. Thus many entrepreneurs become demoralized and leave their companies if they are forced out of the CEO role by their investors or their boards of directors. There are a few entrepreneurs, however, who view their start-ups and their roles within them quite differently. For these entrepreneurs, the thrill is in the process of creating a company and sharing a new vision with the world. Making money or acquiring power is only of secondary importance. I call these entrepreneurs "visioneers." They start a company, shape its vision, and stay with it as it grows, but they may not have any management responsibilities within their company.

Jerry Yang and David Filo of Yahoo! are examples of visioneers. The hallmarks of their style are (1) defining success as public acceptance of the company and its vision, not personal money or power; (2) sticking with the company long-term to play out the vision; and (3) perceiving the company as a community that can offer both fulfillment and a sense of belonging to its employees.

As Yang and Filo have proved, it is possible to have an idealistic approach to starting a company, and yet still become successful. They believed that Yahoo! made a valuable contribution to the world and that their responsibility was to maximize its success in order to maximize its contribution. With the company at the center, rather than the founders, some choices were simpler for them than for other entrepreneurs. They knew that they were not the right people to run the company, so they willingly gave up the top management spots to management professionals. They looked upon the abdication not as a defeat, but as a door to an opportunity to do what they felt was important.

In Yang's case, it was to go out and evangelize the company and its vision. For Filo, it was to continue to shape the technology that drove the company.

Money has a different meaning for the visioneer, also. It is symbolic of independence and commitment. Early on, when Yahoo! was still more of a hobby than a business, Yang and Filo rejected a $2 million offer from Netscape. The pair felt it was more important to take a risk and maintain an independent course. The present-day Yahoo! still covets its independence and has put into place a plan for fending off hostile takeover bids. The belief is that only an independent Yahoo! can maintain the spirit and philosophical direction of the founders. Yahoo!'s breathtaking market valuation seems to communicate investor agreement with its independent strategy.

Yang and Filo are willing to express their commitment to their company with their own money, too. On the eve of Yahoo!'s IPO, for example, the founders were offered $12.5 million in cash each for a portion of their personal shares, but they initially rejected most of the instant wealth because "they didn't want to be viewed by future shareholders as running away from their creation" (Kaplan 1999, 315). They want to remain with the company long-term. As with all visioneers, Yang and Filo are continually motivated to prove that their vision is valid, that it has staying power, and that it can be expanded to something even more profound.

The founders of Yahoo! started their company as a fun and challenging project to do together. As their organization has grown, that lighthearted sense of "playing together" remains. The result is a company whose employees call themselves "Yahoo! brothers and sisters" and who clearly see their organization as a family. It is an example of the connectedness that Silicon Valley entrepreneurs often demonstrate. The informality of the work environment reinforces the theme, with numerous magazine articles showing Yang working in his stocking feet, and Filo sitting on the floor of his office. The family metaphor helps convey to idealistic young employees that they can contribute to a community and still reap personal rewards. It also speaks in particular to engineers, suggesting that even the least socialized of the lot can find a place where they can create, contribute, and belong. Finally, the family theme may have a special meaning for immigrant entrepreneurs, like Taiwanese Jerry Yang, who have been able to make a place for themselves and their brethren in Silicon Valley.

Yang and Filo are the archetypal Silicon Valley entrepreneurs. They have influenced the course of Silicon Valley development as much as they have been influenced by it. At Stanford University, they had access to the Internet and the opportunity to experiment with new ideas there. They also had a bird's-eye view of the exciting businesses starting in the Valley, and were very inspired by those examples. After leaving Stanford, they called upon their network of former classmates to be early employees at their new start-up. They found invaluable support in the habitat, not just from their investors, but from other local start-up companies, like Netscape, who hosted their web site after Stanford could no longer accommodate them. Their wildly successful business model of providing useful free content and services supported by advertising revenues has been adopted by thousands of companies, both in Silicon Valley and elsewhere. Yang and Filo's experience with Yahoo! now serves as an inspiration for a new generation of Internet entrepreneurs.

Acquisition Entrepreneur

> *We don't do R&D, we do A&D: acquire and*
> *develop.*
> —DON LISTWIN, CISCO SYSTEMS[7]

It might be said that the acquisition entrepreneur has a grand vision for his company that he is able to effectuate through the acquisition of numerous other companies, each fulfilling one portion of that grand vision. The reality, however, is that all of the companies and technologies needed to realize the vision may not exist. It may be more accurate to say that the acquisition entrepreneur assimilates the visions of others into one cohesive but continually evolving vision. Clearly, the strength of this entrepreneurial approach is its flexibility and pragmatism.

John Chambers of Cisco is an example of an acquisition entrepreneur. The key elements of his entrepreneurial style are (1) the ability to articulate a high-level vision that can accommodate each acquisition; (2) the talent to create a sustained business success from the assembly of many disparate corporate components; and (3) the ability to maintain an effective management team.

Chambers travels worldwide to promote his vision. He calls it the "new world network," or sometimes the "new network economy," a broad concept with lots of room underneath for the details. He can then talk about how Cisco is well positioned to be central to that vision. In truth, the vision and Cisco's perceived role in that vision have evolved together as the company acquires the technology and ideas of others—more than 50 acquisitions since 1993.

In building a company from acquisitions, the acquisition entrepreneur recognizes that he does not need to be the personal creator of all the details of his business vision. Instead, his role is to recognize, nurture, and promote the new ideas embodied in an acquired company, just as a venture capitalist might. This task does not end with the purchase. Indeed, much of the talent of the acquisition entrepreneur is his ability to use what he acquires most effectively. At Cisco, the 13 percent "R&D" budget is almost entirely devoted to assimilating and integrating the acquired companies into Cisco's technology, customer base, and employee community (Reinhardt 1999).

In making multiple acquisitions, there will inevitably be overlap or conflict in technologies or business models. Acquisition entrepreneurs like Chambers can use these situations to good advantage. He can set up an internal competition to see which alternative his customers favor, or hedge his bets on which way a market will develop. In other instances, he can use the acquisition of a conflicting technology as a way to move from an older technology to a more modern one. For example, Cisco's 1999 purchase of Cerent will eventually help transition current customers from copper wire to fiber optics. In making so many acquisitions, there will always be failures. But the acquisition entrepreneur accepts these failures as the venture capitalist does, as the cost of exploring business possibilities. Like a venture capitalist, Chambers creates a net positive return from Cisco's acquisitions.[8]

Chambers is especially adept at using acquisitions to build his top management team. Managers coming from the acquired companies ease the burden of integrating the newly acquired company, help keep acquired employees from leaving Cisco, and offer a depth of understanding about the acquisition that is vital to its future contribution. Building the management team this way also keeps the players fresh, entrepreneurial, and focused on where Cisco wants to go (not where it was). Chambers wants to retain all employees, not just the senior management, because he believes that, in the final analysis, he is buying the people. *Electronic Business* relates a story about

Chambers deciding against buying a company with the perfect technology and price because he would have had to lay off the people (LaPlante 1997). An interesting counterpoint to the previous story comes from an insider at Cisco who maintains that Cisco's acquisition of Precept Software was not the complete failure outsiders assume it to be, because it brought the company an outstanding CTO.[9]

The Silicon Valley habitat provides important advantages to Chambers as an acquisition entrepreneur. Many companies Cisco targets for acquisition are in the Silicon Valley area. Their founders are part of the local business network. In some cases, Cisco might even be a small investor in the company. When a start-up develops enough to be a suitable acquisition candidate, Chambers probably already knows the senior managers and has a relationship with them. In the case of Cerent, for example, Cisco already had a 9 percent investment in the company. In the rapid style of many Silicon Valley business transactions, Chambers was able to complete the acquisition negotiations for Cerent in just 2½ hours over a three-day period.[10]

Transformational Entrepreneur

> *McNealy has also worked a transformation that may be just as important for the company's future—he's made Sun cool.*
> —DAVID KIRKPATRICK, in *Fortune*[11]

A transformational entrepreneur is a manager who redirects his company's momentum toward a leadership position in a new technology or market. This section focuses particularly on the heads of maturing high-tech start-ups that must change their companies to compete effectively with both established foes and the many innovative new start-ups that are springing up around them. One might argue that good business leaders reshape their companies regularly in order to stay competitive, and that a transformational entrepreneur is hardly a *real* entrepreneur. I have found in Silicon Valley, however, that a company recreated by a transformational entrepreneur can be as profoundly different from the original company as a new venture would be. The transformational entrepreneur turns out to be an important player in sustaining the innovation process in Silicon Valley.

As a start-up matures, it begins to acquire many of the trappings of a traditional company. The company will have an entrenched management structure with enough personnel on board to cover all major job functions. It may also have adopted standardized approaches to important business processes. Finally, the company will surely have acquired competitors, alliance partners, and a customer base with extensive needs and expectations.

After some number of years, the founder inevitably finds himself in the awkward and perhaps unfamiliar position of being a traditional leader in a rather traditional company. The business environment and technological changes that once gave his start-up a chance to enter the market and succeed have continued to evolve. These forces begin to make his products obsolete and create openings for new innovators. At the same time, his successful evangelization of the company has oriented the employees, customers, and investors toward the current business model. Their mindset is reinforced by the weight of the processes and management hierarchies and the sheer size of the installed base, which demand maintenance of the status quo.

The transformational entrepreneur must be able to recognize when the moment has come, in effect, to recreate his company as a new organization, with a new direction, and with the same spirit of adventure as the original start-up. He recognizes that he is compelled to undertake this transition in order to maintain a competitive advantage. This task is a formidable one, perhaps even more difficult than building a new high-tech company from scratch. Let me note the relevance of an old Asian saying: "Building a castle is difficult. Defending and maintaining it is harder still."

Scott McNealy at Sun Microsystems is a transformational entrepreneur. He has embraced the Internet and made it central to his new vision for Sun. For the past four years he has used the introduction of the Java programming language as a vehicle for this transformation. I focus on three characteristics of McNealy's approach to Sun's metamorphosis: (1) capacity to envision the transformed organization; (2) ability to build a new team within the existing company; and (3) ability to learn a new business model, on the job, in real time.

Eric Schmidt, Sun's CTO in 1994, recalled for *Fortune* the moment when he first showed McNealy the Java prototype: "We showed Scott the technology and described how we might want to work with partners to give it broader appeal. He saw it as much more, as a destination for the whole company, and even for the whole industry to pursue. It was like a switch came on" (Schlender 1997). McNealy had just spent years promoting Sun as the premier vendor of engineering workstations and a superior alternative to the Wintel platform in the corporate network servers world. His employees were committed to this vision of Sun, and so was the rest of the world. Yet, at that first meeting on Java, McNealy recognized that Sun needed to pursue a new vision, centered on the Internet, and that this software product would provide the means to reorient the entire company.

McNealy had looked beyond the vision of the company that he himself had tirelessly promoted. He then needed to recreate Sun internally and, more importantly, in the public mind. He has spent the last four years as an evangelist for Java, selling not just a programming language, but a new vision for the entire world of corporate computing, and Sun's central role in furthering that vision. His evangelism has extended well beyond customers and alliance partners; it embraces Sun's management, investors, and employees, as well as the press, industry analysts, the government, and the general public.

The transformation that McNealy envisions for Sun only succeeds if enough people buy into it. Sun's position as a respected and innovative Silicon Valley company gave McNealy's new ideas some additional support, especially from other habitat companies, but McNealy needed to do much more. Creating and promoting the vision of a hardware-independent software platform is an entrepreneurial undertaking of serious proportions for any company. For a maturing hardware start-up with hardware-focused management, it produced an additional challenge for McNealy as a transformational entrepreneur.

Ultimately, it is the management team that effectuates the changes the company head envisions. In *Only the Paranoid Survive*, Andy Grove talks about the need for management to adjust to the new vision: "Simply put, you can't change a company without changing its management. I'm not saying that they have to pack up their desks and be replaced. I'm saying that they themselves, every one of them, needs to change to be more in tune with the mandates of the new environment" (Grove 1996, 157).

McNealy's approach to "reconfiguring" existing management was painful, but effective. He organized Sun into a number of separate "planets," or operating companies, each with its own management and profit-and-loss statements. JavaSoft was named a new planet, giving it high visibility within Sun and attention from the executive management committee. Attention at Sun means a trial by fire for every new idea. Java was no exception. McNealy's management style, which is deeply embedded in the company culture, is intense and confrontational. Sun lost a number of managers in the planet reorganization and subsequent heated debate over the importance of Java. The ones remaining were those most committed to nurturing Java as a technology and as a new direction for all of Sun. James Gosling, one of the creators of Java, described the hazing process in these terms: "We were this small ragtag group of survivors from an atom bomb blasting. We wanted to make sure our technology saw the light of day" (Southwick 1999).

McNealy's interests and talents lay in managing a hardware organization. In order to transform Sun into an Internet company, McNealy had to transform himself as well. He needed to learn the software business as well as the Internet business. He had to learn it on the job while he managed what had been, up until then, a multibillion-dollar hardware company. In contrast to Andy Grove, who learned the software business by studying the strategies of various PC software companies and establishing relationships with their managers, McNealy undertook his personal transformation in his characteristically brash style. He didn't study. He talked up Java and his vision to everyone: the software-savvy developer community, the executives at companies such as Oracle, IBM, Netscape, and Apple, and the software industry analysts. He learned about software from the objections and arguments that he received, and he refined his understanding of what Java was and how Sun could move forward with it. As he learned, he became even more passionate about Java's long-term potential, and he eventually gave up his seat as president to devote more time to transforming Sun and the world.

Serial Entrepreneur

> *Did I want the fruits of a big score? Absolutely.*
> *But what I really wanted was to be ahead of the*
> *curve again.*
>
> JIM CLARK, *Netscape Time*

The serial entrepreneur creates a company, builds it up to a certain point, and then moves on to start another company. Although this entrepreneurial style is a great deal rarer than the other three I have examined, it is the one that gets the most press. Many outside Silicon Valley consider the serial entrepreneur to be the only model of entrepreneurship in the region. The reason for the high profile of serial entrepreneurs is the massive amounts of money they make (and sometimes lose) as they create these new start-ups. As Michael Lewis says of Jim Clark in *The New New Thing*, "All Clark had to do was announce how he next planned to invent the future, and huge sums of money and vast reservoirs of engineering talent came pouring in, intent on proving him right" (Lewis 2000, 87).

Jim Clark is one of the best-known serial entrepreneurs of Silicon Valley. He is currently working on his fourth and fifth start-ups, myCFO and Shutterfly, having created many billions of dollars of wealth for himself and his colleagues in his first three start-ups, SGI (Silicon Graphics), Netscape, and Healtheon. The serial entrepreneur has the ability to (1) articulate a vision with passion, attract all necessary resources, and "make things happen"; and (2) know his limitations.

Serial entrepreneur Jim Clark has refined the art of identifying an important new technology or market, and starting a company to exploit that new idea. Especially for the second and subsequent start-ups, he could choose from his well-established network all of the elements he needed: a good idea, the key engineers, the CEO heir apparent, and, of course, the investors. For multibillionaire Clark, choosing investors is a strategic decision, not a financial necessity. For example, when he started myCFO, he allowed the venture capitalists to buy a 12 percent interest, saying "If I don't let them invest, they'll start a competitor" (ibid., 258). The people and the money are perhaps initially attracted more by his successful track record than by the brilliance of his ideas, but he then knows how to close the deal, selling potential collaborators on his vision with a passionate conviction as well as the lure of great wealth. "When you find someone you want, I tell them, 'Here's exactly what we are going to do and it is going to be huge and you are going to be very, very rich'" (ibid., 114). Finally, he has the fortitude to make an absolute and total commitment of his time, personal attention, and money to the start-up. Some start-up ideas are so unusually risky and ambitious that only the entrepreneur's complete commitment to gamble everything allows the venture to go forward.

The serial entrepreneur also knows how to utilize the press effectively to create buzz about his new company, effortlessly recruiting both customers and new employees. In recent years, Clark has been particularly effective in manipulating public opinion through the press, building up his mystique as a star of Silicon Valley, as someone who creates the future, in a way that was previously thought to be within the exclusive purview of the Valley's venture capitalists. This notoriety of course enhances his ability to organize and create his next new company.

Clark knows his personal weaknesses and manages to exploit them in his bid for success. For example, he has long realized that he is too impatient to deal with the day-to-day management of a company. He knows, too, that he is restless, never satisfied, and needs the stimulation of constant new challenges. Thus he sells his new ideas on the premise that he will set the direction of the company and then relinquish control to a more traditional chief executive. He can walk away from a company that he has worked hard to build up when the company has been assured a financial success. He stays only long enough to build the company up to a valuation of more than a billion dollars, and extract a major part of his personal financial return. He then moves on to begin a new process of creating markets, creating jobs, and, of course, creating great wealth, all over again.

SOME CLOSING THOUGHTS

The great success and wealth of Silicon Valley does not always bring out the best in entrepreneurs. I have seen a rise in recent years in the number of companies that appear to be started solely for the money rather than primarily for the passion to bring a new business idea to the world. Greed, coupled with the abundance of wealth in the Valley, spawns imitative business ideas and a wide range of unhealthy speculative deals. These business ventures of lesser quality divert scarce human resources from ultimately more productive endeavors. Their higher failure rates may also reduce the credibility of all entrepreneurs.

Although not always the case, some of the problems can be attributed to unseasoned entrepreneurs who have never been through hard times. These entrepreneurs see others creating great wealth in a very short period of time, and have unrealistic expectations that they can easily duplicate that success. They have learned to talk to the public about how their companies will change the world. Unfortunately, some of them buy into their own hyperbole and then cannot deliver. In these instances, the Silicon Valley habitat may be a bit too supportive and forgiving.

Another downside to Silicon Valley entrepreneurship is the lack of a philanthropic mindset in some successful entrepreneurs. As the Valley has grown and prospered in the past decade, the level of charitable giving and community service has lagged behind the rest of the country. Only recently has that situation begun to rectify itself. Perhaps it is because the business boom has given more entrepreneurs financial security, or because youthful entrepreneurs now have families and therefore more ties to the community. In any case, many of this new generation of entrepreneurs, led by the examples of a few farsighted business leaders, are now joining the effort to build a strong community through philanthropy and community service.

I want to close with a few remarks about the role of Silicon Valley entrepreneurs in the civic life of the community. Many Silicon Valley entrepreneurs have been very generous with contributions of time and money. They serve on the boards of directors of museums, schools, universities, hospitals, community foundations, the United Way, and environmental organizations. They bring their experience and entrepreneurial talents to the organizations and projects within the organizations. These are individuals who personally lead projects. They do not send their assistants to the meetings, but they go and lead themselves, bringing the same passion, drive, and vision that made them good entrepreneurs.

Harry Saal is a good example of a Silicon Valley civic leader. Saal was the founder and CEO of Network General. He wanted to give back to his community, so he became the president and CEO of Smart Valley, a nonprofit organization whose mission was to provide a test bed for applications of the new information infrastructure that would help create a 21st-century electronic community. He brought to this nonprofit organization and its mission the same entrepreneurial zeal he had brought to his company. He promoted the establishment of programs like Smart Permitting, which used technology to unify the building permit process of 19 area communities, and Smart Schools, which undertook to connect every Silicon Valley school to the Internet. Saal also understood that Smart Valley was an integral part of the Silicon Valley habitat. He therefore fashioned an organization that could give its entrepreneurial employees and volunteers the opportunity, encouragement, and support to "change the world."

David Packard is quoted as saying that there are four things important to his company: "You pay attention to your employees, customers, and shareholders, but you also give attention to your community." As it turns out, paying attention to one's community also has implications for one's business. Valley entrepreneurs have come to understand that to have a strong company, the community must also be strong. Thus building a strong community through charitable giving and civic service rewards the entrepreneur not only through personal satisfaction, but through a positive impact on his business as well.

Silicon Valley entrepreneurs like Harry Saal have learned that they can use their hard-earned experience, their leadership skills, and their extensive business networks to make things happen in the community. Most have also discovered the essential truth of philanthropic endeavors: that those who enrich the community are in turn enriched by it. Their networks of associates are now expanded beyond the borders of their particular set of business activities. Moreover, they gain a perspective and insight about life that is hard to come by in daily business.

We all too often hear about the great wealth and business success of entrepreneurs, but it is also important to recognize their significant contributions to community and civic activities. I personally feel that one of the biggest benefits of being a Silicon Valley entrepreneur has been to give back to my community. Silicon Valley has been my home for 40 years, since I left Korea. My business ideas and hard work have been successful in part because of the energy, talent, and support that the Valley offers. I have therefore concentrated my philanthropic activities in this region, hoping to make a positive difference here and to inspire the current generation of Asian immigrant entrepreneurs to make a difference, too. Writing a chapter for this important book on Silicon Valley is yet another way that I give back to my community by sharing what I have learned about Silicon Valley entrepreneurship.

7

Changing Everything

The Internet Revolution and Silicon Valley

STEVE JURVETSON

"**T**he Internet changes everything." This is a Silicon Valley mantra. And the Internet is synonymous with entrepreneurship. Each is a boon to the other. The Internet has lowered the barriers to entrepreneurship and democratized it. And entrepreneurship is the engine of the Internet's growth.

As a seed-stage venture capital firm, Draper Fisher Jurvetson has been an active investor in the Internet since 1994. We have seen the cycle of rapid innovation and renewal play out many times. We have also seen entrepreneurship flourish and flounder in various regions of the United States, as we have opened venture offices in nine different U.S. locations.

Venture capital is a local business. The venture capitalist works closely with portfolio companies to build the team, form partnerships, sign on key customers, gain awareness in the press, and secure follow-on rounds of financing. All of these elements of "Rolodex power" are themselves network effects in that accumulated investment experience makes the network increasingly powerful. We serve as a network hub. The network grows with each investment, each partnership forged, each acquisition of one of our companies, and each of the 20,000 business plans we receive each year.

We also accumulate knowledge of industry best practices, of particular value in a period of radical change such as today's Internet economy. We look for patterns and strategize about emerging business models. We also serve as confidants, mentors, and cheerleaders for our companies. We help them focus on getting to market early and securing a first-mover advantage. We help build their confidence that they can change the world.

In this chapter, I will discuss the clustering of entrepreneurial zeal and the multifaceted synergy of Internet entrepreneurship. Then I will elaborate on several current and emerging examples of how the Internet changes everything. It is as if business is a game of chess—competitive and rich with strategy—but with the added twist that at any moment, a new company may redefine the plane of play. All of a sudden, an incumbent business may find that the game has a third dimension, and that they have few pieces on the new playing plane. We have seen this radical restructuring of the playing field with the "eyeball bandits," the horizontal e-commerce enablers, the small business aggregators, and the "viral marketing" start-ups—each of which I will cover in detail.

Finally, I will briefly address the question of sustainability: given the flurry of mergers and acquisitions among Silicon Valley start-ups, are entrepreneurs simply seeking to make a quick buck, or are they building sustainable enterprises?

LOCUS OF INNOVATION

At Draper Fisher Jurvetson, we find that there is a positive cycle of entrepreneurship that occurs locally. We have noticed this pattern of entrepreneurial fervor in various pockets around America and overseas. We have opened affiliate VC offices in nine U.S. locations, and we are in the process of opening several overseas offices. In many cases, we are the first venture firm to open an office in a region. From this experience, we are struck by the clustering of entrepreneurial activity. Why does it arise and flourish in some areas and not others? Where should we open our next venture office?

What we have found is that besides universities and a culture that rewards risk-taking, it is important to have local heroes, people who have done it. Seattle has Microsoft and Amazon.com, Salt Lake City has Novell, Los Angeles has NetZero and GoTo.com, Austin has Dell, Reston has America Online, Pittsburgh has Lycos, and Silicon Valley had Intel and Hewlett-Packard, and more recently, eBay and Yahoo! In each case, the founders are heroes, but they are also ordinary people. For those who live in the region, there are many within a couple degrees of separation who say, "Hey, I can do that too! I could be a

Marc Andreessen or a Jerry Yang." The process of entrepreneurship seems less mysterious and daunting to them than to those outside the region, to whom it can seem very magical and mystifying. Distance can be distancing. Those of us in Silicon Valley may not see it since we have entrepreneurship all around us. For us, Hollywood is magical and mystifying. Having never lived there, we can only imagine what it takes to make it in the movies, what steps to take, and whom to talk to. When you are an outsider, it's easier to mentally distance yourself and rationalize that the successful ones are special people in a special place.

Local heroes catalyze fence-sitters. If you have been thinking about starting a company or thinking about joining one, there's nothing like a local success story to give you that extra push. Many of the Internet heroes have been quite young—straight out of school in many cases. Many of the large Internet companies were founded by people in their twenties. They didn't know what "couldn't" be done. They were the pioneers. Many of them have nontraditional backgrounds. Ten years ago you had to be an electrical engineer to launch a high-tech company. Now, with the Internet, it doesn't even take a technical background to found a company. People with marketing and all sorts of business backgrounds can conceptualize a new business model and form a company.

To date, Silicon Valley has been the locus of Internet innovation since it is the center of entrepreneurship. But the Internet lowers the barriers to entrepreneurship. People of all backgrounds and ages and from all regions of the world are working hard at starting Internet companies. The Internet itself is increasing the visibility of entrepreneurial success and providing an alternative way onto the path others have followed. The Internet transcends a local press that often does not celebrate entrepreneurship. Grassroots groups have emerged, like "First Tuesday," which recently had 10,000 entrepreneurs come to its monthly event in Europe. Participants from several countries came together via the Internet. Angel financing organizations like Garage.com are also moving rapidly to Europe and Asia.

An Internet company is not anchored to a particular place or physical assets, other than people. If Hotmail were started today, it could just as easily be started in India as the United States. None of its users know where the headquarters is located. In fact, the Internet can in many cases route around attempted censorship and bad governance.

THE START-UP ADVANTAGE

Most of the economic wealth from the Internet has been generated by start-ups, as opposed to large, established companies. If you look at the major Internet brands and companies today, the vast majority of them did not exist five years ago. When our firm funds a start-up company today, we rarely, if ever, worry about a large company posing a competitive threat. Microsoft, IBM, HP, Sun Microsystems—these companies are not the largest threat to the entrepreneur. Much more worrisome are other start-ups. For every good idea, there is an array of small competitors that spring up contemporaneously. It's amazing how different this is from five years ago. Incumbents used to be credible threats. Today, an existing business franchise is more often an albatross than an asset. It is as if the start-up has an unfair competitive advantage.

So what is the start-up advantage? Like many of the past high-tech advances, the Internet is a disruptive technological dislocation. We are in an economic milieu in which everything is changing quickly. Start-ups have the advantage of being nimble and able to change business plans dramatically on a dime. One of our companies, Beyond News, was a corporate "push" technology company when we funded them, which turned out to be a dead end, and so they transformed into a consumer shopping bot. They changed their name to C2B Technologies and were acquired by Inktomi before they launched their first product. These dramatic, turning-on-a-dime actions and reactions to the marketplace are often found in a start-up. Especially in the Internet era, a company's competitiveness seems to depend on its velocity of thought and action.

And thus we witness "Internet time compression." It took HP 47 years to gain a billion dollars of market capitalization; it took Microsoft about 15 years, Yahoo! about 2 years, NetZero about 9 months. That time compression in economic value creation is an expression of a phenomenon in high-tech: the power of demand-side economies of scale, or increasing returns to scale. These network effects are captured in Metcalfe's Law—that the value of a network grows with the square of the number of nodes. When time is the competitive weapon, a small, nimble company can outmaneuver a large company every time.

The Internet is a substrate for intellectual property growth. It allows good ideas to spread more quickly than ever before. In the physical world, companies have to build factories and inventory; customers can only buy products as quickly as they learn they exist, by going into a store. The pace of the physical world is slow, allowing incumbents time to respond to new entrants. But with the rapid proliferation of Internet companies, the rules have changed, and a good idea can take off like wildfire. Ideas do not require physical assets or a huge capital base to be adopted. Historical advantages to corporate scale are dissolving.

Start-ups also don't have any sacred cows. They can come into a business with a remarkably open mind. And with the Internet, they can ask questions and propose business models unlike any we have seen in the physical world. Many incumbent businesses seem wed to their channel of distribution, their partners, and their way of charging for products; they are not the first movers on new business models. Big companies have more to lose by abrupt change.

The Internet is a new direct distribution channel, and new distribution channels tend to benefit new companies. Incumbents have channel conflicts and business relationships that keep them from selling directly to consumers. In the PC industry, the Internet-based direct mail approach was a boon for Dell and Gateway as new entrants, but Compaq and the other incumbent PC companies failed to benefit. It was too painful for Compaq to embitter its sales force and anger its distributors by competing in a new channel; it was as if Compaq was destined to watch helplessly as Dell took the business.

A start-up company can also partner in a very focused way. When you want to partner with Microsoft, you really never know what you are dealing with— which group, how they might hurt you, or what other part of Microsoft may come around to get you. Start-ups, however, do one thing and one thing only in life, so they can more easily partner broadly outside the core they know best. In terms of market entry timing, that can make the difference between a young company succeeding and failing.

Basically, today's Internet economy is the product of entrepreneurship. Each is important to the other. The Internet has lowered the barriers to entrepreneurship and democratized it. In return, entrepreneurship is the engine that drives the Internet's growth. And so, for other regions of the world that are looking to foster Internet businesses, they have to answer the question, "How can we foster entrepreneurship in our culture?"

The most exciting new industries will arise from the disruptive technologies pioneered by the entrepreneurs of the future. There will be myriad challenges in the new industries of 2005—probably in the fields of nanotechnology, photonics, bio-programming, and, hopefully, several areas we can't even anticipate today.

So far, the Internet has proven to be a wonderfully disruptive technology, allowing the gates of innovation to open for a vast array of new companies. As an early-stage venture capital firm, Draper Fisher Jurvetson tries to identify patterns across companies and opportunities in markets. The next few examples will explore some of the trends we are seeing from the seed-financing front and their impact on the broader IT industry. Several of the examples are drawn from our portfolio, as these are the companies that we know best. Each example illustrates how a start-up can redefine the playing field for competitive advantage. We start with the Internet's revolutionary effect on traditional business and then discuss consumers and retailers. In several of these examples, we also see a common theme of the disaggregated industrial structure. Silicon Valley firms, rather than handling all stages of development, production, and distribution themselves, as in the old vertical model, partner with other small, specialized firms at every stage of the process, and thus gain flexibility.

THE REINVENTION OF BUSINESS PROCESSES

Business-to-business (B2B) electronic commerce is expected to become a $1.3 trillion industry by 2003, according to Forrester Research. Will it be business as usual? Will large businesses move their existing business processes online en masse? Or will they radically restructure because the landscape has changed? The answers to these questions are important since they dictate whether the spoils will accrue proportionately to the industry's incumbents, or whether new companies and new business structures will emerge.

In factory automation, the first step is to optimize the production flow before introducing robotics. The problem with information-age automation is that the substrate is a shifting sand of innovation itself. Rather than a physical world with stable rules of physics, we are automating a virtual world in which the basic assumptions of connectivity, latency, and time and space are subject to change.

Imagine how factory automation would change if, suddenly, all machines could be interconnected with equal ease, products could move instantaneously from machine to machine, and copies of any product could be spawned at any time. Certainly, the factory design and layout would change. Even more interestingly, what if trucks and trains could move a product cross-country as fast as a conveyor belt could move it ten feet? Trading practices and the scope of vertical integration would change. Partnerships with separate companies would be feasible for all process steps in the production flow. Small companies that focus on a core of value-added services would proliferate. Adaptive businesses would be radically restructured. This is not some fantasy, but a description of information-age business. With the Internet, information products can spread globally with near-zero latency.

Most modern businesses are information businesses at their core. The optimal scope of an information technology business is defined by the connectivity and latency of its information systems. Business boundaries have been reinforced historically by the relative hassles of wide-area connectivity and proprietary network integration. Companies became islands of automation.

An analogy can be drawn to the evolution of programming models—from desktop computing to client/server and network computing. This shift in program partitioning between desktop and server is a by-product of the shifts in network connectivity and latency. Just as client/server topologies have become obsolete, so too has the traditional definition of a business.

In the past five years, we have witnessed a radical change in the use of computers—from computation to communication. By improving real-time communications, computerization can improve most business processes, including sales and support, which are fundamentally communication exercises. Trade is a form of structured communication. Excess inventory is a by-product of poor information flow.

Businesses are now starting to use the Internet to tie their business automation systems together. Twenty years ago, you could not assume that your trading partners in any business had computers on their desks. Ten years ago, you could assume that many of them did, but to hook those PCs together would be an expensive custom-development effort. Only recently have you been able to depend on a lingua franca that is understood throughout all businesses. My Macintosh can talk to your PC; we can start building business applications without having to worry about the plumbing. And that is a remarkably liberating substrate for B2B e-commerce.

Computer automation migrates from the desktop to the enterprise to the industry. Once automation is widespread at one level, the opportunity to automate at a higher level of abstraction becomes possible. We have seen a similar pattern playing out in three of DFJ's portfolio companies: Tradex, Magnifi, and Saltare.com.

Tradex initially automated the purchase-order approval process. By replacing a paper-based system, they found that they could reduce the overhead cost of a purchase by a factor of 33. Once procurement automation was adopted within a company, Tradex could offer connections to suppliers' catalog systems and enable intercompany trading. Once several companies were in the network, Tradex could promote industry-level automation by aggregating small-business demand, gaining pricing leverage with suppliers. (Three years after introducing these products, Tradex was acquired for $6 billion, the largest software acquisition in history.)

In the field of marketing automation, Magnifi initially automated the enterprise by building systems that helped users search and retrieve complex media files within a corporate intranet. But most marketing operations—from public relations to media buys—are outsourced to partners. The economic leverage of marketing automation is not to be found within the confines of a company; it is in efficient partner communications. Magnifi found a much larger opportunity in automating the structured sharing of marketing materials across an extranet.

In supply-chain optimization, first-generation companies like I2 and Manugistics delivered centralized systems for optimizing inventory levels within a company. Saltare.com has developed a real-time supply-chain optimization system that runs up and down the entire supply-chain extranet. By sharing information more widely between companies, Saltare.com's distributed intercompany application enables a much larger economic gain in efficiency and inventory reduction.

Once Saltare automates a large portion of an industry, a new level of efficiency and industry automation is possible. Industry capacity, timing, and pricing could be rolled up into a higher-level abstraction—a commodities market. Suddenly, a futures market for production goods could restructure the basis of production planning.

WEB-RESIDENT BUSINESS

The economic leverage of computerization grows at each of these steps to a higher level of automation. There is much more to be gained by industrywide trading networks than by further improvements in personal desktop productivity. E-mail is more important than Excel. Extranets are more important than Enterprise Resource Planning (ERP) systems.

A new group of businesses, called application service providers, are hosting these enterprise- and industry-level applications. Entrepreneurs are not sending us business plans for "software companies" any more. The vernacular has changed. They are developing web-deployed services. These hosted applications allow for frequent (even daily) invisible upgrades, access to real-time data feeds, and easy deployment across all corporate desktops as well as all remote "webtops"—at home and overseas.

Many of the early users of these web services will be small businesses. Small businesses dominate the U.S. economy, yet today they are islands unto themselves. Some of DFJ's portfolio companies, like DigitalWork (web services aggregator) and Everdream (subscription computing for small business), are finally forging effective channels to reach small businesses through the web. With channels in place, small businesses can gain from the sophisticated services that used to require a direct sales force and a complex corporate installation. Procurement automation, marketing automation, and sales force automation will finally be available to small businesses.

The business landscape will undergo further tumult with auctions, dynamic pricing, multilingual trading exchanges, outsourced e-commerce, and a variety of innovations that are not possible in the physical world. It will not be business as usual. And as always with radical change, new companies will be the first to exploit the new paradigm. Like the consumer Internet powerhouses of today, most of the B2B winners will be companies that didn't exist five years ago.

Beyond B2B, the consumer Internet is by no means mature. It, too, is entering a new period of radical restructuring and disaggregation. We are in the first inning of a nine-inning game. Based on what we are seeing in the start-up pipeline, the best is yet to come.

THE EYEBALL BANDITS

In the area of consumer electronic commerce, we are seeing the beginnings of a profound shift in the locus of power on the web, from vertically integrated e-retailers like Amazon to a set of horizontal, "pan-web" service providers like Brodia (for shopping automation), ICQ (for instant messaging), NetZero (an ad-supported free Internet service provider), and Third Voice (an on-line community built on web site annotation). Much like the vertical to horizontal shift in the computer industry—from IBM to Intel and Microsoft—this creates opportunities for new entrants and threatens the incumbents.

The technical underpinnings of this transition can be traced to the browser's transformation into a development platform. Entrepreneurs are enhancing the browser to make it a lot richer than just a window through which you look at relatively static web pages. The browser is finally becoming an "application," one that lets companies offer innovative forms of commerce, community, and communication.

For example, Brodia's on-line wallet service, which stores the user's purchasing information, gives consumers the benefit of "one-click-shopping" across all web merchants. No more forms from hell every time you want to buy from a new merchant, asking for the same information—name, address, credit card number, gender. The wallet also will be a place to maintain a record of prior purchases, receive promotions, track incentive programs, and search for other goods and services, pan-web. In addition to e-commerce, the locus of communication and community is going horizontal and pan-web. Companies like Third Voice let consumers annotate any web site with a note like a Post-It that other users can read. It works across the entire web, putting community building into everyone's hands.

What these new companies have in common is a persistent presence. They don't lose contact with consumers as they click from site to site. With a persistent presence, it's easier to poach customers than ever before. In exchange for free Internet access, NetZero keeps a banner ad on your screen whenever you are on-line. Those banners can make some radically new offers, such as competitive targeting. Catalina built a nice business just offering competitive counter-punch coupons at the grocery checkout stand (e.g., if you buy Coke, you get a Pepsi coupon). The web can make such targeting real-time, prepurchase, and responsive to consumer impulse.

Take this a step further: how much would BuyBooks.com pay to flash its ad at the Amazon.com order page? Imagine that as soon as you added a particular item to their shopping cart, a poaching banner would pop up: "Amazon wants $35 for that John Grisham novel? Click here for a $22 one-click purchase from BuyBooks.com!" This is possible because the "persistent client" companies know who you are and, through the browser, what you are about to buy and the price that was offered.

NetZero's ads are "closer" to the user's eyes in the information stack. The technology is aware of the consumer's location at all times, and can recognize the content and the commerce context. Amazon knows only what happens on its site; it loses all visibility once the consumer goes elsewhere.

Why *wouldn't* you switch sites based on price? Although studies have shown that consumers are not very price-sensitive in practice, that's a legacy of the physical world. When it becomes possible to get the lower price with equal ease—that is, a mouse click here or there—then consumers' preferences for retail brands will shift to back-end issues of fulfillment and customer service.

What's more, with companies like Brodia and NetZero and their persistent customer agents on the desktop, we finally have a compelling delivery and fulfillment vehicle for e-commerce coupon issuers. Although the off-line coupon and promotions business is larger than advertising, until now the web has lacked a universal promotions infrastructure and the power of Catalina-like competitive couponing. Promotions should exceed advertising on the Net in the not-too-distant future, and on-line promotion companies like PlanetU and Netcentives should benefit from this trend.

The eyeball bandits restructure the locus of power in advertising and commerce, two of the basic vehicles for the monetization of human attention on the Web. And this trend is moving off-line. By virtue of their stored television programming preferences, TiVo and Replay Networks, for example, are closer to the consumer and can overlay ads at the point of consumption—in the set-top box at home—thereby abrogating the power of the TV networks. The pattern continues. What's more, it may catalyze a fracture in Amazon.com and the other vertically integrated e-retailers, just as Microsoft and Intel catalyzed a fracture in IBM and the vertically integrated computer companies.

AMAZON.COM IS AN ANACHRONISM

The whole concept of a retail brand is an anachronism on the Internet. The vertically integrated electronic retailer is a holdover from the physical world that is entirely out of place on-line. The Internet empowers consumers over retailers for the first time. E-retailers will no longer be the force—and the bottleneck—that they are in the physical world. A dramatic shift of power in the e-commerce space is under way.

The first approaches in any new medium mimic what is already well understood in prior media. Marshall McLuhan first espoused this idea in the 1960s, and it has played out to this day with remarkable faithfulness. Early movies were "filmed theater," with a single camera angle capturing the view from the audience seat. Early TV shows were televised radio programs. People start with what they understand, and the unique expressions of the new medium take time to emerge.

The Internet has grown much more quickly than any of the preceding media did, but it has not yet matured. Many millions of people are using the web while it is still in the "filmed-theater" phase. Untargeted banner ads, like subway billboards, are simplistic and increasingly ineffective. We have yet to see the widespread adoption of business models that are uniquely derived from the Internet medium and that would not have been feasible in the physical world.

So what do we have so far? On the Internet, one of the first e-commerce metaphors was the shopping mall. MCI and several now-defunct start-ups built on-line versions at which consumers would see rows of retailers and rows of products on their shelves. Some of them even went so far as to create a 3D rendition of the physical shopping experience. Those shopping malls failed in part because they ignored the Internet's power to collapse geographical distance; such an aggregation of commerce sites under one virtual roof was unnecessary when people could go anywhere with a few keystrokes.

The next physical-world model transplanted to the Internet was the "vertically integrated retailer," a single vendor like Amazon.com that handles the shopping experience from product selection to shipment. E-retailers have scaled much more quickly than traditional shops serving a geographic locale, but they do not represent the great step forward that the Internet enables.

Over the next few years, merchandising and product selection will be decoupled from product fulfillment and support. Today they are combined out of habit, because that is what we are used to in the physical world. We browse the products on the shelves, ask a sales clerk for advice, pick a product, pay for it, and take delivery, all from the same store. In the physical world, it is very cumbersome to segregate these activities, allocating each to a different company, as the customer would have to shuttle across town for each step in the buying chain.

The retail store is organized to maximize efficiencies of the physical supply chain—the logistical relationships that move the goods from production to the consumer. The consumer is only engaged in the final step, with the binary option to buy or not to buy from a fixed set of options at fixed prices. Power rests with the store. Geographic constraints defined this optimal retail chain, one that has undergone little change for hundreds of years.

Vertical integration is not optimal for consumers. Let's say you want to decide which DVD player to buy. Do you want to go to a company that is trying to sell you a DVD player? It's probably no surprise that if you look at an Amazon.com review for a CD, you usually see between five and four stars; very few have zero stars. Everything is a great product. Over time consumers are going to start to distrust ratings of this kind.

What if your alternative was a "shopping agent" service with a brand like Consumer Reports, which has no economic incentive to sway you one way or another, will give you honest consumer feedback, and will get to know you and all of your purchase habits across the entire web? Any one merchant knows only what you have done on that particular site. Other companies (like NetZero and the "browser buddies") will stay with you as you surf and thus can make personal recommendations for you based on your buying habits across the entire web.

So for both objectivity and pan-web personalization, there will be separate consumer companies that focus exclusively on product selection and reviews. They can innovate in many ways, like consumer feedback networks, collaborative shopping, and buyer aggregation (imagine ad hoc groups with fleet purchasing power).

When a vertically integrated industry breaks apart, there is rapid innovation at each horizontal layer, just as we saw in the computer industry when IBM ceased to be the one-stop shop for computing. Markets make better decisions than bureaucrats or middle managers. An array of competitors will be more adaptive to change and will move more quickly than a big retail company bureaucracy. Some companies will innovate with pan-web shopping carts and payment. Some will innovate with logistics and support—deploying vans and warehouses for same-day delivery, for example. These and other fulfillment agents will differentiate themselves on service and customer support. These disaggregated, specialized services are easily concatenated over the Internet, and the consumer's shopping agent can provide a uniform front-end view of the myriad services that constitute the buying chain.

In this new world, product merchandising, promotion, and support should migrate from the retailer back to the product manufacturers. We have seen the beginning of this transition from two of our portfolio companies, Kana Communications and Digital Impact, both of which facilitate company-customer interaction based on e-mail. What they have found is that recently even large product-based corporations, from Estee Lauder to General Motors, have had to start talking to customers on a daily basis. For many years, the manufacturers were shielded from direct customer interaction by the channel: the retail stores and dealers. All that changed when the manufacturers put up web sites and the e-mails started pouring in. The web has allowed the pent-up demand for basic product knowledge to migrate back to the product companies.

In this new horizontal model, retail brands won't exist—no Wal-Mart or Toys "R" Us. There will, however, be plenty of powerful brands—the old product brands, like Tide detergent, and the new personal shopping agent brands. These new brands will be customer-centric and built on trust. They are uniquely enabled by electronic networks and will engender the strongest of loyalties.

The Internet dissolves the physical retailer metaphor. The new purchasing paradigm will be consumer-centric, with marketing, merchandising, and logistics all aligned to provide personalized and unbiased information to consumers. The consumer is king.

In a horizontal industry, value accrues from relationships. Positions of power can be most easily maintained at the boundaries of the supply network—at the consumer shopping agent interface and the interface to the product manufacturers. The valuable assets are customer knowledge and exclusive access to product brands and private label products.

These changes will not occur overnight. Although Amazon.com is an anachronism as a simple e-retailer, it is by no means doomed. Shopping habits change at a glacial pace. Amazon.com will likely recognize the transition sooner than IBM did in the mainframe days.

For an in-depth case study of the revolutionary business practices and rapid market share shifts enabled by the Internet, we will take a close look at Hotmail and the viral marketing successes that followed.

VIRAL MARKETING
AND THE POTENTIAL FOR HYPER-GROWTH

The Internet can dramatically boost the adoption of a product or service by "viral marketing," or network-enhanced word of mouth. Communication is so easy on the web that product awareness spreads like wildfire. So once a company reaches critical mass, it can experience increasing returns leading to explosive growth. This principle means that in the new economy, first-mover advantages are greater than ever.

A lot of the energy behind the Internet comes from the way it enables everyone to be a publisher. Consequently, we are all scrambling for a precious commodity: people's attention. Their attention is finite, and rising above the noise of a thousand voices requires creativity. Shouting is not very creative. Just hanging up a web shingle and hoping for visitors is not very creative. Rather, new companies can structure their businesses in a way that allows them to grow like a virus and lock out the existing bricks and mortar competitors through innovative pricing and exploitation of these competitors' legacy distribution channel conflict.

In 1996, Sabeer Bhatia and Jack Smith pioneered a great new product category—free web-based e-mail. But many great ideas and great products have withered on the vine. The special catalyst for Hotmail's torrid growth is what we at Draper Fisher Jurvetson first named "viral marketing"—not because any traditional viruses are involved, but because of the pattern of rapid adoption through word-of-mouth networks. Viral marketing powerfully compounds the benefits of a first-mover advantage. And it's something we eagerly look for when evaluating any Internet start-up company. As a founding investor in Hotmail and a member of their board of directors, I think Hotmail is a great case study of the impact of the viral marketing strategy over its full life cycle.

Hotmail's Amazing Growth

Hotmail grew its subscriber base from zero to 12 million users in 18 months, more rapidly than any company in any medium in the history of the world. To be fair, this is the Internet, after all. But it did so with an advertising budget of $50,000—enough for some college newspaper ads and a billboard. Nonviral competitors like Juno spent $20 million on traditional marketing in the same time period with less effect. What's more, Hotmail became the largest e-mail provider in several countries, like Sweden and India, where it had done *no* marketing whatsoever.

Other companies may have distributed more unit volume of product than Hotmail did in their first year—especially when releasing upgrades or brand extensions to an established franchise. But for a new entrant with a new product, the challenge is more daunting. Subscriptions have their own challenges as well. Users face a trust decision when choosing whether to share their private information and e-mail with an on-line entity. And the user may not be certain that the end product is worth the effort. These are barriers to adoption in the subscription model. How did Hotmail overcome these barriers as an undercapitalized start-up? Viral marketing.

Hotmail originally approached us as JavaSoft, Inc., a web database tools company, and, as *Business Week* recounted, Sabeer and Jack went to see "Draper Fisher Jurvetson, but the investor was unimpressed by their idea for database software for the Net. As they were packing up to leave, [the VCs] asked: 'Do you have any other ideas?' Sabeer said they'd noodled over a scheme to offer free, advertising-supported E-mail over the Web. A week and a half later, the venture capitalists ponied up $300,000, and Hotmail was born" (August 25, 1997).

In our next meeting, Tim Draper suggested that they should append an advertising message to every outbound email: "P.S. I love you. Get your free email at *http://www.hotmail.com.*" It was very contentious at the time. Would users balk at having this automatic addition to the content of their private messages? Hotmail tempered the idea by clearly demarcating the promotional plug and removing the "P.S. I love you." Nevertheless, every outbound message sent by a Hotmail user contained a promotional pitch with a clickable URL. Therein lay one of the critical elements of viral marketing: every customer becomes an involuntary salesperson simply by using the product.

Viral marketing is more powerful than third-party advertising because it conveys an implied endorsement from a friend. Although the promotional message is clearly delineated as an advertisement, the spillover marketing benefits are powerful—much like the efficacy of radio commercials read by your favorite DJ. The recipients of a Hotmail message learn that the product works and that their friend is a user. A key element of consumer branding is usage affiliation: do I want to be a member of the group—in this case, my friends—that uses the product?

Hotmail's business model maps well to the medium. By contrast, Juno does not map well to the medium, despite spending $20 million in advertising. Hotmail did not spend the money, yet gained more than three times as many users in half the time.

Elements of Viral Marketing

We were amazed at how quickly Hotmail spread over the global network. The rapid adoption pattern was that of a network virus. People typically send e-mails to their associates and friends, both geographically close and scattered around. We would notice the first user from an overseas university town, and then the number of subscribers from that region would rapidly proliferate. From an epidemiological perspective, it was as if Zeus had sneezed over the planet. The beauty of it is that none of this required any marketing dollars. Customers did the selling.

Digital viruses can spread internationally more rapidly than biological viruses that rely on the physical proximity of hosts for their spread—via a sneeze or handshake. Hotmail is the largest e-mail provider in Sweden and India despite the fact that they have done no marketing of any sort in these countries. It's a happy day when you discover your business has displaced several entrenched competitors to become the market share leader in a country you have never visited. What's more, Hotmail spread to more than 220 countries, despite the limitation that it was only available in English.

Viral marketing captures the essence of multilevel marketing and applies it to all customers—the "word-of-mouth" spread of the Hotmail message is involuntary. And it's more powerful than many other marketing techniques that lack the implied endorsement of a friend. Hotmail had "Free E-mail" buttons on several other highly trafficked web sites, but they generated comparatively negligible numbers of subscriptions. Juno has shown that advertising is relatively cost-ineffective. It is hard to spend your way to Hotmail-like growth. The snowball effect is a mechanism to effectively leverage a first-mover advantage.

Whenever a product involves people other than the purchaser, then there is an opportunity to market to potential new customers. As more Internet and intranet applications move beyond computation to embrace communication, the viral marketing strategy has wide applicability. E-commerce, groupware, community, messaging, and promotions businesses can all use these techniques to further the Internet explosion.

Hotmail is not an isolated example. Hotmail and the instant messenger service ICQ had an identical number of subscribers (plus or minus 5 percent) at the six-, nine-, twelve-, and eighteen-month points. What do they have in common? Hotmail was typically used as a secondary or personal account for communication to a close coterie of friends—much like ICQ's buddy lists. There appeared to be a mathematical elegance to their smooth exponential growth curves.

A first-order model for viral spread is:

$$\text{cumulative users} = (1 + \text{fanout})^{\text{cycles}}$$

In this model, the exponent *cycles* is the number of times the product is used in the time period since launch (or frequency × time). In the early days, Hotmail and ICQ fanned out to about two new users every month, and they each told two friends, and so on, and so on. By the simple model, one seed user grew to 3 users at the end of the first cycle, 9 by the second, 27 by the third, and so on. Companies with much larger fanouts, such as the free e-mail list managers, have grown more quickly than Hotmail. Those that have provided an economic incentive to spam large groups, like AllAdvantage, which pays users to view advertising, have grown faster still, going from zero to 750,000 users in two weeks. The same formula would apply to traditional word-of-mouth marketing (like MCI Friends and Family discount plans and Tupperware parties), but lacking the involuntary coupling to patterns of communication, the average fanout and frequency are much lower.

For a bit more accuracy, we can factor in the variables that describe the success of the recruiting message and the retention rate as percentages:

$$\text{Cumulative users} = [(1 + \text{fanout} \times \text{conversion rate}) \times \text{retention rate}]^{\text{frequency} \times \text{time}}$$

Working through the variables, the ideal viral product will be used to communicate with many people, will convert a high percentage of them to new users, and will retain a high percentage of them. It will also be used quite frequently.

A more accurate, second-order model would include decay functions on each of the variables, reflecting novelty and saturation effects. For example, Hotmail's variables are tapering as it reaches population saturation. Hotmail now has more than 60 million active users, which is one out of every four people on the web worldwide.

Given our excitement about the power of viral marketing, we have funded several companies that are pushing viral marketing in new directions, and we have suggested the addition of a viral element to an otherwise noncommunicative product. For example, NetZero's e-mail vector of spread is very similar to Hotmail's, but it has higher retention and conversion rates. Totally free Internet access is a more compelling proposition than free e-mail, and so NetZero has grown faster than Hotmail in the United States. It has also grown ten times faster than America Online, becoming the second largest Internet service provider in America. In group-event RSVP management, SeeUthere.com has a much higher fanout, reaching many invitees but with a lower frequency—the rate at which events and parties are held.

Companies as diverse as Inforocket (a marketplace for questions and answers), Third Voice (a pan-web community and information service), and Homestead (personal web pages) have found ways to amplify their growth through viral spread. Inforocket encourages users to forward a question to a friend who is likely to know the answer, and in return, the forwarder gets a cut of the lifetime economics of the new recruit. Third Voice encourages users to share their commentary with friends and colleagues via e-mail, thereby upgrading each recipient's browser with Third Voice. Homestead facilitates the recruitment of coauthors to a family or group web site, eventually bringing the community of users to Homestead.

In the e-commerce world, on-line retailers have gained some viral effects through gift packaging and "refer-a-friend" programs. Mimeo.com has taken it a step further by applying viral marketing to every package it delivers. Mimeo offers web-initiated printing, copying, binding, and delivery—a substitute for waiting in line at Kinko's. Each sender is a Mimeo user, but the multiple recipients are not, so the FedEx-like package is covered with Mimeo evangelism.

Meanwhile, Vivaldi offers viral marketing programs to bricks and mortar retailers through a computerized feedback loop between cash registers and the web. By knowing what and when customers are buying, Vivaldi lets retailers offer powerful promotions like frequent-shopper discounts, refer-a-friend bonuses, and new-product notifications. For the first time, off-line retailers can offer loyalty and recruitment programs that are common on the web but difficult to implement at a traditional store.

Although powerful, dyadic communication products like ICQ recruit new customers one by one. A sneeze releases two million aerosol particles. In the digital domain, this can get very interesting. For example, Tumbleweed Communications enables secure e-mail delivery of documents or newsletters to a huge number of recipients. Every recipient also gets a web link to the enabling Tumbleweed service. So when a single new customer starts to use Tumbleweed, thousands of potential new customers receive the Tumbleweed pitch.

This viral broadcast model can be creatively applied to a variety of products, such as web-hosted address books, calendars, list servers, and newsgroup readers.

Viral Marketing Strategies

A good virus will look for prolific hosts (such as students) and tie to their high-frequency social interactions (such as e-mail and messaging). Viral marketing is most powerful when it taps into the breadth of its customers' weak connections to others. Tapping customers' entire address books is more valuable than reaching only their best friends.

The typical viral entry strategy is to minimize the friction of market entry and proliferation with an eye to building in hooks and barriers to switching for customers. If the service is trying blatantly to monetize its subscriber base in every way imaginable, new users will be reluctant to spread the word. Therefore, many of these services are free, and light on revenue generation, in the early days of their rapid proliferation.

An interesting side effect of geometric growth is that by the time a virus spreads to the point of being an epidemic, its growth curve relative to a new entrant is somewhat daunting. Hotmail was doubling in size each month, but it took several months to reach one million users. Until then, they were under the radar screen of many potential competitors and acquirers. By the time the industry came to realize that free web-based e-mail was indeed a hot idea, Hotmail was adding one million new subscribers per month, and that growth rate was accelerating. A new fast follower would start small and have to grow for several months to reach one million subscribers. But in that same time, Hotmail would have grown to 10 million subscribers. So although Hotmail's followers grew geometrically as well, the absolute difference in subscriber bases widened every month (while the ratio remained approximately constant).

Absolute size matters. One significant effect of Hotmail's absolute size is that their efficiencies of scale allowed them to be the lowest-cost e-mail provider on the planet. Server utilization and bandwidth pricing improved with growth. Also, the perceived gorilla in a category tends to get the dominant share of the business and financial partnerships. Many advertisers and media companies do not want to spend time with small properties. All of this makes it tougher for the smaller new entrant. It also skews the "make versus buy" decision toward "buy" for the large portal companies, which realized en masse that they wanted an e-mail solution with proven scalability.

A challenge for the hyper-growth gorilla is scalability. On a technology level, server scalability is a critical concern. Fortunately, companies like Hotmail are turning software into a service. What was sold as e-mail servers and clients is now offered as a web-based service for which the customer need only have a standard web browser. This makes product upgrades a lot easier; Hotmail can upgrade its server software several times a month without involving, or in many cases even notifying, its large customer base. The customer still uses the same browser.

But once one problem is solved, hyper-growth tends to uncover new scalability bottlenecks. Often the young Internet company finds that its growth is constrained by its ability to hire good people. This is why many of these companies try to engineer around people-intensive elements of their business.

By lowering prices or offering free products, and targeting particular parts of their market, the new entrant can make it very painful for established companies with established distribution relationships to follow them. Although the new market size may be smaller, driven by Internet price efficiencies, the new entrant can gain significant share by restructuring the basis of competition. There may be less revenue in a free e-mail market, but it's tough for Eudora and companies based on selling client software to follow Hotmail's lead.

Viral marketing provides a new distribution channel for almost any Internet application. Although it naturally lends itself to free communications or network applications, viral marketing could also be applied to traditional stand-alone software to accelerate the word-of-mouth spread of good software.

How might this work? ReleaseNow.com can embed in just about any software application an e-commerce engine for electronic software distribution and "try before you buy" purchasing. When a customer gives the application to a friend, it triggers the embedded sales agent to offer a 30-day trial period, after which the new user has to pay for the software. It turns software piracy into a sales opportunity. ReleaseNow can also credit multiple distribution partners involved in the sale with a percentage of the transaction. In this viral marketing model, the customer is treated like a distribution partner, receiving a cut of downstream sales.

This could lead to some interesting consumer behavior. Customers would have an incentive to post software to their favorite download sites or other distribution outlets to maximize the total sales of *their* copy of the application. Not only would the customers help resell product directly, they would innovate and discover new distribution networks. Perhaps these should be called "self-organizing viral distribution networks." Established companies are unlikely to experiment with them because of channel conflict with their legacy partners.

And this is just the beginning. NetMind/Puma offers a free web site update notification service as a presales pilot for enterprise server sales. The free voicemail, fax, and telephony companies use aural marketing to recruit new users. Even Palm Pilot users are beaming viral applications over their infrared ports.

From a mimetic engineering perspective, the *idea* of viral marketing spreads like an adaptive virus. The idea itself evolves as it is retold in society.

SUSTAINABILITY

Given all of the rapid change and hyper-growth in Silicon Valley, a number of people are questioning the sustainability of Silicon Valley companies. They suggest that these companies are, in fact, built to flip, that entrepreneurs and venture capitalists are just out to make a quick buck, that everyone is trying to exploit an arbitrage opportunity.

Certainly acquisitions happen, but they are not rampant, and they are not directed by venture capitalists. No venture firm that I know adheres to a flip strategy. Top tier firms know that selling out quickly just isn't the way to make big, thousandfold returns. It's better than a kick in the teeth, but it won't deliver big profits—especially for the massive funds most top firms are managing.

Therefore, "built to flip" is a poor strategy. You can't orchestrate a sale, and savvy entrepreneurs realize that. Yes, there have been lots of companies lately that were acquired even before they had any revenue. But if you're starting a company, you can't say, "Hey, I'll do that too." That's foolish. When a company wants to sell itself, it doesn't do things it should. It doesn't hire the best people possible: if the founders can hire a great vice president of engineering who's going to cost them equity versus someone who's going to get the company by, they settle for someone who's just adequate. Why dilute the stock if you're only going to get acquired in a few months?

And if you've designed a company whose only exit opportunity is acquisition, you have less negotiating leverage with acquirers. The best acquisitions occur when the target doesn't intend to be acquired. Hotmail said no, no, no, for five months to Microsoft. At first, they turned down $120 million in cash, which was ridiculously low. At the end of the day, they got $400 million in Microsoft shares, which are worth $1.2 billion today. That wouldn't have happened if Hotmail were built to flip.

Even then, we advised Hotmail not to sell when it did. In nearly every case, in fact, we've strongly advised against acquisition. Several of our companies have sold anyway, but there simply is a greater upside in staying independent. Anyone who looks at Hotmail's 60 million active subscribers would see that the company would easily have a multibillion-dollar valuation if it were independent today. Tumbleweed and Kana, two of our other companies, both turned down acquisition offers just before their IPOs. The founders of these companies absolutely want to change the world. We look for that in every deal we do. We ask founders, "Why are you starting this company?" If they say, "We want to build something to sell quickly," we'll turn it away. In the end, it requires dedication and passion to say no to the inevitable buy-out offers that are made to successful companies. The toughest challenge for the founder is to persuade the recent hires, VPs, and their spouses to turn down the quick windfall.

So, if venture capitalists aren't driving this phenomenon, what is? In part, it's the developmental speed that the Internet economy allows—and requires. Network effects, the underlying driver of the Net, allows you to grow like wildfire based on the strength of an idea that spreads without mass or physical assets. In previous generations, companies making physical products had to endure long life cycles to realize success. Now, a good idea can take off instantly. Hotmail is now adding more than 200,000 subscribers a day, seven days a week. That's the rate at which an idea can spread and change the world.

The partnering that's rampant on the Net is accelerating this process. Online, Yahoo! and other companies partner like crazy, and they're successful because of it. The number of links that you have correlates to market share, and those who have tried to be islands have withered and faded. That's a huge change for the economy. In the old days, when geography and shipping costs determined business scope and strategy, the transaction costs of partnering were quite high, so companies integrated vertically to own more of the value chain. Henry Ford saw to it that his company owned everything from rubber production to its dealers.

But the Internet has collapsed the cost and latency of communications, so it's much easier to focus on a core for which value is added and partner for the rest. A business model can be much narrower than before and still be viable. Don't assume that just because a company has only one product or service, it can't make it. The possibility that a new Merck or General Electric will emerge is much lower than a generation ago—and it doesn't have to happen for the economy to thrive. U.S. GDP growth will come from many nimble, small businesses, not from sprawling corporate behemoths.

Internet-age companies can operate at a smaller size than ever before. As a result, start-ups can become potent competitors sooner in their organizational lives. Established players recognize this and react out of fear. If you're Eudora, and you own the electronic mail space, all of a sudden you see Hotmail restructuring your business for you. In periods of rapid growth and technological dislocation, incumbents react with their vertical mind-set. They say, "We have to own this space. We have to acquire it." Microsoft couldn't live in a world in which Hotmail owned a critical business, so it was willing to pay a premium to make the acquisition.

To the extent that flipping exists, that sort of acquirer mentality is driving it. We're in a transitional period in which the IBMs think they have to acquire everything. Their effect is magnified artificially because they typically identify start-ups as competitive threats before a banker considers the same start-up suitable for public offering. This industry is barely five years old, and lots of companies were started in 1996 or 1997. That isn't much time to get to an IPO—but it is time enough for a big rival with cash to pick you off. But that will change with time and maturity. We are seeing the first bumper crop of IPOs finally hitting the market in 1999 and 2000.

Certainly, there are people out there who just want to make a quick buck. I think that sort of thinking is short-sighted, shallow, and potentially self-destructive. As an individual, you want to strive for excellence in all that you do. Life is too short to sacrifice personal fulfillment and play a charade for opportunistic gain. That can be a chase that never ends. Always pursue your passion. At this moment in the Net economy, the pace of work makes it easy to lose sight of that.

But individual fulfillment shouldn't be confused with corporate fulfillment. Entrepreneurs will continue to pursue their dreams, but that doesn't mean that a specific corporate entity should expand forever. What we can say is that even a company like Hotmail has had a huge impact on people's lives in a very short time. Companies can grow more rapidly than ever, and they can have a profound impact sooner than ever. Every one of the founders and VPs of Hotmail have since started new companies. Their identity is not tied to one corporation; the cycle begins anew.

Although every person has a fundamental need for symbolic immortality, the vehicle for its expression need not be the formation of a large company like Hewlett-Packard that will preserve a corporate culture (the "HP Way") and the names of the founders in perpetuity. In the corporate flux of the information age, and with the shift from corporate behemoths to a freelance economy, more people will find fulfillment in the artistic expression of their ideas and in the dramatic impact that small groups can have at the product and project level. A good idea no longer needs a corporate crustacean to change the world. This is no longer an opportunity for a very small number of lucky people. Individuals and ideas are empowered as never before. This is a very exciting time. Bring on the new wave of entrepreneurial democracy!

The Evolution of Silicon Valley

INTRODUCTION

There are reasonable grounds for debating the precise events that launched Silicon Valley on the path to its present eminence in the world of high-technology entrepreneurship. This question is a manifestation of the problem of history: What early events "cause" later ones? There usually is no wholly satisfactory answer, and the Valley's history offers no exception.

One can begin by noting the area's beauty and salubrious climate, assets that have undergone some depletion over time but are still substantial. The first wave of risk-tolerant immigrants, seekers for gold, came to the area in 1849. At least one institution key to today's Silicon Valley dates from the late nineteenth century. Stanford University, founded in 1891, was to become a virtual mother lode of people and ideas for industry. Or one might start with the founding of the Federal Telegraph Company, a radio operating company, in 1909 (with David Starr Jordan, the president of Stanford, as, in current terminology, an angel investor). The early twentieth century also saw the invention and development of the triode vacuum tube in Palo Alto by Lee deForest, followed in the next two decades by the growth of a radio tube industry.

These events can be seen as precursors of a high-tech future, but until World War II and for several years afterward, the Santa Clara Valley—the heart of what was to become Silicon Valley—was mainly agricultural. At the outset of its meteoric rise, the region had no old-line manufacturing or resource-intensive industries, and it lacked the array of legal and financial organizations that support such industries. Having few established firms probably made it easier for those in the Valley to invent new business models in later years. As to the state of thought in the late 1940s about the area's future, one of the uses contemplated for what was soon to become the Stanford Industrial Park was growing fruit trees.

In the Valley's formative years, from the late 1930s to the 1980s, several individuals and organizations played a key role in creating the conditions from which came an efflorescence of enterprises over the decades. James Gibbons (Chapter 10) and Emilio Castilla, Hokyu Hwang, Ellen Granovetter, and Mark Granovetter (Chapter 11) acknowledge the pivotal role played by Professor Fred Terman, later dean of engineering and provost of Stanford. Terman's role as a founding father of Silicon Valley is widely recognized, but it is less well known that he was much influenced by Vannevar Bush of MIT, the author of the seminal post–World War II vision for American science and government. After working for Bush during the war, Terman returned to Stanford, inspired by Bush's view of how universities could work productively with industry. Among organizations, James Gibbons in Chapter 10 identifies five as seminal in the Valley's development: Stanford University, Hewlett-Packard, Fairchild Semiconductor, Xerox PARC, and Apple Computer. We focus especially on two of these organizations: Stanford (in Chapters 10 and 11) and Fairchild (in Chapter 8).

From such beginnings, positive feedback processes then took over. Successes attracted ideas, talent, money, and firms from other parts of the world. That this is a self-limiting process is demonstrated by growing congestion on local highways and real estate prices that cause some programmers to decide to locate elsewhere. But higher value-added activities continue to grow.

Gibbons's chapter on Stanford is based on interviews he conducted some years ago with leaders of Silicon Valley. Although all credited the university with large contributions to their firms and to the Valley, he reports diversity in their views of which were the most important contributions. He also puts forth his pioneering version of what we call the "habitat" in this book (first discussed by him at a meeting on Wall Street in December 1988). The financial value created by what Gibbons in his chapter calls "Stanford start-ups" is extraordinary. Consistent with his general finding is the more recent estimate by the university's "Wellspring of Innovation" project that one-fourth of the top 150 public companies in the Valley were "Stanford-founded" (founded or cofounded by alumni, faculty/staff, or former faculty/staff). Their total revenues in 1999 were more than $90 billion, about 40 percent of the total for all these firms.

This record must be unique in the annals of academia—but, as reported in Henry Rowen's Chapter 9, for more than a century American universities have tended to have closer links with industry than have those in other countries. Although other nations are trying to become more like the United States in this respect, one still does not observe in Europe and Japan the extensive links between faculty members and firms that exist here.

Stanford has changed over the years, partly in response to changes in its environment. One change is in the university's policy toward ideas created by the faculty. It is tricky to get this policy right. Inventors should be rewarded, and the university should be compensated for supporting the faculty and for the facilities that enable their work to be done. As practiced by the Office of Technology Licensing and other university entities, the policies that have evolved try to balance incentives to invent and commercialize ideas with the larger goals of the university. Another change at Stanford is the growth of entrepreneurial activities at all levels, from faculty research and teaching to student clubs and activities, not only in the business and engineering schools, but also in other departments and research centers throughout campus.

The history of Fairchild Semiconductor, another key early organization, is presented by Christophe Lécuyer in Chapter 8. Its leaders, who were regarded as the "Traitorous Eight" by William Shockley, the founder of Shockley Semiconductor Laboratory, whom they abandoned en masse, created the Valley's first major spin-off in Fairchild. Fairchild made major advances in silicon technology, established a productive relationship with the government (in particular, the Air Force), played a large role in bringing venture capitalists to the Valley, and became the source of many spin-offs itself.

Fairchild's involvement with government exemplifies one of several roles government has played in the rise of the American computer industry and of the Valley in particular. Many people, especially foreigners, misunderstand these roles. Contrary to the prevailing policies in most countries, the United States never had "national champion" companies that it backed (on the contrary, it punished its leading firm, IBM). It was rarely protectionist (with certain exceptions, mainly regarding trade with Japan in semiconductors and the buying of supercomputers) and avoided a policy of favoring some regions, such as Silicon Valley, over others.

The roles that it did play, however, as discussed in Chapter 9, were of enormous importance. Often overlooked in accounts of Silicon Valley's rise is how an extensive set of American laws and institutions regarding securities, employment, pensions, bankruptcy, and much more created an environment that made the Valley's rise possible. To be sure, this does not explain why so much happened in the San Francisco Bay Area, rather than elsewhere in California or the United States, but without the American system, this region might be more famous today for its apricot orchards than its seven thousand high-tech firms. Among the government's roles, research support supplied through many, largely independent, channels has been especially important. The diversity displayed in research funding is a distinctive American characteristic, one with its roots in our governmental division of powers. Because Stanford and Berkeley had strong electrical engineering schools and made commitments early to computer science, as government research funds grew, these two institutions benefited and so, in turn, did the region's economy.

Organizations like Stanford and Fairchild Semiconductor had such a great influence on Silicon Valley because of the rich networks of firms and individuals they spawned. Everyone recognizes that networks of relations are crucial to the operations of the Valley, but, in reality, little has been done to study them systematically. Emilio Castilla, Hokyu Hwang, and Ellen and Mark Granovetter provide a progress report on such an effort in Chapter 11. They undertake a formal analysis of who has worked with whom in various organizations, especially newly created companies, over time. The history of the semiconductor industry, with its many spin-offs, involved intricate connections among engineers, inventors, and entrepreneurs, and some individuals (not always the best known to the public) are revealed as central in the semiconductor social network. As observed above, a wide range of people at Stanford, located in many departments and laboratories, participate in these networks, and there are strong interactions among faculty, students, and local industry. The venture capital and legal scenes also display strong network characteristics.

Among the fastest-growing networks in the Valley today are those of the region's many immigrants. Chinese and Indian immigrants, especially, play a key role in the regional economy. AnnaLee Saxenian documents their entrepreneurial successes and growing links with their homelands in Chapter 12. She estimates that Chinese and Indians led 27 percent of the region's high-technology companies started between 1990 and 1998. This was more than double their share during the first half of the 1980s. Saxenian describes an important institution through which immigrants form networks and get help: ethnic associations. These associations, many of which are organized in subgroups (Taiwanese engineers, mainland Chinese engineers, etc.), are a source of mentoring and financing for younger members. The goal of The Indus Entrepreneurs, for example, is to "foster entrepreneurship by providing mentoring and resources" within the South Asian technology community.

The Valley relies on a high level of human capital, and much of that now comes from Asia. It is further increased through graduate education in the United States, and mentoring and work experiences here. It used to be widely thought that this flow of talent created a brain drain on immigrants' countries of origin, but a different view has recently emerged. Significant numbers of highly skilled professionals are returning to their countries of origin and carrying with them skills acquired here. And many immigrants in the Valley act as bridges between entrepreneurs at home and opportunities here. This produces valuable two-way exchanges of products, ideas, and people. This manifestation of globalization as an exchange process is by no means an entirely new phenomenon, but it is becoming an increasingly important one.

Why have these evolutionary developments so far benefited Silicon Valley more than other regions? In the end, there remain debates as to exactly why some regions take off and others don't. It is easier to look back and identify key events, people, and relationships than to forecast the future.

8

Fairchild Semiconductor and Its Influence

CHRISTOPHE LÉCUYER

"It was on the San Francisco Peninsula," reflected Thomas Bay, Fairchild Semiconductor's first marketing and sales manager, "that the silicon industry was invented." Although most of the seminal work in silicon electronics was done at the Bell Telephone Laboratories, and silicon diodes and transistors were first produced by firms in Texas and Southern California, it was Fairchild Semiconductor, a firm located on the Peninsula, which defined the new industry in the late 1950s and very early 1960s. Fairchild delineated the silicon industry's main products and manufacturing processes. It also developed innovative sales and marketing practices, as well as new organizational structures that were later widely adopted by other silicon firms. In addition to its "invention" of the silicon industry, Fairchild also had an enormous impact on the electronics manufacturing complex on the San Francisco Peninsula. It pioneered the phenomenon of "spinning-off" a group to form new firms and brought venture capitalists to the area.

Most accounts of Fairchild's rise present the firm as the creation of a "visionary" technologist-turned-businessman, Robert Noyce. These narratives portray Noyce, the co-inventor of the integrated circuit and the firm's second general manager, as the main force behind the establishment of Fairchild. Noyce, rather than Fairchild's founding group, is also often seen as responsible for the firm's spectacular success.[1]

The role of the Department of Defense has also been much debated (DeGrasse 1987, 77–104; Asher and Strom 1977; Seidenberg 1997, 36–74;

Ceruzzi 1998). Some scholars have argued that the military had little influence on the evolution of silicon technology in the 1950s and early 1960s. Key innovations such as the development of the planar process at Fairchild were developed without government support. These authors have viewed the evolution of semiconductor design processing as driven mostly by internal forces. As a result, the military appears in their accounts as a selecting mechanism for industrial success rather than as a primary driver of technological change. Others have claimed that the Department of Defense shaped the process of technical change in semiconductors and that the military demand for reliable and compact electronics equipment led to major semiconductor innovations such as the silicon transistor and the integrated circuit (Golding 1971; Levin 1982; Misa 1985; Holbrook 1995).

New material shows that the shaping of silicon technology was a group effort rather than the creation of "heroic" individuals such as Noyce. It was also closely coupled with military procurement and the establishment of reliability and performance standards by the Department of Defense. A group of highly creative scientists and technologists (including Noyce) established Fairchild Semiconductor in alliance with a New York investment bank and a medium-sized military contractor on the East Coast. Fairchild's founders reshaped the silicon industry's products and manufacturing methods by adopting the diffusion process recently developed at the Bell Telephone Laboratories. As a result, Fairchild was the first commercial firm to introduce high-frequency transistors to the market. These transistors met a rapidly growing demand for fast silicon components in the emerging field of digital-based guidance and control systems for jet aircraft and missiles.

However, at first Fairchild's transistors did not meet the reliability criteria of the Air Force Minuteman program. Adapting their technologies to meet these reliability standards, Fairchild's founding engineers such as Jean Hoerni, Robert Noyce, and Jay Last made a second round of major innovations. One was the planar process and another the integrated circuit. Fairchild's engineers perfected their production systems and tightened their control of the manufacturing process with the help and under the scrutiny of the Minuteman program. This enabled Fairchild to gain a large share of the military market for high-reliability silicon components. The firm emerged as the leading silicon manufacturer in the late 1950s and very early 1960s.

PROFESSIONAL VALUES, VENTURE CAPITAL, AND THE FORMATION OF FAIRCHILD SEMICONDUCTOR

Fairchild Semiconductor was established in Palo Alto in October 1957 by a group of eight physicists and engineers from Shockley Semiconductor Laboratory to manufacture advanced silicon transistors. These men, Sheldon Roberts, Eugene Kleiner, Jean Hoerni, Gordon Moore, Jay Last, Victor Grinich, Julius Blank, and Robert Noyce, were highly creative and independent-minded scientists with impeccable professional credentials. Five had Ph.D.s in the physical sciences and had done noted research work in spectroscopy, metallurgy, and solid-state physics. Noyce, a solid state physicist from MIT, was the only one with a strong semiconductor background. Like Noyce and Last, Roberts, a metallurgist, was an MIT Ph.D. and Moore, a physical chemist from Cal Tech, had worked on the spectroscopy of hot gases for the missile re-entry program at Johns Hopkins. Finally, Hoerni was a physicist from Switzerland with two Ph.D.s from Oxford and the University of Geneva.[2]

The group also had three engineers. Kleiner, an Austrian émigré, had studied mechanical and industrial engineering in the United States before designing cigar-making machinery at the American Shoe Foundry Company and making relays at Western Electric. Blank, a mechanical engineer, had held a variety of technical and engineering positions at Babcock & Wilcox and Western Electric. Finally, Grinich, the group's only electrical engineer, had received a doctorate in circuit theory from Stanford University. At the Stanford Research Institute, he designed transistor circuits for color television and the ERMA computer, the first computing machine for banking applications.[3]

This unusual group had joined the Shockley Semiconductor Laboratory, a small semiconductor operation on the San Francisco Peninsula, in the spring of 1956. Although small and far from major scientific and technological centers, the firm offered an interesting opportunity for young and ambitious scientists with an interest in the promising semiconductor field. William Shockley, the firm's founder, had developed the junction transistor in 1948, an invention for which he later received the Nobel prize in physics. Shockley had also directed much of the Bell Telephone Laboratories' extensive solid state physics activities and helped transform it into the premier center for semiconductor research in the United States.

Figure 8.1. The founding group, Fairchild Semiconductor Corporation.
Photo courtesy of Eugene Kleiner.

The eight Shockley recruits were also attracted to the Bay Area by its beauty and proximity to the Sierra Nevada Mountains. Frederick Terman, Stanford's provost, who was interested in attracting new electronics-based businesses to the area, had strongly encouraged Shockley to locate his new lab in the university's vicinity. More importantly, Shockley was a native of Palo Alto and his mother lived in the area. Shockley was interested in being near her.[4]

The new laboratory was to develop and manufacture advanced transistors and other components based on two technologies in which Shockley saw much industrial potential: silicon and solid state diffusion. Silicon, although less used than germanium, was considerably cheaper and allowed the fabrication of more durable and temperature-resistant devices. Solid state diffusion, recently developed at the Bell Telephone Laboratories, promised to revolutionize silicon components. It offered a much more precise and controllable way of forming transistor and diode junctions, and made possible the fabrication of higher-frequency devices.

Shockley's team set out to develop double diffused silicon transistors. "It was pretty much research on developing the basic technology," Moore later recalled, "trying to repeat some of the things that had been done [at the Bell Laboratories], understand some of the problems that we still had because neither the processing nor the physics of [silicon] was well understood. We were just exploring the technology and figuring out what could be done, and we had a lot of things to make work before we could try to build something. We were far from developing a commercial device."[5]

Besides fundamental studies on currents in silicon crystals, much of the group's work was on diffusion phenomena. The group also experimented with mesa transistor structures, which had recently been developed at the Bell Telephone Laboratories. Adopting the Bell process, the Shockley recruits built and tested experimental mesa structures.[6]

Working with Shockley did not prove easy. In less than a year, seven of his eight recruits rebelled against him (Noyce was the exception). They asked Arnold Beckman (of Beckman Laboratories), the laboratory's backer, to remove Shockley from the day-to-day management of the laboratory. They wanted to replace him with "a professional manager to whom [they] could report."[7] The group's rebellion was motivated by Shockley's heavy-handed management style, as well as by sharp disagreements about the laboratory's direction. While the rebels admired his physical intuition and command of solid state physics, they were increasingly unhappy with his mercurial temperament and his poor treatment of the laboratory staff. Shockley not only routinely threatened employees with immediate dismissal, but he also staged public firings and called for lie detector tests to be given for a trifling issue.[8]

Moreover, Shockley closely supervised their projects, which left them with little creative liberty and no real sense of pride in their work. The insurgents were further disconcerted by the laboratory's seeming lack of focus. Wavering between engineering commercial devices and doing advanced research in solid state physics, Shockley regularly shifted his staff back and forth from research projects to product development. He constantly promoted new ideas and directed his staff to abandon the projects they were working on to turn to new ones.[9]

The group also strongly objected to Shockley's decision to shift the laboratory's focus from transistors to PNPN diodes, a specialized device recently invented by Shockley for telephone switching applications, and one that they believed to be a poor prospect for a first product. Instead, the rebels urged that the lab return to its original goal of manufacturing double diffused silicon transistors. No corporation, they argued, had yet been able to produce and commercialize these devices. They could meet the high-speed requirements of digital circuits, an application that members of the group had been sensitized to through their research projects at MIT, Philco, and the Stanford Research Institute.[10]

When they failed to convince Beckman to remove Shockley and reorient the lab, the insurgents found themselves in an uncomfortable position. Unwilling to stay at Shockley Semiconductor, they could not easily find jobs in the area, either. The local tube and instrumentation firms had no interest in silicon componentry and little demand for people with their skills. Intent upon staying in the area, keeping the group together, and pursuing their work on diffused silicon transistors, the rebels contacted Hayden, Stone & Company, a small investment bank in New York with which Kleiner's father had an account. In a bold move, the rebels asked the bank to help them find a corporation interested in hiring them collectively and in setting up a silicon operation on the San Francisco Peninsula. "Because of seemingly insuperable problems with the present management," the Shockley insurgents wrote to Hayden Stone,

this group wishes to find a corporation interested in getting into the advanced semiconductor device business. If such suitable backing can be obtained the present group can reasonably expect to take with them other senior people and an excellent supporting staff totaling about thirty people. Thus a backer has the opportunity to obtain at one time a well-trained technical group by supplying enlightened administration and support. It is the aim of the group to negotiate with a company which can supply good management. We believe that we could get a company into the semiconductor business within three months which would represent a considerable saving in cost and time. The initial product will be a line of silicon diffused transistors of unusual design applicable to the production of both high frequency and high power devices. It should be pointed out that the complicated techniques necessary for producing these semiconductors have already been worked out in detail by this group of people, and are not restricted by any obligation to the present organization. We [also] have an excellent supporting staff. Because of this experienced staff, and also because of the group's own attachment to the lower San Francisco Peninsula area, we would want to establish the operation here south of San Francisco. It is estimated that the establishment of this new enterprise and its efficient operation in the first year will require an expenditure in the neighborhood of $750,000.[11]

The letter soon attracted the attention of a young security analyst, Arthur Rock, and a managing partner, Alfred Coyle, who had a keen interest in science-based industries. While Hayden Stone traditionally had been oriented toward established industrial sectors, the bank, under Coyle's leadership, had recently expanded into electronics. These men had also followed the emergence of the venture capital industry and, in particular, firms such as J. H. Whitney and Company and American Research and Development, which had provided financing to new chemical and instrumentation firms since the late 1940s. Inspired by these examples, Rock and Coyle were interested in developing new types of financial services for such firms and, in particular, in helping new electronics firms secure early rounds of financing from established corporations. While riskier than the underwriting of securities, these activities could potentially bring very large financial returns to the company.[12]

Rock and Coyle flew to California. They were impressed by the defectors' intellectual abilities and their capacity to work as a group and were aware of the potential of the semiconductor business. The Hayden Stone representatives made them an unusual proposition. At a time when very few scientists and engineers started new business enterprises, Rock and Coyle suggested that the group establish its own corporation rather than look for collective employment. Furthermore, they offered to secure capital among corporate backers. In return, they asked for a small interest in the new company. Their proposal was a startling one for the group. Socialized in academic science rather than entrepreneurship, they had never thought of establishing their own firm and assumed that they would always work in corporations. The group, however, found Rock's proposal appealing for personal and professional reasons. They saw the formation of a new firm as a way of staying in California and, more importantly, as a means for controlling their own technical work and, as Last put it, "being their own boss."[13] Acting as the group's agent, Rock approached more than 30 potential corporate backers, including many East Coast electronics firms and large aerospace corporations such as North American Aviation. Rock encountered considerable difficulties in raising the needed capital. Some firms were taken aback by the risks in supporting a group with no product and, more importantly, little management experience. Others had already started their own research programs in silicon and did not feel a need for the defectors' expertise. More importantly, most corporations deemed the project impractical if not disruptive. Because they had never financed a company outside their own business, many managers did not see how they could structure such a deal. They also worried about the effect on their own employees. They feared, in particular, that it would lead them to set up their own businesses and compete with their former employer.[14]

Only Fairchild Camera and Instrument, a medium-sized military contractor based in Long Island, expressed an active interest in the idea. It had no internal silicon expertise and was willing to consider unorthodox proposals. Established in the early 1920s by Sherman Fairchild, the wealthy scion of an IBM executive, to manufacture aerial cameras, the firm had expanded in the immediate postwar period into other military businesses such as high precision potentiometers for analog computers and military avionics equipment. By the mid-1950s, Fairchild had seen its sales decline from $42 million in 1954 to $36 million two years later and its earnings dwindle from $1.6 million to $260,000 during the same period.[15]

To reverse the company's sagging fortunes, Sherman Fairchild, who was also IBM's largest shareholder, reoriented the company toward electronics and especially data gathering, transmitting, and storing technologies. He hired a group of young managers with electronics experience such as Richard Hodgson, a Stanford electrical engineer who had headed a small television tube manufacturer on the West Coast. The firm then acquired a number of system businesses such as the teletypesetter division of AT&T and a manufacturer of magnetic tape transports for digital computing. These men were also looking for opportunities in the transistor business but were taken aback, as they later recalled, by the scarcity of "qualified personnel, the very large capital investment [required], and the prospect of years of research before production might be feasible." Hence their interest in the Shockley rebels. They offered a group steeped in the latest silicon techniques, which had nearly mastered the manufacturing processes, and was reasonably close to the production stage. They provided a fast and relatively cheap entry into the silicon industry.[16]

Exploiting Fairchild Camera's keen interest in the rebels' proposal, Hayden Stone negotiated, on their behalf, one of the first venture capital agreements on the West Coast. Fairchild Camera financed the establishment of a new firm, Fairchild Semiconductor Corporation, with a loan of $1.38 million for its first year and a half of operation. The new firm was jointly owned by Hayden Stone, the seven rebels, and Noyce, the charismatic assistant director of research at Shockley, who joined as its technical leader. While Hayden Stone owned roughly one-fifth of Fairchild Semiconductor, the remaining shares were distributed equally among the eight entrepreneurs. Fairchild Camera controlled the firm's board of directors and, in conjunction with Hayden Stone and the California group, had the right to choose its general manager. The contract further specified that, in case the new firm became successful and met certain profitability requirements, Fairchild Camera had the option of acquiring it for $3 million after two years or $5 million after eight years.[17]

The new corporation would make high-performance silicon transistors for the military. Although the group had done no formal market research prior to the firm's establishment, they sensed that the military sector offered by far the most promising market. Interested in the high-temperature characteristics of silicon components, the Department of Defense (DoD) was the largest user of silicon transistors and diodes by the mid-1950s and had expressed a strong interest in the application of solid state diffusion to the making of silicon transistors. Finally, only the military and large weapon system contractors, Fairchild's founders reasoned, would have the financial resources to buy such complex and expensive products.[18]

The founders decided that it would also be a manufacturing organization. Unlike other electronics component firms on the San Francisco Peninsula that had often started as contract engineering firms, Fairchild was to concentrate on the highly profitable volume production of silicon transistors. Indeed, it had no interest in military research contracts. Benefiting from generous financing, Fairchild Semiconductor did not need military patronage for research and product development. Furthermore, the founders deemed military research contracts detrimental because they would give the DoD control of the firm's research program and product line, leading it in directions of interest to the military but of little industrial potential. Finally, because of their one- to three-year duration, military research contracts would also restrict the firm's ability to adjust rapidly to new technical and market opportunities in a fast-evolving industry.[19]

BRINGING A NEW PRODUCT TO MARKET

The eight entrepreneurs set up shop in Palo Alto in October 1957. Besides setting up suitable facilities and building specialized equipment, their first task was to build a strong technical and management team. The group hired former co-workers from Shockley's lab as well as local electronics technicians. Many had worked in the Peninsula's power and microwave tube industries and brought with them knowledge of chemical handling, glass working, and vacuum techniques. Under Hodgson's guidance, the founders also recruited managers from component firms in Southern California. They appointed Thomas Bay, a former marketing manager at Fairchild Camera's potentiometer division in Los Angeles, as the head of sales and marketing. Edward Baldwin was recruited as the firm's general manager in February 1958. Baldwin, an important recruit with experience in directing product engineering at Hughes Semiconductor, also brought a large contingent of manufacturing and instrumentation engineers from Hughes. Bay also hired some of Hughes Semiconductor's best and most aggressive salesmen.[20]

The new team proceeded to identify potential users of the firm's products before developing their first transistors. Noyce and Bay, benefiting from Sherman Fairchild's close contacts with IBM, visited its Federal Systems Division, which specialized in the design and manufacture of advanced military computers, and discovered that there was an emerging market for double diffused silicon transistors in military avionics, especially in new digital-based guidance and flight control systems.[21]

Starting in 1956, the Air Force championed the digitization of avionics. Until that time, aircraft and missiles had been controlled by analog techniques, especially analog computers. Analog-based avionics systems, however, depended on failure-prone electron tubes and a multitude of moving parts that were sensitive to vibration and wear and tear. As a result, analog autopilots, bomb sights, and navigation instruments failed on the average every 70 hours. Digital computers, the Air Force reasoned, had a number of advantages. They were more accurate and could calculate the trajectory of ballistic missiles more precisely. Digital computers could also operate at speeds far outstripping those of mechanical and electromechanical machines and could therefore control very complex weapon systems in real time. They were also general-purpose machines and could be used for a variety of functions. Furthermore, they promised to be more dependable than analog machines (Ceruzzi 1989, 15–16, 20–30, 51–57, 80–111; Fishbein 1995, 111–21; Bridges 1957, 1–7).

As manufacturers of navigation and flight control systems such as Sperry, Arma Bosch, and Hughes gradually shifted from analog to digital techniques, they started building high-speed digital computers from which came a market for high-performance digital components. Going further, the Air Force insisted that avionics firms employ silicon transistors as much as possible. Only silicon components met the reliability, miniaturization, and high temperature demands of airborne systems.

Fairchild's founders also identified a pressing need for switching transistors in computer memories. The engineers at IBM's Federal Systems Division needed a transistor for the navigational computer for the B-70 aircraft. Fairchild's founders realized that only a silicon device, faster and of higher power than any on the market, would drive the computer's core memory planes. This product would fill "a vacant area in transistors" and find a ready market in military airborne computers.[22]

The Fairchild group decided to develop core drivers that would meet IBM's engineering specifications and negotiated the terms of a purchase order with its Federal Systems Division. Because the engineers who designed the navigational computer had concerns about the firm's production capability and financial soundness, the Fairchild group enlisted the help of Hodgson and Sherman Fairchild. These men visited Thomas Watson Jr., IBM's chief executive officer, to "convince him that [buying transistors from the new firm] was a safe thing to do." As a result of this timely visit, Fairchild received a purchase order for one hundred mesa transistors at the hefty price of $150 a piece in February 1958. Although the device's polarities (NPN or PNP) were left for the group to choose, IBM's engineers carefully specified the transistor's electrical parameters. Furthermore, they impressed upon the Fairchild group the importance of supplying reliable components. They asked that Fairchild "cut out all random catastrophic failures" in its production lots, use high-quality packages for its transistors, and apply special procedures to test them.[23]

The development of these radically new transistor products offered very substantial difficulties. The group could rely on sophisticated physical theories developed at Bell Labs for the design of mesa transistors, but the production techniques required to make them were fraught with difficulties. To develop a process applicable on a production scale the founders made risky and innovative process choices that contrasted sharply with those of Western Electric, Bell's manufacturing arm. While Western Electric employed proven techniques such as metal masking and gallium diffusion, the Fairchild group chose to exploit very advanced processes that ironically had been developed at Bell Labs. The group specifically decided to use oxide masking and photolithography. Although these techniques were more complex and difficult to use than metal masks, they promised more precise control of transistor dimensions and ones with better electrical characteristics. In addition to photolithography, the Fairchild group also settled on boron and phosphorus diffusion as well as aluminum deposition, all techniques that later became standard in the silicon industry.[24]

In less than five months, the team transformed these and other laboratory techniques into reproducible and economical fabrication processes. Experimenting by trial and error and relying on their rich and varied scientific and technological skills, these men made numerous innovations, ranging from improvements in crystal-growing techniques to the development of a novel procedure for attaching gold wires to the transistor chips. Key among these was the development of a controllable photolithography process and its attendant equipment. In particular, Noyce and Last designed, along with Kleiner, a step-and-repeat camera to make masks and devised an innovative method for aligning them.

In conjunction with their work on masking, Last and Noyce improved upon existing photoresists, the photographic emulsions used to selectively etch the wafers, which did not meet the exacting requirements of silicon processing. To solve these problems, Last and Noyce, working in collaboration with Eastman Kodak, transformed the photoresists' chemical composition and purified them so as to eliminate contaminants and make them adhere to the silicon wafer.[25] The group also sought to better understand the boron and phosphorus diffusion processes and to engineer controllable and economic diffusion techniques. Finally, the Fairchild group developed a novel fabrication technique to deposit ohmic or nonrectifying contacts on top of the transistor dice in order to connect them to the package's wires. While Western Electric used two different metals, aluminum and silver, for its contacts, Moore developed an all-aluminum process. This was an important innovation, as aluminum later became the metal of choice for making contacts in the silicon industry.[26]

Fairchild's engineers also faced the problem of packaging double diffused transistors that needed to be shielded from outside contaminants and had to withstand the high temperatures and vibrations that are characteristic of military aircraft. At IBM's request, Fairchild's engineers used the highest-quality packages then on the market: hermetic metal cans that incorporated very advanced seals developed originally for the manufacture of power tubes. More importantly, Fairchild engineers devised new ways of assembling the transistor chip or die to its package. Texas Instruments had attached the silicon chips to their cans through dangling wires, which made its transistor products sensitive to shock and vibrations and earned them a reputation for unreliability. Instead, Fairchild engineers directly soldered the chips to their containers. As a result, Fairchild's transistor products were much more rugged than those of its competitors.[27]

Because the NPN version of the core driver was more advanced in its design than its PNP counterpart, Fairchild put it into production first, in May 1958. To produce this revolutionary transistor, Kleiner and the engineers from Hughes borrowed practices from the silicon industry, such as the use of process manuals, the employment of relatively unskilled female workers, and the establishment of a preproduction engineering group whose sole responsibility was to scale up the process. These men also made important innovations in production. They, in effect, pioneered a new form of silicon manufacturing. First, they built an unusual production line with both a batch component and a continuous flow element. In the first part of the manufacturing process, the devices were batch produced. Groups of wafers containing hundreds of transistors were diffused and oxidized at the same time. The second part of the process was an assembly affair, reminiscent of the production lines in the mechanical industries. The wafers were sliced and the individual transistor dice or chips were hand-soldered to the base of the transistor cases. Finally, gold wires were attached to the transistor contacts, and each unit was hermetically sealed.[28]

Second, Fairchild's manufacturing engineers gave considerable attention to cleanliness. They dust-proofed and air-conditioned the firm's processing and assembly areas. They also enforced no-smoking rules to limit environmental contamination to a minimum. As a result, Fairchild's production line was substantially cleaner than those of other silicon corporations. It had more stringent cleanliness standards than the manufacturing areas of other electronics component firms on the San Francisco Peninsula, such as microwave tube firms that had pioneered the building of clean rooms in the late 1940s and early 1950s.[29]

Third, Kleiner and other Fairchild engineers tightly controlled a very complex and unforgiving process by imposing an unprecedented level of industrial discipline on the workforce. They developed process manuals that were much more detailed than the specification books used by other silicon corporations, carefully specifying the complex procedures operators had to perform in the factory. "The specification books [were produced] in several editions," recalled Kleiner, the first head of manufacturing at Fairchild, "so very often the manuals had to be revised several times, before they became clear enough to be followed by a relatively unskilled person."[30] Hundreds of pages in length, these process manuals described in excruciating detail the production operations, from crystal growing, to diffusion, photolithography, metallization, assembly, and testing. To ensure that operators followed the manuals, Fairchild's engineers imposed highly regimented work tasks and closely supervised the operators and dismissed those who did not carefully follow the procedures. "We had to have a great deal of discipline on the production line," Kleiner later recalled.

Fairchild Semiconductor made its first product delivery to IBM in the early summer of 1958 and introduced its NPN transistor on the market at Wescon, the western electronics trade show, in August of the same year. At Wescon, the Fairchild group discovered with relish that they were the first ones to commercialize a double diffused silicon transistor. "We scooped the industry," Noyce reported gleefully at a Fairchild policy meeting a few days after the trade show. "Nobody [is] ready to put something like this on the market. [Moreover]," he added, "[there is] no prospect of anybody getting in our way in the immediate future."[31] Only Western Electric had succeeded in manufacturing double diffused transistors, but it did not pose any competitive threat as its devices were used exclusively by the Bell system. In effect, Fairchild Semiconductor had become the only supplier of double diffused silicon transistors available on the open market and kept its monopoly on these devices for nearly a year and a half.

ENGINEERING ULTRARELIABILITY

The standard sales practice in the electronics component industries at the time was to approach the procurement officers of large military contractors. Reasoning that contractors were interested mostly in supplier dependability and viewed small, untried firms such as Fairchild with suspicion, Bay and his salesmen circumvented them. They approached, instead, the design engineers in charge of developing airborne computers and avionics systems. These engineers, Bay surmised, were concerned mostly with performance and reliability and were looking for the most advanced components. Because few design engineers then knew about transistors, let alone diffused silicon ones, Fairchild made another marketing innovation. Unlike other manufacturers of silicon components, it gave strong technical support to its customers. The firm's application engineering laboratory, under Grinich, wrote notes describing the unusual electrical characteristics of Fairchild's device and explained how it could be used and tested. These notes also proposed circuit arrangements around the firm's transistor that customers could copy in their own designs.[32]

Fairchild rapidly built up a substantial business using these tactics. It also benefited from the fact that the NPN transistor fortuitously met the requirements of a wide range of avionics applications. While Fairchild had $65,000 in sales in August and September 1958, its revenues jumped to $440,000 in the fall of the same year, reaching $2.8 million in the first eight months of 1959. An overwhelming share was in the avionics sector, with large purchase orders from Hughes, Sperry, Arma Bosch, and other companies developing digital computers and avionics systems for jet aircraft and missiles.[33]

Fairchild received an especially important procurement contract from Autonetics, a division of North American Aviation, which was developing the guidance and control system of the Minuteman missile. This system had the unusual performance specifications of guiding a missile to a target in the Soviet Union with a precision of a few hundred meters. It also had to be extremely reliable: the Air Force wanted the Minuteman to be fired without long warm-up periods, be easy and inexpensive to maintain, and operate without failures for more than a year at a time. This implied a mean time between failures of seven thousand hours, a hundred-fold improvement over the average reliability of avionics systems at the time. To meet these extraordinary specifications, Autonetics selected an all-digital design. It also chose to use the fastest and most reliable components: solid state devices and, wherever possible, silicon diffused semiconductors. Autonetics granted a contract to Fairchild, the only supplier of double diffused silicon transistors, with the understanding that the company would improve the reliability of its devices by several orders of magnitude (Reed 1986; Wuerth 1976).

At this stage, Fairchild Semiconductor soon ran into a serious crisis. A customer, possibly Autonetics, discovered that Fairchild transistors had a major reliability problem. Merely tapping the transistor cans with a pencil would produce unstable voltage characteristics and make the transistors unfit for operation. After months of unsuccessful inquiries, a Fairchild technician found out that these failures were caused by particles shaken loose in the transistor can that would short the junctions and cause their premature breakdown. Although the occurrence of transistor failures was reduced by applying tapping tests at the end of the production line, Fairchild's engineers could not eliminate the problem entirely: it was an intrinsic failure mechanism linked to the transistor's structure. Solving the tapping problem was imperative. The survival of the company was at stake.[34]

To eliminate tap failures, Fairchild's engineers, in a burst of technological creativity, developed revolutionary products and processes. Indeed, solving the tapping and contamination problems of mesa transistors led Hoerni to make the most important innovation in the history of the silicon industry. He developed a new process, the planar process, which made possible the manufacture of ultrareliable transistors and diodes, as well as the development of a new component, the integrated circuit. The Fairchild group learned at a meeting of the Electrochemical Society in May 1958 that a research group at Bell Labs had discovered that a thermally grown oxide passivated or electrically stabilized the silicon surface. Independently, Hoerni, along with Noyce and Moore, had experimented with these oxides at Shockley Semiconductor. Following up on this work, these men developed at Fairchild a transistor in which the oxide layer was left on top of the emitter junction after processing. They discovered that this new device had much-improved electrical parameters.[35]

Building on these results, Hoerni developed a new manufacturing process that relied heavily on the masking and passivating properties of silicon oxide, motivated, in part, by the rejection of his PNP transistor by Moore a few months earlier. Hoerni grew an oxide layer on top of the wafer at the very beginning of the process. Using the photolithographic techniques developed for Fairchild's first transistor, he later selectively etched this layer to diffuse dopants and form the transistor junctions. More importantly, Hoerni, in a very innovative move that went against all accepted knowledge in the silicon community, left the oxide layer on top of the wafer after transistor processing. This layer passivated the crystal's surface and protected the transistor junctions from outside contaminants. Applying these techniques to the fabrication of Fairchild's first NPN transistor, Hoerni obtained a device characterized by its flat or planar surface—a feature that gave its name to the new process. This device, Hoerni discovered, was vastly superior to its mesa equivalent. In particular, it had much-improved electrical characteristics. While Fairchild's first transistor had a low gain, the planar transistor amplified electrical signals much better. It also had very little leakage. More importantly, planar transistors were much more reliable than their mesa counterparts. "The most interesting thing [with these devices]," Hoerni reminisced, "was once they were sealed then you could tap forever—nothing would happen."[36]

Noyce and Moore, who had emerged as the company's main managers, decided to develop the planar process and bring it to production. Although this decision might appear obvious with hindsight, it was not evident at the time and involved much technological risk. In particular, planar transistors were extremely difficult to make. "The yield," Hoerni later recalled, "was terrible."[37] At an early stage in their development, the yield of Fairchild's first NPN mesa transistors had been in the 25 to 30 percent range. The yield of planar devices did not exceed 5 percent, a fact that cast doubts about their ultimate manufacturability. Indeed, Bell Laboratories, which devised a process similar to Hoerni's at about the same time, decided to forgo its further development because of its seeming lack of manufacturability. In contrast, Fairchild's management chose otherwise. It saw the planar process as the solution to the company's severe tap failure problem and as a way to manufacture the highly reliable transistors specified by Autonetics. "The reason why [Noyce and Moore] eventually went to the planar," Hoerni later reminisced, "was because they had to solve this damn tap test problem. Marketing was after them."[38] Unlike Bell's component groups, which served the needs of a telephone monopoly, Fairchild was oriented mainly toward avionics applications, which had very high reliability requirements and put enormous pressure on the company to eliminate its products' catastrophic failures.[39]

Two other factors further encouraged the decision to bring the planar process to production. Impressed by its reliability potential, Autonetics actively pushed the company to perfect the new process and bring it to production. "Autonetics was a big force behind the development of the planar," Moore later recalled. "They wanted us to go with planar technology."[40] Crucial to the decision was Autonetics' willingness to buy Fairchild's future planar transistors. Thereby the avionics contractor offered a large market for the new components, which would help Fairchild recoup its heavy investments in process and product engineering.

A second factor was the new competition Fairchild faced in the mesa transistor field. Motorola and Texas Instruments had active engineering programs in mesa transistors and introduced copies of Fairchild's first NPN mesa transistor to the market in late 1959. The main competitive threat, however, came from Fairchild's own engineers. Enticed by the large profits in the silicon business, Baldwin (the firm's general manager) and the engineers he had brought in from Hughes left Fairchild to start Rheem Semiconductor in March 1959. Bringing with them Fairchild's process manuals, these men set out to produce the firm's mesa transistors at lower cost than Fairchild. To compete with Rheem, Fairchild had to introduce new and better devices. Bringing the planar transistor to market would give the company a major competitive edge.[41]

Because of these pressures, Noyce and Moore dedicated very substantial engineering and financial resources to the further development of Hoerni's fragile process and the design of planar products. Although little is known about Fairchild's effort to transform Hoerni's laboratory techniques into a stable and reproducible manufacturing process, it is clear that the firm's research laboratory devoted substantial efforts to understanding this very complex process.

In conjunction with developing a stable manufacturing process, Hoerni and other engineers at Fairchild designed a series of ultrareliable planar products that were a major breakthrough in transistor technology.[42] Hoerni then went one step further in the commercial exploitation of his process in the spring of 1959 by designing a planar diode for computing applications that was faster and more reliable than any mesa product on the market. Seeing a ready market for such a diode at Autonetics and in the avionics industry, Fairchild's engineering groups designed a large family of ultrareliable planar diodes. The company also set up a new plant dedicated exclusively to diode manufacture in Marin County, north of San Francisco, in October 1959.

Fairchild's engineers also developed a radically new planar component, the integrated circuit. Unlike discrete devices, the integrated circuit incorporated an entire electronics circuit, which included transistors, diodes, capacitors, and resistors, into the silicon crystal. Avionics reliability was once again the driver of this development. Many system failures were due either to faulty connections between the silicon die and the electric wires of the component packages, or errors in the assembly of electronics components to the systems' printed circuit boards. By integrating a whole circuit into a silicon die and by depositing an aluminum film to interconnect its various components, the potential for such failures was substantially reduced.[43]

Fairchild's engineers also saw integrated circuits as a way to further miniaturize electronics systems. The use of discrete silicon devices had helped avionics manufacturers miniaturize their systems by dispensing with the bulky air-conditioning equipment required by germanium components. Integrated circuits represented a further step in that direction. Fairchild also saw integrated circuits as a way of "automating" transistor and diode assembly. The assembly of transistor dice to their packages was a very labor-intensive operation. By integrating a number of components into the same silicon die, they would reduce the workforce and improve the productivity of assembly stations.[44]

Noyce conceived of the integrated circuit in January 1959. Although the circumstances surrounding his invention are obscure, it is likely that his work derived from Hoerni's planar process. Asked by the lawyer in charge of filing the planar patents about how Hoerni's idea could be extended, Noyce thought of using the planar process to fabricate a complete circuit rather than individual components. The planar process, Noyce reflected, had two unusual features: it permitted the manufacture of hundreds of devices on the same slice of silicon, and it had the unusual characteristic of leaving an oxide layer on top of the wafer. This oxide layer, in addition to its masking and passivating properties, could also act as an electrical insulator. As a result, Noyce reasoned, one could connect electrically the different components on the same wafer by evaporating and properly etching an aluminum film on top of the silicon oxide. To obtain a functional electronics circuit, Noyce also devised ways of making other standard components in electronics circuits such as resistors and capacitors with diffusion and photolithographic techniques. Finally, he conceived of using diodes mounted back to back to electrically isolate the different devices on the same die.[45]

The integrated circuit idea, soon patented by Fairchild, was put into silicon and productized in the next two years by a group directed by Jay Last. This was a revolutionary step. Building a functional integrated circuit, Last and his group discovered, was extremely difficult because of the very close tolerances required. It also presented the challenge of electrically isolating the transistors, diodes, resistors, and capacitors on the same die or silicon chip.

Using a new and innovative process, Last's group developed a family of digital integrated circuits, which the firm introduced to the market in March 1961. These circuits were peripheral to Fairchild's transistor- and diode-oriented product line. Because of their high price and low performance, they could only be used in a small number of applications. However, they constituted an important breakthrough in silicon technology and promised major improvements in system reliability, performance, and miniaturization.[46]

MANUFACTURING ULTRARELIABILITY

In tandem with designing reliability into its products at the component and circuit levels, Fairchild perfected its production systems to meet the tight reliability specifications of military avionics. Autonetics forced Fairchild to improve its manufacturing operations by setting very high reliability criteria. It also financed and closely supervised Fairchild's efforts to enhance its production systems by instituting a comprehensive "reliability improvement program." The goal of this program, which applied to all Autonetics' subcontractors, was to drastically improve the reliability of solid state components by transforming the ways in which they were manufactured. Autonetics sought to reinforce its suppliers' manufacturing disciplines, tighten their process controls, and augment their testing procedures.[47]

Autonetics' program was closely patterned after similar efforts at the Bell Telephone Laboratories, which developed very reliable components for undersea telephone cables in the 1940s and early 1950s. Adopting many of Bell's methods and applying them to semiconductor manufacturing, Autonetics required all its suppliers to implement a comprehensive "reliability improvement program" that touched all aspects of their manufacturing operations. Suppliers of solid state devices were asked to document carefully their manufacturing processes and had to build "high reliability lines" using such techniques as "assembly in dust-free environments, carefully spelled out operator instructions, and close monitoring by Quality Control personnel" (Smith 1963, 434–40, 436; McNally et al. 1957, 163–88).

Second, modeling its program after Bell's, Autonetics requested its vendors to serialize their components in order to follow the history of each part so they could trace those that had failed to the materials and processes with which they had been produced. This required an enormous record-keeping effort as Autonetics' suppliers made hundreds of thousands of components for the Minuteman program. And Autonetics asked its subcontractors to isolate their products' failure modes and identify their causes, demanding that they apply statistical control techniques to their manufacturing processes in order to monitor process variations and achieve narrower distributions of parameter characteristics.[48]

Third, Autonetics required its subcontractors to establish very strict testing procedures to screen out defective products. They demanded that the subcontractors apply the life tests pioneered by Bell for electron tubes to solid state components to evaluate their reliability and determine the best temperature and voltage conditions under which these devices had to be operated.

Autonetics closely supervised its suppliers. Resident inspectors were stationed at its subcontractors' plants. These inspectors were "free to walk into the line and look at every step," and they had the authority to make changes in the manufacturing process. Autonetics also established an in-house component engineering group that closely followed the subcontractors' engineering efforts and evaluated their progress toward the Minuteman reliability goals (Stranix 1960, 90–104).

Autonetics had a major impact on manufacturing at Fairchild. To meet its specs, Fairchild made substantial advances in manufacturing that were lavishly funded by Autonetics. "The Minuteman contract," Kleiner recalled, "was a very good contract, not only from the income point of view but to advance the state of the art of manufacturing. It certainly advanced our knowledge and increased our experience. It increased our quality control procedures and testing procedures, which we had to some degree. But the quality requirements of this Minuteman program were much higher than [those] you have in commercial use."[49]

The Minuteman contract helped Fairchild to acquire a solid competence in testing and enabled them to gather vast amounts of data on the reliability of its products. While the firm had relied in its early days on a rather limited set of testing instruments, it designed a wide variety of electrical and mechanical testers for the Minuteman program. More importantly, Fairchild set up a new division, the reliability evaluation division, whose sole objective was to appraise the dependability of its mesa transistors. The division conducted extensive life tests of hundreds of thousands of mesa and, later, planar transistors. By 1961 it had accumulated more than 150 million transistor hours, which "gave Fairchild experience orders of magnitude higher than those results from previous evaluations in the industry."[50]

As a result of these systematic efforts, the reliability of Fairchild's mesa transistors improved very substantially between 1959 and 1961. While the failure rate of Fairchild's first NPN transistor had been 0.1 percent per thousand hours in 1959, it reached 0.004 percent in early 1961. By the time the Minuteman missile was fully operational, the failure rate had dropped to 0.00009 percent. This was an average of less than one failure in 10,000 years. Fairchild's devices became, by far, the most dependable transistors used in Autonetics' guidance and control system. Autonetics' program also had another important effect: it helped Fairchild tighten process control and thereby improve its yields and reduce its manufacturing costs. These advances were quickly applied to the firm's other mesa transistors and, later, to its planar products as well.[51]

GROWTH

The Minuteman also sanctioned the firm as a manufacturer of high-reliability products—which gave it considerable visibility in the military sector in the late 1950s and early 1960s. "The Minuteman program," Bay later recollected,

> took a company that was a little nothing and put us on the map if you will—because we were compared to TI and Motorola. We were a contender in the semiconductor business. It was not a big contract in terms of lots of devices and lots of dollars. But it was a contract that proved the reliability of our device. The value of the [Minuteman contract] to the company was much more in the reputation it gave us than it was in the dollars that it generated by itself, although by the time the program was going and the Minuteman was being produced, it was substantial volume.[52]

As a result, Fairchild was well positioned to take advantage of the rapid growth of the military market for silicon components in the late 1950s, which almost tripled from $32 million in 1958 to $90 million two years later. Avionics contractors, which had used silicon transistors in their digital prototypes in the mid-1950s, required them in large volumes when they moved these new systems to production at the end of the decade. At the same time, a new military market emerged for silicon transistors in ground-based equipment. Intent upon improving the reliability of radio communication, telemetry, and other ground-based systems, the military required its suppliers to employ silicon rather than germanium transistors.[53]

Aggressively exploiting this rapidly expanding market, Fairchild saw its sales grow explosively, from $500,000 in 1958 to $21 million in 1960. To meet this demand, in addition to the diode plant in San Rafael, Fairchild opened a new factory dedicated to transistor production in Mountain View in the summer of 1959. While Fairchild had 180 employees on its payroll in February 1959, one year later it employed 1,400 operators, engineers, and technicians. In short, in less than three years, Fairchild had become one of the biggest electronics component manufacturers on the San Francisco Peninsula. The firm was also the second largest manufacturer of silicon components after Texas Instruments, as well as the leading producer of diffused silicon components in the United States.[54]

CONCLUSION

Fairchild's founders and the engineers and managers they hired defined the silicon industry's products, processes, and manufacturing systems, as well as its marketing and sales practices, in the late 1950s and very early 1960s. Key to the reshaping of the industry was their adoption of the solid state diffusion process recently developed at Bell Laboratories. To bring this complex process to quantity production, the Fairchild group drew upon a wide variety of industrial practices and bodies of scientific and technical knowledge. In addition to solid state physics, they relied on their expertise in optics, metallurgy, chemistry, and electrical and mechanical engineering. These men also drew upon techniques coming out of the photography, metalworking, and electron tube industries. Out of this vast array of skills and practices, the Fairchild group built radically new products and designed innovative fabrication methods and manufacturing systems. They also developed creative sales and marketing techniques and closely coupled product development with market demands.

Because of their focus on military avionics, they were constantly under enormous pressure to meet the reliability standards of avionics system manufacturers and, more indirectly, of the Air Force. Because of these demands and the group's internal dynamics, Fairchild's entrepreneurs made major process and design innovations in the late 1950s and early 1960s. In close succession, they developed the planar process and the integrated circuit, both of which made the engineering of highly reliable electronics systems possible. Finally, under the guidance and scrutiny of Autonetics, Fairchild's manufacturing engineers also perfected their production systems and tightened their control of the manufacturing process in order to produce highly reliable diodes and transistors.

In a few years, Fairchild profoundly transformed silicon manufacturing. It revolutionized the industry's products by introducing high-performance and reliable devices that other firms later copied. As an example, by the summer of 1960, the firm's first transistor was produced by Rheem, Motorola, Texas Instruments, Pacific Semiconductors, and Hoffman Electronics, among others. Fairchild also developed radically new component designs such as the integrated circuit, which became the industry's mainstay in the 1960s. It also radically transformed manufacturing methods. Whereas Texas Instruments,

Hughes, and other firms had used the grown junction and alloy junction techniques in the mid-1950s, Fairchild's founders reoriented the industry toward solid state diffusion. More importantly, the corporation developed the planar process, which revolutionized the manufacture of diffused components and rapidly became the standard process for making silicon components. Corporations that did not readily adopt Fairchild's innovations went out of business in the early 1960s.[55]

Fairchild Semiconductor had an enormous impact on electronics manufacturing on the San Francisco Peninsula. Fairchild's founders and their allies at Hayden Stone played a major role in the formation of the venture capital industry in the area. Arthur Rock, who had been instrumental in Fairchild's formation, established the Peninsula's first venture capital partnership with Thomas Davis. They formed Davis and Rock in 1961. To muster the required capital, Rock raised monies among Bay Area industrialists. Fairchild's founders, each of whom had received $250,000 after the sale of Fairchild Semiconductor to Fairchild Camera in 1959, were among the first he approached. Four Fairchild entrepreneurs invested in Davis's and Rock's fund. In addition to their investments in Rock's partnership, Fairchild founders also independently financed new science-based firms in the area. Out of these activities emerged yet another venture capital partnership, Kleiner Perkins. This fund, as well as Rock's, was rapidly emulated. As a result, the San Francisco Peninsula became one of the largest centers for venture capital in the nation in the late 1960s and early 1970s.[56]

The rise of the venture capital industry, along with Fairchild's spectacular success and the numerous business and technical opportunities arising from its research and development efforts, led to an extraordinary entrepreneurial expansion on the Peninsula in the 1960s. Twenty-six silicon firms were founded in the area between 1960 and 1969. They were almost all established by former Fairchild engineers and managers. Two waves of Fairchild spin-offs can be distinguished. The first corporations were established by engineers and managers closely involved in the development and marketing of Fairchild's first products, especially integrated circuits, in the early 1960s. Following up on a suggestion from Rock, who had financed the formation of Teledyne, a military conglomerate, three Fairchild founders, Hoerni, Last, and Roberts, established Amelco, Teledyne's silicon subsidiary, in 1961. In the same year, a group of engineers who had worked under Last on the development of the integrated circuit incorporated Signetics to make custom integrated circuits. Other integrated circuit engineers, in collaboration with Fairchild's first salesmen, set up Molectro and General MicroElectronics in 1962 and 1963 respectively.[57]

A second and much larger wave of start-ups followed in the late 1960s. They were often funded by Rock and other venture capitalists. In an entrepreneurial explosion, former Fairchild engineers and managers established nineteen firms between 1966 and 1969. Among the most notable were Intersil, another Hoerni venture, and Intel, founded by Noyce and Moore in 1968. In parallel with the formation of these new enterprises, technicians who had worked at Fairchild set up semiconductor manufacturing equipment companies such as Kasper and Electroglas. The establishment of these companies, along with Fairchild's and other firms' move into the commercial markets, account for the extraordinary expansion of the industry on the Peninsula in the 1960s. While Fairchild had a workforce of 1,400 in 1960, the firm and its spin-offs employed 12,000 technicians, engineers, and operators on the Peninsula ten years later.[58]

9

Serendipity or Strategy

How Technology and Markets Came to Favor Silicon Valley

HENRY S. ROWEN

The rise of Silicon Valley might tempt one to believe that businesspeople in this region have figured out the one best way to succeed in high-tech entrepreneurial innovation. But putting its history in perspective, one sees that the Valley has not always been (and may not always be) the epicenter of the computer industry. For years, New York's IBM dominated the industry, and it was joined in the 1960s by firms in the Boston area. In this chapter, following an argument developed by Timothy Bresnahan, I argue that the success of Valley companies is due not only to the region's favorable environment for starting firms, but also to advances in technology and markets that fit the Valley's industrial structure particularly well (Bresnahan 1999).[1]

Fundamental to this geographic shift were advances in technology that drastically lowered the cost of computing and greatly increased computer use, together with radical changes in the structure of the industry (Grove 1996). These combined to bring about a shift from an industrial structure that Bresnahan has labeled the "IBM system" to a new one that he labels the "Silicon Valley system."

I also address here the view that government must have been directly responsible for the rise of the Valley, a belief held less often by Americans than by some foreigners. The role of the government is often misunderstood. Government played a large role in the rise of the American computer industry, and therefore of the Valley's firms, but there was never any special treatment of this region by the government.

To explain how the new computer industry emerged, this chapter first explores why American firms have dominated this industry throughout its existence. This might not have seemed likely a priori given the scientific strengths of Europe, the superior manufacturing talents of Japan, and the abundant human capital in both places. The first part of the chapter argues that much of this success must be attributed to unique properties of the American system of innovation. The second part explores the ways in which recent changes in technology and markets have favored Silicon Valley within that system.

DISTINCTIVE FEATURES OF THE AMERICAN SYSTEM

The computer industry operates within a distinctive American system: a national system of laws, regulations, and conventions for securities, taxes, accounting, corporate governance, bankruptcy, immigration, research and development, and more. This system is decentralized—but with more coherence than is evident at first glance. It is decidedly market-oriented and aims to protect people through transparency and disclosure rather than microregulation. Its rules encourage competition. Unlike many other governments, that of the United States never selected any computer firms as national champions. On the contrary, on antitrust grounds it held back its leading firm, IBM, for several decades.

The U.S. system is also more favorable to new business ventures than are those of virtually all other countries. For example, according to the Organization for Economic Cooperation and Development (OECD), in Europe it takes on average twelve times as long to set up a company as in the United States and costs four times as much (Summers 2000). The politics of most, if not all, other nations give more weight to protecting established institutions, such as firms, banks, and labor unions. Because these governments have tried to preserve existing firms they—usually inadvertently—have erected obstacles to the entry of new ones. Striking evidence of the distinctive American attitude toward established companies is the decline of IBM, the supreme computer industry icon, which occurred with no political fuss.

The labor laws of other countries make it difficult to lay off workers—which creates a disincentive to hire them. Until recently, finance has come largely from banks that are not accustomed to lending to young firms without collateral. Stock options in lieu of wages have been little used. And to be listed on the stock exchanges in many countries has required years of operations, and sometimes years of profits, a formidable barrier for high-tech start-up companies. Such practices have been great disadvantages in the fast-moving computer industry.

The distinctive American system of innovation, with its overarching emphasis on diversity and competition, encompasses much more than laws affecting the formation of firms and the labor market. It affects all aspects of the process of creating new products and bringing them to market. There are circumstances in which central control of technology is appropriate, indeed essential, as in the Manhattan Project during World War II or the race to the moon. But the record shows that when there is rapid technological change, as in the computer industry, and much uncertainty about which of many possible paths will be successful, a decentralized system in which many ventures are tried is more likely to succeed than a centralized one.

From the origins of the American system, decentralization in public funding of higher education, and therefore of much research, has been assured by much of it coming from 50 state governments rather than from a single, national one. The existence of many private universities has further contributed to educational and research pluralism. Competition is pervasive among universities for faculty, students, and research funds (Mowery and Rosenberg 1993). These characteristics are difficult to find so strongly elsewhere.

Funding supplied by the states also affected universities' ties with business. Because state politics were geared to commercial opportunities, the custom of close university-industry ties was established long ago. Professors at state-funded universities have long worked with farmers, on mining problems, with coal and steel companies, and in many other sectors. Such connections were markedly weaker in Japan and Europe. In those regions, institute researchers and academics at state universities are civil servants who, unlike their American counterparts, have long faced obstacles in operating in the private sector. According to Michael Sharp, "A researcher at a CNRS laboratory in France, or a Max Planck Institute Laboratory in Germany, is a full time employee of that institution. . . . As a full time employee, he/she will not find it easy to undertake the mix of research frequently undertaken by an American professor, who combines an academic post with consulting in the private sector." In Europe, most spin-offs are found in the United Kingdom, a country whose organization of academic science most closely resembles that of the United States (Sharp 1989).

In the United States, World War II saw a significant increase in the role of the federal government in universities, especially at MIT (Mowery and Rosenberg 1993). After the war, national support for university research in science and technology burgeoned, with much of it coming from agencies with focused missions that were overseen by different congressional committees with independent powers.[2] This money more often went to universities—that is, to institutions often close to industry—than did comparable funds in Europe and Japan, where more of it went to specialized research institutes and government laboratories that were distant from industry.

The decentralized and competitive character of the U.S. innovation system has helped the American computer industry throughout its history. The United States was initially favored by having the world's largest market for computers and, at the outset of the industry's development, by having the world's leading computer firm, IBM (Bresnahan 1999). This gave the United States a clear advantage as the industry began to take off. But France soon had Bull; Germany had Siemens; Japan had NEC, Fujitsu, Hitachi, and Mitsubishi. These companies never lacked for scientific and engineering skills, but none could match IBM's technology and management. Their governments used various devices, including government procurement from domestic firms and pressure on government-dependent firms to also buy from domestic firms, but two decades into the computer era, in the early 1970s, one assessment of Japan's efforts was that they were "dominated by the long shadow of IBM, the globe-straddling giant, that dominated every computer market in the world and controlled half of Japan's" (Callon 1995).

As technology continued to advance and minicomputers emerged, computing costs fell. American firms such as Digital Equipment, Hewlett-Packard, and IBM pioneered these advances. Many of the advantages discussed above came into play for U.S. firms. Competition was intense, there was government support for academic computer centers, and there was an established pattern of university-business links (illustrated by Digital Equipment's founder, who had been at MIT). These new companies established strong positions in foreign markets, selling to many more users. They had early mover advantages and benefited from strong economies of scale.

The microcomputer revolution in the 1980s repeated the process. IBM gave big advantages to Microsoft and Intel by selecting their operating system and microprocessor, respectively, for its PC. This created the Wintel standard that opened the field for computer "box" makers and applications suppliers. This shift from proprietary operating systems to an open standard reduced barriers to entry and opened the door for the firms able to move fastest. These firms were overwhelmingly ones able to benefit from the strengths of the American system: in computers, IBM, Compaq, Apple, Dell, Sun, and HP; and in software, Microsoft, Lotus, and Oracle, among others. As earlier with mainframes and minis, these firms quickly moved abroad to exploit economies of scale (which are especially significant in software and network computing) and to establish dominant market positions.

Firms in other countries were starting behind and having to run faster while depending on institutions that were not well suited for this task: finance, labor markets, university-business ties, and government rules. These countries lacked habitats that enabled people with technical ideas or new applications to put together teams quickly, raise risk capital, and enter new markets. Although their firms and universities had strong technologists, they have had many fewer successful start-ups than the United States. Here, universities were important sources of scientific knowledge and entrepreneurship in minis and micros—MIT notably in minis, and Stanford and the University of Texas for workstations and micros. Outside the United States, only Cambridge University has played a similar, but lesser, role.

THREE WAYS GOVERNMENT HELPED
THE COMPUTER INDUSTRY

Many visitors from abroad assume that Silicon Valley's successes are due to government. The government has, indeed, been integral to the success of Silicon Valley, but not in the way that some assume. The government has helped the American computer industry most through indirect means, by establishing rules favorable to entrepreneurship, rather than by direct means, although it has done much of the latter also.

The federal government has acted in three capacities: 1) as setter of the rules by which firms operate; 2) as buyer of their products; and 3) as financier of research and early system development. The indirect rule-setting role has arguably been more important than the direct buying and funding ones.[3]

Government as Rule Maker

One category of rules established by the government is those related to taxation and finance, such as the tax treatment of capital gains and of stock options. The lowering of the top capital gains tax rate from 49 percent to 28 percent in 1978 and then to 20 percent in 1981 made risky investments more attractive. Another rule favorable to entrepreneurship is taxing options only when exercised, not when granted, a rule not widely adopted around the world. Another rule change, also made in 1978, decreed that investments in venture partnerships by pension funds are consistent with the "prudent man" rule under which these funds operate; this change greatly increased funds available to venture partnerships. Other rules include permitting general partners of venture firms to be on the boards of their portfolio firms; limiting the liability of limited partners to the money they invest; the nontaxation of partnerships; accounting rules aimed at making a firm's financial status transparent; bankruptcy laws that do not burden failed entrepreneurs so that they have difficulty in starting over; and requirements for listing stocks of firms on public exchanges that do not include having a history of profits.

The rule on labor that favors worker mobility in Silicon Valley is that employment is at the choice of either employer or worker—a markedly different rule from countries in which workers effectively have tenure. For firms in California the unenforceability of noncompete clauses in labor contracts further encourages worker mobility.[4]

Changes in the patent system have increased intellectual property protection, which is probably a good thing for fostering innovation. Patents are sometimes significant in the computer industry, although companies do not rely heavily on them (much less than in biotechnology). Firms need access to a diverse array of intellectual properties, and with technology moving fast, new products or processes often overlap with others developed by many different parties. As a result, patents are usually legal bargaining chips rather than the traditional prize for winning a technology tournament.

The virtues of certain of these American institutions are increasingly being recognized abroad. Several countries have created NASDAQ-like stock markets with listing requirements less stringent than for firms on their established exchanges. Japan, especially, has been active in removing obstacles to venture finance. It had a rule requiring many years of profits before stocks could be listed on an exchange—and consequently had few high-tech start-ups—but recently amended it. In 1997, Japan's top individual marginal tax rate was lowered from 65 percent to 50 percent, and corporate pension funds were allowed to make venture-fund investments. In 1998, a limited partnership act was passed, listing requirements were relaxed, and a law was passed enabling universities to set up technology licensing offices. And in 1999, there was drastic deregulation of pre-IPO requirements; a law was passed permitting the equivalent of American-type Small Business Investment Companies; and the Ministry of International Trade and Industry (MITI) decided to guarantee loans to start-ups without collateral who borrow from commercial banks. Legislation that establishes defined contribution pension plans is forthcoming; this will aid worker mobility.

The Federal Government as Buyer

As Chapter 8 on Fairchild Semiconductor shows, the government played an important role as a customer in the Valley's early history. The main market for silicon transistors in the late 1950s and early 1960s was for Air Force avionics and missile guidance and control systems. Intimate and productive interactions between the Air Force's system contractor (the Autonetics Division of North American Aviation) and Fairchild led the latter to make important innovations in silicon semiconductors. This business enabled Fairchild to become a leader in the increasingly important silicon transistor sector, in which commercial demand soon outstripped government requirements.

In the computer systems market, the National Security Agency and the nuclear weapons laboratories have been major customers for supercomputers. Although this market helped advance computer technology, it did little directly to advance Silicon Valley, a place that came to specialize in components, smaller machines, and software.

In hindsight, it seems that Silicon Valley's lack of defense industry—with the exception of the Lockheed Missile and Space Division—was an advantage. Firms such as those in Southern California and Massachusetts that worked with the Department of Defense had to be skilled in dealing with government bureaucracies, a skill not compatible with Silicon Valley's entrepreneurial character. Recognizing this problem, neither Fairchild nor Hewlett-Packard would accept R&D contracts with government agencies—though they would sell products to them.

Government as Financier and Early-Stage Developer

In its most direct supporting role, the federal government has funded research in electrical engineering, including semiconductor and telecommunications technologies, with around $1 billion per year since the 1970s. Support for computer science went from $180 million in 1976 to $960 million in 1995 (in constant 1995 dollars), most of which went to university and industry researchers for work in computers and communications. The recipients of these funds were not arbitrarily chosen by officials, but rather determined by competition between individuals and teams (*Funding a Revolution* 1999).

Such support has constituted about 70 percent of total university research in these fields and, as a by-product, has helped educate many students; more than half of the graduate students in these fields at MIT, Stanford, the University of California at Berkeley, and Carnegie-Mellon are supported through federal funds. In 1997, 27 percent of graduate students (and 50–60 percent of PhD students) in electrical engineering and computer science received federal funds. Countrywide, more than half of the papers cited in computing patent applications acknowledge government funding. (Even so, these numbers show that nonfederal sources of funds have been significant.)

A few universities that were to become leaders in the field created computer science departments early—Stanford and Carnegie-Mellon in 1965, and MIT in 1968. Those decisions helped establish them as major centers. In the San Francisco area, significant advances in technology at Stanford and Berkeley were federally supported. The National Science Foundation financed computer centers at several universities. In the San Francisco Bay Area it supported, for example, the Ingres program at Berkeley on relational databases, and Reduced Instruction Set Architecture (RISC), which was pioneered at IBM but further developed by David Patterson at Berkeley and by John Hennessy at Stanford (who also created MIPS Computers). The Defense Department's Advanced Research Project Agency (ARPA, later known as DARPA) also supported Forest Baskett at Stanford who, with Andreas Bechtolsheim, created the Stanford University Network (SUN). Bechtolsheim, together with two Stanford MBAs, Vinod Khosla and Scott McNealy, and Bill Joy from Berkeley, then went on to create Sun Microsystems.

Although the National Science Foundation spread its money widely among universities around the country, ARPA, more insulated from congressional pork-barrel pressures, concentrated much of its computer science support on MIT, Carnegie-Mellon, and Stanford. However, it also helped organizations in Boston, Philadelphia, Dallas, Austin, St. Louis, and Los Angeles, among other locations. ARPA's Very Large Scale Integration program supported about a dozen computer centers around the country. Government funding of high-performance computing also went to IBM, the Control Data Corporation, and Cray Computers (the latter two firms in Minneapolis). In short, Stanford and Berkeley undoubtedly attracted Department of Defense research funds not supplied to many universities, but funds were available to any university with the requisite talent.

The history of the Internet impressively demonstrates the role of the federal government as a systems developer. In the mid-1960s, a vision of the power of computer networks emerged from ARPA, an organization with the resources to pursue it. (Significantly, in contrast to the civil servant model dominant in other countries, ARPA's professionals come from outside government and serve for only a few years.) ARPANET was originally conceived of as a tool to support scientific research, but soon other applications emerged, including the ability to send e-mail and move files (*Funding a Revolution* 1999). ARPA's financial support for networks was joined by the National Science Foundation in 1980 and by other federal agencies, who were the main supporters of specific research areas such as energy or space, and who wanted to create their own networks. After further innovation, by the early 1990s the Internet had been born.

A very different kind of financial help came via the Small Business Act of 1958. Under it, government funds could be matched with private ones in Small Business Investment Corporations (SBICs). Several were formed in the Valley in the late 1950s and early 1960s. SBICs were the most popular vehicle for venture financing during the 1960s, but from the late 1960s on their role declined as the limited partnership format became dominant. Limited partnerships avoided SBIC regulations, were attractive to large institutions, and had greater potential. According to Kenney and Florida, "The SBICs as an organizational form proved to be a critical stage in the creation of a free-standing venture capital. After performing this service, the SBICs disappeared as important funders of high-technology firms" (Kenney and Florida 2000). Incentives to take greater risks than the government would guarantee led to its collapse (Gompers and Lerner 1998). Later changes in its rules have led to some recovery, but this program no longer plays a significant high-tech role.

Thus it would be quite wrong to think that the American computer industry, and Silicon Valley, would have thrived without government support. But as the above discussion shows, government did not get involved directly in the affairs of companies, and it did not support preferred regions.

HOW TWO REVOLUTIONS IN TECHNOLOGY AND MARKETS HELPED THE VALLEY

The outstanding characteristic of the computer industry is its extraordinary rate of technological advances. Inevitably associated with such rapid advances are large and unexpected changes in the industry. There have been two epochal changes in the past fifteen years. The first was the emergence of a "new" industry caused by the combination of ever-cheaper computers and open standards. The other is the arrival of the Internet.

Emergence of a New Computer Industry

Lowered computing costs, along with a move toward open standards, produced a radical change in the industry's structure in the late 1980s and 1990s, a change that was well matched to the Valley's industrial structure (Bresnahan

1999). Firms in the "old" (mainframe and minicomputer) industry assembled components, software, and networks, each with its own proprietary operating system and standards. The customers for these (by today's standard) costly machines were large organizations. Although scientific and engineering users generally knew how to use them, users in large business and government organizations usually got help from service firms such as EDS and American Management Systems.

This was, in effect, a top-down, "host" system of supply. AnnaLee Saxenian has described well the pattern of semi-independent corporate "pillars" that made up the industrial landscape of the Route 128 (Boston) area (Saxenian 1996). In contrast, Silicon Valley had a broad mixture of firms in every segment of the industry, making components, notably semiconductors, and, from the 1970s, computer systems and software. Then, in the 1980s, came the arrival of IBM's personal computer, the success of Apple's Macintosh, and the entry of other suppliers into the microcomputer market, including Compaq, Dell, and HP.

During this period, computing costs continued to plummet; the cost per million instructions per second fell by a factor of 500 between 1982 and 1998. These developments not only greatly expanded the market for computers, they were also accompanied by a shift from proprietary to open standards, specifically the combination of Microsoft's DOS operating system and Intel microprocessors: the Wintel standard. A parallel—but less complete— move toward open standards came with the emergence of powerful workstations for scientific and engineering applications using the Unix operating system (incomplete because the major manufacturers adopted variants of Unix that were not wholly compatible).

The move from proprietary to open standards led to the dis-integration of the old, vertically integrated industry and to the formation of a new, horizontally structured one. Figure 9.1, taken from Grove 1996, shows both the old and the new industry structures, the former organized by firm and the latter by industry segment.

Upstream suppliers developed powerful general-purpose programs that made it much easier for a multitude of applications to be developed by downstream intermediate suppliers and final users. As Grove describes it, from the mid-1980s most computers were using Intel microprocessors and, therefore, were becoming more alike; this, in turn, enabled software producers to develop

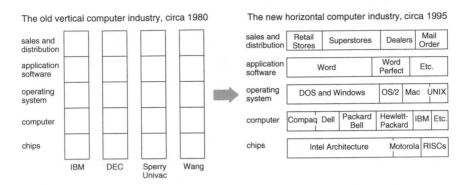

Figure 9.1. The transformation of the computer industry.

FROM *Only the Paranoid Survive*, by Andrew S. Grove, © 1996 by Andrew S. Grove. Used by permission of Doubleday, a division of Random House, Inc.

software for fundamentally similar computers made by many firms. By the end of the 1980s, many large, vertical computer firms were cutting back and many new firms, such as Compaq, were taking off.

Changes in the sources of invention. During the late 1980s and early 1990s, dramatic changes took place as small, networked computers rapidly displaced large hosts (Bresnahan and Greenstein 1997). The mainframe share of the market had fallen from 1970 until the mid-1980s as minis and micros became important. Then, in the early 1990s, smaller computers came to be used in large data centers, mainly as servers, and PCs took over many of the interface tasks with people.

Realizing the vast potential created by the reduction in computing costs and the great expansion in the number and variety of users changed the locus of invention from "hosts" (mainframes and minis) to a mixture of "servers" and "clients" (users) of computers, that is, a shift toward "co-invention" (Bresnahan 1999). The result has been a burst of inventions: in finance (ATM machines, on-line credit card processing), organizational computing (Enterprise Resource Planning), logistics (tracking of goods), marketing and new business models (on-line selling of books, auctions, stocks, business-to-business transactions), and much more.

The computer is a general-purpose technology—that is, one with wide applications and revolutionary consequences (Bresnahan and Trajtenberg 1995). Famous antecedents are the inventions of movable type in printing, the steam engine, and the electric dynamo. Such technologies need many other inventions before their potential can be fully realized. These other inventions involve a large and diverse set of contributors supplying different technologies, and they can be long in coming.[5] This has been the case with computers, with advances being made in semiconductors, semiconductor equipment making, data storage, printing, optics, displays, relational databases, and software applications over many years.

Changes in the character of competition. In the old mainframe industry, firms such as Burroughs, Sperry, National Cash Register, and IBM competed in offering different and incompatible packages to large firms and government agencies. The rise of minicomputers increased the number of firms supplying computers to the market, which was expanding but continued to be composed largely of scientific, engineering, and business customers. Competition was still largely among proprietary systems.

The big change came with the move to open standards, which shifted competition from the vertical to the horizontal dimension, as shown in Figure 9.1. One competition was among operating systems, in which Microsoft's DOS beat Apple's Mac OS (despite the latter's greater ease of use, Apple made strategic errors). At the same time, Intel's progressively faster microprocessors became the hardware standard. With open standards, the computer systems ("box") makers had much less opportunity to distinguish themselves through different technologies. They had to devise different business models; hence, for instance, the rise of Dell, which was better than others at tailoring products to consumer demand and at supply chain management.

There is now intense competition not only within each horizontal segment, but also among them. As an example of the latter, Intel is now producing web appliances (using the Linux operating system, not Windows, for televisions, cars, and telephones. More generally, the line between hardware and software, or between applications and services, is becoming blurred. If an equipment maker develops a browser for the Internet and combines that with a portal, the maker could become the user's guide to the Internet. But telephone operators such as Vodaphone AirTouch also want to bring the Internet directly to users; Microsoft has links with an operator, British Telecom, and with a hardware company, Ericsson; and it also competes with Ericsson for the operating system because Ericsson backs the Symbian OS. The outcome, to say the least, is highly uncertain (*Financial Times* 1999).

Geographic shifts. These changes—and surprises—are best exploited in places with highly skilled and mobile workforces; experienced venture capitalists, universities as sources of entrepreneurship, trained people, and new ideas; local knowledge spillovers; and makers of components of final products. The United States best fits this description and, within it, Silicon Valley more so than any other region.

Major changes in technology have been associated with changes in the geographic center of the industry. In the mainframe era the center of the computer industry was at IBM's R&D and production locations in New York, although the company had important outposts such as its San Jose laboratory, which did pioneering work on magnetic memories. When minicomputers came along, the center remained in the Northeast, where IBM continued to be a major supplier, but Digital Equipment, Data General, and Wang emerged in Boston along Route 128. Hewlett-Packard was a Western outlier. With the advent of the microcomputer, and especially network computing, the center shifted west—to Washington (Microsoft, Amazon), Texas (Compaq, Dell, and long-established Texas Instruments), and, above all, to Silicon Valley (HP, Intel and other semiconductor makers, Apple, Sun, Applied Materials, Silicon Graphics, Cisco, Oracle, Informix, Sybase, Netscape, Yahoo!, e-Bay, and many more). Silicon Valley had experienced engineers, marketers, and managers, seasoned venture capitalists and lawyers who knew how to bring people and money together, and good universities as sources of ideas and trained people. As a consequence, there was a veritable explosion in the number of start-up firms in the Valley from the late 1980s through the 1990s.

The Internet Revolution

Following fast on the heels of the new computer industry was the sudden transformation of network computing from a set of links among scientists and within large organizations to an open, worldwide system: the Internet. Its emergence gave a further boost to the Valley.

In 1990, computers had long been linked in networks, notably in the pioneering ARPANET, followed by the NSFNET and various proprietary net-works. NSFNET was soon to be handed from government to commercial providers, but another crucial invention was needed to further its enormous potential: the world wide web. Tim Berners-Lee and Robert Cailliau at CERN, motivated by the desire of physicists who were at widely dispersed centers to distribute their papers quickly, created a system of hypertext links among different sources of information. That soon led to the invention by Marc Andreessen at the University of Illinois of the Mosiac browser, which connected audio, video, and graphics, as well as text. It allowed users to point and click with a mouse on a menu or to search for information. The great browser war was soon underway (*Funding a Revolution* 1999).

The Internet is the ultimate open system. It is accessible at low and falling costs (but with telephone company charges an obstacle in some countries) and is independent of computer operating systems. It opened up a wealth of applications to those who could move fast and offer the right services. What these would be was, to say the least, hard to determine at the outset. The only way to find out was to make inventions and move to the market quickly. This required a host of new firms, and in the mid-1990s Silicon Valley was the region best equipped to create them.

MIGHT ANOTHER TECHNOLOGICAL SHIFT UNDERMINE THE VALLEY'S POSITION?

Given that the region benefited from the transition from the old to the new computer industry and from network computing to the Internet, might another technology or market shift work against it? Wireless communications is a candidate. Europe and Japan, following their top-down, government-regulated tradition, adopted uniform standards for mobile telephony early, while the United States, following its customary (and usually successful) practice, encouraged many alternatives while leaving the ultimate standard to be determined by the market. So far, this has resulted in the United States having several incompatible mobile phone systems; this has held down demand and slowed market penetration compared with the other countries. Meanwhile the wireless technologies are burgeoning, and most of the demand is outside the

United States. The game isn't over, but one wonders if the historically successful American way of "letting a hundred flowers bloom" before converging on a standard will be a winner this time.

There have been enough surprises to make any forecast suspect. The continued high rate of change of information technologies, however, implies that a place that can generate new firms in response to new opportunities in the unique way characteristic of Silicon Valley will continue to succeed. Despite the region's possible disadvantage with respect to wireless technologies, Silicon Valley will very likely continue to be the world leader in the computer industry.

10

The Role of Stanford University

A Dean's Reflections

JAMES F. GIBBONS

As Dean of Stanford University's School of Engineering from 1984 to 1996, I had the privilege of observing first-hand Stanford's critical role in fostering Silicon Valley entrepreneurship during a period of very significant economic growth. I also had the opportunity to discuss Stanford's role with senior leaders in Silicon Valley, who added a perspective that would have been difficult to secure within the university. This paper presents a summary of those conversations, with a particular focus on the conditions that improve the chances of success for a start-up company.

My work on this subject began with a conversation I had with Bill Hewlett shortly after I became Dean of the School of Engineering. Bill pointed out that, for most of its history, the Santa Clara Valley had been covered with apricot and prune orchards, and he speculated that even as late as the mid-1960s, fruit orchards in the Santa Clara Valley probably produced more revenue than electronics firms. Indeed, until the early 1970s, the popular name for the Santa Clara Valley was the Valley of the Heart's Delight, not Silicon Valley. Bill saw the 30-year period from 1938 to 1968 as being distinctly different from the subsequent 20 years, and his question to me, slightly rephrased, was this: What role did Stanford play in transforming the Valley of the Heart's Delight for farmers into the Valley of the Heart's Delight for high-tech entrepreneurs and those that support them?

This paper is a slightly expanded version of a talk that I first developed for the Stanford Alumni Association in 1988.

As we thought about that question further, we recalled several different theories that were commonly advanced to explain Stanford's role in the transformation. One of the most popular was that Stanford's principal role was in transferring technology from its laboratories to commercial companies. But this hypothesis raises the question of whether the transfer occurred primarily through existing firms that licensed technology created at Stanford, or through the formation of new companies by students, staff, and faculty who saw the commercial possibilities of bringing laboratory technology to the marketplace. And there was also the possibility, of course, that Stanford's principal contribution was not in transferring technology at all, but rather in educating engineering and business students to continually build the intellectual pool.

As we studied these possibilities, it became clear that, although all of them are important in general, their relative importance to any given firm changes with the age of the firm. In addition, specific industries and segments within industries seem to depend on one of these roles more than others. For example, the university has been a rich source of start-ups in the biotechnology sector, but Stanford's principal contribution to the pharmaceutical part of that industry has probably been in licensing intellectual property (e.g., the Cohen-Boyer gene-splicing patent) to large companies that can afford to spend large sums over long periods of time to develop it. By contrast, when we consider companies in the computing and information networking area, such as Silicon Graphics (SGI), Sun Microsystems, and Cisco Systems, it is clear that Stanford's principal contribution to this industry has been (and continues to be) made through companies that are founded by faculty, staff, and students using technology they either developed or learned about while at Stanford. The same is probably true for firms in the medical devices area, and in the microelectron-mechanical systems (MEMS) area as well.

On the other hand, for the silicon semiconductor industry, Gordon Moore, a co-founder of both Fairchild Semiconductor and Intel, believes that Stanford's principal contribution to Silicon Valley is in replenishing the intellectual pool every year with outstanding graduates at both the masters and Ph.D. levels. Important device and fabrication technologies for the semiconductor industry are indeed developed at Stanford and elsewhere; but most of the development of semiconductor technology occurs in the industry itself. And in any case, new semiconductor technologies only add to a very large body of existing technology that has been developed over many years.

So there is no single answer to the question: What is Stanford's principal role in creating and supporting the Silicon Valley economy? The principal contribution is different for different industry sectors. It will also change over the life of a particular company. Firms that are started to commercialize a specific technology will, if they are successful, create their own flow of new products and services over time. And although some of these new products may come from Stanford, the university's principal contribution to mature firms is providing them with both well-educated new employees and opportunities for continuing education for their existing employees.

Although it is useful to recognize several different types of contribution, no such classification can capture the vitality of Silicon Valley over the last 30 years or adequately describe Stanford's role in it. For that, we need to look directly at how Silicon Valley revenues have grown since 1975. And to assess Stanford's role in that growth, we need a serviceable definition of a Stanford start-up company. It is important to be at least reasonably rigorous in making and using such a definition, because it is otherwise easy to exaggerate Stanford's role.

The definition that I wish to use for this purpose is as follows: *A Stanford start-up is a company in which both the technology for the first product and a majority of the founding team came from Stanford.* The definition is not intended to distinguish between technology that was actually developed by the founders at Stanford and technology that they learned about in the normal course of educational programs.

An alternative method of determining which start-ups are associated with a given university is to count all of those companies in which at least one of the company's founders attended that university. The difficulty with this definition will be clear from an example. Intel was founded by two individuals, with a collection of four degrees from four separate institutions. It would seem inappropriate to regard any one of these colleges or universities as playing a principal role in the founding of Intel. Furthermore, the founding technology had little to do with work that either of the founders did at the universities they attended. It is clear from this example that Intel is best regarded as a pure Silicon Valley start-up, without specific affiliation with any university. That is also the way the founders themselves have described the company.

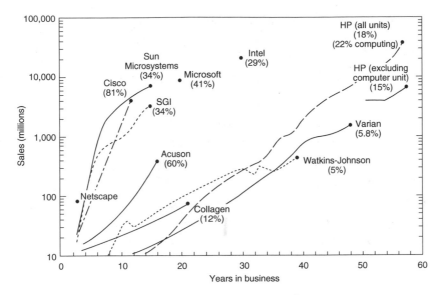

Figure 10.1. Sales versus years in business. Endpoints are 1996 sales; percentages are annual compound growth rates estimated at the end of fiscal year 1996.

We can use the definition given above to estimate the relative importance of companies that started life as a Stanford start-up in the economy of Silicon Valley. For that purpose, Figure 10.1 plots the 1996 revenues of a number of companies that began as Stanford start-ups versus the age of the firm in years. We also show data for Intel, Microsoft, and Netscape as examples of non-Stanford companies (and in Microsoft's case, also non–Silicon Valley). Since the vertical scale is logarithmic and the horizontal scale is linear, a straight line on this plot is interpretable as a compound annual growth rate. The revenue history for each Stanford start-up is also plotted.

One of the first things we see in this figure is that the historical growth rates of firms that are less than 30 years old tend to be considerably higher than those of older firms. Part of this has to do with the difficulty of trying to grow a very large business at the same speed that a smaller business with a large market potential can grow. But there is clearly much more than this involved. The businesses that are less than 30 years old are in personal computing, net-working, and biotechnology—fields that are themselves less than 30 years old. And Hewlett-Packard's growth since about 1975 has been dominated by the fact that they entered the computing business then. As suggested in Figure

10.1, Hewlett-Packard's noncomputing businesses (now spun off as Agilent) are growing at about 15 percent per year compared to the growth of more than 20 percent taking place in their computing and computer peripherals business. Broadly speaking, the data confirm Bill Hewlett's speculation that the last 30 years have been different. New companies have been founded at an extraordinary rate.[1] These companies are based on new technologies that serve new, very large markets that are developing rapidly. These companies are responsible for the transformation that Bill Hewlett observed.

It is also interesting to observe the importance of specific technology drivers in the data, and the time it has taken for paradigm-changing technologies to develop in the information industry. Intel was formed in 1968. Their first product was a one-kilobyte semiconductor memory chip. Fortunately for Intel, the microprocessor was invented at the company in 1972. The first microprocessor that was commercially available was designed to handle four bits of information at a time. Microsoft was formed ten years later, when, according to co-founder Paul Allen, microprocessors had reached a level of sophistication high enough that it "made sense" to write code for them.[2]

The combination of advances in microprocessor architecture and capability, memory technology, and software over the next decade and a half made possible the development of increasingly sophisticated desktop and personal computing equipment. These advances created in turn a demand for workstations, servers, and the technology to connect them. This led to the formation of companies such as Sun Microsystems, Silicon Graphics, Cisco, 3Com, Adobe, and others, changing the nature and importance of information technology in the global economy. So nearly 2½ decades elapsed between the invention of the microprocessor and the emergence of data networking.

By collecting basic economic data for several hundred companies, one can estimate the importance of Stanford start-ups in the Silicon Valley economy. This is done by comparing the total Silicon Valley revenues with those generated by the one hundred firms that account for most of the revenue generated by Stanford start-ups.[3] Such comparisons are provided in Table 10.1 for the years 1988 and 1996.

What is evident from this table is that, with HP included, Stanford start-ups accounted for about 60 percent of total Silicon Valley revenues in both 1988 and 1996. Taking HP out of the comparison, so that the largest firm in

Table 10.1 Stanford Start-Ups' Revenues
Compared to Total Silicon Valley Revenues, 1988 and 1996

	1988		1996	
	WITH HP	WITHOUT HP	WITH HP	WITHOUT HP
Silicon Valley	~$40 BIL	~$30 BIL	~$100 BIL	~$66 BIL
100 companies started with Stanford teams and technology	~$25 BIL	~$15 BIL	~$65 BIL	~$32 BIL

the area will not have a disproportionate effect on the total, the percentage drops somewhat, to 50 percent. And although it is clear that a firm's growth over several decades is only distantly related to its origins, it is also clear that Stanford start-ups have succeeded in growing into firms that create a major fraction of the Silicon Valley economy.

But it is also clear that about half of the revenue of the region is created by firms that are not Stanford start-ups, which suggests that there is something in the environment itself that is equally beneficial for Stanford start-ups and non-Stanford start-ups alike.

With this observation in hand, we interviewed a group of senior leaders from a representative set of Silicon Valley companies (Stanford and non-Stanford start-ups), asking the question: "What factors were most important in starting your company?"

What we found was reasonably broad agreement on what we will call the four requirements for a successful start-up venture. These are not, of course, requirements in the formal sense of the term. They are more correctly described as highly desirable conditions that will measurably increase the probability of success for the start-up. But for shorthand purposes, we will call them requirements.

REQUIREMENTS FOR A SUCCESSFUL START-UP

The Right Product

The first requirement is that the start-up have either a prototype product or an idea for such a product that 1) can be developed rapidly, 2) ideally enjoys patent or other legal protection that can serve as a barrier to entry for others, and 3) appears to have significant market potential.

The new technologies and the new product ideas around which a start-up can be organized arise naturally in corporate and university research laboratories. This represents a major contribution of the research community in general and Stanford in particular to Silicon Valley. However, new product ideas also arise from an entrepreneurial analysis of a market need. This analysis may be performed by a small technical and managerial team that is already in the general field, and whose members may become the founders of the start-up.

Examples of firms for which the prototype for the first product was developed at Stanford include Hewlett-Packard, Cisco Systems, Sun Microsystems, and Silicon Graphics. Other firms are based on ideas that came from corporate research laboratories. The technologies for the Apple Macintosh, and those that led to the formation of such firms as 3Com, Metaphor, and Adobe, for example, came from the Xerox Palo Alto Research Laboratories. Gordon Moore, a co-founder of both Fairchild Semiconductor and Intel, argues that many of the technologies that were used to start semiconductor companies in Silicon Valley came from the Fairchild Semiconductor Research Laboratories. Indeed, the relative ease with which an entrepreneurial group working at a broadly based research laboratory inside a company can start a new company in Silicon Valley persuaded the founders of Intel that they should not create a corporate research laboratory of the type they had previously established at Fairchild.

These start-ups were based on technology developed in university or corporate laboratories. In contrast, Intel and Netscape are examples of what we might call pure Silicon Valley start-ups: companies formed by an entrepreneurial team that saw a market need they could fill using technologies that were largely in existence, though they needed to be collected and developed to produce a prototype product.

The Right Team

The second requirement for a successful start-up is that the founders comprise a high-quality, highly dedicated team. The commitment of every member of the team to the success of the start-up is critical, as is their willingness to work very long hours, often at much lower salaries than they could (or did) make at established firms in Silicon Valley. Arthur Rock, a very successful venture capitalist, has often said that he believes the quality of the team is perhaps the single most important predictor of the eventual success of the start-up.[4]

Some of these team members may bring the technology for the start-up with them, so start-ups are often populated with people from the university or corporate labs where the technology was developed. Or, the team is formed directly in Silicon Valley by people who are in the same field, either at the same company or at different companies. There are of course legal constraints that can effectively prevent the inappropriate use or conveyance of intellectual property, and the start-up will need to have clear, legal access to the technology it requires.

Often these teams are not functionally complete. In particular, teams composed largely or entirely of technologists often lack sufficient experience in sales, finance, marketing, and operations to create a solid company, in which case significant venture funding will depend on the willingness of the founding team to create a management team that can measurably improve the probability of success. Members of the team may also have different visions of what constitutes success, which can easily lead to failure of the overall effort. Over time members of a successful start-up team may also reach a limit in their effectiveness or interest, perhaps necessitating replacement at a critical stage of development. CEOs of start-ups are especially vulnerable.

Sources of Capital

The third requirement is a source of capital to fund the start-up. Over the past two decades or so, this funding has come from three main sources.

Angel investors. The largest single source of capital for start-up ventures comes from individuals and groups that are collectively called angels. Historically, angels have been friends and family members of the start-up team who, in addition to having an interest in the field of the start-up, also have a personal interest in members of the team. They often provide both money and a great deal of emotional support for the start-up team. More recently, angel investing is being done by individuals in loosely organized groups using financial resources they have acquired over time, often from previous investments in start-ups that were successful.[5]

Previously successful entrepreneurs starting a new company may also invest personal resources that they acquired from their previous start-up. These sources of funding create a vehicle for further growth of Silicon Valley because entrepreneurs tend to stay in areas in which their success in a previous start-up is a significant asset in hiring a new team, attracting other funding, and fulfilling the other conditions for a successful start-up. There is some evidence to suggest that previously successful entrepreneurs are also more likely to succeed than those who are entrepreneurs for the first time, a fact that is important in raising new money from angels and venture capitalists.

It is estimated that in 1997, angel investors in the United States were responsible for a total investment in excess of $62 billion. The majority of this was invested in very small ventures, not typically high-tech, and likely to create only a local success. Nearly a third of the total, however, was invested in high-tech start-ups of the type we are discussing. These investments were in the seed round, when the company was at too early a stage in its development to secure an investment directly from a venture capital firm.

Professional venture capitalists.[6] When a firm has reached a stage at which it has at least a prototype product and a defined market of sufficient size, the next round of funding will often come from the venture capital market. Professional venture capitalists sometimes also invest in the seed round, depending on the nature of the product and the market it is to serve.

Professional venture capitalists are especially interested in the management team, and will often seek to strengthen it as a condition of their investment. They will also normally take a seat on the board of the company. They are directly interested in the financial success of the company, which they want to use to provide an exit for themselves and their limited partners. They are not normally long-term investors; that is, they do not normally stay on the board of a company that has gone public. Whether their exit opportunity is provided by taking the company into the public market or through the acquisition of the start-up by a larger firm is relatively unimportant if the price is right.

It is estimated that in 1997 venture capital firms invested approximately $11 billion in start-ups, mostly in second- and third-round financing. Their goal is to invest in start-ups that they believe have the potential to return five to ten times the invested capital in a period of five to seven years. This corresponds to about a compound annual growth rate in the range of 25–40 percent.

To get these rates of return, of course, involves considerable risk. Data collected by the venture capital industry suggests that, on average, in a portfolio of ten investments, seven will lose money, two will be profitable in seven years but not at high rates of return, and one will perform at or even well above the 40 percent compound return indicated above. This gives a basic statistical measure of the financial risk associated with venture investing. Second- and third-round investments in successful start-ups may also increase the value of the investment portfolio and hence reduce the long-term financial risk.

Large industrial firms. For some time in the late 1970s and early 1980s, there was a significant effort within large industrial firms to make venture investments, often in companies that were at the stage at which they would attract venture capitalists. These large firms, however, typically had a specific interest in the technology the start-up company was attempting to develop, so that if that development did not work out exactly as planned, the large firm tended to regard the investment as unsatisfactory. Since start-ups often end up changing direction, large industrial firms had an unsatisfactory experience as venture capitalists. Professional venture capitalists are generally not concerned about whether the original idea or business plan works if a modification of it is seen to be of major economic value. The difference in interests between the large firm and venture capitalists leads to different forces affecting the start-up.

More recently, large industrial firms have taken a somewhat different stance toward start-ups that come from within the firm itself, occasionally offering to partially fund a spin-out rather than have the team leave the parent firm completely. This can occur for several reasons. For example, the large firm will have an existing set of markets it needs to defend; and if the new technology and market do not lie along its strategic path, the new idea is unlikely to receive the support required to create a success. However, the field of the new venture may still be of considerable long-term interest, and a partially funded start-up is an opportunity to capture some of the value that would otherwise devolve entirely to others. An additional motivation for a large firm to spin out technology and a start-up team into a partially funded start-up is that the competition for funding of projects within the large firm, and the limited resources that have to be allocated to the entire set of internal projects, may lead to both inadequate funding and inadequate focus for the new venture, even when the venture may lie along the strategic path of the larger firm. These realities tend to favor the start-up, with the result that some firms spin out technology and partial funding with the right of first refusal to reacquire the spin-out at a later point in time.

Appropriate Infrastructure

The fourth requirement, which we describe as appropriate infrastructure, was the most difficult requirement to piece out of the interviews, even though it is of critical importance. There are three aspects of the infrastructure, each of which is important.

Technical characteristics. The first of these is the technical characteristics of the infrastructure. This includes appropriate space in which the start-up can set up its operations, and easy access to high-quality, basic technology. This latter category includes, for example, software development, chip design, chip fabrication, circuit design and fabrication, glass blowing, sheet metal work, and a large variety of services that can be purchased so that the start-up can focus entirely on its strategic objectives. Almost any piece of technology a start-up needs is available to it in Silicon Valley. And it is available from relatively small, specialized firms, which can probably do it better, faster, and cheaper than the start-up can. This group of specialized firms thus provides a supply chain of basic technology for the start-up, allowing the start-up to focus entirely on building its product and getting it to market in the shortest possible time.

Use of the technology supply chain reduces the technical risks for the start-up significantly. Producing technology that is available outside the start-up takes time and costs money, so it may simultaneously increase market, technical, and financial risk.

Speed, or a short time to market, is very important for a start-up. Donald Valentine, an extraordinarily successful venture capitalist, says that if the three things important in the real estate market are location, location, and location, then the three things critical for a successful start-up are speed, speed, and speed.[7] Effective use of a fully developed infrastructure increases speed and reduces risk.

Social characteristics. A second, very important feature of the infrastructure is its social characteristics, by which we mean the qualitative, emotional nature of the intellectual and business climate that supports start-ups. One of the things that surprised us most was the degree to which senior leaders in Silicon Valley uniformly and repeatedly cited "the Santa Clara Valley as a place to live and work" as being extremely important in the development of the region.[8] The temperate climate, the lifestyle, and the pioneering attitude that is prevalent in the western United States were also cited as critical factors in increasing the success rate of Silicon Valley start-up ventures.

Beyond that, three specific characteristics of the social infrastructure are seen as very important. First, in Silicon Valley it is okay to start a company that fails. According to the venture capital statistics cited earlier, most of them do. And in order to have a flourishing economy that is driven by start-ups, it is necessary to encourage their formation. If it were not acceptable to fail, there would be many fewer start-ups. Beyond that, entrepreneurs often learn through their failures things they need to know to succeed in their next venture. This tolerance of a productive failure is a cultural characteristic of Silicon Valley that is perhaps very difficult to reproduce. More than that, the heroes in Silicon Valley are the entrepreneurs who can both start and grow successful companies, and this also encourages entrepreneurs to start new ventures.

Second, it is acceptable to leave a company and form a start-up that directly competes with it. The start-up must of course have a legal right to the technology it expects to commercialize. But within this broad guideline, there is the opportunity for entrepreneurial teams to build new products that address the markets of the existing company in a new way, or address markets the existing company cannot effectively address.

Finally, it is acceptable to talk to competitors about general problems in your industry. As long as the discussion does not inform others about the company's strategic plans, conversation is acceptable and even desirable. What this means is that each executive does not have to learn by himself or herself what is known in the Valley. Sharing of information means that Silicon Valley is a very good learning environment for new business ventures.

Educational resources. The third very important characteristic of the infrastructure is the range and depth of its educational resources. Mark Myers, Senior VP for Corporate Development at Xerox, generalizes this characteristic by arguing that entrepreneurship flourishes in an information-rich environment, which includes the entire educational and research community in Silicon Valley.[9]

Within this category we need to identify several different types of educational institutions, all of which are important to the health and vitality of Silicon Valley. First, there is a collection of exceptional research universities: Stanford, U.C. Berkeley, and U.C. San Francisco. These institutions conduct research that is relevant to high-tech start-ups in many fields, and they also replenish the intellectual pool for Silicon Valley (as do other universities across the country and around the world) by training graduate students at both the master's and Ph.D. levels.

Second, there is a group of institutions that provides high-quality education in the basic engineering disciplines and engineering sciences. The research universities do that as well, but the need for baccalaureate engineers is far greater than can be met by the research institutions.

A third critical component of the educational hierarchy is the community colleges, offering two-year training programs as well as engineering programs for students proceeding to universities. For example, Foothill College has a program for training semiconductor technicians that is highly regarded worldwide. Students in these programs obtain education that is absolutely essential to Silicon Valley. Sematech, a U.S. government/semiconductor industry partnership focused on semiconductor manufacturing research and techniques, found the Foothill College curriculum for semiconductor technician training to be an excellent core for the program that they developed and duplicated at community colleges around the country where semiconductor manufacturing was being conducted.[10]

Finally, in addition to these various levels of education for engineers and scientists, Silicon Valley companies, both start-up and established, profit significantly from the high-quality programs in business education that exist not only at Stanford and Berkeley but also in evening programs at Santa Clara University. Employees also have the opportunity to receive business and technical education at their workplaces if necessary.

REPRESENTATIVE VIEWS OF STANFORD
FROM SILICON VALLEY LEADERS

In addition to asking senior leaders to discuss the general conditions necessary for a successful start-up and the role that Stanford played in that process, we also asked them to focus more precisely on what they thought Stanford's principal contribution to their company might be. The answers fell broadly into three categories.

Increasing Technical Advantage

> *We depended on the research done at Stanford [the graphics chip developed by Jim Clark and his students at the Center for Integrated Systems] to start our company. And we profit from continuing interactions with faculty and students.*
>
> *We drew a ten-minute commute circle around Hoover Tower [on the Stanford campus] to define acceptable locations for our company.*
> —ED MCCRACKEN, CHAIRMAN AND CEO,
> SILICON GRAPHICS, INC.

Deciding to locate a company with the potential size of SGI within a ten-minute commute of Hoover Tower is an expensive decision. It would only be made because the company believed that high-quality, nearly instantaneous interaction with faculty and students who do work on computer graphics is critical for the company. Placing the company within easy commuting range of Stanford has surely facilitated regular interaction between the Stanford computer science and electrical engineering departments and the research staff at SGI. More than that, it is likely true that the research agenda at Stanford is to some degree shaped by the insights faculty and staff receive from these interactions, even though SGI would not have exclusive right to the research output. The decision to locate near Stanford was therefore made in part to reduce technical risk and increase technical advantage.

Educating Entry-Level Professionals

> *The most important contribution Stanford*
> *makes to Silicon Valley is to replenish the intel-*
> *lectual pool every year with new graduate*
> *students.*
>
> —GORDON MOORE, CHAIRMAN, INTEL

Moore's view is clearly very different from the one held by Ed McCracken. This is because they see Stanford's contributions from the perspective of different industries: the computer industry on the one hand, and the semi-conductor industry on the other.

Of course, Silicon Valley needs more graduate students than Stanford can supply, or even than all of the research universities in the San Francisco Bay Area can supply. Many universities make a similar contribution. The central point here is that, where the semiconductor industry is concerned, it is not patents or technology transfer that is of primary importance to the industry. It is students educated as entry-level professionals in the field.

Providing Continuing Education

> *Stanford's TV [distance learning] program allows*
> *our engineers to take graduate courses wherever*
> *they are [including sites across the United States*
> *and around the world]. By providing this oppor-*
> *tunity, Stanford has increased the productivity of*
> *its professors without sacrificing the quality of the*
> *educational experience.*
>
> —JOHN YOUNG, CEO, HEWLETT-PACKARD

John Young, during the time that he was CEO at Hewlett-Packard, focused on a different feature of Stanford's program. To see why distance learning was so important to Hewlett-Packard, it is useful to mention that at the time Young made that statement, HP had about eight thousand engineers. Two thousand of those had at least one degree from Stanford; and many of those graduates, as well as other employees within HP, had taken at least one course over the Stanford TV network.

Engineers at HP are attempting to design new products and manufacturing processes that take advantage of the state of the art. They need to stay up-to-date, so access to a high-quality graduate program is very important to them. Such access not only provides them with up-to-date information; it also means that HP engineers at all of the HP locations have a common background for discussing problems.

We have, then, several different, complementary insights into Stanford's contributions to Silicon Valley. For some companies, particularly pharmaceutical companies, technology transfer through licensing is very important. For firms in the computing and information-networking field, Stanford's contribution is research and the formation of new companies that can bring new products to the market quickly. For established firms in high-tech markets, it is the graduate education, which on the one hand replenishes the intellectual pool, and on the other provides, through distance learning programs, continuing education for engineers in industry.

CONCLUSION

As one looks at the history of Silicon Valley, five firms and institutions, and one individual in particular, stand out as being central to the formation and long-term development of the region. The individual is Fred Terman. It was his frustration with the lack of jobs for graduates of the Stanford electrical engineering department that led him, beginning in 1936, to energetically encourage several of his former pupils to start their own businesses, thus initiating Stanford-related high-tech entrepreneurship in the region.[11] He saw that the growth of these companies could provide agreeable employment for new graduates and consulting opportunities for faculty.

The most successful company formed from Terman's personal efforts was Hewlett-Packard, incorporated in 1939. Terman was the angel investor for the firm, providing $500 in seed capital. Bill Hewlett and Dave Packard created a firm that set a standard for product excellence, company management, and employee benefits that has been emulated many times by other firms in Silicon Valley and elsewhere. Hewlett-Packard represents the first successful Stanford start-up in the area of electronic instrumentation and equipment.

A second organization crucial to the development of Silicon Valley is Fairchild Semiconductor Corporation, founded in 1957 (for more on Fairchild Semiconductor, see Chapter 8). Among its contributions were the development of the silicon bipolar transistor as a commercial device; the invention and development of the integrated circuit; and the creation of a research laboratory that, according to Gordon Moore, was the source of much of the technology used by firms that eventually spun out of Fairchild. These firms are the ones that actually produce integrated circuit chips in Silicon Valley. But for all of this to happen, it was first necessary for Fairchild to spin out of the Shockley Semiconductor Laboratory, thus proving that employees could leave the company they were working for and start a competitor to it. According to Moore, this set the stage for the repeated spin-outs that have occurred in Silicon Valley since then in nearly all industries represented here.

Apple Computer, of course, has to be listed as one of the five organizations, for two reasons. First and most important, it was a central participant in starting the personal computer revolution. But its first products were not as useful as the founders wanted. Their greatest success came when they recognized that technology being developed at the Xerox Palo Alto Research Center had practical applications and used that technology to shift their focus from the original Apple models to the Macintosh.

The Xerox Palo Alto Research Laboratories also have to be listed as a key organization in the development of Silicon Valley. In addition to the technologies that led to the Macintosh, Xerox engineers invented the Ethernet, the laser printer, software for word processing, software for printing systems, and a collection of other technologies that have been critical in the development of the region.

Finally, for the many reasons mentioned throughout this chapter, Stanford itself plays a major role in many ways, a role that differs for each sector of industry that has grown up in this region. The depth and breadth of this contribution are hardly captured by this chapter, but some indications of it are apparent from the data presented and from the comments of senior leaders in Silicon Valley who have profited from it.

The Stanford contribution can be traced to a number of sources, including especially a group of faculty, staff, and students that tend to be highly entrepreneurial in their own right. In addition, imaginative leadership at the university, starting with Fred Terman, recognized the benefit of close relationships between Stanford and the high-tech companies that could be formed by entrepreneurs who came from or had access to Stanford.

In addition to mentioning these organizations, it is fitting to end with a statement made above. It captures the essence of Silicon Valley perhaps as well as it can be captured in a single sentence: *The heroes in Silicon Valley are the entrepreneurs who can start and grow successful companies.* As long as the conditions for starting and growing a business in Silicon Valley remain in good health, the region will continue to be the Valley of the Heart's Delight for entrepreneurs and the entourage that surrounds them.

11

Social Networks in Silicon Valley

EMILIO J. CASTILLA, HOKYU HWANG,
ELLEN GRANOVETTER, AND MARK GRANOVETTER

"The most crucial aspect of Silicon Valley is its networks." There is no proposition so universally agreed upon and so little studied. We see two main reasons for this. The first is that the analysis of social networks has been mainly the province of sociologists, but only in recent years have they become interested in industrial organization. The second is that methods for systematic study of social networks are of very recent origin.[1]

Sociologists' earlier theoretical concerns led them to focus network analysis on small groups (like children in schools). But more recent work has treated larger groups and even entire industries (see, e.g., Granovetter and McGuire 1998). In this chapter we outline a project in progress, "Networks of Silicon Valley." Ultimately, we hope to achieve a systematic mapping of the Valley's networks and their evolution over time. This means also accounting for how networks of individuals literally outside the Valley's industrial activity, but playing a vital role, articulate with and sometimes become "insiders." The most obvious such groups are educators, venture capitalists, lawyers, headhunters, engineers, and industrial/civic associations and trade groups. Financial, commercial, educational, and political institutions are linked not only to information technology firms, but also to one another in this region, since industries do not arise and exist in a vacuum, but in a distinct institutional context. Variations in these contexts may well explain why the myriad attempts to replicate Silicon Valley in utterly different contexts, by copying only the features of its firms, are rarely fruitful. This broader account is essential for understanding how regional economies operate. The distinctive inclination of sociologists is to investigate how different institutional arenas mesh with one another, rather than focusing on the technical, economic, legal, educational, or political aspects of a situation. In Silicon Valley, where such linkages are an important and distinctive feature of economic success, this is an especially vital topic.

Thus, in this chapter we will introduce some key ideas about social networks, sketch some of the vital institutional sectors in Silicon Valley where they operate, and present an initial exploration of the formal analysis of how these sectors articulate with one another.

SOCIAL NETWORKS IN THE ECONOMY

A "social network" can be defined as a set of nodes or actors (persons or organizations) linked by social relationships or ties of a specified type. A tie or relation between two actors has both strength and content. The content might include information, advice, or friendship, shared interest or membership, and typically some level of trust. The level of trust in a tie is crucial, in Silicon Valley as elsewhere. Two aspects of social networks affect trust. One is "relational"—having to do with the particular history of that tie, which produces conceptions of what each actor owes to the other. The other is "structural": some network structures make it easier than others do for people to form trusting relationships and avoid malfeasance. For example, a dense network with many connections makes information on the good and bad aspects of one's reputation spread more easily.

An extensive literature shows the importance of social networks in the economy—from small start-up companies to large multinationals, from emerging industries such as biotechnology to traditional ones such as automobiles, from regional industrial districts such as Silicon Valley to national and supranational entities such as the European Union. (For a general review, see Powell and Smith-Doerr 1994.) In Silicon Valley, networks have special importance in the movement of labor, the evolution of influence and power, and the actual production of innovation.

Networks of Access and Opportunity

One of the most important aspects of Silicon Valley is the way its labor market works. Extensive labor mobility creates rapidly shifting and permeable firm and institutional boundaries and dense personal networks across the technical and professional population. The ability of Silicon Valley to restructure itself when conditions change through rapid and frequent reshuffling of organizational and institutional boundaries and members (which, in the Eastern European context, Stark [1996] has called a "recombinant" process) is one of the factors that underlie the dominance of Silicon Valley in the new economy.

Scholars have written extensively on the role of social networks in allocating labor (see Granovetter 1995a). Recruitment often occurs not through close friends, but from what Granovetter (1973) called the "strength of weak ties." Close friends know the same people you do, whereas acquaintances are better bridges to new contacts and nonredundant information. Firms benefit from employees' social networks, and employers are thus willing to pay monetary bonuses to them for successful referrals (Fernandez and Weinberg 1997; Fernandez, Castilla, and Moore 2000). Workers' social connections are considered resources that yield economic returns in the form of better hiring outcomes. Employees hired though social networks tend to quit less, experience faster mobility inside an organization, and perform better than those recruited through other means.

Commenting on Silicon Valley's exceptionally high rates of interfirm mobility, Saxenian (1994) has argued that "The region's engineers developed loyalties to each other and to advancing technology, rather than to individual firms or even industries" (28). The result of this unique culture and vast network of weak ties is that engineers in the Valley move frequently from one project or company to another. High mobility reinforces the dense networks, strengthening their role as channels through which technical and market information, as well as other intangibles—organizational culture and trust, for example—are diffused and shared among firms.

Engineers not only hop around firms in the same industry; they also move from one industry and/or institutional sector to another—from technical firms to venture capital firms or to university research centers—creating cross-institutional ties and loosely integrating different institutional nodes in Silicon

Valley. Many venture capitalists, for example, once worked in technical sectors of the Valley. Eugene Kleiner, the founder of the preeminent venture capital firm, Kleiner Perkins Caufield & Byers, had worked for Fairchild Semiconductor before moving on to finance. Similarly, John Doerr had been an Intel employee prior to his excursion into venture capital, and Regis McKenna had worked at National Semiconductor before founding his own, now famous, public relations firm.

Networks of Power and Influence

In addition to mediating labor flows, networks can also be an important source of power and influence. Research on interlocking directorates among financial and industrial corporations (e.g., Mintz and Schwartz 1985) shows how influence can flow from financial institutions to the industrial corporations to which they lend. In Silicon Valley, venture capitalists and lawyers play more than their conventional roles; they influence the structure and future development of their client companies. The lawyers are deal makers as well as counselors (Suchman 1994; Suchman and Cahill 1996). As deal makers, "Silicon Valley attorneys employ their connections in the local business community to link clients with various transactional partners" (Suchman 1994, 96). For example, lawyers help by providing connections to venture capital, giving Valley firms access to their accumulated knowledge about the region and high-technology industries, and offering general business advice, like conventional business consultants (100).

Venture capitalists not only provide necessary financial resources to start-ups and spin-offs, but often play the multiple roles of broker, management consultant, and recruiter. Their vested interest in the firms for which they provide financial resources makes them more likely to intervene in the operations of their start-ups. From the knowledge of high technology that they have accumulated from their broad portfolios of successes and failures, venture capitalists offer invaluable advice as to what does and does not work. Many start-ups and spin-offs are founded by engineers who are naive about management; venture capitalists can access an informal and formal network of experts to further the long-term viability of newly created firms. Further, venture capitalists often (re)organize the boards of directors of their start-ups, sometimes reducing the role of original founders and even severing the original founders from their own creation; Cisco Systems and Silicon Graphics were two famous cases.

Networks of Production and Innovation

Finally, social networks function as a distinct governance mechanism, a "social glue" that binds actors and firms together into a coherent system. In high-technology industries in particular, social networks help transmit information and knowledge among different firms and individuals and produce innovation. In Silicon Valley, getting the right product out at the right time has become crucial for the survival and growth of a firm in a rapidly changing environment. Networks enhance the capacity to do this by enabling people to mobilize capital, find relevant and reliable information quickly, and link to appropriate outlets. Innovation is so central to high-technology industry that it is not an exaggeration to say that effective social networks determine a firm's chance for survival.

Such a network governance structure is a typical way to regulate the inter-firm alliance practices, such as collaborative manufacturing, found in industrial districts. Piore and Sabel (1984) argue that a new logic of production—"flexible specialization"—emerged as a challenge to mass production once markets for standardized goods were saturated, and higher quality and more specialized goods attracted consumers. Into this volatile environment have stepped flexible producers who can respond quickly to changing market conditions. To meet the demands of this changing marketplace, firms adopt new modes of organization that spread production across diversified interfirm linkages of suppliers, subcontractors, and end users. In the regions of north central Italy and southwestern Germany, for example, a complex division of labor among small and medium-sized companies has developed, supported by local political, financial, and educational institutions, which allows firms to produce a wide range of industrial products (Herrigel 1996).

Saxenian (1994) shows that Silicon Valley shares many of the characteristics of European industrial districts, and thus promotes collective learning among specialist producers of interrelated technologies. In this decentralized system, dense social networks and open labor markets encourage entrepreneurship and the ongoing mobilization of resources. Companies compete intensely, but simultaneously learn about changing markets and technologies through informal communications, collaborative projects, and common ties to research associations and universities. High rates of job mobility spread technology, promote the recombination of skills and capital, and aid the region's development. Silicon Valley companies, just as those in Germany and Italy, trade with the whole world, but the core of knowledge and production remains local. One way the Valley accomplishes this recombination of knowledge and capital is through spin-offs, which have contributed to the construction of dense social networks of entrepreneurs, inventors, and other institutional actors.

Part of the importance of these spin-offs is that most organizations resist changing their core technologies and structures (compare Stinchcombe 1965; Hannan and Freeman 1977; 1984). This resistance based on past success is what Clayton Christensen calls the "innovator's dilemma" (Christensen 1997). Thus, upgrading of a regional economy occurs especially through new organizations rather than through transformation of existing ones. While the founders of spin-offs explore new ideas and possibilities, they build upon the know-how they have gained from previous employment. In this regard, ties between new spin-offs and previous organizations through founders are an important way in which information and experience are transmitted, as we show in detail in the network analysis of the following section. Any region whose institutions or networks resist spin-offs or new entrants may face stagnation. Larson's (1992) and Nohria's (1992) research on the development of successful start-up companies stresses that social networks to other firms are a means for quick access to resources and know-how that cannot be produced internally.

NETWORKS AND INSTITUTIONS

In this part, we sketch the application of social network ideas and methods to some of the main institutional sectors of the Silicon Valley industrial district, including the region's educational, industrial, financial, and legal activities. We want to know how Silicon Valley's networks attained their current structure—what growth process took them from the modest and small-scale enterprise of

William Shockley's semiconductor laboratory in 1957, for example, to the world-dominating structures of the early twenty-first century? We address such questions by illustrating how formal techniques of network analysis can uncover patterns not easily found by casual inspection. Our emphasis will be not only on networks within a sector, but also on how networks from different sectors mesh with one another.

Networks and Genealogy: A Semiconductor Industry Case Study

Part of the legend of Silicon Valley is the story of how Shockley's company begat Fairchild Semiconductor via defection of the "Traitorous Eight," and how Fairchild later begat the many "Fairchildren" firms such as Intel, which in turn gave birth to still new generations of important firms. Many Silicon Valley firms have a "genealogy chart," first developed by journalist Don Hoefler and later maintained by the trade association SEMI, hanging in their lobbies, tracing their ancestry back to Fairchild. In this section, we undertake the first systematic analysis of the data in this chart, by techniques of network analysis and network visualization. By doing so we hope to illuminate the continuing significance of patterns laid down in the initial set of foundings and spin-offs that gave the Valley its distinctive industrial organization.

History of the semiconductor industry. In 1947, William J. Shockley and his collaborators at Bell Laboratories in New Jersey introduced the first successful transistor, which would eventually earn them the Nobel prize. This was important for Silicon Valley because Shockley, a Stanford graduate, with the encouragement of Frederick Terman, Stanford's legendary engineering dean and provost, decided to start his own company in his native Palo Alto to capitalize on the invention (Hoefler 1971; Riordan and Hoddeson 1997).

Shockley's ability to spot and recruit talented people contributed to the growth of what would eventually become Silicon Valley. Shockley Semiconductor Laboratories was founded in February of 1956. Drawing on established firms such as Raytheon, Motorola, and Philco, and on top engineering and science programs such as those at MIT and Cal Tech, Shockley soon had the core of the firm, and of the nascent semiconductor industry, in place. Robert

Noyce and Gordon Moore, both in their late twenties, would later go on to found Fairchild Semiconductor and Intel. In addition to Noyce and Moore, by mid-1956 Shockley had successfully recruited Jay Last and Sheldon Roberts from MIT and Dow Chemical Company, respectively.

Despite his ability to recruit, Shockley's eccentric and authoritarian managerial style did not match his Nobel laureate stature. Both Last and Roberts thus joined Noyce, Moore, Julius Blank, Jean Hoerni, Victor Grinich, and Eugene Kleiner to become the "Traitorous Eight" who left Shockley to form Fairchild Semiconductor in 1957, indelibly changing the future development of Silicon Valley's semiconductor industry. (For a full historical account, see Chapter 8.)

At Fairchild, the integrated circuit was first developed sufficiently for commercial production, with Noyce receiving the first patent in 1961. But the "Traitorous Eight" contributed more to Silicon Valley than a breakthrough in technology. Robert Noyce had a vision for this newly emerging industry that explicitly rejected the hierarchical East Coast corporate culture (Wolfe 1983). For example, there was no reserved parking at Fairchild, which was conceived of as a democratic community rather than a hierarchical workplace. And this new approach diffused as employees from Fairchild spun off to start their own companies. Everywhere the Fairchild émigrés went, they took the "Noyce approach" with them. It was not enough to start up a company; you had to start up a community in which there were no social distinctions. The atmosphere of the new companies was so democratic, it startled businessmen from the East. As Tom Wolfe reported:

> Some fifty-five-year-old biggie with his jowls swelling up smoothly from out of his F. R. Tripeler modified-spread white collar and silk jacquard print necktie would call up from GE or RCA and say, "This is Harold B. Thatchwaite," and the twenty-three-year-old secretary on the other end of the line, out in the Silicon Valley, would say in one of those sunny blonde pale-blue-eyed California voices: "Just a minute, Hal, Jack will be right with you." And once he got to California and met this Jack for the first time, there would be, the CEO himself, all of thirty-three years old, wearing no jacket, no necktie, just a checked shirt, khaki pants, and a pair of moccasins with welted seams the size of jumper cables. Naturally the first sounds out of Jack's mouth would be: "Hi, Hal." (1983, 360–61)

And, of course, there was the start-up culture. Fairchild engineers, even those who were among the founders, started their own companies—often in direct competition with their mother company. Fairchild spin-offs produced another round of spin-offs and spin-offs of spin-offs and so on. The spin-off of all spin-offs was founded in 1968 when Noyce and Moore, with Andy Grove, left Fairchild to start Intel. Their intention was not to compete with Fairchild and other already-established semiconductor firms, but to carve out a new niche, in semiconductor memory. Intel grew to become a company with sales of $66 million by 1973, employing more than two thousand workers (Wolfe 1983).

The early history of the semiconductor industry is replete with similar stories of spin-offs, some encouraged and some discouraged by parent companies. These spin-offs led to rapid technological breakthroughs created by networks of scientists and engineers building on the accumulated knowledge of their predecessors, and their experience in previous firms.

Social network analysis of the semiconductor industry. Although all accounts stress how crucial these spin-offs were for the spectacular stream of innovation that came from this region, there has been no systematic analysis of this spin-off process. Our own research on this is at an early stage, but it is interesting to see what can be gleaned from the well-known Semiconductor Genealogy Chart, originally developed by journalist Don Hoefler (with the concept by Jack Yelverton), and later maintained by the trade association Semiconductor Equipment and Materials International, or SEMI (updated information provided by H.T.E. Management). This chart indicates that more than 372 people started and built the semiconductor industry since 1947.

In the chart, we have identified 129 firms (including spin-offs, spin-offs of spin-offs, etc.) that existed between 1947 and 1986, after which the chart was no longer updated. In Figure 11.1 we plot the number of companies founded each year from 1947 to 1986.

We use a computer graphics program called MAGE (Richardson and Richardson 1992), which displays dynamic three-dimensional images to explore and evaluate the social structure of engineers, inventors, and entrepreneurs.[2] The resulting image represents the social network as a set of actors and the ties between them. Such a picture is like an X ray, laying bare the struc-

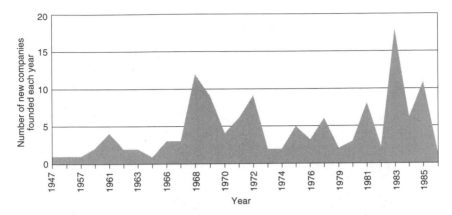

Figure 11.1. Number of new companies in the semiconductor industry founded each year, 1947–86.

ture of social ties, but needing a substantial amount of interpretation, and often raising more questions than it answers. Thus, social network analysts are "social radiologists," who use such pictures as heuristic devices to initiate more systematic probes of how structures arise and change over time, and as preludes to more complex quantitative analyses (such as those described in Wasserman and Faust 1994).

The graph of those who started and built the semiconductor industry in Silicon Valley is presented in Figure 11.2.[3] Each point (or "node") represents a person, and the lines connecting the points represent the ties. Since the presence of a tie between two people is coded from the semiconductor industry genealogy chart, it means that they were co-founders of at least one Silicon Valley semiconductor company. Thus, for any two persons in the sample, a tie is either present or absent.[4]

Not surprisingly, important actors in the semiconductor industry such as Jean Hoerni, Julius Blank, Eugene Kleiner, Jay Last, and Sheldon Roberts are the ones who are connected to more than ten people in the network. Shockley, on the other hand, appears with quite a low average number of co-founder ties. One important task is to discover how a person's position in a network may both reflect and confer or reinforce a position of influence. Roughly speaking, actors who are more central, in the sense of having more ties to others ("degree centrality"), or being crucial linkages that actors must go through to reach others ("betweenness centrality"), can often be shown to be more in-

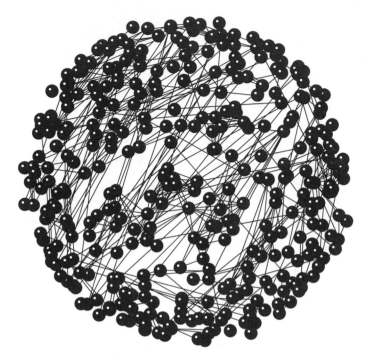

Figure 11.2. The founders of the
semiconductor industry.
SOURCE: SEMI Semiconductor Industry Genealogy Chart.
First conceived by Dan Hoefler, later maintained by SEMI.

fluential.[5] Jean Hoerni is the actor with the highest betweenness centrality in
the network we computed from the genealogy chart. The analysis also highlights other less well known actors who appear to be quite central in the development of the semiconductor social network. Among these are Gifford,
founder of companies such as Advanced Micro Devices in 1969 and later
Maxim Integrated Products in 1983; Araquistain, Baldwin, Bower, Breene, El-
binger, Koss, Marchman, Valdes, and Wiesner, all founders of Rheem Semiconductor in 1959 (and some of whom also worked for Fairchild Semiconductor); and, finally, Weindorf, who had previously worked for Fairchild
Semiconductor and Rheem Semiconductor. One virtue of network analysis is
that in its impartial way it may point to the need to look more closely at individuals whose centrality has not been captured in the many impressionistic
and journalistic accounts of Silicon Valley history.

The meaning of centrality, however, depends on a network's definition. In a network of ties computed at a single point in time, individuals with the highest centrality are quite likely to be powerful and influential by virtue of their position, because of which much vital information must flow through them before it reaches others. But the network we display here, where ties indicate co-founding, is quite different, as it spans nearly thirty years. Here, central individuals are those who provided vital linkages among industry sectors, making Silicon Valley the "small world" that it is. Though this was a crucial role in shaping the Valley's unique character, those who played it need not have been highly visible. Recent research on the "small world problem" (known to the general public as the issue of "six degrees of separation") shows that a remarkably small number of strategically placed ties can dramatically increase the connectivity of a network (see Watts 1999).[6]

Higher Education and University-Industry Networks:
The Role of Stanford

To study the evolution of connectedness among industrial firms in Silicon Valley is already a challenge. But as we stress repeatedly, much of what is unique in this region and accounts for its "edge" is how industry relates to other sectors. In this section and the next, we choose two such sectors—education and venture capital—and discuss how the social networks within these sectors and with Silicon Valley industry helped shape outcomes. This is followed by an illustrative network analysis of IPOs that shows how the different sectors work together on a particular activity. A fuller account would treat other institutional sectors such as law, public relations, and real estate, and give much more extensive attention to connections. Here, however, we want simply to sketch out the issues.

The educational sector has been especially vital because the constant movement back and forth between industry and university has blurred the boundaries of both and created elaborate social networks that keep academic research focused on practical problems, and infuse industrial activity with up-to-date science. Though a number of educational organizations have been important in this way, we focus on the key actor in Silicon Valley's early history, Stanford University.

In the 1950s, two institutional innovations—the University Honors Cooperative Program and the Stanford Industrial Park—brought together university researchers and nascent industry interests. Stanford Industrial Park (now called Stanford Research Park), conceived by Stanford provost Frederick Terman and officially founded in 1951, was the first of its kind. No university had previously allotted large tracts of its own land for industrial uses (in part because few other universities had Stanford's more than 8,000 acres of land to allot). Varian Associates moved its R&D and administrative operations to Stanford in the late 1940s, and other companies such as General Electric, Eastman Kodak, Admiral Corporation, Hewlett-Packard, and Watkins-Johnson joined Varian. By 1962 there were 25 companies in the park (Saxenian 1994, 23–24). Although the park is still home to many influential players in the Valley, such as the law firm Wilson Sonsini Goodrich & Rosati and the legendary Xerox Palo Alto Research Center, Silicon Valley has outgrown its birthplace.

The Honors Cooperative Program, founded by Frederick Terman in 1953, made it possible for local companies to send their engineers and scientists to pursue advanced degrees at Stanford as part-time students while working full-time. The program "strengthened the ties between firms and the university and allowed engineers to keep up to date technically and to build professional contacts" (Saxenian 1994, 23).[7]

In addition, Stanford students and faculty formed new companies, such as Hewlett-Packard, Sun Microsystems, and Yahoo!, among many others, that were crucial to regional growth. As Silicon Valley matured, research and commercial interests proliferated and the business community came to assume the role of innovator, developing and commercializing innovations. The university's emphasis has shifted to maintaining its relations with already-established firms as the source of cutting-edge scientific knowledge and expert labor. Currently, innovative ideas produced at Stanford find their way to industries through licensing via the Stanford Office of Technology Licensing and various research centers that have proliferated over the past two decades. Further, given Stanford's prominent role in the evolution of Silicon Valley and its accumulated ties to the region's different sectors, Stanford is the one place where outsiders can gather information about Silicon Valley. It is also an important port of entry to the Valley for many high-technology firms from overseas through its various affiliates programs. Now foreign firms can send their employees to Stanford to study Silicon Valley for a nominal fee. In fact, one of Stanford's main current roles is to attract people from all over the world to the region, which is a crucial matter, as Silicon Valley start-ups are increasingly formed by nationals of foreign countries (see Chapter 12). It does so in part from its reputation as past midwife of successful firms, and in part from the international reputation of its engineering departments. The School of Engineering, typically rated at or near first in the United States, regularly provides the region with a highly skilled labor force and attracts top researchers from around the United States and the world.

One of the crucial links between the university and the surrounding Silicon Valley community is provided by its approximately 50 research centers, which provide for the university and the business community a forum in which they can maintain close contact. These centers also make it easier for foreign companies aspiring to learn the "Silicon Valley way" to introduce themselves into its sometimes arcane culture. The centers and programs are surprisingly informal and decentralized. Though they must be approved by the university administration, the university is not directly involved in their decision-making processes and their daily workings. They receive little financial support from the university, raising funds internally through corporate memberships.

The recruitment of firms to these centers occurs through already-established personal networks between professors or researchers and businesses. In particular, a research center director's role is to identify companies that are interested in the center's activities and to set up collaborations with the Stanford faculty. Usually a director has extensive experience working with both industry and universities. For example, the director of the Center for Integrated Facilities Engineering had worked both in industry and for various universities before joining Stanford University to set up the center, and had particular experience working in the area of university-industry collaboration.

Research centers are avenues through which information about the current state of research activities at Stanford flows to industry. Most member companies of research centers or affiliates programs work through particular faculty members as their liaisons to Stanford; through the liaisons they have early access to research reports. In addition, companies are invited to conferences held on campus and can have individual meetings when needed. They can set up courses geared specifically toward their design problems through the affiliates programs. This is a cost-effective way to tackle specific problems with the help of cutting-edge researchers and engineers. And some affiliates programs include opportunities to send their employees as corporate visiting scholars both to the programs and to an academic department. As a result, companies learn more about students and researchers who work on their problems, and some companies exploit this opportunity as a recruiting tool.

These centers and programs also provide funding opportunities for researchers in the Stanford community. Funding is used to support graduate students, to purchase equipment, and to support administrative assistants. Money is received from industry in the form of affiliates' fees, which do not go directly to the researchers, but through research centers. Compared to most government funding sources, the process of funding research is much more efficient and informal, and entails far less "overhead" cost than traditional grants.

The research centers provide a means by which university researchers can develop or commercialize their ideas. Here, researchers and faculty can legitimately pursue applied knowledge, which is at times difficult to do in an institution of higher education. This is not only allowed but encouraged, as the primary role of the centers and programs is to connect the university and industry. Through meetings such as annual affiliates days and other public events hosted by the centers, to which previous and current affiliates and individuals who have been involved in the program or centers are invited, industry and university come into direct contact with each other with the common purpose of university-industry cooperation. Student internship opportunities are provided through networks created in the research centers and programs. Professors can utilize concrete issues, topics, and materials brought to them by industry for their classes. Students enjoy and benefit from learning by doing.[8] This, in turn, helps departments to attract highly motivated students.

Key individuals move back and forth from industry to academic positions in research centers and affiliates programs. For example, a former director of one Stanford interdisciplinary research center, who now works for a high-tech company in the region, had also worked in industry before joining the center. As the industry liaison for the center, his past experiences and networks in industry were invaluable in developing its industry sponsorship program and in raising funds for the center.[9] Moreover, his career and current relationship with this center typify the evolving Stanford–Silicon Valley relationship. After receiving a Ph.D. in computer science, he joined a renowned research organization in Silicon Valley, and then a large industrial corporation. He subsequently started his own companies, one of which is now publicly traded on NASDAQ. Then he did consulting work for financial companies in the region. Years later, he joined the Stanford center to develop the affiliates program. Now back in industry, he still maintains an informal relationship with the center and can imagine returning some day.

Speaking more abstractly, the personnel of these research centers constitute "boundary spanning units" (Hirsch 1972), a category of organizational actor crucial in situations in which brokers must connect disparate institutional sectors.[10] The centers create social networks that ramify into every corner of the region's high-tech industry. Because of the proliferation of such boundary-spanning units, unusual in institutions of higher education, Stanford University continues to be a central forum for both academic and industrial researchers to benefit from the exchange of information.

Key Financial Institutions

It is widely agreed that the venture capital industry has been the financial engine of Silicon Valley. Harmon reflects a popular belief in asserting that

> the venture capitalists (VCs in finance parlance) are the new power brokers, banks, management providers, gurus, and mothers who hold the hands of the newbie idea-ites [the founders of new companies], taking them past the training wheels stage into rocket racers. It is smart money, the people and their capital. It has to be smart—there is no time to make the wrong moves in a world where every great idea has a dozen imitators in sixty seconds. (Harmon 1999, 3–4)

Wilson's 1985 study is probably the first systematic analysis of American venture capital. In his words, "Born in New York, nurtured in Boston, and almost smothered in Washington, venture capital did not really come of age until it moved to California and joined forces with the brash young technologists who were using bits of silicon to create an information revolution as profound as the industrial revolution a century earlier" (Wilson 1985, 31). With the formation of venture capital firms such as Draper, Gaither & Anderson, and Western Business Assistance Corporation in 1958, the basic foundations of today's venture structure were laid.

Experienced venture capitalists now manage billions of dollars. Half of the venture capital firms in the United States are now in Silicon Valley, which attracted $3.3 billion in venture capital funding in 1998 alone. This is about half of the venture capital invested in the top ten technology regions of the United States, which include Atlanta, Austin, Boston, Dallas, Denver, Phoenix, Portland, Raleigh-Durham, Salt Lake City, and Seattle (Joint Venture: Silicon Valley Network, "Index of Silicon Valley," various issues).

While Silicon Valley industry attracted venture capital firms, the presence of venture capitalists attracted entrepreneurs from all over the country and the world. Employment grew accordingly, and in 1998 Silicon Valley added an estimated 19,400 new jobs. The number of initial public offerings (IPOs) and mergers and acquisitions (M&As) in Silicon Valley indicates how successful entrepreneurship and companies are in the region. The Valley still produces the highest number of initial public offerings (IPOs) in the country (Joint Venture 1999). Sand Hill Road, in Menlo Park, California, is now the "*de facto* headquarters for venture capital activity on the West Coast" (Saxenian 1994, 40). Today it is probably the most powerful venture capital enclave in the country and a center of gravity for international venture capital.

Networks of engineers, entrepreneurs, and wealthy investors were crucial to the development of venture capital. These networks were fed by major inflows of technical entrepreneurs, venture capitalists, management talent, and supporting services from other regions. By the early 1980s, Silicon Valley venture capital was dominated by individuals who had migrated from industry rather than from backgrounds in finance (Wilson 1985, 50–51). For this reason, venture capitalists play a more active role in Silicon Valley than in other regions of the United States and the world (Saxenian 1994; Florida and Kenney 1987; Nohria 1992).

History of venture capital in Silicon Valley. In the 1950s, when the practice of venture capital did not yet have a name, the patterns for investment were established by rich men pursuing some risk investing in an informal but disciplined way. Three stand out among those who began to put risk capital on a more permanent institutional base. Laurance S. Rockefeller (third of the five sons of John D. Rockefeller Jr.) and John H. Whitney were rich, prominent prewar venture experimenters; and Georges F. Doriot, a French Harvard Business School professor, was very influential as teacher of a course about entrepreneurship and as president of the American Research & Development Corporation, founded in 1946. In the latter position, he organized capital and support for scientist-entrepreneurs in the Boston area. Government also stepped in by creating the Small Business Investment Company (SBIC) program in 1958, which "created hundreds of venture investors overnight" (Wilson 1985, 13), and later by reshaping the tax system to promote equity investing. One of the most successful pioneers was Frank G. Chambers. Chambers raised $5.5 million in 1959; his Continental Capital Corporation is believed to be the first SBIC in Northern California. Chambers and his brother, Robert, were greatly influenced by Doriot's teaching at Harvard, and started Magna Power Tools in San Francisco. "Chambers was already part of the informal luncheon-and-investment club that constituted San Francisco's venture capital community at the time, and he joined a few small investments" (Wilson 1985, 23). Aside from Chambers's SBIC, the only venture investment group of any magnitude in California was Draper, Gaither & Anderson in Palo Alto. DG&A was formed in 1958 by some of the biggest investors on the West Coast, William H. Draper Jr. (former vice president of Dillon, Read & Company), Rowan Gaither (founder of Rand), and Frederick L. Anderson (a retired Air Force general). DG&A had also raised money from the Rockefeller group.

An important Wall Street investment banker, Arthur Rock, moved himself and his "quiet passion for backing entrepreneurs" (Wilson 1985, 31) to San Francisco in 1961. His name is closely associated with the evolution of Silicon Valley. Rock played a significant role in the creation of Fairchild Semiconductor by the "Traitorous Eight" and accumulated considerable profits from his investments in companies like Scientific Data Systems, Intel, and Apple, among others. Rock's experiences in California convinced him that there was an important business investment opportunity in the West. In 1961 Rock and Tommy Davis, a lawyer who was president of Kern County Land Company, raised $3.5 million from several of the Fairchild Semiconductor founders, and opened an office in San Francisco. Davis and Rock and their principle—"back the right people"—became a model for later venture groups. The partnership between Rock and Davis lasted until 1968, when Davis started a partnership with Wally Davis to form the Mayfield Fund.

The "Boys Club" or "the San Francisco Mafia" (Wilson 1985) refers to a 1960s venture capital network that grew up in San Francisco. "One noontime each month they would troop up Nob Hill to the University Club for a meeting of the Western Association of Venture Capitalists, ideas and gossip flowing with the martinis. Deals were put together over lunch at Jack's or Sam's, venerable Financial District restaurants where the sole was dependable and the sourdough fresh. 'We'd get together and listen to the entrepreneur's story,'" recalls Reid Dennis, a charter member of "The Group" (Wilson 1985, 49).

During the 1970s, the Group moved down from the San Francisco Financial District to Sand Hill Road in Menlo Park, just a few miles from Stanford University. It is then that Silicon Valley became the most powerful venture capital enclave in the country. Venture capitalists were sharing the same physical space, now close to the inventors and entrepreneurs and to many of the young technology companies near Stanford.

Simultaneously, the number of venture capital firms increased enormously, as a result of spin-offs and new venture capital firms started by managers and engineers of companies in the computer industry. The evolution of the venture capital industry followed a pattern similar to that of new high-technology companies. Proliferation by spin-offs from preceding generations was prevalent in both industries. Some of the prominent examples of spin-offs in the venture capital industry are documented by Florida and Kenney (1987, 20–21). For example, Reid Dennis and Burton McMurtry founded Institutional Venture Associates (IVA) in early 1974. Out of IVA, two new important venture firms were built in the 3000 Sand Hill Road complex. Dennis's Institutional Venture Partners raised $22 million and invested successfully in Seagate Technology, a firm making disk drives for personal computers; and David F. Marquardt joined McMurtry and James J. Bochnowski to form Technology Venture Investors (TVI) which raised $24 million. McMurtry later brought in Pete Thomas from Intel, James A. Katzman from Tandem Computers, and Robert C. Kagle from the Boston Consulting Group. TVI had a chance to invest $1 million in Microsoft, which had been founded in 1975 by Harvard sophomore Bill H. Gates and Paul Allen.

Donald Valentine, formerly head of marketing at Fairchild, moved to Sand Hill Road in 1972 and formed Capital Management Services (which later became the important venture capital firm Sequoia Capital). "Everybody in the Valley knew Don Valentine, and if Valentine did not know them, he usually knew somebody who did" (Wilson 1985, 59–60). Valentine's connection to Fairchild Semiconductor salesmen led him to invest in Atari, entering the home video game industry. In 1976 Atari was bought by Warner Communications, which brought large returns to Sequoia. The founder of Atari, Nolan Bushnell, subsequently referred Steve Jobs, who worked for Atari, to Valentine. Jobs approached Valentine in 1977 in his quest to found Apple Computer; though Valentine passed on this funding opportunity, he did connect Jobs to his ultimate financial supporters.

In 1972, the first venture capital team taking up residence at 3000 Sand Hill Road was Thomas J. Perkins and Eugene Kleiner, predecessor of the now top-ranked firm Kleiner Perkins Caufield & Byers. Sandy Robertson, founder of an investment banking firm on San Francisco's Montgomery Street, was the matchmaker for this successful venture fund. Perkins was an engineer from MIT, had been a Harvard Business School MBA student who took classes with Georges Doriot and had worked for David Packard. Kleiner, one of the "Traitorous Eight," was a mechanical engineer from Brooklyn Polytechnic Institute who moved to California to work at Shockley Semiconductor Laboratory. Kleiner and Perkins decided to go into venture capital and to take an active role in designing and building the companies they backed. But they went a step further, encouraging their associates and partners to start companies of their own, such as Tandem Computers, Genentech, and Hybritech. This made Kleiner and Perkins not only a venture capital firm, but also a group of entrepreneurs able themselves to start and run their own companies.

Social network analysis of West Coast venture capital firms. Ultimately we aim not only to describe the historical development of the networks, but also to show how the particular structure of social networks in Silicon Valley stimulated higher growth and development compared to other regions. But the historical evolution of venture capital networks during the key period from 1958 to 1983, if narrated in full detail, would be too confusing and complex for our more modest purpose here. Our first goal has been to identify all early venture capital firms that contributed to the development of the West's venture capitalism. We compiled our data from the second well-known Silicon Valley firm "genealogy chart": "West Coast Venture Capital—25 years," created by the Asset Management Company (AMC) in 1984. This chart indicates that more than three hundred people in more than a hundred companies built West Coast venture capital in the 25 years between 1958 and 1983.[11]

We have identified 129 venture capital organizations (including spin-offs) in the Western region between 1958 and 1983. In Figure 11.3 we plot the cumulative number of such firms by year. The rate of founding remained relatively stable until 1967–68, after which it grew rapidly. An explanation for this trend is that during the late 1960s, the limited partnership became a common form of organization, and even large financial institutions became willing to invest as limited partners. After 1983 (not displayed), the number of venture capital firms in the Western region of the United States continued to grow, mainly as a result of spin-offs from existing venture capital firms.

Next we provide a preliminary glimpse into the network of venture capital firms.[12] As with the semiconductor industry, we use the computer program MAGE to illustrate the connections. In the semiconductor genealogy graph of Figure 11.2, each point (or "node") represented a person; here, each point represents a firm, and the lines connecting the points represent the ties between these organizations. In this case, the presence of a tie between two firms indicates that they share at least one founder.

There are 129 firms (or nodes), and 232 lines.[13] Unlike Figure 11.2, in which the nodes are more or less uniformly connected, Figure 11.4 shows two clear-cut clusters of venture capital firms.[14] One, on the upper right, is composed of 57 firms that are highly interconnected with each other. In this cluster, we find some of the oldest and still the most central and influential VC firms in Silicon Valley today, such as Kleiner Perkins, Crosspoint Venture Partners, Hambrecht & Quist Venture Capital, Institutional Venture Partners, and Mayfield Fund. It is remarkable how many of these firms have common founders, which indicates how close-knit this collection of firms was. We expect that the enormous influence of these firms derives not only from their early position of dominance, but also from the dense network of contacts they maintained among themselves. This network would have provided important conduits of information and flows of resources including advice, gossip, and referrals of opportunities that a given firm could not take advantage of at a

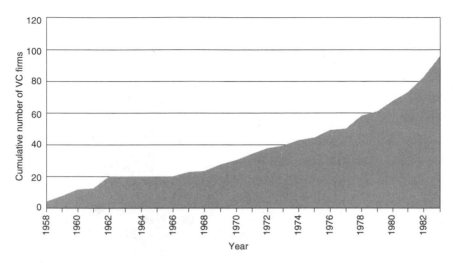

Figure 11.3. Cumulative number of venture capital firms per year, 1958–83.

given moment. In this clique, however, are also firms of more recent (1980s) origin, such as Melchor Venture Management and Lamoreaux & Associates. These newer firms appear to have gained their influence as spin-offs of the older and more influential ones.

The second cluster is a group of individual firms with very few or even no co-founder links among themselves. They are more or less randomly connected when connected at all, and include many "isolates"—which in this context means firms whose founders neither came from other VC firms nor started any new ones. Some of the firms in this incoherent cluster are nevertheless influential, such as Davis and Rock, and Sierra Capital.

This picture belies the idea that connections in Silicon Valley are dense everywhere and that everyone is connected to everyone else. The very different structure of these two distinct and completely disconnected groups of firms also suggests that there are at least two different strategies by which venture capital firms exercise their influence. Moreover, at least for venture capital, firms that are not involved in spin-offs or in dense networks of other such firms may find other ways to make their mark. Further research will be required to suggest what these ways are, but one possibility is that firms in the second cluster, appearing isolated in their absence of co-founder relations to other firms, may have other kinds of personal relations to fellow venture capital firms, and

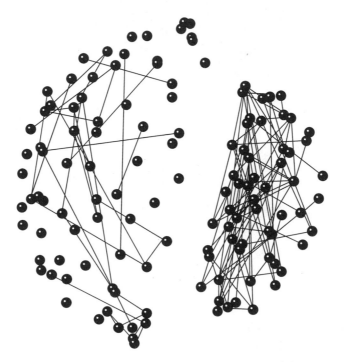

Figure 11.4. Connections among venture capital firms.

SOURCE: Asset Management Company's Genealogy Chart, 1958–83.

be more tightly integrated than the first cluster with firms *outside* the venture capital sector, such as law and accounting firms, educational institutions, and the technical sector itself.

Finally, although we do not show the figure here, we have also examined the social network of venture capitalists who started and built the venture capital industry in the Western region. There are 348 people involved in the construction of venture investing, according to the AMC's genealogy chart, and over 2,200 ties.[15] The average number of ties per person is 6.41, which means that each person in the network is connected as a co-founder of a venture capital firm to 6 other people in the network on average. This corroborates, once again, the importance of networks of human relations for Silicon Valley venture capital.

One of the interesting findings in the network analysis of individuals is that actors such as Arthur Rock, Tommy Davis, Eugene Kleiner, and Frank Chambers, who historically had important roles in the institutionalization of venture investing in Silicon Valley, are not necessarily as central as one would have expected. The most central actors in the co-founder network of venture capitalists all appear to have worked in the 1970s and early 1980s for venture capital funds started by important U.S. and regional banks (such as Citicorp Venture Capital Ltd., Bank of America Capital Corporation, Wells Fargo Investment Company, and Western Bancorp Venture Capital Company). These "venture capital" banks are not only "training grounds for inexperienced venture capitalists" (Kenney and Florida 2000), but also excellent places for them to expand their personal networks. Most of these venture capitalists, after learning about venture financing by working for a bank, left and started their own limited partnership or joined a more prestigious existing venture capital fund.[16]

An analysis of the network of companies confirms that employees of venture banks such as Bank of America Capital Corporation and Citicorp Venture Capital Ltd. founded a large number of new firms. Likewise venture capital firms such as Small Business Enterprises, Westven Management Company, and Fireman's Fund were also quite central to the development of the industry. The venture capital funds such as Hambrecht & Quist, Institutional Venture Partners, Interwest Partners, and Kleiner Perkins and their current venture fund descendants are among the firms that were and still are the most central and influential VC firms in the financing of companies, not only in Silicon Valley, but also elsewhere in the United States, where new investment opportunities are emerging. There are also venture partnerships that were started during the mid- to late 1980s (e.g., Menlo Ventures, and Burr, Egan, Deleage & Company, among many) or even earlier (Sierra Capital) that have become central in the current structure of venture capital.

Institutional Infrastructure:
An Analysis of the Silicon Valley Regional Economy

Dense networks not only within but between sectors of engineers, educators, venture capitalists, lawyers, and accountants are important channels for the diffusion of technical and market information. Although we have frequently mentioned the importance of such cross-institutional ties, and have given important qualitative examples, we have not yet attempted systematic analysis of this phenomenon.

Mapping the relationships among different institutional sectors in the Valley is a must for a systematic understanding of the regional economic system, but it presents daunting challenges. Many domestic as well as foreign attempts to imitate the success of Silicon Valley have failed because the Valley's results depend on its particular institutional configuration rather than on the features of particular firms. But it is not obvious how to explore systematically the way different institutional sectors articulate with one another.

As a first step in developing such exploration by network analysis, we chose to study the case of IPOs. IPO deals allow us to observe the infrastructure of the economy at work, since at least five firms from four different institutional sectors take part: the new industrial firm itself (the "issuer"), a lead underwriting investment bank (usually as part of a syndicate), the issuer-side law firm, the underwriter's law firm, and an auditing accounting firm.

To illustrate the kind of analysis we believe will be fruitful, we take a small special case: the data on California firms involved in 1999 IPOs in a single four-digit SIC code, SIC 7375—"information retrieval services"—which includes such familiar firms as Ask Jeeves, Inc., Broadband Sports, Inc., and McAfee.com Corporation. In SIC 7375, the total number of issuer firms that filed for IPO in the United States in 1999 was 148, of which 19 came from California. In these 19 IPOs, 14 different law firms, 9 lead investment banks, and 6 accounting firms participated. The difference between the number of law firms and the number of accounting firms reflects the difference in industry concentrations. The audit industry is highly concentrated, and the Big Six (Arthur Andersen, Ernst & Young, Bailey, Mark & Co., KPMG, Lumer, Marc & Company, and PricewaterhouseCoopers) take up a disproportionate share of the audit market.[17]

We define two firms as having a network tie when both are involved in the same IPO. The structure of connections among the different companies involved in the filing of IPOs is presented in Figure 11.5, computed with the MAGE program previously described. The issuer firms themselves do not appear in the picture, only the infrastructural firms that supported the IPOs. Law firms, investment banks, and accounting firms are each represented. Firms are connected by lines if they participated together in at least one of the nineteen IPOs, and the length of the line is inversely proportional to the number of co-

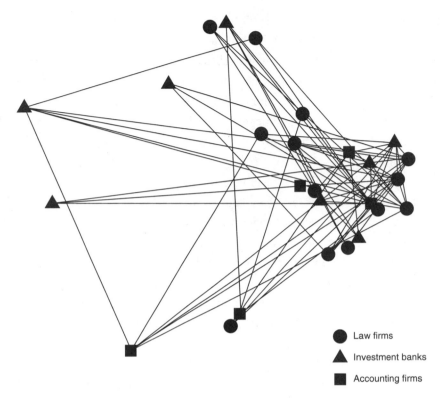

Figure 11.5. Network of IPO deals in the
information retrieval services industry in California.
SOURCE: 1999 IPO deals from www.ipodata.com

participations; we may think of this as a measure of the "strength" of the
tie—the longer the tie, the weaker the relationship.[18]

Although the network as a whole is densely connected, one can single out
a group of eight firms (with the highest score in all centrality measures such
as nodal degree, closeness, and betweenness) that are relatively more densely
connected to one another: three law firms (Wilson Sonsini Goodrich & Rosati,
Brobeck Phleger & Harrison, and Cooley Godward), three investment banks
(Goldman, Sachs & Co., Morgan Stanley Dean Witter, and CS First Boston),
and two accounting firms (PricewaterhouseCoopers and Ernst & Young).[19]

We note some interesting findings in the graph. First, there is a status dimension to this collection of firms. All eight firms are leading firms in their

own industries (see Podolny 1993 for the status hierarchy of the investment banking industry and Han 1994 for the audit market). Both the investment banks and the accounting firms are well-recognized firms. While legal practice is more localized by state-level licensing, the three law firms are all big, corporate law firms. Wilson Sonsini has long been an institution in its own right in the Valley. Both Brobeck Phleger & Harrison and Cooley Godward are San Francisco–based law firms with branches around the country, employing hundreds of lawyers.

Second, although the profile of investment banks and accounting firms suggests the national scope of the markets for financial services and audit services, the market for legal services appears to be distinctively local. Although legal practice is circumscribed by state-level licensing, the emergence of national law firms (with branches in multiple states) and international law firms means that the market does not necessarily need to be as localized as it appears in this analysis. And the high concentration of legal services in our data departs from the more general national pattern. For example, the law firm of Wilson Sonsini Goodrich & Rosati participated in nine of our nineteen IPOs, either from the underwriter's or from the issuer's side.

Given that there are fourteen law firms in the data, this is a remarkable figure, equaled only by the accounting firm PricewaterhouseCoopers. But there are only six accounting firms in the data, reflecting the domination of the audit market by a small number of national firms. By contrast, concentration in law, compared to other service industries, is normally quite low. We do not have good recent data, but Galanter and Palay (1991) show that in 1982, percentages of total receipts were .9 percent and 3.6 percent for the four and twenty largest law firms, respectively, compared to 16.9 percent and 34 percent for the largest accounting firms. We do not have reason to think that these national patterns have changed dramatically. Yet in our data, the three most central law firms appeared twenty times in the nineteen deals. This is out of a possible 38 showings (since there are two law firms for each deal, one for the issuer and one for the underwriter), and thus these three occupied more than 50 percent of the slots in these deals—an extraordinarily concentrated market, far different from the national pattern for legal services.

From our preliminary study of IPO deals within a single SIC code, we begin to see the contours of the institutional articulation of the economy and can point to the local aspect of this configuration. It is this background of financial, commercial, and legal institutions linked to each other that characterizes Silicon Valley. Results for a single SIC code in a single year can only be illustrative. Differences in outcomes between years and industrial sectors would help us see why different sectors evolve in different ways. We would like to know, for example, whether the high concentration of legal services is a regional effect, an industry effect in this particular SIC code, or a temporary blip in a less concentrated pattern over time. We plan to explore many different permutations of this type of analysis in our effort to understand how Silicon Valley industrial and nonindustrial infrastructure has interacted and fitted together.

The development of Silicon Valley was highly dependent on this particular institutional context, which cannot easily be replicated in other regions. Our analysis also suggests that attempts to merely copy the structure and features of firms, as though they were independent actors, cannot be fruitful. Understanding how the networks of Silicon Valley have been built and are interrelated is essential for understanding regional differences in development.

CONCLUSION

This chapter has had two aims. First, we tried to describe and explain the crucial importance of social networks for the functioning of the Silicon Valley regional economy. Our emphasis has been not only on the important networks within institutional sectors, but also on the flow of people, resources, and information among sectors. It is our view that these intersectoral flows are what make Silicon Valley unique, and that in the history of the world's economy, the ability to leverage value by shifting resources among previously separated sectors has always provided a vital edge for regions able to do so.

Because of the enormous attention paid to this highly successful region, the general idea that networks are important has attained widespread currency, and so our emphasis will not surprise even casual observers. But we have also tried to connect this theme to the large and growing academic literature on the sociology of the economy, which indicates that Silicon Valley is not unique in having its outcomes derive from social networks. Instead, these networks underlie the economic structure of many regions, including some that are far less successful and have drawn much less attention. This means that the interesting problem is not whether networks are important in a region, but what kinds of networks are associated with what kinds of outcomes.

The literature on industrial organization has begun to consider this question. Saxenian (1994) presented a systematic argument that network structure in Silicon Valley was quite different from that in the Route 128 corridor of the Boston metropolitan area, for a variety of historical, economic, and cultural reasons, and that this difference translated into what she called, in her book's title, a distinct "regional advantage" for the Valley. Increasingly, when analysts question network interpretations of economic outcomes, they turn not to non-network stories, but to different and more refined network accounts. Thus, several recent studies challenge the idea that the "Third Italy" produces uniformly successful outcomes in its textile industry through elaborate networks of ties among small firms, outcompeting previously dominant but now ponderous and slow-moving large firms. Locke (1995) proposes that such outcomes are in fact quite variable, because only some regions have the institutional infrastructure to support such elaborate networks; and Lazerson and Lorenzoni (1999) point to situations where what really matters is what kind of ties connect networks of small firms to larger firms that can in turn connect them to global partners and suppliers. In such a scenario, the analytic problem shifts from whether large or small firms will triumph, to how the regional economy links firms of various sizes and competencies together, and with what results.

Such an emphasis should be important in Silicon Valley as well, because although most attention has gone to the network of small firms and connections among them, it is amply clear that the Valley's success also depends crucially on the Hewlett-Packards, the Intels, and the Cisco Systems. These firms do not compete to the death with small firms, but instead have an elaborate and complex relation to them that has been a source of vitality not yet adequately charted.

The second goal of this chapter, and of the project from which it reports, is to develop systematic methods to analyze the networks of Silicon Valley, and to enable us to make the distinctions between network structures that lead to stronger or weaker outcomes. The important work in industrial organization that has pointed to the centrality of networks cannot progress further without an adequate toolkit of methods for clear and detailed analysis of the complex data presented by the actual networks in particular regions and industries. We present here exploratory analyses from the beginnings of a long-term project.

As in most fields, methods lag behind theory, and at present, our technology and computer programs are a patchwork of materials borrowed from other settings, which need to be further developed and integrated. We believe that the network studies reported here show the promise of such further development, without establishing the definitive results that systematic analysis aspires to. But we also believe that such analysis is an indispensable step in developing a more sophisticated understanding of this and other industrial economies. In studying Silicon Valley's networks, we are probing its deepest and most enduring source of vitality, which will determine whether its world-dominating position can survive very far into the twenty-first century.

12

Networks of Immigrant Entrepreneurs

ANNALEE SAXENIAN

Silicon Valley is the home of the integrated circuit, or IC—but when local technologists claim that "Silicon Valley is built on ICs" they refer not to chips, but to Indian and Chinese engineers. Skilled immigrants are a growing presence in Silicon Valley, accounting for one-third of the engineering workforce in most technology firms and emerging as visible entrepreneurs in the 1980s and 1990s. In fact, well-known technology companies like Yahoo!, which have immigrant founders, are the tip of a much larger iceberg. This chapter documents the growing contribution of skilled Chinese and Indians to the Silicon Valley economy as entrepreneurs as well as engineers. It also demonstrates how these first-generation immigrants have constructed vibrant ethnic networks to support their professional advancement within the region, while simultaneously building long-distance connections to markets and sources of capital and skill in Asia.

SILICON VALLEY'S NEW IMMIGRANT ENTREPRENEURS

Asian immigration to California began in the eighteenth century, but its modern history can be dated to the Immigration Act of 1965, often referred to as the Hart-Celler Act. Before 1965, the U.S. immigration system limited foreign entry by mandating extremely small quotas according to nation of origin. Hart-Celler, by contrast, allowed immigration based both on the possession of scarce skills and on family ties to citizens or permanent residents. It also significantly increased the total number of immigrants allowed into the United

States. For example, Taiwan, like most other Asian countries, was historically limited to a maximum of 100 immigrant visas per year. As a result, only 47 scientists and engineers immigrated to the United States from Taiwan in 1965. Two years later, the number had increased to 1,321 (Chang 1992).

The Hart-Celler Act thus created significant new opportunities for foreign-born engineers and other highly educated professionals whose skills were in short supply, as well as for their families and relatives. The great majority of these new skilled immigrants were of Asian origin, and they settled disproportionately on the West Coast of the United States. By 1990, one-quarter of the engineers and scientists employed in California's technology industries were foreign-born—more than twice that of other highly industrialized states such as Massachusetts and Texas. The Immigration and Nationality Act of 1990 further favored the immigration of engineers by almost tripling the number of visas granted on the basis of occupational skills from 54,000 to 140,000 annually. In so doing, it fueled the already burgeoning Asian immigration to urban centers such as Los Angeles and San Francisco.

These changes in the immigration system coincided with the growth of a new generation of high-technology industries in Silicon Valley and in turn transformed the regional workforce. Silicon Valley's pioneers in the 1950s and 1960s were virtually all white engineers from the East and Midwest. As the demand for skilled labor in the region's emerging electronics industries exploded during the 1970s and 1980s, so too did immigration.[1] By 1990 one-third of Silicon Valley's scientists and engineers were immigrants. Of those, almost two-thirds were Asians—and the majority were of Chinese and Indian descent. In fact, according to the 1990 census, more than half of the Asian-born engineers in the region were of Chinese (51 percent) or Indian (23 percent) origin, and the balance included relatively small numbers of Vietnamese (13 percent), Filipinos (6 percent), Japanese (4 percent), and Koreans (3 percent). The disproportionate representation of Chinese and Indian engineers in Silicon Valley's technology workforce explains the focus on these two groups in the balance of this chapter. Although we must await the 2000 census for more recent data on skilled immigrants in the technology workforce, immigration to the region accelerated markedly during the 1990s. The Asian population in Santa Clara County alone increased by 24 percent between 1990 and 1996, with more than 60,000 net new Asian migrants to the region—a significant proportion of whom were undoubtedly foreign-born professionals, as a result of the higher limits established by the Immigration and Nationality Act of 1990 (State of California, Department of Finance 1996).

The Chinese engineering workforce in Silicon Valley was initially dominated by Taiwanese immigrants, although mainland Chinese engineers are a fast-growing presence in the region. In the 1970s and 1980s more than one-third of the region's Chinese immigrant engineers were of Taiwanese origin. This strong Taiwanese presence has had important implications for both Silicon Valley and Taiwan. It has also distinguished the region's Chinese community from the less educated, more established mainland and Hong Kong–born community in San Francisco's Chinatown.

The increased presence of mainland Chinese engineers during the 1990s is difficult to document but quite visible in Silicon Valley. One indicator is the shifting balance of graduate degrees to foreign-born students. The University of California at Berkeley, for example, granted graduate degrees in science and engineering to a fast-increasing proportion of students from mainland China, whereas the proportion granted to students from Taiwan declined correspondingly in the same period. By the mid-1990s, more than half of the degrees were granted to students from China, compared to only 10 percent in the early 1980s. The number of graduate degrees granted can be seen as a leading indicator of labor supply in Silicon Valley, as most graduates find jobs in the region's technology companies.

National trends in graduate science and engineering education mirror these trends. Between 1990 and 1996, the number of doctorates in science and engineering granted annually by U.S. universities to immigrants from China more than tripled (from 477 to 1,680), and those to Indian immigrants doubled (to 692), whereas those to Taiwanese remained stable (at about 300). These three immigrant groups alone accounted for 62 percent of all doctorates in science and engineering granted to foreigners in the United States between 1985 and 1996 (Johnson 1998). Moreover, California's universities grant engineering degrees to Asian students at more than twice the rate of universities in the rest of the nation. In short, we can expect the 2000 census to show a dramatic increase in mainland Chinese and Indian engineers in the Silicon Valley workforce since 1990.

In the 1970s and 1980s, many Chinese and Indian engineers in Silicon Valley claimed that a "glass ceiling" inhibited their professional advancement. A 1991 survey of Asian professionals in the region found that two-thirds of those working in the private sector believed that advancement to managerial positions was limited by race. This is striking, as Indian and Chinese workers in Silicon Valley are significantly better educated than their white counterparts. In 1990, 55 percent of Indian and 40 percent of Chinese technology workers in the region held graduate degrees, compared to only 18 percent of the white population. Moreover, concerns about a glass ceiling increased significantly with the age and experience of the respondents. This perception is consistent with the finding that Chinese and Indian engineers remain concentrated in professional rather than managerial positions, despite superior educational attainment. It is notable, however, that those surveyed attributed these limitations less to "racial prejudice and stereotypes" than to the perception of an "old boys' network that excludes Asians" and the "lack of role models" (AACI 1993).

Lester Lee, a native of Szechuan, China, who moved to Silicon Valley in 1958, describes the feeling of being an outsider that was common for Asian immigrants in that period. "When I first came to Silicon Valley," he remembers, "there were so few of us that if I saw another Chinese on the street I'd go over and shake his hand." This sense of being an outsider was reinforced in many ways. Lee notes, for example, that "nobody wanted to sell us [Chinese] houses in the 1960s."[2] Although immigrants like Lee typically held graduate degrees in engineering from U.S. universities and worked for mainstream technology companies, they often felt personally and professionally isolated.

Immigrants like Lee responded to the sense of exclusion from established business and social structures in two ways. Many responded individually by starting their own businesses. Lee became the region's first Chinese entrepreneur when he left Ampex in 1970 to start a company called Recortec. Entrepreneurship was an attractive option for early Chinese engineers, who often felt as if they were seen as "good work horses, and not race horses" or "good technicians, rather than managers." David Lee, for example, left Xerox in 1973 to start Qume after a less experienced outsider was hired as his boss. Lee was able to raise start-up capital from the mainstream venture capital community, but only on the condition that he hire a non-Asian president for his company. David Lam similarly left Hewlett-Packard in 1979 after being passed over for a promotion and started a semiconductor equipment manufacturing business,

Lam Research, which is now a publicly traded company with $1.3 billion in sales. Not surprisingly, these three have become community leaders and role models for subsequent generations of Chinese entrepreneurs.

As their communities grew during the 1970s and 1980s, these immigrants responded to the sense of professional and social exclusion in a second way as well—by organizing collectively.[3] They often found one another socially first, coming together to celebrate holidays and family events with others who spoke the same language and shared a similar culture and background. Over time, they turned the social networks to business purposes, creating professional associations to provide resources and support structures within their own communities. The institutions they created mirrored those created in an earlier generation by native engineers in the region. These two responses—the individual and the collective—are clearly interrelated.

The growth of immigrant entrepreneurship is one of the most dramatic changes in Silicon Valley in recent decades. In contrast to traditional immigrant entrepreneurs, who are concentrated in low-technology services and manufacturing sectors, these new immigrant entrepreneurs are a growing presence in the most technologically dynamic and globally competitive sectors of the Silicon Valley economy. One measure of the presence, and success, of immigrant entrepreneurship is the growing number of Chinese and Indian companies that are publicly traded. By 1999, Chinese immigrants had started more than 40 public technology companies in the region while their Indian counterparts had started more than 25. The existence of so many immigrant-run publicly traded companies suggests a significantly larger population of private, immigrant-founded companies.

It is difficult to get accurate data on broader trends in immigrant entrepreneurship. One can estimate the trends, however, by identifying all Silicon Valley businesses run by CEOs with Chinese and Indian surnames in a Dun & Bradstreet database of technology firms started. According to this count, close to one-quarter (24 percent) of Silicon Valley's technology firms started between 1980 and 1998 had Chinese or Indian executives. Of the 11,443 high-technology firms started during this period, 2,001 (17 percent) were run by Chinese and 774 (7 percent) by Indians. These numbers may understate the scale of immigrant entrepreneurship in the region because firms started by Chinese or Indians with non-Asian CEOs are not counted. Interviews suggest that this

Table 12.1 Chinese- and Indian-Run Companies as Share of Total Silicon Valley High-Technology Start-Ups, 1980–1998

	1980–84		1985–1989		1990–94		1995–98	
	NO.	%	NO.	%	NO.	%	NO.	%
Indian	47	3	90	4	252	7	385	9
Chinese	121	9	347	15	724	19	809	20
Other	1,181	88	1,827	81	2,787	74	2,869	71
Total	1,349	100	2,264	100	3,763	100	4,063	100

SOURCE: Dun & Bradstreet database, 1998.

has frequently been the case in Silicon Valley, where venture capital financing has often been tied to the requirement that non-Asian senior executives be hired. This seems a more likely source of bias than the opposite scenario, that is, firms started by non-Asians that hire a Chinese or Indian CEO.

These businesses are creating significant wealth and employment in Silicon Valley. In 1998, these companies collectively accounted for more than $16.8 billion in sales and 58,282 jobs. Moreover, the rate of immigrant entrepreneurship in Silicon Valley has increased significantly over time. Chinese and Indians were at the helm of 13 percent of Silicon Valley's technology companies between 1980 and 1984, but they were running 29 percent of the region's high-technology companies started between 1995 and 1998 (see Table 12.1). The following sections suggest that the growth of entrepreneurship has been fueled both by the emergence of role models and by supportive networks within the ethnic communities in the region, as well as by growing ties to Asian markets and sources of capital and manufacturing capabilities.

THE ORIGINS OF SILICON VALLEY'S ETHNIC NETWORKS

The previous section portrays Chinese and Indian entrepreneurs as individuals or as collections of unrelated individuals. This conforms to the popular image of the entrepreneur as a lone pioneer. In reality, however, Silicon Valley's immigrant entrepreneurs—like their mainstream counterparts—rely on a diverse range of informal social structures and institutions to support their entrepreneurial activities. During the 1970s and 1980s, Asian immigrants in Silicon Valley saw themselves as outsiders to the region's mainstream technology community, and they created social and professional networks among themselves on the basis of shared language, culture, and educational and professional experiences.

Scholars have documented nonmarket mechanisms, or "ethnic strategies," ranging from information sharing and labor pooling to rotating credit associations, that immigrants use to mobilize the resources needed to build successful businesses (Portes 1995; Light and Bonacich 1988; Waldinger and Bozorgmehr 1996). Yet this literature locates immigrant entrepreneurs almost exclusively in sectors that are marginal to the mainstream economy, such as restaurants, small-scale retail, and garment manufacturing. These industries are typically characterized by low barriers to entry, minimal skill requirements, and limited technical change. Although the mobilization of ethnic resources in such communities allows immigrants to make more economic progress than they would as individuals, this progress tends to be limited by their location in peripheral, low-productivity segments of the economy.

Silicon Valley's new immigrant entrepreneurs, by contrast, are highly educated professionals who are active in dynamic and technologically sophisticated industries. It might appear that the ethnic strategies used by less-skilled immigrants would be irrelevant to these university graduates who possess the language and technical skills as well as the credentials needed to succeed as individuals. Yet as the region's Chinese and Indian engineering communities have grown, their associational activities have multiplied as well. This section describes how Silicon Valley's immigrant engineers rely on local social and professional networks to mobilize the information, know-how, skill, and capital needed to start technology firms. In so doing, they have enhanced their own entrepreneurial opportunities as well as the dynamism of the regional economy.

Table 12.2 lists the professional and technical associations organized by Silicon Valley's Chinese and Indian immigrant engineers during the 1980s and 1990s.[4] These organizations are among the most vibrant and active professional associations in the region, with memberships ranging from several hundred in the newest to more than one thousand in the established organizations. Although this study focuses on Chinese and Indians, the phenomenon of ethnic networking and mutual support among skilled immigrants in Silicon Valley is not limited to these groups. There are now professional associations or less formal forums for networking among the region's Iranian, Korean, Japanese, Israeli, French, Filipino, and Singaporean immigrant engineers.

These associations combine elements of traditional immigrant culture with distinctly high-technology practices: they simultaneously create ethnic identities within the region and facilitate the professional networking and information exchange that aid success in the highly mobile Silicon Valley economy. They are not traditional political or lobbying organizations. With the exception of the Asian American Manufacturers Association (AAMA), the activities of these groups are oriented exclusively to fostering the professional and technical advancement of their members.

It is notable that the region's Chinese and Indian immigrants have organized separately from one another—as well as from Silicon Valley's mainstream professional and technical associations, such as the American Electronics Association, the Institute of Electrical and Electronic Engineers, and the Software Entrepreneurs Forum. They also join the mainstream organizations, to be sure, but they appear to be less active in these than they are in the ethnic associations. There is virtually no overlap in the membership of Indian and Chinese professional associations, although there appears to be considerable overlap within the separate communities, particularly the Chinese, with its multiplicity of specialized associations.

There are ethnic distinctions within the Chinese technology community as well. The Monte Jade Science and Technology Association and the North American Taiwanese Engineers Association, for example, use Mandarin (Chinese) at many meetings and social events—which excludes not only non-Chinese members, but even Chinese from Hong Kong or Southeast Asia who speak Cantonese. More recently, immigrants from mainland China have spawned a whole new generation of associations, sometimes replicating existing Taiwanese organizations, as in the case of the North American Chinese Semiconductor Association (mainlanders) and the Chinese American Semiconductor Professionals Association (Taiwanese).

In spite of the distinct ethnic subcultures and the greater number and specialization of the Chinese associations, these associations share important functions. All mix socializing—over Chinese banquets, Indian dinners, or family-

Table 12.2 Indian and Chinese Professional Associations in Silicon Valley

Name	Year founded	Membership	Description
INDIAN			
Silicon Valley Indian Professionals Association (SIPA)	1991	1,000	Forum for expatriate Indians to contribute to cooperation between United States and India. Web site: www.sipa.org
The Indus Entrepreneur (TiE)	1992	560	Fosters entrepreneurship by providing mentorship and resources. Web site: www.tie.org
CHINESE			
Chinese Institute of Engineers (CIE/USA)	1979	1,000	Promotes communication and interchange of information among Chinese engineers and scientists. Web site: www.cie-sf.org
Asian American Manufacturers Association (AAMA)	1980	> 700	Promotes the growth and success of U.S. technology enterprises throughout the Pacific Rim. Web site: www.aamasv.com
Chinese Software Professionals Association (CSPA)	1988	1,400	Promotes technology collaboration and facilitates information exchange in the software profession. Web site: www.cspa.com
Chinese American Computer Corporation (NBI)	1988	270 corporate members	Mid-technology cluster of PC clone system sellers, majority from Taiwan. Web site: www.killerapp.com/nbi
Monte Jade Science and Technology Association (MJSTA)	1989	150 corporate, 300 individual	Promotes the cooperation and mutual flow of technology and investment between Taiwan and the United States. Web site: http://montejade.org

centered social events—with support for professional and technical advancement. Each organization, either explicitly or informally, provides first-generation immigrants with a source of professional contacts and networks within the local technology community. They serve as important sources of labor market information and recruitment channels and they provide role models of successful immigrant entrepreneurs and managers. In addition, the associations sponsor regular speakers and conferences that provide forums for sharing specialized technical and market information as well as basic information about the nuts and bolts of entrepreneurship and management for engineers with limited business experience. In addition to providing sessions on how to write a busi-

Table 12.2 *(continued)*

Name	Year founded	Membership	Description
		CHINESE	
Silicon Valley Chinese Engineers Association (SCEA)	1989	400	Network of mainland Chinese engineers to promote entrepreneurship and professionalism among members and establish ties to China. Web site: www.scea.org
Chinese American Semiconductor Professionals Association (CASPA)	1991	1,600	Promotes technical, communication, information exchange, and collaboration among semiconductor professionals. Web site: www.caspa.com
North America Taiwanese Engineers Association (NATEA)	1991	400	Promotes exchange of scientific and technical information. Web site: http://natea.org
Chinese Information and Networking Association (CINA)	1992	700	Chinese professionals who advocate technologies and business opportunities in information industries. Web site: www.cina.org
Chinese Internet Technology Association (CITA)	1996	600	Forum and network for Chinese Internet professionals and entrepreneurs to incubate ideas, learn from each other, and form potential partnerships. Web site: www.cita.net
North America Chinese Semiconductor Association (NACSA)	1996	600	Professional advancement in semiconductor sector, interaction between the United States and China. Web site: www.nacsa.com

SOURCE: Interviews.

ness plan or manage a business, some of the Chinese associations give seminars on English communication, negotiation skills, and stress management.

Many of these associations have become important forums for cross-generational investment and mentoring as well. An older generation of successful immigrant engineers and entrepreneurs in both the Chinese and the Indian communities now plays an active role in financing and mentoring younger generations of co-ethnic entrepreneurs. Individuals within these networks often invest individually or jointly in promising new ventures, acting as "angel" investors who are more accessible to immigrants than the mainstream venture capital community and who are also willing to invest smaller amounts of money. The goal of The Indus Entrepreneur (TiE), for example, is to "foster entrepreneurship by providing mentorship and resources" within the South Asian technology community. Similarly, both the AAMA and the Monte Jade Science and Technology Association now sponsor annual investment conferences aimed at matching potential investors (often from Asia as well as Silicon Valley) with promising Chinese entrepreneurs.

This is not to suggest that these associations create entirely self-contained ethnic businesses or communities. Many Chinese and Indian immigrants socialize primarily within the ethnic networks, but they routinely work with native engineers and native-run businesses. In fact, there is growing recognition within these communities that although a start-up might be spawned with the support of the ethnic networks, it needs to become part of the mainstream to grow. It appears that the most successful immigrant entrepreneurs in Silicon Valley today are those who have drawn on ethnic resources while simultaneously integrating into mainstream technology and business networks.[5]

THE GLOBALIZATION OF SILICON VALLEY'S ETHNIC NETWORKS

At the same time that Silicon Valley's immigrant entrepreneurs organized local professional networks, they were also building ties back to their home countries. The region's Chinese engineers constructed a vibrant two-way bridge connecting the technology communities in Silicon Valley and Taiwan; their Indian counterparts became key middlemen linking U.S. businesses to low-cost software expertise in India. These cross-Pacific networks represent more than an additional "ethnic resource" that supports entrepreneurial success; rather, they provide the region's skilled immigrants with an important advantage over their mainstream competitors who often lack the language skills, cultural know-how, and contacts to build business relationships in Asia.

The traditional image of the immigrant economy is the isolated Chinatown or "ethnic enclave" with limited ties to the outside economy. Silicon Valley's new immigrant entrepreneurs, by contrast, are increasingly building professional and social networks that span national boundaries and facilitate flows of capital, skill, and technology. In so doing, they are creating transnational communities that provide the shared information, contacts, and trust that allow local producers to participate in an increasingly global economy (Portes 1996).

As recently as the 1970s, only very large corporations had the resources and capabilities to grow internationally, and they did so primarily by establishing marketing offices or branch plants overseas. Today, by contrast, new transportation and communications technologies allow even the smallest firms to build partnerships with foreign producers to tap overseas expertise, cost-savings, and markets. Start-ups in Silicon Valley today are often global actors from the day they begin operations: many raise capital from Asian sources, others subcontract manufacturing to Taiwan or rely on software development in India, and virtually all sell their products in Asian markets.

The scarce resource in this new environment is the ability to locate foreign partners quickly and to manage complex business relationships across cultural and linguistic boundaries. This is particularly a challenge in high-technology industries in which products, markets, and technologies are continually being redefined—and where product cycles are routinely shorter than nine months. First-generation immigrants, like the Chinese and Indian engineers of Silicon Valley, who have the language and cultural as well as the technical skills to function well in both the United States and foreign markets, are distinctly positioned to play a central role in this environment. They are creating social structures that enable even the smallest producers to locate and maintain mutually beneficial collaborations across long distances and that facilitate access to Asian sources of capital, manufacturing capabilities, skills, and markets.

These ties have measurable economic benefits. Researchers at the University of California at Berkeley have documented a significant correlation between the presence of first-generation immigrants from a given country and exports from California. (For every 1 percent increase in the number of first-generation immigrants from a given country, exports from California to that country go up nearly 0.5 percent.) Moreover, this effect is especially pronounced in the Asia-Pacific region where, all other things being equal, California exports nearly four times more than it exports to comparable countries in other parts of the world (Bardhan and Howe 1998).

Silicon Valley's immigrant entrepreneurs have helped to construct these new transnational (and typically transregional) networks. Taiwanese engineers have

forged close social and economic ties to their counterparts in the Hsinchu region of Taiwan—the area, comparable in size to Silicon Valley, that extends
from Taipei to the Hsinchu Science-Based Industrial Park and is the home of
some nine hundred technology companies. They have created a rich fabric of
professional and business relationships that supports a two-way process of reciprocal industrial upgrading. Silicon Valley's Indian engineers, by contrast,
play a more arm's-length role as middlemen linking U.S.-based companies
with low-cost software expertise in localities like Bangalore and Hyderabad. In
both cases, the immigrant engineers provide the critical contacts, information,
and cultural know-how that link dynamic—but distant—regions in the global
economy.

THE SILICON VALLEY—HSINCHU CONNECTION

In the 1960s and 1970s, the relationship between Taiwan and the United
States was a textbook First World–Third World relationship. American businesses invested in Taiwan primarily to take advantage of its low-wage manufacturing labor. Meanwhile, Taiwan's best and brightest engineering students
came to the United States for graduate education and created a classic "brain
drain" when they chose to stay to pursue professional opportunities here.
Many ended up in Silicon Valley.

This relationship has changed significantly during the past decade. By the
late 1980s, engineers began returning to Taiwan in large numbers, drawn by
active government recruitment and the opportunities created by rapid economic development. At the same time, a growing cohort of highly mobile engineers began to work in both the United States and Taiwan, commuting
across the Pacific regularly. Typically Taiwan-born, U.S.-educated engineers,
these "astronauts" have the professional contacts and language skills to function efficiently in both the Silicon Valley and Taiwanese business cultures and
to draw on the complementary strengths of the two regional economies.

K. Y. Han is typical.[6] After graduating from National Taiwan University in
the 1970s, Han completed a master's degree in solid state physics at the University of California at Santa Barbara. Like many Taiwanese engineers, Han
was drawn to Silicon Valley in the early 1980s and worked for nearly a decade

at a series of local semiconductor companies before joining his college class-mate and friend, Jimmy Lee, to start Integrated Silicon Solutions, Inc. (ISSI). After bootstrapping the initial start-up with their own funds and those of other Taiwanese colleagues, they raised more than $9 million in venture capital. Their lack of managerial experience meant that Lee and Han were unable to raise funds from Silicon Valley's mainstream venture capital community. The early rounds of funding were thus exclusively from Asian sources, including the Walden International Investment Group, a San Francisco–based venture fund that specializes in Asian investments, as well as from large industrial con-glomerates based in Singapore and Taiwan.

Han and Lee mobilized their professional and personal networks in both Taiwan and the United States to expand ISSI. They recruited engineers (many of whom were Chinese) in their Silicon Valley headquarters to focus on R&D, product design and development, and sales of their high-speed static random access memory chips (SRAMs). They targeted their products at the personal computer market, and many of their initial customers were Taiwanese moth-erboard producers, which allowed them to grow very rapidly in the first several years. And, with the assistance of the Taiwanese government, they established manufacturing partnerships with Taiwan's state-of-the-art semiconductor foundries and set up a facility in the Hsinchu Science-Based Industrial Park to oversee assembly, packaging, and testing.

By 1995, when ISSI was listed on NASDAQ, Han was visiting Taiwan at least monthly to monitor the firm's manufacturing operations and to work with newly formed subsidiaries in Hong Kong and mainland China. Finally, he joined thousands of other Silicon Valley "returnees" and moved his family back to Taiwan.[7] This allowed Han to strengthen the already close relationship with their main foundry, the Taiwan Semiconductor Manufacturing Corpo-ration, as well as to coordinate the logistics and production control process on a daily basis. The presence of a senior manager like Han also turned out to be an advantage for developing local customers. Han still spends an hour each day on the phone with Jimmy Lee, and he returns to Silicon Valley as often as ten times a year. Today ISSI has $110 million in sales and 500 employees world-wide, including 350 in Silicon Valley.

A closely knit community of Taiwanese returnees, "astronauts," and U.S.-based engineers and entrepreneurs like Jimmy Lee and K. Y. Han has become the bridge between Silicon Valley and Hsinchu. These social ties, which often build on pre-existing alumni relationships among graduates of Taiwan's elite engineering universities, were institutionalized in 1989 with the formation of the Monte Jade Science and Technology Association. Monte Jade's goal is the promotion of business cooperation, investment, and technology transfer between Chinese engineers in the Bay Area and Taiwan. Although the organization remains private, it works closely with local representatives of the Taiwanese government to encourage mutually beneficial investments and business collaborations. Monte Jade's social activities, like those of Silicon Valley's other ethnic associations, are often as important as its professional activities. The annual conference draws more than one thousand attendees for a day of technical and business analysis and a banquet.

This transnational community has accelerated the upgrading of Taiwan's technological infrastructure by transferring technical know-how and organizational models as well as by forging closer ties with Silicon Valley. Observers note, for example, that management practices in Hsinchu companies are more like those of Silicon Valley than of the traditional family-firm model that dominates older industries in Taiwan. As a result, Taiwan is now the world's largest producer of notebook computers and a range of related PC components, including motherboards, monitors, scanners, power supplies, and keyboards.[8] In addition, Taiwan's semiconductor and integrated circuit manufacturing capabilities are now on a par with the leading Japanese and U.S. producers; and its flexible and efficient networks of specialized small and medium-sized enterprises coordinate the diverse components of this sophisticated infrastructure.

Taiwan has also become an important source of capital for Silicon Valley start-ups—particularly those started by immigrant entrepreneurs who historically lacked contacts in the mainstream venture capital community. It is impossible to accurately estimate the total flow of capital from Taiwan to Silicon Valley because so much of it is invested informally by individual angel investors, but there is no doubt that it increased dramatically in the 1990s. Most observers estimate that formal investments from Asian sources (not including Japan) exceeded $500 million in 1997.[9] These investors often provide more than capital. According to Ken Tai, a founder of Acer and now head of venture fund InveStar Capital, "When we invest we are also helping bring entrepreneurs back to Taiwan. It is relationship building. . . . We help them get high level introductions to foundries (for manufacturing) and we help establish strategic opportunities and relationships with customers."[10]

The growing integration of the technological communities of Silicon Valley and Hsinchu offers substantial benefits to both economies. Silicon Valley remains the center of new product definition and design and development of leading-edge technologies, whereas Taiwan offers world-class manufacturing, flexible development and integration, and access to key customers and markets in China and Southeast Asia. This appears a classic case of the economic benefits of comparative advantage. However, these economic gains from specialization and trade would not be possible without the underlying social structures and institutions provided by the community of Taiwanese engineers, which insures continuous flows of information between the two regions. Some say that Taiwan is like an extension of Silicon Valley, or that there is a "very small world" between Silicon Valley and Taiwan.

The reciprocal and decentralized nature of these relationships is distinctive. The ties between Japan and the United States in the 1980s were typically arm's-length, and technology transfers between large firms were managed from the top down. The Silicon Valley–Hsinchu relationship, by contrast, consists of formal and informal collaborations between individual investors and entrepreneurs, small and medium-sized firms, as well as divisions of larger companies located on both sides of the Pacific. In this complex mix, the rich social and professional ties among Taiwanese engineers and their U.S. counterparts are as important as the more formal corporate alliances and partnerships.

BANGALORE'S SOFTWARE BOOM

Radha Basu left her conservative South Indian family to pursue graduate studies in computer science at the University of Southern California in the early 1970s. Like many other skilled immigrants, she was subsequently drawn into the fast-growing Silicon Valley labor market, where she began a long career at Hewlett-Packard (HP). When Basu returned to India to participate in an electronics industry task force in the mid-1980s, the government invited her to set up one of the country's first foreign subsidiaries. She spent four years establishing HP's software center in Bangalore—pioneering the trend among foreign companies of tapping India's highly skilled but relatively low-cost software talent. When Basu returned to Silicon Valley in 1989 the HP office in India employed four hundred people, and it has since grown to become one of HP's most successful foreign subsidiaries.

Radha Basu was uniquely positioned to negotiate the complex and often bewildering bureaucracy and the backward infrastructure of her home country. She explains that it takes both patience and cultural understanding to do business in India: "You can't just fly in and out and stay in a five-star hotel and expect to get things done like you can elsewhere. You have to understand India and its development needs and adapt to them."[11] Many Indian engineers followed Basu's lead in the early 1990s: they exploited their cultural and linguistic capabilities and their contacts to help build software operations in their home country. Indians educated in the United States have been pivotal in setting up the Indian software facilities for Oracle, Novell, Bay Networks, and other Silicon Valley companies.

However, few Indian engineers choose to live and work permanently in India. Unlike the Taiwanese immigrants who have increasingly returned home to start businesses or to work in established companies, Indian engineers—if they return at all—typically do so on a temporary basis. This is due in part to the difference in standards of living, but most observers agree that the frustrations associated with doing business in India are equally important. Radha Basu explains that the first HP office in India consisted of a telex machine on her dining room table, and that for many years she had to produce physical evidence of software exports for customs officials who did not understand how the satellite datalink worked. She adds that when the Indian government talked about a "single window of clearance" to facilitate foreign trade, she would joke, "where is the window?"[12]

Business conditions have improved dramatically in India since Basu arrived. The establishment of the Software Technology Parks (STPs) scheme in the late 1980s gave export-oriented software firms in designated zones tax exemptions for five years and guaranteed access to high-speed satellite links and reliable electricity. The national economic liberalization that began in 1991 greatly improved the climate for the software industry as well. Yet even today, expatriates complain bitterly about complex bureaucratic restrictions, corrupt and unresponsive officials, and an infrastructure that causes massive daily frustrations—from unreliable power supplies, water shortages, and backward and extremely costly telecommunications facilities to dangerous and congested highways.

In contrast to the close collaboration between Taiwan's policymakers and U.S.-based engineers, there has been very little communication between Silicon Valley's Indian engineers and India's policymakers—even those concerned directly with technology policy. Moreover, young engineers in India prefer to work for U.S. multinationals because they are seen as a ticket to Silicon Valley: software companies in Bangalore report turnovers of 20–30 percent per year, primarily because so many workers jump at the first opportunity to emigrate. Of course, some U.S.-educated Indians return home and stay, but, on balance, the "brain drain" of skilled workers to the United States continued throughout the 1990s.

Silicon Valley's Indian engineers thus play an important, but largely arm's-length, role in connecting U.S. firms with India's low-cost, high-quality skill. Although some, like Basu, have returned to establish subsidiaries, most do little more than promote India as a viable location for software development. As they became more visible in U.S. companies during the 1990s, Indians working in U.S. companies were increasingly instrumental in convincing senior management in their firms to source software or establish operations in India. The cost differential remains a motivating factor for such moves: wages for software programmers and systems analysts are ten times lower in India, and the fully loaded cost of an engineer is 35–40 percent what it is in the United States.

The availability of skill is, of course, the essential precondition for considering India; and it is of growing importance for Silicon Valley firms facing shortages of skilled labor. The low wages are a viable trade-off for working in an environment plagued by chronic infrastructural problems. In addition, the time difference makes it possible to work around the clock, with programmers in India logging on to a customer's computers to perform relatively routine testing, coding, or programming tasks once a U.S.-based team has left for the day.

As a result, most economic relations between Silicon Valley and regions like Bangalore are still conducted primarily by individuals within the large American or Indian corporations. There are few Taiwan-style "astronauts" or U.S.-educated engineers who have their feet sufficiently in both worlds to transfer the information and know-how about new markets and technologies or to build the long-term relationships that would contribute to the upgrading of India's technological infrastructure. And there are no institutionalized mechanisms—either public or private—that would both facilitate and reinforce the creation of more broad-based interactions between the two regions.

Communications between the engineering communities in India and the United States are growing fast, however, especially among the younger generation. Alumni associations from the elite Indian Institutes of Technology (who have many graduates in Silicon Valley) are starting to play a bridging role by organizing seminars and social events. A growing number of U.S.-educated Indians report a desire to return home, while others have left the large Indian companies to try their hand at entrepreneurship in Silicon Valley. In short, there is a small but growing technical community linking Silicon Valley and Bangalore—one that could play an important role in upgrading the Indian software industry in the future.

CONCLUSION

Skilled immigrants are an increasingly important, but largely unrecognized, asset for the Silicon Valley economy. Over the past decade, Chinese and Indian engineers have started hundreds of technology businesses in the region. These new immigrant entrepreneurs have generated jobs, exports, and wealth for the region, and they have simultaneously accelerated the integration of California into the global economy. The long-distance social and economic linkages they are constructing contribute at least as importantly to the region's economic dynamism as the more direct job and wealth creation.

These emerging global ties allow start-ups and established firms in Silicon Valley to continue to flourish in spite of growing labor shortages at home. They have also accelerated the industrial upgrading of regions in India and Taiwan. The challenge of economic development in coming decades will increasingly involve building such transnational (or translocal) social and professional linkages. The rapid growth of Israel's technology industry, for example, has been coordinated by networks of returning Israeli engineers and venture capitalists, and parallels the Taiwanese experience in many respects (Autler 1999).

This research underscores important changes in the relationship between immigration, trade, and economic development in the 1990s. In the past, the primary economic linkages created by immigrants to their countries of origin were the remittances they sent to those left behind. Today, however, growing numbers of skilled immigrants return to their home countries after studying and working abroad, and even those who stay often become part of transnational communities linking the United States to the economies of distant regions. The new immigrant entrepreneurs thus foster economic development directly, by creating new jobs and wealth, as well as indirectly, by coordinating the information flows and providing the linguistic and cultural know-how that promote trade and investment flows with their home countries.

Economic openness has its costs, to be sure, but the strength of the U.S. economy has historically derived from its openness and diversity—and this will be increasingly true as the economy becomes more global. The experience of Silicon Valley's new immigrant entrepreneurs suggests that we should resist the assumption that immigration and trade are zero-sum processes. We need to encourage the continued immigration of skilled workers, while simultaneously devoting resources to improving education and training for native workers.

The fastest growing groups of immigrant engineers in Silicon Valley today are from mainland China and India. The mainland Chinese, in particular, are increasingly visible in the computer science and engineering departments of local universities as well as in the workforces of the region's established companies. Although still relative newcomers to Silicon Valley, they appear poised to follow the trajectory of their Taiwanese predecessors. Some have started their own companies. And they are already building ties back home, encouraged by the active efforts of Chinese bureaucrats and universities—and by the powerful incentive provided by the promise of the China market. Ties between Silicon Valley and India will almost certainly continue to expand as well. Reversal of the "brain drain" is not yet on the horizon, but a younger generation of Indian engineers now expresses a desire to return home, which distinguishes them from many of their predecessors.

Whether the emerging connections between Silicon Valley and regions in

China and India will generate broader ties that contribute to industrial upgrading in these nations—as well as creating new markets and partners for Silicon Valley producers—will depend largely on political and economic developments within those nations. Whatever the outcome, the task for policymakers remains to maintain open boundaries so that regions like Silicon Valley continue to both build and benefit from their growing ties to the Asian economy.

III

A Clustered Community

Valley lawyer's role during the start-up process, including helping entrepreneurs avoid early mistakes, serving as gatekeepers, evaluating business strategy, and more.

Intimate involvement in the process and outcome of decision making for firms is a theme expanded on by Thomas Friel (Chapter 17), an experienced matchmaker between high-level executives and high-level jobs. In executive search, as in other service areas, local practitioners have broken new ground to serve the distinct needs of Valley firms. Friel discusses pioneering efforts in employee benefits, both formal and informal, especially in complex compensation packages involving equity.

James Atwell's depiction of his expansive accounting practice (Chapter 18) shows a consultant working creatively with clients on how to move across never-before-mapped terrain, rather than someone simply applying accounting rules. This presents a challenge and an opportunity for accountants in Silicon Valley, where official rules and regulations of the SEC and Financial Accounting Standards Board are often a step behind the latest business models. As Atwell illustrates, whether evaluating an acquisition, working with new equity financing, guiding firms in revenue recognition, or preparing for an IPO, accountants can add value—both financially and in terms of know-how—for entrepreneurs.

The section concludes with Regis McKenna's "Free Advice: Consulting the Silicon Valley Way," (Chapter 19), which highlights a prevailing feature of the Valley's habitat: the free circulation of information. This free flow underscores the defining features of the Valley's clustered community: dense networks of relationships, collaborative and ongoing advice, and highly productive and innovative practice.

13

Venture Capitalists

The Coaches of Silicon Valley

THOMAS F. HELLMANN

What do Cisco Systems, Genentech, Intel, Sun Microsystems, and Yahoo! all have in common? Apart from being household names of successful Silicon Valley companies, a commonality among all of these companies is that they were financed by venture capital. The financing of start-ups by venture capitalists is a central ingredient in the economic success of Silicon Valley. Although twenty years ago the term "venture capital" was hardly known outside its little industry, venture capital today has become a widely talked about phenomenon.

What is venture capital? While there is no precise definition, a reasonable approximation might be "professionally managed, equity-like financing of young, growth-oriented private companies." Three things are worth noting here. First, venture capital is professionally managed money. Although venture capitalists are sometimes portrayed as freewheeling risk seekers, the truth of the matter is that they are professionals who invest on behalf of a set of investors in a well-defined and structured fashion. Second, venture capitalists hold equity-like instruments. Although there may be some complexity to the deal structure, an essential element is that they participate directly in the business risk of the companies they finance. Accordingly, venture capital involves not only the spectacular financial returns that get reported in the press, but also significant risk. Third, venture capitalists typically invest in young companies, often those that have yet to reach profitability, sell any product, or even have a product developed. Venture capitalists, however, do not invest in what would commonly be called "small businesses." Indeed, they are only interested in firms that are willing to follow an aggressive (albeit risky) growth path. Put simply, venture capitalists invest in infant giants, not small firms.

What role has venture capital played in the extraordinary success of Silicon Valley companies? To use a sports analogy, entrepreneurs are like athletes, who compete in the actual game and get the glory if they win. The venture capitalists are like the coaches, who choose which athletes get to play, who train and motivate them, and who try to create the most favorable conditions for them to succeed. Without coaches, inexperienced athletes would spend extraordinary effort on the wrong tasks. Similarly, venture capitalists can provide the mentoring and guidance that helps the entrepreneurs to turn their efforts into successes.[1]

How many of these coaches are there? Until recently, the venture capital industry was quite a small industry. In 1980 the total amount of money newly invested by venture capitalists was estimated at $610 million. By 1990 this figure had increased to $2.3 billion, and in 1998 it reached $12.5 billion. The number of companies that received venture capital similarly rose, from 504 in 1980 to 1,176 in 1990 and 1,824 in 1998. This explosion is all the more remarkable given the limited focus of venture capital. The two main industry segments that venture capitalists invest in are information technology (such as computers, telecommunications, semiconductors, and, recently, Internet companies) and life sciences (mainly biotechnology, medical instruments, and medical services). Outside the two main sectors, venture capitalists make relatively few investments, mostly in consumer services. The coaches of Silicon Valley are remarkably focused, only coaching those ventures that they can truly understand and for which they can provide some added value.[2]

And where can we find these coaches? Even though it wasn't invented there, venture capital has grown most significantly in Silicon Valley, arguably the most dynamic center for innovative activity in the world. In 1998, 46 percent of all investments were made in California, the lion's share in Silicon Valley. The next important state was Massachusetts (with its Route 128), accounting for 12 percent of investment. Outside the United States, venture capital is much smaller. In Asia, Japan and China (including Hong Kong) are the largest markets, with $992 million and $998 million invested in 1997 respectively. Like other large Asian countries, India has only a tiny venture capital market ($101 million). The total Asian venture capital market amounted to $4.6 billion in 1997, although this was a 17 percent drop from the previous year, reflecting the "Asian Flu." The numbers have to be interpreted with care, however, because the definition of venture capital varies across different countries.[3]

What companies receive this kind of coaching? Venture capitalists invest in young technology companies long before they reach the point of economic viability. In 1998, 11 percent of the number of deals (5 percent of total dollar investments) were provided to companies in the start-up phase, which includes firms at the idea stage as well as firms somewhat further along. Thirty-one percent of deals (33 percent of total dollar investments) went to companies at the development stage, those that have a clear notion of the technology and markets they want to target, but that have not yet completed their product development. Fifty-four percent of deals (59 percent of total dollar investments) went to companies that were shipping their product, but that had not yet reached profitability. Only 4 percent of the companies were profitable at the time they received venture capital financing.

But these numbers alone cannot convey the distinctive qualities of venture capital financing.[4] Venture capital is a unique method of financing that is very different from traditional bank financing or market financing from stock or bond markets. In fact, it can be argued that the distinctive feature of venture capital isn't really the mere provision of money. The following section therefore discusses the close relationship between venture capitalists and start-ups, and how venture capitalists select companies and then guide them through the early stages of development. Sports coaches may well participate a little in the profits, but they are not the ultimate owners of teams. Similarly, venture capitalists, although well compensated, are ultimately working with other people's money. The relationship between venture capitalists and their own fund providers is discussed in the next section. Finally, the success of any team does not depend only on the coach: the coaches themselves depend on a whole network of other helpers. Similarly, Silicon Valley provides a unique infrastructure and network, which allows venture capitalists to do their business more efficiently. The fourth section thus discusses how venture capitalists benefit from (and contribute to) the Silicon Valley environment. The fifth section concludes with some speculation on the future of the venture capital industry.

VENTURE CAPITALISTS
AND THE COMPANIES THEY FINANCE

A lot of things must happen before a team can win and its coach can be celebrated. Many of these steps are rather mundane, yet all of them are necessary. Similarly, there are a number of important milestones that entrepreneurs and venture capitalists must pass before they can congratulate themselves on the creation of yet another successful company.

The first step for any athlete to get on the winning team is to be selected by the coach. Venture capitalists need to be extremely careful selecting companies to work with. First, they have to invest in ideas that they believe in, and that they can deeply understand. This requires coaches to be extremely qualified and up-to-date themselves. Second, it has to be worthwhile for a venture capitalist to coach a company. This means, first and foremost, that the company is pursuing a large opportunity. Some venture capitalists would say a rising tide lifts all boats. For this reason venture capitalists have been frantic to invest in Internet companies, mostly because they believe that the Internet has opened up vast new market opportunities. The converse argument is probably even more important: if a start-up isn't addressing a substantial market, it won't be able to generate substantial returns, no matter how hard it tries. But a large market alone is not enough. It is also necessary that the company be fast in order to take advantage of the opportunity before competition erodes all the potential profits. This is where the help of venture capital can become crucial.

But before the venture capitalist can move into action and coach the entrepreneurs, one more step is necessary. We know very well from professional sports that nothing happens unless there is a contract. Similarly, the entrepreneur and the venture capitalists must first agree on a deal that specifies not only the division of the financial rewards, but also their respective roles and control rights. Once we understand the varied interests and strengths of these two parties, it is easy to understand the type of financial contracts used.[5]

Fundamentally, venture capitalists invest in company stock; that is, they are equity holders who participate in the success of the company if it does well, but also bear the risk of poor performance.[6] This ensures that the incentives of the investors and entrepreneurs remain aligned as closely as possible.[7] Venture capitalists, however, rarely give a company all the money it needs to become self-reliant. Instead, they prefer to sequence their commitments through a number of smaller rounds. The terms of subsequent rounds are rarely fixed in the previous rounds, implying that competitive dynamics determine the price of subsequent rounds. It makes the fraction of shares retained by the entrepreneur highly contingent on performance, since a better performance is likely to get rewarded with better valuations for subsequent rounds of investment.[8] The staging of financing also gives investors a useful method of control, although it is only one of several control instruments. In particular, venture capitalists tend to have a strong representation on the board of directors and they hold a majority of voting rights, even if they only control a minority of the cash flow rights.

Once the contract is in place, the entrepreneur and the venture capitalist can look forward to a long relationship. As one venture capitalist used to say, "the average duration of a relationship between a venture capitalist and the entrepreneur is probably longer than the average duration of a marriage in California, and rarely less intense."

Consider the case of a young venture capitalist named Jeffrey Drazan, who identified a company called Centex Telemanagement (see Sahlman 1988). He saw a lot of potential in their concept, but many flaws in their strategy and the execution of the idea. He therefore spent considerable time helping the founders to create basic bookkeeping functions, improving the marketing approach, solving complex regulatory issues, and attracting talented employees and managers (including a new CEO) to the company. Without the interventions of Drazan the company would almost certainly have remained a minor player at best, but in fact it grew extremely fast and was acquired after four years at a substantial profit.

The business expertise provided by venture capitalists can often be a critical factor in the development of an entrepreneurial company. Venture capitalists can be helpful in shaping the overall strategy of the firm, often simply by mentoring the founders. Venture capitalists also play a crucial role in attracting talent into start-ups. Jim Barksdale had been the CEO of McCaw Cellular Communications and then AT&T Wireless Services, following the merger of AT&T and McCaw Cellular Communications. It was John Doerr who convinced him to leave that position to become first a board member and then the CEO of Netscape, all before the company was even one year old.

Having a network of business contacts thus helps venture capitalists identify potential talent for the company, and the presence of venture capital typically makes employees and executives more confident about leaving their current employment for the start-up. Some of the most prominent venture capital firms also leverage their networks to forge strategic alliances for their portfolio companies with other firms, sometimes other companies from their own portfolio. Kleiner Perkins, for example, prides itself on its "keiretsu" structure (named after the Japanese quasi-conglomerate structures), in which it tries to facilitate contacts between its portfolio companies. Indeed, the recent merger between Excite and @Home was largely engineered by Kleiner Perkins, which had been an investor in both companies.

Does coaching and support by venture capital truly help companies to perform better? To answer this fundamental question, Manju Puri and I set out to gather some systematic evidence of the impact of venture capital on the strategic performance of firms (see Hellmann and Puri 1999). We sampled more than 170 high-technology companies in Silicon Valley and gathered a large variety of data, both on their business plans and on what actually happened to the companies. We then subdivided these companies into two broad groups: those companies that pursued a truly innovative strategy, and those whose strategy was better characterized as differentiator or imitator. We first asked which group was more likely to obtain venture capital, and found that innovators were indeed more likely to obtain venture capital. Next we asked whether obtaining venture capital affected the subsequent performance of these firms. We noted that after obtaining venture capital, companies were indeed faster at bringing their product to market. Interestingly, this effect was particularly strong for innovator companies, for which the challenge of preempting the competition to establish first-mover advantages is of particular strategic importance. This kind of evidence clearly suggests that the claims about the importance of venture capital are not merely anecdotal, but are more generally valid.

The presence of an active venture capitalist can thus bring a lot of advantages to the start-up firms. But this does not exclude the possibility of conflict. One area of frequent conflict concerns the founders' role. Although company founders often have considerable talent for getting the company started, few prove to be able managers as their companies become much larger. I have mentioned that venture capitalists are instrumental in attracting senior managers, including CEOs, into start-ups, but what happens when the founders resist such change? A less publicized aspect of venture capital is the strong control exercised by venture capitalists over the companies they finance. In another study we performed (Hellmann and Puri 1999), we found that in more than half of all venture capital–backed companies, the founder was no longer the CEO by the time we observed them (when they were 6.5 years old, on average). While some of these departures appeared to be friendly (often with the founder remaining in the company), others essentially constituted the firing of the founder (although typically presented in more favorable language). Similarly, in the story of Centex Telemanagement, all four of the founders had left the company two years after the first venture capital investment. This control dimension of venture capital may seem surprising at first, but upon reflection it is clear that it is an integral part of a coaching relationship. Without control, the coaches risk not being heard and losing their money in the process. Many entrepreneurs are excessively concerned with control and often have difficulty fully comprehending the trade-off between owning and controlling a small firm, and owning a significant stake in a large firm but without control. The control held by venture capitalists allows firms to transcend their founders, so venture capital becomes an instrument of financing entrepreneurial companies, not just entrepreneurs.

VENTURE CAPITALISTS AND THEIR PROVIDERS OF FUNDS

Coaches don't own the sports teams they coach. Although typically well paid by the owners, the coaches are ultimately only hired help for the actual owners of a team. Similarly, the venture capital firms have their own owners, and the structure of the firms and the compensation of the venture capitalists have to be chosen appropriately. More than 80 percent of all venture capital funds are private independent funds. The ultimate investors in these funds are pension funds (37 percent), corporations (23 percent), foundations and endowments (16 percent), families and institutions (12 percent), and others (12 percent).[9] The largest investors are thus the pension funds, which are also often called "institutional investors." They consist of private pension funds (e.g., General Motors Pension fund), as well as public pension funds (e.g., CALPERS). They are primarily concerned with long-term capital gains, and investments in venture capital constitute only a small fraction of their overall investment portfolio. Foundations, endowments, families, and institutions have a similar investment orientation.

Although these investors thus have straightforward financial objectives, other venture capital funds are owned by corporations, which have their own distinct strategic goals. One example is "Adobe Ventures L.P.," a venture capital fund financed by the software maker Adobe, but run by Hambrecht & Quist, a prestigious investment bank with a reputable venture capital division. Another well-known example is the Java fund, a venture capital fund operated by Kleiner Perkins, but financed by a consortium of eleven corporations that all shared a strategic interest in promoting Java as a new platform for software development. A close examination of the Java fund, however, reveals some of the potential problems for corporations making strategic investments through venture capital funds. The Java fund was designed to invest in companies that have some Java developments. One of the companies, Calico Technologies, although initially experimenting with Java, frequently found it in its best interests to develop applications based on the Microsoft NT platform, the direct competitor of Java. As a venture capitalist interested in maximizing fund returns, Kleiner Perkins would have no interest in dissuading the company from doing so, but for the eleven funding companies this investment might not have had the desired strategic effect. Indeed, in order to gain more control over the investment process some companies prefer not to go through an independent venture capital fund, but rather to operate their own venture capital fund. Apple Computer, for example, operated a venture capital fund in the late 1980s that was supposed to promote the Apple platform over the emerging IBM-PC platform (see Hellmann, Milius, and Risk 1995). The problem with directly controlled venture capital funds, however, is that the very strategic control that companies hope to derive from the fund can frequently be a turn-off for entrepreneurs. Dan Eilers, who managed the Apple Computer Venture fund, often found that the fear of strategic interference overshadowed the potential value added and name recognition that Apple would bring to the table. The irony of the Apple fund was that in order to counteract a reputation for strategic meddling, it early on established itself as *not* pursuing strategic objectives against the interest of the entrepreneurial companies. In one of its first transactions it invested in a company that needed reorganization. One of its products was sold to Microsoft, which turned it into PowerPoint. This became one of the cornerstones of the Microsoft Office suite, which was key in taking away market share from Apple Computer. The irony of this highlights the overall difficulty of corporations participating in the venture capital industry.

Some of the institutions that are notably unimportant in the financial landscape of Silicon Valley are banks (see also Hellmann 1997). Less than 5 percent of all venture capital funds are owned and operated by banks, and even those funds tend to be more active in later stage deals where the risks are lower. There are only a few specialized banks, such as Silicon Valley Bank, that specialize in the debt needs of entrepreneurial companies. The overall lack of banks is widely believed to be not a consequence of regulation (indeed, the fact that some banks are active in the venture capital market is proof that regulations are not preventing banks from participating), but rather a consequence of the more conservative practices and mentalities of banks. This is not only true for loans, but also for equity investments. We researched the behavior of those banks that actually choose to participate in the venture capital market (see Hellmann, Lindsey, and Puri 1999). We found that these banks tend to be more reluctant to make early stage deals than their independent venture capital counterparts. And if they do, they tend to only invest in deals for which there are also other investors, presumably to diversify risk and possibly share the blame in case of failure.[10]

If most of the venture capital funds are private independent firms, how are they structured? Typically we find some kind of limited partnership, in which the investors are called the limited partners and the fund operators (i.e., the venture capitalists) are called the general partners. In return for managing the venture capital portfolio, the general partners get some base compensation, and a share of 20 percent of the profits generated by the venture capital fund. This provides high-powered incentives for the general partners to generate high returns. Unlike the close relationship between entrepreneurs and venture capitalists, the relationship between general and limited partners is very hands-off. The limited partners are prevented by law from taking any significant management role, and they cannot unduly influence the general partners in their investment decisions. In essence the limited partners hand over the money to the general partners, who regularly update the limited partners on the progress of the fund. They distribute cash or stock when they feel like it, as long as it is within a prearranged time frame (typically ten years). Although the legal structure of venture capital funds may afford relatively little protection to the limited partners, there are nonetheless economic incentives for the general partners not to misuse the funds. Although a venture capital firm will raise a ten-year fund, most of its investment will be made in its first three years. Once the fund is fully invested, the venture capital firm will want to raise another fund. At this point, the reputation of how it managed the previous fund will determine whether the firm can raise a new fund (see Sahlman 1990).

Most financial intermediaries, such as banks, want to diversify their portfolios so as not to be exposed to negative shocks in individual market segments, such as specific industries or narrow geographical areas. In contrast, the investments of venture capital funds are not well diversified at all. Most funds invest in only one or two industries, and many venture capital funds do not invest in companies that are more than two hours away by car. The only diversification in venture capital is in terms of the stages of companies. Few venture capital funds invest only in early stage deals; most prefer to include some later stage deals that have a more predictable return pattern. Some venture capital companies recently added some public market investments, where they invest in companies that are already listed, but that have difficulty raising additional stock on the public market. The pattern of limited diversification is precisely the consequence of the fact that venture capital investors are highly specialized investors. They need to have specific industry knowledge in order to select and nurture their portfolio companies: accordingly, they focus on some particular areas in which their partners have some expertise, and try to achieve any diversification through mixing companies at different levels of maturity. The logic of a venture capital portfolio is thus entirely different from other financial intermediaries such as banks. A bank will try to hold a portfolio that matches the diversification requirements of its clients, including a large number of small depositors. By contrast, a venture capital fund will hold a very high-risk but high-return portfolio, which is only a small part of a much broader portfolio held by their ultimate investors. It would be unproductive to ask the venture capitalists, who have specific coaching expertise, to also run a diversified investment fund.

The provision of expertise by venture capitalists comes at a price itself. At the Stanford Graduate School of Business, no job is more desired by outgoing MBA students than that of a venture capitalist, partly because of the challenge and excitement, but also partly because of the exceptional pay. Venture capitalist base pay is very generous, and by the time somebody becomes a partner, the profit sharing can become highly lucrative. An interesting question is why these lucrative returns are not competed away? Why is the market for venture capitalists not a perfectly competitive labor market?

There are two central elements to the answer. First, the generous compensation provides protection against opportunistic behavior. In old times, the guards of a bank safe would be paid very well so that they were less likely to run away with the money themselves. In more modern times, a high level of compensation, combined with a strong incentive component, provides similar safeguards against opportunistic behavior. The second reason venture capitalists extract considerable profits is that each develops unique expertise. Consider Eugene Kleiner, the co-founder of Kleiner Perkins. He was one of the famous eight engineers that left Shockley Semiconductor in 1957 in order to found Fairchild Semiconductor. After the tremendous success of Fairchild, Eugene Kleiner not only had a vast knowledge of all the aspects of the semiconductor business, he also had a wide set of contacts and a stellar reputation that put him in a unique position to invest in the next generation of semiconductor start-ups. Indeed, venture capitalists tend to come from three main types of backgrounds: technological, financial, and managerial/entrepreneurial. Kevin Fong (a contributor to this book), for example, held a variety of technical positions at companies like Plantronics and Hewlett-Packard before joining Mayfield; Ruthann Quindlen had a distinguished career as an investment banker at Alex, Brown & Sons before joining Institutional Venture Partners; and Mitch Kapor, the famous idiosyncratic founder of Lotus Development Corporation, is now one of the partners at Accel Partners. Many venture capitalists combine several of these skills. Yogen Dalal, another partner at Mayfield, had not only participated in two successful software start-ups, he was also involved in the Ethernet development team at Xerox PARC and the TCP/IP protocol while a student at Stanford.

Venture capitalists also gain significant additional experience and contacts in the course of practicing their profession. After leading a few companies to success, venture capitalists become more sought after by potential entrepreneurs, which allows them to pick better companies, which further enhances their reputation. There is a social recognition process that gives high visibility to successful venture capitalists, which in turn will allow them to perform even better. The important point to note, then, is that this expertise and reputation is mostly linked to the person, not the venture capital firm. Benchmark became one of the leading venture capital firms in less than five years. The reason for this was that the firm was founded by a number of experienced partners that had left other venture capital funds. They carried their personal reputations and business contacts with them. The ease with which venture capitalists can take these valuable assets with them also means that disagreements about the sharing of the profits of the partnership can easily lead to a breakup of a venture capital firm. These frequent changes in the composition of these groups may seem like a manifestation of needless disagreements and selfishness, which could undermine the stability of venture capital firms. Yet it can also be argued that it is a feature of a very adaptable system in which venture capital teams reform themselves frequently in response to changes in their environment.

THE ROLE OF INSTITUTIONAL INFRASTRUCTURE

Venture capitalists do not operate in an institutional vacuum. There are many complicated interactions between venture capital and its environment; here I focus on a few of the most important ones. Probably the most frequently mentioned institution that is believed to affect the viability of venture capital is the availability of a stock market. Upon reflection, this is a rather surprising claim. Financial institutions' methods are frequently depicted as ranging from "arm's length" to "relationship-based," with stock markets being an extreme form of arm's length and venture capital an extreme form of relationship-based methods of financing. Moreover, the United States is considered to have a financial system based on arm's length interactions, yet it is also the country with the most vivid venture capital market. How can we explain the co-existence of these two distinct types of financial institutions?

We have seen before that venture capitalists make investments in young growth-oriented companies that cannot be expected to generate fast profits, let alone pay out dividends. There is thus a fundamental question of how venture capitalists will be able to get a return on their investment within a reasonable amount of time. Given the inability of firms to pay out dividends, the venture capitalist is looking for some other agent to buy their stock. One solution is to have the founders buy back the equity in their own firm. This was attempted, for example, in the early days of European venture capital. It poses several problems. The founders may be unable to raise any money (in particular debt from banks) to buy back the stock. Even if they raise the money, it is difficult to establish the true value of the stock. And because of risk diversification the founders may not even want to own all of the stock.

A large body of research characterizes the value of having a stock market. It provides a source of funding, a tool for risk diversification, and a competitively determined valuation. It allows venture capitalists to cash out their investments once they have reached a certain stage of maturity. Cashing out the investment is important since it allows venture capitalists to focus their attention on companies in their early stages. Hence, the presence of an arm's length stock market is important for the relationship-intensive venture capital relationship, precisely because it allows investors to transition out of the close relationship (see also Black and Gilson 1997).[11]

What is probably less well understood is the importance of acquisitions as an alternative method for cashing out venture capital investments. Although an IPO is a highly visible event that receives considerable press attention, only a handful of acquisitions receive much public attention. In 1998, for example, 77 venture capital–backed companies went public, yet 190 were merged or acquired. The decision to take a company public or have it acquired has strategic implications, since it leads to alternative boundaries of the firm (i.e., whether the start-up becomes an independent firm or a division of another company). As a consequence, this decision can be highly strategic. When Microsoft bought Hotmail, the Internet e-mail provider, there was a clear implicit threat: either they sell to Microsoft, or they can expect Microsoft as a competitor.[12]

The difference between an IPO and an acquisition can be quite significant, and a potential source of conflict between the entrepreneurs and the venture capitalists. An acquisition may often be feasible earlier than an IPO, since the acquiring company can make a deal prior to the start-up satisfying all the stock market listing requirements. But while a fast exit may appeal to the venture capitalist, the founders may prefer to retain their independence and wait for the company to go public.[13]

One of the most difficult questions to answer is what role the government played in the development of the U.S. venture capital market. Venture capitalists can prove to be rather human when they attribute their success to themselves and their problems to others, the government being an ideal candidate. We should therefore not be misled by some of the industry's "triumph-of-the-free-market" rhetoric. Indeed, it is clear that the government played an important role, at least in the early days of venture capital. In particular, the Small Business Investment Corporation (SBIC) program provided cheap access to funds in the early days of venture capital. It offered government funds to match private ones at favorable rates. A key feature of the SBIC program was that it was meant to help the private markets to function better, rather than to crowd out any private market activity. Even if many of the SBICs performed somewhat poorly, they provided a learning experience and training ground for the first generation of successful independent venture capitalists.[14]

More generally, one could describe the approach of the U.S. government to venture capital as one of enabling the industry to grow, rather than promoting it through direct intervention. For example, one of the key stepping stones in the development of the U.S. venture capital market was the relaxation of rules for institutional investors in 1978 (the so-called ERISA rules), which allowed institutional investors to invest in high-risk assets such as venture capital. It is also often argued that low capital gains taxation in the United States was a critical enabling condition for the development of venture capital, although those who researched this claim more carefully never found any persuasive evidence for it (see Gompers and Lerner 1998). Probably a much more important enabling factor was the generous access to federally sponsored research. The importance of MIT and Harvard for Boston's Route 128, and Stanford and Berkeley for Silicon Valley, has been widely recognized. Federal funding of research, however, did not go solely through the universities, but also went to research institutions such as NASA's Ames Research Center and the Lawrence Livermore laboratory. Moreover, the early venture capital investments, such as in semiconductors, were indirectly spawned by the Department of Defense's demand for high-technology products.

It therefore seems clear that the success of venture capital cannot be separated from a whole set of government policies. Interestingly, this does not contradict the claim that the lack of direct intervention was also an important factor in the development of the venture capital market. The more general point is that there is no such thing as a neutral government. Government actions will always have an effect on the development of the venture capital industry. Because of the need for flexibility and speed, the government is unlikely to be a central actor in the industry itself. But it still plays a crucial role in providing an enabling environment. A current reminder of the importance of government to the venture capital market is the growing attention of Valley businesspeople to politics and the growing fund-raising by politicians here (see "Politics and Silicon Valley" 1999).

The existence of exit options and an enabling government are two elements of the business environment that are critical for the vitality of a venture capital industry. There are many more factors that are important, although it is sometimes hard to determine exactly how important each is. Clearly, the regulation of venture capital funds can have a significant impact on the size of the venture capital industry. Maybe less obvious but probably more important are labor market regulations. The ease of returning to work for a large corporation after working for a start-up, as well as the ease with which people can move from working as venture capitalists to a more traditional financier's career, has a first-order effect on venture capital. The ease with which companies can be created is also affected by the technology and business environment. Can universities easily license their intellectual property? Can start-ups easily contract with established firms to find suppliers of technology and other inputs? Are there channels of distribution that the entrepreneur can hope to access? And the ease with which companies can be restructured is critical. Some start-ups emerge when employees of established companies are either laid off or anticipate future layoffs. Probably more important, the ability to shut down a money-losing venture is critical to preserving good rates of return on venture capital investments. The United States has been widely considered to have the most favorable conditions along these lines, although recently a number of European and Asian countries have begun reforms that bring them considerably closer to the United States in those dimensions.

These conditions are important in understanding the overall success of venture capital in the United States. Yet, within the United States, venture capital tends to be geographically concentrated in a few locations. One point made above was the availability of universities and research centers as one of the local characteristics of Silicon Valley and Boston's Route 128, the two predominant clusters of venture capital. But these are not the only factors that make these two locations particularly suitable for venture capital.[15] Silicon Valley is composed of a cluster of interacting institutions that support each other.

One set of professionals that is important to venture capital is investment bankers. A number of new investment banks emerged in the Bay Area that explicitly specialized in the financing needs of high-technology companies, the most famous being Hambrecht & Quist, and Robertson, Stephens and Company. These investment banks work closely with venture capitalists, and many of them set up venture capital funds themselves, both to have an inside perspective on the venture business, and to participate in later stage rounds of companies for whom they would like to provide investment banking services. Similarly, venture capitalists tend to have close relationships with some law firms (such as Wilson, Sonsini, Goodrich and Rosati and the Venture Law Group) that specialize in the needs of start-up companies. The presence of an experienced law firm can significantly reduce the amount of time it takes for an entrepreneur and a venture capitalist to close a deal. Similarly, venture capitalists make frequent use of a few accounting and consulting firms that have specialized personnel for start-ups. For recruiting executives they are also assisted by specialized headhunters. All of these professionals facilitate the work of venture capitalists and entrepreneurs, allowing them to outsource some of the tasks that can be standardized.

Another symbiotic relationship that is becoming increasingly important is the relationship between so-called angel investors and venture capitalists. Angel investors are private individuals that invest their own wealth in start-ups of entrepreneurs that are not directly related to them through family or prior friendship. Just like venture capitalists, they hold equity and hope to make significant returns. There is much heterogeneity among angel investors, but in the 1990s a particular type of angel investor became important in Silicon Valley, namely the successful executive that had made his or her fortune on a recent IPO. For a variety of reasons many founders and executives of successful start-up companies leave their companies a few years after a successful IPO. Because of their familiarity with the entrepreneurial process, as well as their industry experience, these executives are uniquely positioned to invest in the next generation of entrepreneurs. But while they may well be in a position to seed a company, providing maybe the first million dollars, they are rarely able to fund companies all the way up to an IPO. This is where the relationship between venture capitalists and angel investors becomes very important. The venture capitalists will want to maintain close contact with angels in order to participate in this deal flow. The interesting implication of this is that angel investors are not really a substitute to venture capital, but they can frequently become the ones that provide promising leads for venture capital investments.[16]

Why are all these institutions important for venture capital? It is easy to see that there are symbiotic relationships between venture capitalists as specialized financiers and other specialized professionals, such as the lawyers and investment bankers. To some extent this is nothing but the standard working of the market, where specialization is limited by the extent of the market, and where the large entrepreneurial activity facilitates this amount of specialization. But as Paul Krugman (1995) pointed out in his seminal work of economic geography, the interaction between local institutions can lead to feedback mechanisms that create an agglomeration force where the whole is worth a lot more than the sum of its parts. Geographic agglomeration, however, occurs only if there is a need for these interdependent organizations to be located in close geographic proximity. Precisely because venture capital is more than the provision of capital, geographic proximity is important. Indeed, Silicon Valley venture capitalists rarely invest outside the Valley, and many of them make it an explicit policy not to invest in any company that is more than, say, two hours away from their office. The venture capitalists' emphasis on geographic proximity is thus one example of how a high level of interdependency creates agglomeration economies.

THE FUTURE OF VENTURE CAPITAL

The venture capital industry has experienced phenomenal growth over the last twenty years, catapulting it from an obscure niche business to one of the fastest growing and most visible segments of the financial service industry.

Probably the most controversial question at this point is what the limits of this growth are. Optimists see venture capital as still at the beginning of its era, while pessimists predict a looming crisis in the industry. Few, however, disagree that the industry is experiencing a considerable transformation, the outcome of which remains unclear.

Consider the following data. The median size of a venture capital investment increased from $3.1 million in 1995 to $5 million in 1998, and the median pre-money valuation increased from $9.8 million to $17 million. What this means is that venture capitalists are investing more money in companies without getting a larger fraction of the returns. Has the market for venture capital grown too fast or too large? Although there are no reliable estimates on the rates of return in venture capital, it appears that the venture capital business is highly cyclical. The success of a few well-known venture capital firms has created a large number of imitators that hope to do just as well, if not better. A similar boom existed in the industry in the mid-1980s, followed by a significant decline in the late 1980s. In their analysis of these events, Bygrave and Timmons (1992) note that many new venture capitalists had done very poorly in the downturn, while the established funds continued to perform well. A similar danger exists today. The high returns that a seasoned venture capitalist may achieve are not the result of random bets, but rather the outcome of an intensive process of selecting and nurturing entrepreneurial companies. Newcomers to the industry are unlikely to notice these subtleties, or are simply unable to perform these tasks as well. It may thus be reasonable to expect a good portion of the new venture capital funds not to perform well, especially if the exceptional growth in the stock market were to subside. A different, maybe more worrisome change is that even for the established players, the game of venture capital seems to be changing. Some of the funds that used to excel in investing in the early stage deals have raised unprecedented amounts of funds without much concern for how this would affect their business strategy. But with this much money to invest, it seems that they can only flood start-ups with more money than is needed, or move out of the early stage venture business altogether. And although it is easy to increase the amount of funds tenfold, the number of good coaches cannot be increased at the same rate. If experienced venture capitalists will be replaced with fortune-seeking financial engineers from Wall Street or inexperienced rookies, it is uncertain that the value-adding dimension of venture capital will remain intact.[17] Another interesting implication is that the early stage market might experience some significant changes: maybe angels will become more important? Moreover, there have been some attempts to better organize angel investing through semiformal networking organizations, such as Garage.com, The Band of Angels, and The Angels' Forum. These kinds of organizations are likely to become increasingly important.

Two other organizational changes are also either already happening or likely to happen soon. First, established corporations have taken a renewed interest in corporate venture capital. Many of these are reacting to the threat of the Internet, and the amounts of money they are willing to put into venture capital are quite significant. The most likely outcome of this is a flurry of strategic alliances that will go nowhere. Those venture capitalists who truly understand the corporation's interest in venture capital, however, are likely to do very well. Second, it is quite conceivable that some venture capital funds will seek to become listed on the stock market. The fact that such arrangements failed in the 1960s is probably long forgotten. More importantly, there is a growing interest among the general public to invest in venture capital. Why should it not be possible to have venture capital funds offered to the general public through mutual fund supermarkets such as Charles Schwab? I suspect that small investors are going to ask for a vehicle to invest in venture capital. Whether, however, these venture capital funds will be able to overcome the disadvantages of being listed on the stock market, especially if there is a downturn in the market, remains unclear.

However alarmed one may be about the recent changes in the venture capital market, there is probably more reason to be optimistic than paranoid. Although the organization of the venture capital market is rapidly changing, the functional need for venture capital remains unchanged. As long as there are athletes, there is always a need for coaches. Similarly, as long as there are start-ups, there is a need for a closely involved investor such as a venture capitalist, to help companies through the difficulties of growing up. The inspiration that leads people to establish new companies has survived for a long time, and there is no reason to believe that it will abate. As a consequence, it seems that the venture capital business is here with us to stay for a long time.

14

The Valley of Deals

How Venture Capital Helped Shape the Region

DADO P. BANATAO AND KEVIN A. FONG

Although investing in high-risk ventures has an honorable history that can be traced back at least as far as the Middle Ages, modern venture investing has evolved as a uniquely American phenomenon. The developed nations in Europe and Asia have as yet been unable to build a strong venture capital infrastructure. Traditionally, they have found it difficult to place large sums of capital in the hands of small, untried enterprises for which failure, rather than success, is the norm. In contrast, the entrepreneur is honored in the United States, to the extent that Jeff Bezos, the entrepreneurial founder of Amazon.com, became *Time* magazine's Person of the Year in 1999. The past several decades, and the last few years in particular, have seen a celebration of the entrepreneur not witnessed since the Gilded Age of the great industrialists like Andrew Carnegie, John D. Rockefeller, and Henry Clay Frick. The venture capital community, with its ability to pool large sums of capital for investment in new ventures, is an indispensable element in this story.

The effect of having pools of capital available to back the technological innovations that began to spring up after World War II cannot be exaggerated. During most of the last hundred years, entrepreneurs had to rely on the money they could garner from family, friends, local merchants, and one or two rich individuals willing to invest in something risky. But in the last three decades venture capital has evolved from being a hobby or a sideline of the rich into a legitimate way for banks, pension funds, universities, and wealthy individuals to realize a higher return than they could get in the stock market or from a bank. This institutionalization of venture investing is what propelled the extraordinary technological changes of the last half of the twentieth century. Venture capital backed the nascent semiconductor industry beginning in the late 1960s, the biotechnology and personal computer industries in the 1970s, the workstation and networking industries in the 1980s, and the commercialization of the Internet and the resultant changes in the telecommunications industry in the 1990s.

Many reasons have been advanced as to why Silicon Valley was so conducive to entrepreneurial activity. These range from the weather to the Valley's adaptable social and educational institutions. Stanford University is sometimes cited as a key reason. Yet any number of states have prestigious universities and lots of sunshine. What Silicon Valley possessed in abundance was the willingness of individuals and institutions to take financial risks. People with business experience rather than financial backgrounds—people like Tommy Davis, who founded Mayfield Fund, Paul M. Wythes and William H. Draper III, who formed Sutter Hill Ventures, and Burton J. McMurtry and Jack Melchor of Palo Alto Investments—saw that there was a lot of money to be made in financing new companies. Banks like the Bank of America Corp. pushed into venture capital as early as 1959. Bank of America not only provided start-up backing for companies such as Dataproducts, Memorex, Teledyne, and Advanced Micro Devices, but by 1970 it was estimated to have been responsible for three-quarters of the lending to California electronics companies.

It has been said that venture capital was born in New York and nourished in Boston but truly came of age in California. Venture capital had its origins in the East, where a few rich individuals such as Laurance Rockefeller and Jock Whitney began backing new ventures. Up in Boston, American Research & Development Corp. had been founded in 1946 to provide a source of capital and support for Boston's large base of scientist-entrepreneurs. When Robert Noyce and seven fellow engineers left Shockley Semiconductor Laboratories in 1957, they went east looking for capital to start their own venture. The "Traitorous Eight," as William Shockley called them, got their financing from Fairchild Camera and Instrument but chose to stay in the West to begin manufacturing semiconductors in Mountain View. Many historians trace the entrepreneurial beginnings of Silicon Valley to this venture, Fairchild Semiconductor (see Chapter 8). The silicon revolution that began with Fairchild placed the cutting edge of technology firmly in California. Understanding the power of semiconductors led to an understanding of what came after—personal computers, workstations, networking equipment—that the East did not catch on to until it was too late. Between 1966 and 1969, 27 new chip companies were formed by ex–Fairchild employees. The pattern of engineer as entrepreneur was firmly established.

The first Eastern venture capitalist to make the move to the West was Arthur Rock, a Wall Street investment banker who helped put Robert Noyce and the defectors from Shockley Semiconductor together with Fairchild. Convinced that there were important venture opportunities in the West, Rock moved to San Francisco in 1961. Rock and Tommy Davis, who went on to found Mayfield Fund, had been looking at investments in high technology for cash-rich Kern County Land, where Davis was a vice president. They raised a $3.5 million fund, which ran for seven years, and produced one giant hit— Scientific Data Systems, which ended up being sold to Xerox for just short of $1 billion in stock. As an individual investor, Rock also backed Intel.

The Western venture capital community in the 1960s primarily resided in San Francisco, where a group of men began their own quiet revolution—the institutionalization of venture investing. The community then consisted of a number of individual investors who met at the University Club on Nob Hill in San Francisco at the monthly meetings of the Western Association of Venture Capitalists. Members included Reid Dennis, Jack Melchor, Burt McMurtry, Don Valentine, and Wally Davis. It was not until the 1970s that "The Group," as they were called, began to make their way south to the tract of land at 3000 Sand Hill Road. Many of the firms formed in the 1970s, such as Mayfield Fund, Sequoia Capital, and Kleiner Perkins Caufield & Byers—all of whom were among the first venture firms to set up offices on Sand Hill Road—are still in residence and actively investing in new companies. They have been joined over the years by other firms—Institutional Venture Partners (IVP) and Mohr, Davidow Ventures in the 1980s and Accel Partners and Benchmark Capital in the 1990s, to name a few. Today, of course, this development between the Stanford University campus and Menlo Park has become virtually synonymous with venture investing. With this move from San Francisco, venture capital became inextricably linked with the fortunes of Silicon Valley.

THE TECHNOLOGIST AS KING

In the early days, prominent venture capitalists such as Arthur Rock and Tommy Davis were not technologists themselves. Instead, they relied on their instincts about people when making decisions. Rock backed Noyce, Gordon Moore, and Andy Grove without ever looking at a business plan when they started Intel. Davis always said that the key to making a winning investment was to "back the right people."

Although people remained an essential ingredient in any investment decision, venture capitalists quickly found they also needed to be able to assess the technology they were being asked to fund. To quote what Tom Perkins liked to call "Perkins's Law": "Market risk is inversely proportional to technical risk." Simply put, the harder a product is to develop, the better chance it will have in the market, because competitors will have a hard time duplicating it. The semiconductor industry, a major focus for venture investing in the 1970s, was still in its infancy. There was much uncertainty about how technology would evolve and what the market would demand. Ideas that looked good on paper might end up being technically impossible to design or manufacture. It was also critical for investors to understand where the threat to an established technology might be coming from. If one grasped the significance of the personal computer (and not everyone did), then investing in a company with a new dedicated word processor would be a bet on the past, not the future. Thus technical risk was a key element in any VC strategy, especially that of Kleiner Perkins Caufield & Byers. The entrepreneurs looking for funding were, for the most part, highly skilled engineers or scientists who had served their time at bigger companies and now wanted a chance to make it on their own.

It is not surprising, then, that more and more of the people joining venture firms had engineering backgrounds themselves and had worked at large technology-driven companies such as Hewlett-Packard, Intel, National Semiconductor, IBM, and AT&T. Among the early venture capitalists, Gib Myers, who joined Mayfield Fund a year after it was founded, worked at Hewlett-Packard; Don Valentine, who started Sequoia Capital, had worked in sales and marketing at Fairchild and then at National; and Eugene Kleiner, a mechanical engineer, went from Western Electric to Shockley Semiconductor Laboratories, then to Fairchild, and even started his own small company before teaming up with Tom Perkins in the venture business. Venture capitalists still often come from the ranks of technologists, although, as we shall see, a technology background is becoming less important as more Internet start-ups are focusing on on-line business and commerce.

By the early 1980s, more money and new deals really began to flow into the Valley. This was driven, in part, by a change in Washington in the interpretation of the 1974 Employee Retirement Income Security Act (ERISA). Initially, ERISA seemed to restrict all pension funds to investing only in safe investments such as blue-chip stocks and bonds. In 1978, however, the Department of Labor clarified ERISA to allow pension funds to put part of their assets in so-called "riskier" investments that offered a higher rate of return. Endowments were also affected. Although endowments had never been ruled by ERISA, they operated under the "prudent man rule" enunciated more than 150 years before. With ERISA opening the door to venture capital investing for pension funds, the endowments decided that the "prudent man rule" might include such investments as well. When it came to higher returns, technology investments were clearly in the forefront. A $1.4 million investment in Tandem Computers in 1975 was worth $152 million in 1984; a $200,000 investment in Genentech in 1976 grew to $47 million by 1984.

As more money became available there was already a loose confederation of entrepreneurs seasoned by jobs at earlier start-ups and of venture capitalists who not only understood technology risk, but also the nuts and bolts of getting a product to market. At the same time, as fund sizes grew larger along with the number of deals, venture firms began looking for experienced teams who could absorb the large amounts of capital they were ready to invest. Although the venture successes of the past had been built around brilliant engineers with little or no management experience, now the venture people wanted to see a little more in the way of a business plan, product development, and a management team. Although technology was still important, now it needed more of a business structure at the beginning.

Arthur Rock may have funded Intel based on the credentials of Noyce, Moore, and Grove. But when Bob Metcalfe, a brilliant scientist who was responsible for creating Xerox's Ethernet local area network, showed up with his business plan, the centerpiece of which was a series of what looked like clouds drawn on yellow paper, he had a hard time convincing anyone that his was a serious venture. The venture capitalists he approached did not think he had the skills necessary to become a leader of a start-up, nor could they envision his new architecture. Only after beating the bushes for some time did he get funding for his company, 3Com, from Mayfield Fund, NEA, and Jack Melchor. Yet without the local area networks that were enabled by 3Com and Ethernet, the Internet might not be as pervasive as it is today.

Although Metcalfe eventually received venture funding, he did not enjoy the venture process. Founders of many first generation start-ups like Hewlett-Packard and National, which were not financed by venture capital, complained about the process for other reasons. They felt that the new venture-backed start-ups were draining their best management and engineering talent, and perhaps even stealing their trade secrets. The term "vulture capital" crept into the language to express this view of venture capitalists as birds of prey that ripped apart going concerns to satisfy their appetite for making money. The argument from the established companies went like this: The money being poured into hundreds of companies making similar products was money wasted, since 90 percent of the makers of PC software or disk drives would not survive. Rather than spreading capital among companies whose chances of success were slim, it would be better used bolstering already-successful companies as they engaged in competition with foreign competitors like the Japanese.

By the 1990s it had become clear that, rather than weakening America's high-tech competitiveness, venture funding had strengthened it. While the Japanese relentlessly pursued computer memory, new American chip companies, backed by venture funds, began focusing on new types of microprocessors, graphics chips, and networking chips. The Japanese bet on mainframes and minicomputers, completely missing the workstation revolution that was begun by Sun Microsystems, a venture-funded company.

The development of the Internet is a perfect example of venture funding working hand in hand with creative entrepreneurs. For the Internet to become pervasive and easy to use, whole new classes of telecommunications equipment had to be developed for routing and switching data signals over a network designed for voice traffic. Start-up companies were the first to seize on this opportunity. The browser created by Netscape, a venture-funded company, was critical to making the Internet user-friendly. Search engines like Yahoo! and Excite first provided a means of finding information easily, and then evolved into portals to provide consumers with personalized information. It is fair to say that the Internet as we know it is as much the creation of venture capitalists as it is of the government, which put the network together decades ago. Lacking this entrepreneurial activity, other developed countries have been slow to exploit the Internet and its potential.

THE ROLE OF THE VENTURE CAPITALIST

The venture capitalist, by his or her decisions, exerts an enormous power over what new products, services, and industries will shape the economy. Yet this power rests in the hands of only a thousand venture firms at most, covering a limited geographic spread—California, Massachusetts, Texas, and New York account for the lion's share of venture firms and of the money available for investment. Historically, venture capital investing was more like a club than a profession. It consisted of white males who could access the money of limited partners, such as big universities, when starting a new fund. Everyone knew everyone else who was a participant. They invested in each other's deals, networked at conferences and industry shows, and may have gone to the same universities. As we shall see later in this chapter, this world is becoming larger as more and more money pours in for investment.

Big changes in venture investing in 2000 include, first, the probable doubling of the number of venture firms from 1995 to 2000; second, increases in the amounts of capital; and third, the expansion of the number of sources of investment capital, including large corporations. The size of the markets attractive to venture capitalists has also changed. In 1989, a market of $100 million was sufficient to interest a venture firm: today these same VCs speak of $1 billion markets. This has created a tier of individuals, only some of them venture capitalists (others include individual angel investors), to invest in firms with more modest potential. But for most of its history, venture capital has been the purview of an elite.

Venture capital firms involve themselves in every stage of a company's development, from the idea to the IPO. In his book *The New Venturers*, veteran

Business Week reporter Jack Wilson described the role of the venture capitalist this way:

> At the less cosmic level of the individual investment, the venture capitalist can serve as the catalyst, organizational architect, and strategic designer of the new firm—or simply a minor figure in the background, writing checks and waiting for a payoff. . . . The best venture capitalists are far more than checkbook investors, and the best entrepreneurs have too strong a vision of their enterprise to brook much interference in its planning and operations. Success in venture capital comes most often from a creative partnership in which the investor's lengthy and often painful experience in the company's formation process is combined with the entrepreneur's management skills and detailed knowledge of a market or technology. But as many venture capitalists have expensively learned, companies are not built or operated from the boardroom. The venture capitalist can counsel and assist, but in the end it is the abilities of the entrepreneur that determine the outcome of the investment. (Wilson 1985, 5–6)

One of the first roles a venture capitalist plays is as a filter for the dozens of funding proposals that cross his or her desk every day. The majority of these proposals come from entrepreneurs who have been recommended by other venture capitalists, industry heavyweights, successful entrepreneurs, and, increasingly, lawyers. For entrepreneurs, lawyers provide a more objective view of financing possibilities than other participants, steering them to an angel investor or an established venture firm depending on the entrepreneur's needs.

But a venture capitalist must still engage in due diligence, using an extensive list of contacts to research the viability of markets, the background of the entrepreneur, likely competition already in place or on the horizon, and, if the business is to be built around technology, the extent to which the intellectual property is protected. At this stage, the venture capitalist's contacts in his Palm Pilot are his best friend.

Some venture funds, like Mayfield, rely heavily on the past record of the entrepreneur. The expression "we bet on the jockey, not on the horse" means that if an entrepreneur has been successful in the past, his newest idea is less important in the gating process than his past performance. This is why certain names keep popping up over and over. An entrepreneur's failure at his previous venture is not an insurmountable negative, however. Failure is not considered a stigma but rather a learning experience that could well lead to success the next time out.

Consider Kamran Elahian, a Silicon Valley veteran and co-founder of six companies. Following two successes, with CAE Systems and Cirrus Logic, Elahian crashed with Momenta, a pen-based computer company that went bankrupt. That failure did not prevent Elahian from receiving funding for three more companies. The latest, Centillium Communications, a fabless semiconductor company developing communications chips, had received more than $60 million in three rounds of venture financing by the end of 1999.

Senior-level people from top Silicon Valley companies who are ready to break out on their own are also among the most attractive candidates. These people already have a feel for technology or the products the market needs. Dr. Pehong Chen was working at database developer Sybase as president of multimedia technology when he came up with the idea for BroadVision. Dr. Chen had previously founded Gain Technology, which had been acquired by Sybase. Two Mayfield partners, Yogen Dalal and Gib Myers, had been encouraging Dr. Chen to come up with an idea for a new venture, so they were extremely receptive when he approached them about backing a company that would enable businesses to provide secure electronic commerce and financial services. Back in 1994, when Dr. Chen came up with his idea, the Internet was still largely a network for the computer savvy. Electronic business was still in the future. Dalal and Myers placed a bet on Dr. Chen based on his track record. Today, BroadVision is a successful billion-dollar-plus public company and the leading worldwide supplier of personalized electronic business applications.

Venture funds like Sequoia, however, focus more on the available market for a company's products or services. Don Valentine, Sequoia's founder, firmly believed that a company serving a market where demand was high would be a better investment than a company having to pioneer a market. Although Valentine was willing to take risks with people and product development, he was not comfortable with market risk. Sequoia's Michael Moritz, an early backer of Yahoo!, follows much the same philosophy: serve an existing market, don't try to invent one. "This game is not big-bang creationism," Moritz told *Fortune* magazine in 1996 ("How to Make $400,000,000" 88). A year earlier, Moritz had run across two engineering graduate students who were running a new web guide called Yahoo! out of a trailer. Sensing a cheap way to tap into the Internet craze that was just beginning to build, Moritz invested.

Kleiner Perkins's John Doerr, on the other hand, is famous for backing concepts for which he believes there *ought* to be a market. But Doerr's passion for GO, a pen-operated computer company, was a disaster. Doerr believed that pen computing was the next natural evolution of the computer interface. Two things were wrong with the GO concept. One, the technology never worked as advertised, and two, people were not so uncomfortable with keyboards that they were willing to put up with flaky technology. But with Netscape, Doerr correctly predicted that the growing throng of web surfers would embrace a new browser that made their journey easier.

STAGES OF VENTURE INVESTING

Most venture firms today begin investing when it is clear what business plan the entrepreneur will follow, what markets will be addressed, and what the product will be. Companies at this first stage usually have management and engineering teams in place. The amount of money put into a first-round deal varies, but it has been escalating rapidly over the last several years. It is not uncommon for a company to receive from $5 million to $10 million at this stage. Additional rounds of financing are usually required, and at any point during this additional capitalization other venture firms may join the original investors.

Not all entrepreneurs approach a venture firm with a full-blown business plan, product direction, and management team. Mayfield Fund has been a pioneer in incubating new companies by forming very active partnerships with entrepreneurs that include a small amount of investment capital, office space and support staff at Mayfield's headquarters, and direct access to partners. Silicon Graphics was one of the companies Mayfield incubated. Other venture firms such as Kleiner Perkins have also created incubation programs. During the incubation stage a venture firm will provide the entrepreneur with help in formulating a business plan and recruiting key engineering and management talent.

As more money has become available for new ventures, the institutionalized venture firms have been dramatically increasing their involvement in incubation in order to be sure that they get in early on the best deals. Incubation provides a relatively inexpensive way to invest since at this stage valuations are low. Kleiner Perkins Caufield & Byers, for example, provided Juniper Networks with space in its offices (and also contributed $200,000 in a seed round). Juniper was one of 1999's most successful IPOs and now has a market capitalization of more than $20 billion. The Palm Pilot was developed when Merrill, Pickard, Anderson & Eyre incubated Palm Computing in the early 1990s.

Another tactic for taking advantage of early stage opportunities is the entrepreneur in residence (EIR) program. A number of firms have EIR programs, some in addition to their incubation efforts. Typically an EIR is a seasoned business manager with a number of important contacts. EIRs are given office space, a salary, and access to the partners, their contacts, and their flow of business plans. In return, they meet with the executives of potential investments, advise existing investments, and participate in strategy sessions. Eventually EIRs will choose a company with which to affiliate, either as the CEO or in another key management position. The host venture firm will then often get the first look for investment purposes.

The next stage of venture involvement comes at what is known as the seed round. During the 1980s there were firms that specialized in these very early investments. Crosspoint Venture Partners and Alpha Partners, created by Wally Davis when he left Mayfield, were two of the most prominent. Today, however, this level of financial support, which may be in the $2 million range or less, is increasingly being taken over by angel investors. Only if the entrepreneur is well known, or has a good relationship with a particular venture partner, can he expect help from a venture firm with refining his business plan and getting early financing. Some venture firms do, however, work closely with angel investor groups.

Later financings are often referred to as first, second, and third rounds. Sometimes investors mention mezzanine rounds. Different venture firms define these terms slightly differently. A good way to look at these sequences of funding, however, is in terms of the stage of the company. At an early stage the company will have a business plan, management, and a product in development. Late stage companies are those far enough along to be close to an IPO. The characteristics of the middle stage, between the two, are less definite. Normally the company is at an early stage when it receives its first round, the first institutional money it receives, though it may be at a middle or even late stage.

From the perspective of the multiple of capital—the difference between the initial investment and the final IPO price—investing in early stage companies, although riskier than waiting for a company to become more mature, is far more lucrative. If you pay $1 for each share of company stock in its early stage, when the company goes public at $20 a share, your multiple of capital is a lot better than if you paid $10 a share in a later investment round.

VC firms fund companies with plans for an exit strategy. These could range from being acquired or merged to doing an IPO. The best outcomes from an investment perspective are for the company to have a successful IPO or to be acquired for a significant sum. Sometimes the exit strategy means pulling the plug on the company. It cannot be stated too often that the majority of venture firm investments either fail completely or go on to produce lackluster returns on the capital invested. While the long bull market has reduced the ratio of failures to successes, venture investing still is risky.

CHANGES IN THE VC WORLD

From today's perspective, it seems that in the early days venture capital was less institutionalized and more about one-to-one relationships between a venture firm and its portfolio companies. Without the extensive infrastructure that exists today (the banks, law firms, manufacturing operations, consultants, and advertising and public relations firms), venture capitalists needed to perform many of these roles themselves. Venture people who have been in the business for ten years or more remember when they might actually have had to take over some management function for a short time when one of their investments ran into trouble. If manufacturing was having a problem, it was not unheard of for a partner with manufacturing experience to wade in, roll up his shirtsleeves, and get things sorted out.

It is nearly impossible for the venture capitalist to have this kind of involvement today. Although the period from the late 1960s into the 1990s was a period of exponential growth (with the usual peaks and valleys) in venture investing, the curve has suddenly started to go straight up. In 1999 Mayfield invested $339 million spread over 80 deals. In comparison, in 1993 Mayfield invested $64 million in 49 deals.

Concurrently, the time from first funding to IPO has shortened dramatically. In the past, no one expected a company to go public for at least five years. Today it is not uncommon for a company to reach an IPO in a year and a half. In this short a time, there are no allowances for fine-tuning. An IPO, however, is not the only outcome that guarantees success. Acquisition of a company before it goes public can also prove highly lucrative for both the venture capitalist and the entrepreneur. Although company building is still the main business of venture investing, increasingly, finding a well-heeled buyer for a nascent company's technology and customers is an important part of realizing a return. This is particularly true in the telecommunications field. Established companies like Cisco Systems, Lucent Technology, and Nortel have found that buying the technology they need to keep up with the fast pace of change in this industry is far better than trying to develop these technologies themselves. In some cases, the prices paid for these acquisitions are as good as or better than a company would have gotten with an IPO.

Venture firms themselves have not been untouched by the explosion of Internet deals. Benchmark Capital emerged in 1995 from the dissolution of two old-line firms, Merrill Pickard and TVI, to focus on the Internet. Among the companies whose IPOs have given Benchmark considerable clout in the venture community are Ariba, eBay, Juniper Networks, and Red Hat. And 1999 saw the virtual "merger" of two 20-year-old firms, Brentwood Associates and IVP, when six partners (three from each firm) set up a new company, Redpoint Ventures, to focus on Internet investments. As part of this merger, IVP and Brentwood also spun off their health science partners into another firm, Palladium. Although it is common for individual venture capitalists to change firms, it has been rare for long-standing firms with well-known names and more than twenty partners each to dissolve. Such is the payback on Internet deals, however, that the Redpoint partners felt they needed a new brand to take advantage of the Internet opportunities.

Both Benchmark and Redpoint suggest that there may be more consolidation of power in the venture business in the future. Increasingly, there is a growing gap between the top dozen or so venture firms and the rest of the thousand or so other venture firms in the world in terms of their ability to raise funds and their returns on their investments. The top-tier funds continue to be able to raise more and more money and to invest in the best deals.

In an interview with *Upside* magazine in January 2000, Reid Dennis, who founded IVP in 1980, said: "There is a sadness that creeps into all of us that we couldn't build a vibrant, continuing operation." But, Dennis told *Upside*, one of IVP's hottest partners, Geoff Yang, felt that he was being slowed down by venture capitalists who weren't versed in the new Internet markets such as e-commerce, new media, and Internet infrastructure technology.

Traditional venture firms are also encountering new competition for deals from corporate venture investments. Corporations are not new to the venture game. Looking for diversification into exciting new growth areas, many corporations in the late 1960s set up venture operations. General Electric, Ford Motor, and Exxon were just a few of the corporations to try the venture game with little or only modest success. In the 1980s, all the talk among corporations setting up venture subsidiaries was about having a window on the new technologies that were remaking the industrial landscape, with profit as a secondary motivation. Although companies like a General Electric and Exxon understood their own technologies very well, they floundered when it came to picking winners in the emerging information technologies.

However, several corporations of late have been enjoying considerable success at funding companies that not only contribute to the corporation's own success, but are extremely lucrative as well. What distinguishes this corporate investment from what came before is that the corporations like Intel and Microsoft are investing in technologies they understand. Intel's Corporate Business Development Group has $2.5 billion under management and invested $830 million in 1998. Intel made 130 investments in all in 1998, including later stage investments. Its biggest winner was Inktomi, with a return of 633.3 percent. Although Intel's investment emphasis is on expanding the market for Intel products, that mandate is so broad it encompasses investments in a range of Internet companies, including Stamps.com, ThingWorld.com, and @Home. Microsoft also has an investing arm that funds technology that theoretically has some synergy with Microsoft products. Microsoft was an investor in VeriSign, which went public in 1998, as well as NorthPoint Communications, ThingWorld.com, and Audible.

There is often a working relationship between corporations and the venture community. At later stages in a company's funding, the venture firms may seek to bring in corporate investment not only as a way of raising additional capital, but as a way of providing a company with strategic partners who have a financial stake in the company's success. Most often, these corporate investors plan to use the company's product or service.

Earlier on we discussed how venture firms incubate companies. A growing trend is for funds to be set up whose sole purpose is to incubate companies. The February 2000 issue of *Venture Finance*, the monthly newsletter that tracks the venture business, listed 100 companies incubating high-tech start-ups. These firms—with names like Innovation Factory, incubate.com, Ideas Hub, TechFarm, eCompanies, and eHatchery—provide a range of incubation services, from simply providing space to providing a full range of services.

In a back to the future move, some of the roles once played by traditional venture capital firms are again being filled by wealthy individuals known as angel investors. While these investors do not have the sums of money available to venture funds, they are redefining the role angel investors have played in the past and changing the ways in which web start-ups receive their financing. With the size of the average venture capital fund more than doubling in the last decade—it reached $183 million in 1998 according to the U.S. Global Entrepreneurship Monitor, a study conducted by Babson College and the London Business School—venture capitalists tend to look at bigger deals. A company that only needs $1 million to get started is of less interest than one that needs $10 million. After all, it requires almost as much work to put together a small deal as a large one. Angel investors have moved in to fill the need for smaller amounts of start-up capital. Alliance of Angels, The Angel Network, Tech Coast Angels, the Angels' Forum, International Angel Investors Institute, The Dinner Club, and Garage.com are just some of the organizations dedicated to angel investing.

Those small amounts can quickly add up, however. According to the U.S. Global Entrepreneurship Monitor study, during 1998 alone, non–venture capital sources invested $56 billion into launching companies in the United States. Angels are doing an estimated one-third to one-half of the deals that get started today. Historically, angel investors have been the elder statesmen of technology—the Robert Noyces and Gordon Moores, both of whom were angel investors. They might have spent years building companies and their own fortunes before becoming angels. Today, thanks to the insatiable desire on Wall Street for Internet IPOs, entrepreneurs can go from rags to riches in only a few years. People in their twenties and thirties now have substantial sums available to invest in early stage companies. And because the investors most often made their money in an Internet-focused company, they feel comfortable helping bankroll other Internet entrepreneurs, providing advice and contacts. Even some venture capitalists are beginning to do their own angel investing. This trend will likely continue as long as the market continues to boom.

Ron Conway, a longtime Silicon Valley entrepreneur who launched Altos Computer in 1979, has taken the hands-on involvement of angel investing and combined it with the portfolio diversification of venture firms in creating Angel Investors. In 1999 Conway raised $130 million from such high-profile entrepreneurs as Netscape pioneer Marc Andreessen and Marimba founder Kim Polese to invest in early stage companies. During the first nine months of 1999, Angel Investors placed $30 million in 80 start-ups, including on-line trading community ePace, voice services provider Lipstream Networks, and unified messaging service ThinkLink. Conway's investors are anything but passive investors. They are asked to pass along business plans, help evaluate a start-up's prospects, and in some cases even advise the fund's companies.

Functioning somewhere between venture firms and angel investors is Garage.com, whose CEO is Guy Kawasaki. Kawasaki, former Apple evangelist and now venture "gapatalist," says Garage.com fills the gap between what Kawasaki likes to call the "three F's in fundraising (Friends, Family and Fools)" and venture capitalists who are willing to make investments of $5 million or more. The company makes full use of the Internet, including reviewing e-mailed business proposals. Garage.com even has its own form for proposal submissions. Garage.com invests in its portfolio start-ups and helps them raise between $1 million and $5 million in their early fund-raising round. Once an investment has been selected, using criteria common to all venture firms, Garage.com purchases 5 to 7 percent of the company's common stock and promotes the company to other investors, including venture, corporate, and angel investors, by placing it in Heaven, a password-protected portion of the Garage.com web site. In 1999, its first full year of operation, Garage.com invested in 60 companies.

Garage.com illustrates the way in which the Internet is leading to a democratization of venture financing. Not only do entrepreneurs from outside the major centers of venture financing now have the opportunity to pitch their ideas, but web sites filled with information about how to get your ideas heard are springing up daily. Not all of these sites are equally valuable, but they point toward a day when it may no longer be necessary to live in Silicon Valley, frequent the same restaurants and health clubs, or know somebody who knows somebody to find the ear of someone interested in investing. Where once entrepreneurs were technologists building technology companies, the Internet has opened up the world for entrepreneurs who could never have founded a semiconductor or network switch company. Practically anyone with a good idea and the skill and energy to execute it can now start an Internet company.

Another approach to venture investing is represented by CMGI and its @Ventures funds. CMGI, a 30-year-old, publicly traded company that recently remade itself into an Internet company, has under its umbrella perhaps the largest, most diverse network of Internet companies in the world. These companies include both CMGI operating companies and a growing number of Internet investments made through @Ventures. What distinguishes CMGI from a typical venture firm is that it selects companies not only for their growth and return potential, but also for their ability to fit into the CMGI network. The company sees its network of companies as an extended family in which each company's technology, content, and market reach can be leveraged for the benefit of other companies in the network. Thus CMGI's pitch to entrepreneurs is that the company will provide not only funding, but also the opportunity to take advantage of valuable infrastructure support, mentoring, and partnerships. Compaq, Intel, Microsoft, and Sumitomo hold minority positions in CMGI. The list of @Ventures investments ranges from publicly traded companies such as Lycos and Critical Path to consumer and business-to-business web sites. Because CMGI is publicly traded, individual investors who would like the high risk/high return of a venture capitalist can buy shares in CMGI. Safeguard Scientifics, another venturelike company, even allows investors in its stock to purchase stock in its portfolio companies when they go public, giving them a double chance at striking it rich.

CONCLUSION

All of this new wealth is a cause of both pride and dismay for people living in Silicon Valley. The rest of the world looks with envy at the success of the Silicon Valley entrepreneur and his ability to drive the U.S. economy. At the same time, the influx of IPO money into the Valley has sent housing prices soaring drastically, created traffic jams on U.S. 101 for most of the day, and pushed what would have traditionally been called Silicon Valley companies eastward across the San Francisco Bay. Where once only a few people could have envisioned becoming an entrepreneur or a venture capitalist, today almost everyone at least toys with the idea of starting a company and getting rich. Stanford engineering graduates commonly join start-ups, whereas in the past the normal career path was to join an established company like Hewlett-Packard or Intel.

A big worry of those who have been around the Valley for a while is that all of this success is having a corrosive effect, similar to that of Wall Street in the mid-1980s. Expectations are so high that people have developed short attention spans. Rather than concentrating on building lasting companies, entrepreneurs are focused on their exit strategy, getting acquired, or going public.

Still the money keeps pouring in, and company creation continues unabated. In the first quarter of 1999, venture capital investments in U.S. companies passed the $4 billion mark for the first time, increasing by more than 40 percent over the same period in 1998, according to Pricewaterhouse-Coopers. Technology-based companies accounted for $3.6 billion or 84 percent of all first quarter venture capital investments. Companies located in Silicon Valley hit a record $1.74 billion, while New England–based companies gathered only about $552 million in funds.

Today there is unprecedented opportunity for the venture community. That is because it is at one of those rare points at which, because of the Internet, everything is being remade. Not since the industrial revolution has there been such a rich opportunity to invest in change. The deals that cross desks up and down Sand Hill Road today are exceptional in their promise of financial return. Whereas up until a few years ago venture firms invested in technology, today they are investing in companies that are changing business processes by leveraging technology. The companies being built today are as fundamental to the economy as the chip companies that started the Silicon Valley revolution.

15

Fueling the Revolution

Commercial Bank Financing

JOHN C. DEAN

Do not regard Silicon Valley as some sort of economic machine, where various raw materials are poured in at one end and firms such as Apple and Cisco roll out at the other, but rather as a form of ecosystem that breeds companies: without the right soil and the right climate, nothing will grow.
— *The Economist*, MARCH 29, 1997

The Economist certainly got it right when it called Silicon Valley an "ecosystem," with all that word implies: change, evolution, and, above all, growth. Even though I've spent the past seven years at Silicon Valley Bank (after many years as a banker and bank executive in markets as diverse as Seattle and Oklahoma), I continue to be astonished by the fecundity of this locale. And, short-term bumps in the road notwithstanding, I am confident that the next several years will be just as exciting in terms of new businesses, new sectors, and new opportunities. These are exhilarating times in the Valley, and the pace of innovation and entrepreneurialism continues to accelerate.

It is a wonderful accident that Silicon Valley has emerged as the force that it is: an extraordinary confluence of events helped incubate this particular ecosystem. But that shouldn't prevent us from trying to articulate the elements that created this region, for two reasons. First, it's in the interests of everyone—from the bankers and financiers who fuel the revolution to the workers, investors, and consumers who ultimately profit from rapid innovation—to ensure that the elements that feed this ecosystem continue to be nurtured. And second, even though Silicon Valley may be unique, we have already seen other regions, in the United States and around the world, emerge as entrepreneurial ecosystems. We need to understand the similarities and differences among these regions.

My own perspective as a commercial banker may have a narrower focus than that of the economist or business historian, and it is admittedly biased. But when I consider the question, "Is a robust commercial banking capability a precondition for Silicon Valley–type success?" my answer is a resounding yes. Commercial banking, and in particular the kind of commercial banking we've embraced at Silicon Valley Bank, has played an important role in shaping this ecosystem. I'm equally confident that there's a continuing role for us to play here, as well as in other "Silicon Valleys" emerging around the world, from San Diego to Boston, from Israel to the Pacific Rim. But to really understand the role of commercial banking in the entrepreneurial space—past, present, and future—a little history is in order.

THE RAW MATERIALS FOR INNOVATION

What does an actual ecosystem require to thrive? Raw materials, in the form of water, oxygen, nutrients, and energy. The Silicon Valley ecosystem evolved because the raw materials, the primordial soup, came together at the right time: academic and engineering talent, a few early pioneers and visionaries, and some key technology waves. These raw materials included Stanford University (today complemented by other robust academic institutions in the Bay Area), the two men who founded Hewlett-Packard in 1939, and a series of very fertile, high-growth economic sectors: semiconductors, PCs, software, biotechnology, and—of course—the Internet. What was the spark that transformed walnut and orange groves into the center of high technology? Opinions differ, but a good choice would be Stanford's post–World War II dean of engineering, Frederick Terman. He was among the first to recognize the potential of the university as an intellectual resource that could form the basis of the electronics industry.

But whatever spark ignited Silicon Valley, the synergy among its elements formed a critical mass in the Valley that turned a spark into explosive growth. Good engineering and technology (and good jobs for their practitioners) helped attract engineers and technologists. New companies and new industries attracted competitors and spawned descendants (think of Fairchild Semiconductor, one of the first companies to commercially develop integrated circuits, which led in turn to the creation of Intel and a host of other start-ups). And all this burgeoning economic activity attracted professional services to support it, from real estate and accounting firms to legal and financial services. These services represent the infrastructure for entrepreneurial activity.

One could argue that business and professional services represent the infrastructure for all economic activity, which is certainly true. But they play a much more important role for emerging growth companies because they enable entrepreneurs to concentrate on what they do best—innovate, create, and build. Although some entrepreneurs are also great executives, being an entrepreneur requires a different set of skills from being a successful manager. Entrepreneurs rely on professional services to an even greater extent than companies in more traditional industries as a way to extend their resources. The infrastructure of professional services providers is one more vital ingredient of Silicon Valley's success.

IT TAKES MORE THAN A VILLAGE

Professional services, however, only get you so far; entrepreneurs also need capital, the primary resource for turning good ideas into good (and occasionally great) companies. As we've seen in dramatic fashion over the last couple of years, no region has been as good at attracting capital as Silicon Valley. And just as an infrastructure of service providers emerged to support the Valley's entrepreneurs, an infrastructure of capital providers has also emerged to enable their growth and success.

From angel investors who are eager to seed tomorrow's companies to the venture capitalists who populate Menlo Park's Sand Hill Road, the conduits for infusing equity capital are substantial, both in number and in size. As Stanford University's Thomas Hellmann, and Dado Banatao and Kevin Fong of the Mayfield Fund, observe in this book, these early financiers play a vital role in intermediating capital from those who have it to those who need it—not unlike the great bank financiers of the nineteenth century.

But the world of venture capital is fundamentally different from the traditional world of bank financing, and the difference can be summed up in one word: equity. Equity is the price of admission in Silicon Valley. It's hardly an unreasonable price, given the central fact of life in Silicon Valley: risk. Many, if not most, entrepreneurial ventures fail. For every Intel or Cisco Systems, for every Netscape or Yahoo!, there are dozens of companies that become the Valley equivalent of roadkill. The rewards, in other words, have to be substantial for capital intermediaries to assume the risks associated with venture capital investing. Accordingly, the exchange of equity for capital is commonplace in Silicon Valley. (Could there be a connection between the pioneering spirit of the West—westward expansion and the gold rush—and the risk-embracing culture of Silicon Valley?)

Given the fact that venture capital has become the primary currency of the Valley, what role does the commercial bank play? To put it differently: Why didn't the large and successful commercial banks in San Francisco—which has been the financial center of the western United States since the gold rush era—turn their attention to the phenomenon that was going on in the Valley?

I submit that for *most* commercial banks, the entrepreneurial mindset simply does not mesh with traditional forms of financing. The prevailing culture of banks, particularly large ones, is risk-averse; it isn't suited to the freewheeling, risk-embracing ethos of Silicon Valley. Not surprisingly, then, commercial banks, in the aggregate, have not fared well here. Their presence as a resource has been extremely volatile, with the largest players, including Bank of America and Wells Fargo, dipping into and out of the market, testing the waters but not jumping in.

There's plenty of capital in the Valley, of course, but there is room for commercial banking because every company is going to need a checking account, cash management services, letters of credit, or lease financing—to cite a few examples of commercial banking products. These and other services are our core competencies (which is why venture capital firms often refer their portfolio companies to us). The reluctance of the big commercial banks to deal with entrepreneurs left a void in the market space and, eventually, led to the creation of Silicon Valley Bank.

In fact, it was a small group of frustrated executives who, over a poker game one evening in Santa Clara, decided to launch Silicon Valley Bank in 1983, just as the first "mass market" technology wave (the personal computer) was beginning to build momentum. The founders of Silicon Valley Bank recognized two important trends. First, they were relatively quick to realize the importance and potential of entrepreneurs. Sixteen years ago, technology was nothing more than one component of the total economic picture—not the driving force it has become today. And second, these founders recognized that even if venture capitalists were catalysts for entrepreneurial ventures, those young companies would still need corporate banking services. And that's how Silicon Valley Bank got started—at a time, it's worth remembering, when very few people in this country would have considered starting a bank.

I should add here that serving the entrepreneur wasn't the sole focus of Silicon Valley Bank in our early days. The founders envisioned a banking business with three legs: real estate lending, corporate lending, and emerging growth (primarily technology) lending. You don't have to be much of a student of banking history to recall that real estate lending in the 1980s turned out to be a problem, reaching speculative and, ultimately, unsustainable levels that led to significant credit problems for commercial lenders in the late 1980s and early 1990s. Moreover, the traditional corporate lending market has largely evaporated, the result of disintermediation and the consolidation of large banks.

And so, we identified the third leg of the Silicon Valley Bank stool—emerging growth companies—as the core of our future success. As the bank entered the 1990s, our destiny was clear: we intensified our focus on technology and growth companies and began to overhaul our product and service offerings to be valuable to them and profitable for us. And we deepened our ties throughout the vibrant Silicon Valley community (as well as its counterparts in other regions of the country) so that we could become the bank of choice for entrepreneurs—whether they needed financing or just a checking account. We believed that if we could speak their language, understand their concerns, and, most important, deliver services they valued, we could succeed. We were right, but it took a lot of work.

BROADENING OUR PRODUCT LINE

Sixteen years ago, Silicon Valley Bank's primary commercial lending product was a working capital line of credit. We would lend against assets, primarily accounts receivable. We believe we were the only bank in the country to make such loans to companies that were, in the parlance of bankers, "preprofit."

Today, obviously, the idea of lending to a preprofit company isn't the least bit preposterous; Internet and other companies that are preprofit, and even prerevenue, receive debt capital from various lenders. But in our early days at Silicon Valley Bank, this kind of lending was a substantial challenge. We were able to rise to that challenge because we knew the venture capitalists, and that gave us confidence about whom we were lending to. Our VC relationships gave us (and continue to give us) an entrée into promising young companies— all of whom, eventually, need corporate banking services. We recognized then what is common knowledge today: that the assets in an information-age economy are often intangible, including patents, processes, business plans, and other intellectual property. And those assets are as bankable as plants and equipment—often more so, at least in today's economy.

We had to become willing and able to lend creatively. We introduced a broad array of products to help entrepreneurs realize their vision (Silicon Valley Bank today offers 36 different lending facilities), such as factoring loans and a variety of asset-based financing products. We pioneered new lending vehicles for specific market niches and for critical stages in a company's life cycle and evolution. We worked with the equity financiers, the venture capitalists, and the angels to supplement and complement their efforts; this made their equity investments more effective. We added all kinds of products with the needs of the entrepreneurs in mind, like cash management, so entrepreneurs could focus on doing business, not balancing checkbooks; and letters of credit to facilitate international transactions. In short, we transformed ourselves into multifaceted providers of financial services focused on the entrepreneurial space. And that enabled us to cross-sell, to broaden our ties to emerging companies and to build with them enduring relationships.

All this also helped us define our market space. We don't act as venture capitalists, for example, but we do serve as a complement to them. In fact, VCs

are a vital source of deals for us, and, because we can be useful to their portfolio companies, we're an additional resource for them. For the entrepreneur,
a bank loan is often a much more palatable and effective source of ancillary
financing than a new infusion of equity capital. Bank financing is, obviously,
much less dilutive; we occasionally take warrants as part of the terms of a deal,
but that always has a smaller impact on the entrepreneur's stake than straight
equity. And sometimes, for an entrepreneur in the early to middle stages of a
company's evolution, commercial bank financing can play a meaningful role
in helping to achieve a particular goal, thereby increasing the likelihood of
long-term success. It might be as simple as ensuring positive cash flow until
payment for a large order is received, but a loan might also help a company
get further financing or facilitate some other kind of transaction, such as an
acquisition or merger.

Bank financing may not play the central role that seed money or venture
capital does in fueling emerging growth companies, but ask an entrepreneur
who has benefited from a Silicon Valley Bank credit facility and you will realize that the role we play is often crucial. But it takes more than just a willingness to lend to succeed in the Valley; it takes a special kind of expertise.

DECOMMODIFYING CREDIT

"Everybody's money is green." You hear this a lot in the Valley. It's true
enough: cash is a commodity. But *capital* clearly isn't. This is why start-ups
don't always sign on with the first person willing to write a check; they know
that although everybody's money may be green, the experience, expertise, and
network of connections venture capitalists bring to the table differ enormously. And just as VC firms work to differentiate themselves by the quality
of their partners or the added value their sponsorship can create, Silicon Valley Bank has tried to add value to credit. How? By approaching credit from
a position of knowledge, insight, and experience. And by establishing a spirit
of partnership.

Bankers serving traditional industries strive to codify the process of supplying credit as much as possible. A credit committee establishes certain parameters. Loan officers evaluate opportunities. A commitments committee

looks at the numbers and says "yea" or "nay." But in Silicon Valley—a place where new businesses and new business models are invented every day—it takes more than a set of formulas to make good decisions. It takes insight, knowledge, and judgment. In short, it takes more than money.

Talk to any successful venture capitalist and you'll hear some version of this story: "We want to be a partner with the companies we invest in." The best of them really mean that, seeking to add value through operating expertise, relationships, and contacts. Silicon Valley Bank recognized early that it had to fill the same kind of role.

We have a lot more in common with our clients than we do with other bankers. I've been a banker all my career, but many bankers here have hands-on work experience in the technology and entrepreneurial spaces (and all are focused on emerging markets). In addition, all of them work in teams that are not just targeted at specific sectors but deeply entrenched within them.

We strive to function as a valuable partner, as the bank that brings something extra to bear on the issues and challenges of emerging growth companies. And the fact is that our experience, along with our sector-specific knowledge, gives us insights into the issues our clients are facing, often before they've even identified them. We know, for example, that a growing software company will, at some point, have to enter the European market; we can help them with the financial and logistical challenges of doing so, providing letters of credit and expertise in export finance, currency exchange, and correspondent banking, for example. We know what kind of roadblocks and pitfalls face, say, an emerging biotechnology company, and that knowledge can be as important as the capital we might provide. And of course we know people and companies that can be valuable to our clients, for strategic relationships, joint ventures, and partnerships.

Knowledge is power in another way: it helps us stay the course when times are bad. If you know what the entrepreneur's journey is like from garage to corporate campus, from raising $25,000 from friends and family to going public, you're well equipped to be a good lender to that business. That insight helps us help the entrepreneur anticipate and deal with problems; perhaps even more important, it gives us endurance. For many commercial bankers, a quarterly revenue "blip" means tightening the credit reins; at Silicon Valley Bank, we have learned to distinguish between blips and secular declines. If you understand the trends in a given market, you're far better able to help your borrower deal with the inevitable ups and downs. Knowledge is directly related to judgment.

Do we work within a set of constraints and parameters? Of course we do. Do we use analytical tools and guidelines as an aid to the decision-making process? Of course we do. Are we supremely careful about the risks we take, on the individual and portfolio levels? Of course we are. But being prudent doesn't always mean saying "no." When we say "yes," we're doing so from a position of knowledge. Remember, too, that commercial banking is nothing if not diversified; there are more than 4,000 names in our portfolio; even an aggressive VC firm might have 40 in its. Our risk is considerably less concentrated. What sets Silicon Valley Bank apart is our ability to apply the insight and information we have developed over the years to the relatively uncharted waters of the entrepreneurial space.

We never set out to be all things to entrepreneurs, but we did set out to be a comprehensive provider of commercial banking services, lending as well as cash management and other banking services. We are, after all, in the business of providing and managing credit, and our success depends on our ability to do that. Succeeding in this environment has meant embracing the concept of the networked enterprise (and doing so long before that phrase had much currency). We've sought out relationships with other firms and businesses that can benefit us and our clients, from venture capitalists (we have an office on Sand Hill Road) to legal, accounting, and other business services. Moreover, we stayed in the game, even as larger banks came and went. And we continued to embrace new sectors and new ways of doing business.

THE INTERNET CHANGES EVERYTHING

The cliché about the Internet—that it changes everything—becomes more obviously true with each passing day. Yes, the valuations are (or maybe they just seem to be) absurd. Yes, many of them will not survive to become the great companies of tomorrow. Yes, there will be continued, and possibly greater, volatility in the sector. But the Internet is not like the industrial revolution in terms of its impact, and its effects are likely to be even more far-reaching and dramatic. As more companies in more sectors are discovering, the Internet provides powerful opportunities.

The Internet is one of the best entrepreneurial engines since the microprocessor—and it will probably prove to be better. Nearly $5 billion of new investment (venture stage) poured into the sector in 1998, and approximately 36 percent of 1998 IPOs were Internet-related. In 1999, the Internet was even more prominent: Internet-related companies attracted $12 billion in VC investment, and as of September 30, 1999, more than 57 percent of the year's VC capital commitments. Some 205 IPOs were Internet-related, as of December 1, 1999. It seems you can't open a business magazine without reading about a twenty-something overnight Internet multimillionaire. The conclusion is inescapable: the Internet is spawning new businesses and new opportunities at a fantastic rate, generating more potential business for firms like Silicon Valley Bank.

Perhaps even more important than the new clients the Internet offers us are the new opportunities it offers in terms of channel and delivery. We can do more, and do more for less, using the Internet. Of course, we're not alone in that: the Internet lowers the barriers to entry for banking, just as it has done for book and CD buying, to cite just two examples. Internet-only banks like Wingspan and Netbank are already chipping away at the retail sector. (From a structural vantage point, the existing framework of bricks-and-mortar branches, the traditional distribution system for retail banking, can only get smaller.) The corporate banking arena is surely next, and we recognized early that we could either embrace the Internet or watch our business get clicked away to Internet-savvy competitors. So we launched eSource, a Silicon Valley Bank–sponsored portal offering business services specifically intended for our entrepreneurial clients.

And eSource is just the first step of our Internet strategy. We also plan to web-enable more of our banking products such as cash management and foreign exchange. In part, of course, it's because our customers want us to, and it's a useful way to deepen the ties that connect us—to forge the kind of networked enterprise that will be the defining organization model in the new century. In the parlance of the Internet, eSource enables us to build "stickier" relationships. But it's also because the Internet offers us a tremendous source of leverage—the ability to transact business and forge relationships with more companies using fewer human resources.

Obviously, that's an important goal for any business, but it's doubly so here in Silicon Valley because of the importance of identifying opportunities that are indicative of the future direction of entrepreneurial financing. A couple of years ago, we launched a new practice group called Emerging Technologies, specifically designed to enable us to serve the earliest stage of start-up companies (some are even pre-start-up—that is, they are still putting together their business plan). The services are basic, but so are the needs for these very early stage companies: checking accounts, a corporate credit card, perhaps an asset-backed line of credit. These companies lie outside the purview of the major venture capital firms, which, quite often, are focused on larger investment opportunities.

A few years ago, $500,000 was a reasonably large first round of venture capital financing. Today, it's $3 million to $5 million and often quite a bit more. Those at the very beginning, often backed by angel investors and new intermediaries like Garage.com (in which we are an equity investor), need our banking services as much as their more mature counterparts do. But to handle higher volumes of these clients and continue to be profitable, we need a lower-cost delivery system. The Internet is the ideal solution.

The growth opportunities in our Emerging Technologies Practice are very real. In just two years, we've gone from zero to more than one thousand clients. Not all of these companies will make it; very few will succeed on the scale of today's blockbuster IPOs. But some will. Many more will make it to a certain level before being acquired or merged. And we are building a good business by serving them with a sound, economically delivered portfolio of products and services. By banking with us, start-ups and entrepreneurs get solid financial tools and the opportunity to move ahead a little bit faster. And we build relationships with tomorrow's potential giants.

Our ability to successfully take advantage of these new opportunities around the world will always be a challenge, one that we are eager to embrace. Silicon Valley Bank has built a corporate culture that combines the ethos of the entrepreneur with the expertise and professionalism of an established bank. And that gives me confidence in our future in this region and in all the "Silicon Valleys" that are emerging elsewhere in the country and the world.

16

Advising the New Economy

The Role of Lawyers

CRAIG W. JOHNSON

As an undergraduate at Yale in the 1960s, I noticed when I first arrived on campus that there were lots of buildings named after or attributed to someone called Sterling. The Sterling Memorial Library, with its stained-glass windows, gargoyles, and fairyland metal castles on the roof, was a whimsical and imposing structure. There were Sterling professorships. The residential colleges had been built by money contributed by Sterling. Whoever Sterling was, he had obviously done well and was a loyal Yale alumnus.

Upon inquiry I discovered that they were all named after or funded by John W. Sterling, an 1864 graduate of Yale and the cofounder (in 1873) of the worldwide law firm of Shearman & Sterling, which now has more than 850 lawyers. Sterling joined the Wall Street bar just at the time the United States was trying to cope with massive growth and geographic expansion, post–Civil War reconstruction, and financial scandals, many of which centered around an aggressive and controversial "robber baron" named Jay Gould, who was then battling Cornelius Vanderbilt for control of the Erie Railroad and was trying to corner the market in gold. It was a time of financial Darwinism, when many businesses were being started and bankrupted, technologies such as the railroad and the telegraph were changing American business, and there was much financial speculation and a plethora of business and legal dealings and disputes. In short, it was a good time to be a lawyer!

Shearman & Sterling became the legal and business advisor to Gould, who, with the firm's help, seized control of the Union Pacific Railroad in 1875. Gould

325

was involved in a variety of other new business enterprises, including Western Union and the telegraph. Sterling also played a key role in advising many other early stage enterprises, including a small New York bank that would eventually become Citibank, an important Shearman & Sterling client even today.

Sterling died in 1918 and left most of his estate to Yale. By 1931 this gift had grown to $29 million—a huge sum in those days (hence the gargoyles and fairyland castles on top of the library). Sterling had the great good fortune to practice law in New York City—then the center of the financial universe—at a time when America was starting to flex its industrial muscle. The railroad and telegraph industries, the oil and gas industries, the automobile industry, the chemical and steel industries, the banking conglomerates that financed them—Sterling was there at the beginning, and he and his colleagues played an important role in developing many of these industries.

Sterling provided something that the "robber barons" of that explosive age needed—good business and legal advice. A law firm was a natural place to look for this advice. A good corporate lawyer comes into contact with a variety of businesses and business problems, and has the breadth of experience and per-spective that even the most successful entrepreneurs often lack. It was natural for corporate lawyers to evolve into business partners with their clients and even become entrepreneurs themselves—which was much easier in Sterling's day, when the businesses that would dominate American business by the mid-dle of the twentieth century were still in their embryonic stages.

Fast forward to today—and Silicon Valley, where my law firm (Venture Law Group, started in 1993 and with more than 90 attorneys at present) is right in the middle of the Internet/e-commerce and telecommunications explosion, having helped to start companies like Yahoo!, eToys, WebTV, Chemdex, Hot-mail, Foundry Networks, Cerent, and many others. I suspect that John Ster-ling would be at home in this place and time. Whole new industries and enor-mous wealth are being created, just as in his era. Small law firms have grown into enormous institutions to serve these new businesses, just as Shearman & Sterling did. Wilson Sonsini Goodrich & Rosati, my old firm, had 10 attor-neys when I joined in 1974, but has more than 600 lawyers today. We even have our own technology "robber barons" (Bill Gates, Larry Ellison, Scott McNealy, and Ted Turner, for example). Instead of breaking up Standard Oil, the government is trying to break up Microsoft. The parallels are uncanny. So it shouldn't be a surprise to find similarities between the lawyer's role on Wall Street then and in Silicon Valley today.

Lawyers are better positioned than other professionals to provide the kind of business advice and contacts beginning entrepreneurs need. Accountants, marketing consultants, and headhunters rarely attend meetings of the board of directors, but Silicon Valley attorneys almost always do, so the lawyers stay closer to their clients and their businesses and are better able to see the big picture and give relevant advice. Successful business executives can also be good coaches, but they usually have seen only a few companies up close, while an experienced venture lawyer has seen hundreds. Only the venture capitalists have comparable business experience, and in many cases the lawyers have more, although they lack the operational backgrounds investors usually have. Many business problems (such as financings or mergers) also have important legal components, which the lawyer is specially trained to handle. Lawyers also work closely with venture capitalists and other entrepreneurs. This allows them better to develop relationships of trust and makes them better sources of introductions and contacts than other professionals. It is often a lawyer's ability to make a key introduction to a potential source of funds or corporate partner that a beginning entrepreneur values most.

When I use the phrase "Silicon Valley lawyer" I really mean a lawyer whose clients are primarily technology companies, regardless of where that lawyer is located. Regions of technological innovation and start-ups are sprouting up in many parts of the world (Boston, Austin, Seattle, London, Tel Aviv, San Diego, and Hong Kong, for example), and there are lawyers in these areas who perform much the same role as do Silicon Valley lawyers. But the focus of this book is on the development and functioning of Silicon Valley, so I will discuss the way lawyers work here.

SILICON VALLEY LAWYERS AS BUSINESS ADVISORS

The business lawyer's role in Silicon Valley is very different from that of a corporate lawyer. For lawyers working with large, mature corporations in places like New York City and Cleveland, their role is more mechanical and circumscribed. They are paid well to draft and proof documents following SEC rules and form books. They can add creativity, energy, and value to their deals (and often do), but they generally report to a general counsel or assistant general counsel who is very fee-conscious, not to the founder or president of the business. With few exceptions, they are generally neither expected nor encouraged to participate in determining the strategy or direction of the business, only to carry out a specific mission in facilitating a particular transaction. It's an important but much narrower role.

Although start-up lawyers in Silicon Valley draft documents and follow form books, too, they usually play a much larger role in the businesses being started. They are often dealing with people with very limited or no business experience. These people need help in defining and pursing their business goals. They can go in many different directions and have many questions they need answered. Should they leave their present jobs or can they work on their new company idea while remaining with their current employers? How should the founders divide the initial stock ownership? Who should be on their board of directors? Whom should they use as patent counsel? Which financing sources should they consider? At what valuation and on what terms? Is their business strategy sound? How should it be modified? What should they do first? Second? Not at all? The start-up lawyer is writing on a clean slate, and there are no clear rules.

Most of these questions have significant legal components, so the entrepreneur tends naturally to seek out the lawyer's advice first. Entrepreneurs also feel the need to have someone on their side in the often bewildering and scary process of starting and building a company. They need an advocate and ally, a role that other professionals cannot fill. Entrepreneurs know that what they tell the lawyer is confidential, and they understand from generations of TV shows that the lawyer is supposed to be on their side, not just a neutral advisor. An accountant is seen as an umpire or referee, while the lawyer is the coach—always wanting to help the entrepreneur and the team to win the game.

HELPING ENTREPRENEURS AVOID EARLY MISTAKES

Seemingly minor structuring or strategy mistakes at the beginning of a business can have very adverse effects later on. As I've often explained to my start-up clients, starting companies is a lot like launching rockets: if you're a tenth of a degree off at launch, you may be a thousand miles off downrange.

A classic example is the story of VisiCorp in the late 1970s and early 1980s. Two Harvard Business School classmates watched as one of their professors struggled to erase and recalculate a set of financial projections for a business on the blackboard. The Apple II computer had just come out, and it occurred to them that perhaps software could be written to automate the recalculation process and save a lot of drudgery. One of them wrote the software, and the world's first spreadsheet program, VisiCalc, was born. Apple agreed to promote it to help sell more computers, and it was an enormous hit. The two founders, however, decided that they wanted to live in different places. One (the technical wizard) started the company Software Arts, based in Boston, to do the technical development. The other (the marketing guru) went to Silicon Valley to start a company (Personal Software, later VisiCorp) that would sell the software and pay a 50 percent royalty to Software Arts.

It all went fine until Software Arts decided it should develop future products for which it would get 100 percent of the revenues, not just 50 percent. The IBM PC had just been introduced, and Software Arts was focused on developing an obscure formula-solving program (TKSolver!) rather than doing a version of VisiCalc for the PC. Lawsuits were filed, and one of the key managers at VisiCorp, Mitch Kapor, quietly left and started his own company (Lotus) to a do a VisiCalc-like spreadsheet for the PC called 1-2-3.

VisiCorp and Software Arts eventually settled their lawsuit, but they never recovered. One eventually went out of business and the other was acquired. Meanwhile, Lotus became an enormous success. In hindsight, the flaw in the initial structuring of VisiCorp and Software Arts seems obvious, since one party made its money on stock and the other on royalties. Interests were misaligned, and failure inevitably occurred. The right advice at the beginning (which might have come from their lawyer) would have saved a lot of grief and large legal fees later on.

PROVIDING EMOTIONAL SUPPORT

A good lawyer for an entrepreneur should play the role of coach, mentor, and teacher. Good legal advice is important but is not all that entrepreneurs really want—they want business advice and the credibility and access that a good lawyer can provide. At the beginning stages of a company, even the most competent entrepreneur the first time out welcomes the steady hand on the tiller and advice of an experienced counselor. The student will grow up, and the lawyer's role will diminish in importance as the company expands and the direction of the business becomes clearer. But the bond established between the legal advisor and entrepreneur in the early days will often survive the reduction in the lawyer's role. Entrepreneurs remember who helped them when their success wasn't assured.

A lawyer for a business at the start-up stage also acts as a friend and cheerleader for the business and team. It's often lonely and frightening to the founders and their families to start a new business. They are giving up the security of well-paying jobs to live off their savings and seed capital. They need someone who has been successful with other businesses to believe in them and give them hope when things look bleak (as they will for almost all businesses at some time or another). The relationships between the young clients and their lawyers are often emotionally close.

Other professionals aren't as well positioned to provide this emotional support. Accountants are supposed to remain independent and aloof. They are there to keep entrepreneurs honest and to certify their financial results to shareholders. Headhunters, marketing consultants, and public relations agencies all have specific tasks to do that don't lend themselves to continuing and intimate relationships. Only the lawyer is there with the entrepreneur every step of the way, from start-up to IPO and beyond, experiencing the ups and downs of the business almost as vividly as the founders do.

SEQUENCING

The biggest challenge a young company has is sequencing, or getting things in the right order. Knowing what to do and in what sequence is critical, since the entrepreneur has very limited time and resources. Like a complex biochemical reaction in the body that involves numerous steps requiring certain enzymes and catalysts, starting a company requires a series of small steps that have to be taken in the correct order or the reaction will stop and the company will die. A lawyer who has been through the start-up process many times can help the young entrepreneur identify these steps and keep them in the right sequence.

A classic example of poor sequencing is the start-up that believes the market opportunity for its product is about to explode and decides to build a large sales force before the product has been fully developed, lest it leave an opening for a competitor. If there are delays in product development (as there often are), the costly sales force sitting idle can eat up valuable cash just at the time when investors may be starting to lose confidence that the product can be built. Companies are generally better off building the product first and then the sales force if there is significant technological risk in getting the product to work. Competitors will probably have the same challenges in developing the product, so waiting to develop a sales force until the product is ready will probably not put a company at a significant disadvantage.

Another role the start-up lawyer can play is in evaluating and modifying the business strategy. Often entrepreneurs have not thought things completely through, and the questions a good lawyer can ask encourage them to reconsider the issues. I call this the Heisenberg Uncertainty Principle of business strategies (modeled after the physics law that states that the mere act of trying to observe a particle's position changes that position due to the energy of the photon used to make the observation). For many start-ups, just the act of asking questions about their business strategy causes the strategy to change. I won't accept a new company as a client until I have what I call "target lock" on the business strategy for how the company will succeed (imagine Darth Vader trying to get "target lock" on Luke Skywalker's fighter when chasing him down the canyons of the Death Star). In trying to achieve this "target lock," the company's founders, not surprisingly, often change their strategy.

SILICON VALLEY LAWYERS AS GATEKEEPERS AND FILTERS

A business lawyer in Silicon Valley is also a source of valuable contacts. A would-be entrepreneur (many of whom come from other countries) often lacks credibility and has great difficulty reaching the right people who can help the new business. By enlisting the services of an experienced business attorney and law firm, the entrepreneur can be introduced to potential investors and board members who otherwise would not be willing to spend the time.

Silicon Valley can be thought of as a network of networks, with certain people acting as gatekeepers. The successful business lawyer is one of those gatekeepers. Others in the network value their judgment and experience. If the lawyers involve themselves with a new venture, it becomes more credible and people will be more likely to consider it and be attracted to it. Many venture capitalists will not look at a new business plan unless it is sponsored by someone—perhaps a lawyer—whose judgment they trust.

Until recently it was relatively easy for a new entrepreneur to get the attention and services of a good lawyer in Silicon Valley. Business lawyers maintained an open door, since they never knew if the two unlikely young persons in front of them would start the next Apple Computer or Yahoo! They often would not expect to be paid anything for their services unless and until the new company received funding.

But recently experienced lawyers in Silicon Valley have had to become much more selective in the clients they take. With the advent of the Internet it has become easier than ever before to start a new business, and the very high valuations the stock market has placed on these companies have been a powerful magnet for all kinds of people to start new companies. It is no longer necessary to have a strong technology background to start a new Internet business, making the universe of potential entrepreneurs much larger. At VLG we have even been approached by high school students wanting to start companies! Start-ups take much more time and handholding than later stage companies, so lawyers have to be even more careful in the clients they take on.

Most law firms let the individual partners decide what business to take on and provide an incentive for them to do so and build the biggest "book of business" they can. At VLG we do exactly the opposite. We have had for some time a New Business Committee that has the sole power to accept new clients. We won't accept a client unless we can properly staff it and it ranks high on our "fun and opportunity" matrix. It's not a question of paying our fees—we assume that all our clients will do that (historically more than 99 percent have). We want clients with whom we can have fun, for whom we can add value, and who provide us with an opportunity, which may take the form of representing a company in an exciting new industry or receiving stock in the company. Today we are able to accept as clients on average fewer than 5 percent of the companies that approach us for representation.

Choosing which start-up to take on as a client is a very difficult task. Whether a start-up company will be successful is not obvious even to the most experienced attorney. It's like trying to look at a one-year-old child and decide whether he or she will win the Nobel prize.

Take an example from my own experience. In late 1994 I was asked by one of my partners to meet with two young Stanford Ph.D. students who were considering whether to start a business around their hobby, which was surveying web sites in their spare time and posting them on their own Internet directory. I thought immediately that they were trying to build a Yellow Pages for the Internet, which sounded like a good idea, but they said no, that the web was growing far too rapidly to be able to do that. Instead they just surfed around, and when they found something interesting, they posted a link on their site. I asked if they could protect their listings, and again they said no—the full directory was visible to anyone, and people were already copying it. I asked if there was any way to make money from the service, and they said it was free in the spirit of the Internet, but maybe they could sell some ads on it. It didn't sound very promising (incomplete, nonproprietary, and without the prospect for significant revenues), but we took them on as clients anyway. Their site was already getting hundreds of thousands of hits per day, so something was going on, even if we couldn't figure out exactly what.

The company of course was Yahoo!, which today has a market capitalization in excess of $80 billion five years later. I suspect the lawyer who initially accepted Apple Computer as a client felt similarly puzzled as Steve Jobs and Steve Wozniak tried to explain their vision for the personal computer and how they would sell their Volkswagen bus and Hewlett-Packard calculator to raise funds to start the company.

It was easier in John Sterling's day, when the concepts of railroads, telegraphs, and banks were well understood. But the uncertainty and sense of potential are what get Silicon Valley business lawyers excited—just as they do for people visiting Las Vegas! The difference is that the lawyer can play a significant role in improving the odds of the company's success.

FACILITATORS, NOT ADVERSARIES

A lawyer in a booming economic environment must facilitate transactions, not obstruct them. In more mature economic settings, in which fighting over the pie is more important than creating it, a litigator's attitude and an "I win/you lose" mentality may be common. But in environments like Silicon Valley, where wealth is being created much more quickly than it can be divided, lawyers are prized for their "win/win" attitude and an ability to keep everyone focused on common goals and make things happen smoothly. Contentious-ness, formality, an emphasis on status, and unpleasantness are all qualities that will drive clients away.

Studies (such as the one Robert Gordon, then a Stanford law professor, con-ducted a number of years ago about the role of the lawyer in the boom years of the Wisconsin lumber industry) have found similar patterns in other times of economic prosperity. Clients want lawyers who can help them achieve their goals as efficiently as possible. They are focused on creating new wealth, not taking it away from others.

As an economic boom area matures, the role of the lawyer changes, too. The focus shifts gradually from wealth creation to wealth preservation. Practice areas such as estate and tax planning and litigation become more important.

This transition happened earlier in the twentieth century on Wall Street, and the beginnings of the same change can be seen in Silicon Valley, where a wealth creation ethic still dominates but where disputes over wealth division, estate planning, and litigation are becoming more common. Firms such as Cravath Swaine & Moore, which started as primarily a business law firm, started to develop major litigation practices in the 1930s. Other firms, like Milbank Tweed, developed major practices by focusing on the estate planning needs of wealthy families such as the Rockefellers. The same transition has been happening in Silicon Valley over the past 15 years. Firms such as Wilson Sonsini and Gray Cary went from primarily corporate practices to more var-ied ones in which litigation and other wealth preservation specialties now employ hundreds of attorneys. Large law firms from outside the area are open-ing branches in Silicon Valley, hoping to crash the party by offering their much deeper experience in big case litigation, employment and intellectual property disputes, and other areas.

A CASE STUDY OF THE SILICON VALLEY LAWYER'S ROLE: GARAGE.COM

One example of the role a lawyer can play in defining a new business occurred in my practice in August 1997. I was approached by two individuals with whom I had had professional contact in the past—Guy Kawasaki, then an Apple Computer Fellow and the former Macintosh software evangelist and author, and Rich Karlgaard, then editor in chief of *Forbes ASAP* and now publisher of *Forbes*. Kawasaki and Karlgaard wanted to start a business called "Boom Cities" (an Internet site about who's who and what's hot in the major technology cities in the world) and wanted me to represent the new business.

Even though Venture Law Group had had great success helping to start Yahoo! a few years earlier, I was still skeptical about advertising revenue–based Internet business models (it seemed like a very hard way to make money) and told Kawasaki and Karlgaard so. Over lunch I said I would really like to work with them, but couldn't we find a more interesting business to build? At that time I was preparing a speech I would be giving the next week to two groups of chief financial officers and Taiwanese investors and entrepreneurs about recent changes in angel and corporate investing in Silicon Valley. In my speech I explained that, although both types of investment were increasing, it was still very difficult for early stage entrepreneurs to find qualified angel and corporate investors and vice versa. It seemed like a perfect application for the Internet—to bring entrepreneurs and investors together in an efficient way. I suggested it as a substitute for the "Boom Cities" idea, and by the end of our lunch a new business was born. The Garage.com name was the idea of Beth Kawasaki, Guy's wife.

Having the idea for the business, however, wasn't enough. We needed a business strategy and funding to get it started. Fortunately, Kawasaki and Karlgaard had recruited a team of engineers, salespeople, and editors from Apple and Forbes, so we had the beginning of a great team. But we needed to lock up access to high-quality start-ups that needed advice and funding. So we used my introductions and prior contacts with leading Silicon Valley institutions (Silicon Valley Bank, PricewaterhouseCoopers, Heidrick & Struggles, Wilson Sonsini Goodrich & Rosati, and others) to get initial seed funding and sponsorship agreements. I introduced Stanford law professor Joseph Grundfest (a former

SEC commissioner and a leading expert on Internet securities law) to the company, since it was clear that Garage.com would raise novel legal issues the SEC had not yet considered. Step by step the business started to take form.

My principal role was to provide the contacts and correct sequencing for the development of the business, which mainly meant raising enough money to keep the doors open as we built the business. It was not an obvious idea for a business, and the top venture capitalists we initially approached turned us down. But we did find an investor, Advanced Technology Ventures, which had discovered us by accident: one of their partners was the brother-in-law of our webmaster and heard about Garage.com over a family dinner.

At each stage it was necessary to evaluate whether our strategy was working, much like trying to steer a sailboat out of a crowded harbor to the open sea in a brisk breeze. I had the most experience in getting companies started, so the team members often looked to me for guidance.

Today Garage.com is clearly a success, having brokered more than $100 million in funding for 40 companies in 1999 and established a solid record of profitability. Offices have been set up in Israel, London, Boston, Austin, and Seattle as well as Palo Alto. In Garage.com's development over the past two years I have had to play all of the roles I described above (conceptualizer, cheerleader, sequencer, and source of contacts and introductions).

Of course it helps to have a great team, which Garage.com has, and a charismatic leader such as Guy Kawasaki. But I had been through the start-up process many times more than the founders had, which allowed me to add value throughout the growth process. I have had this experience with numerous other companies, including Financial Engines, SnapTrack, and, most recently, Grassroots.com, which intends to change the political process through the use of the Internet. It's an enjoyable and creative process. Most Silicon Valley lawyers involved with start-ups feed off their energy, and I do, too. Financial returns are only a by-product of the fun in creating these companies.

THE INTERNET BOOM: THE LAWYER AS ENTREPRENEUR

It's commonly said that the Internet is changing everything, and that applies to the role of the business lawyer in Silicon Valley, too. There are a number of reasons for these changes.

First, the Internet boom has created an unprecedented number of Internet/e-commerce and networking equipment start-ups and entrepreneurs. Lawyers who in the past accepted all new clients are now being forced to be more selective in choosing clients. This selectivity is allowing lawyers to ask for and receive larger fees and stock ownership positions in the companies they take on. This is just a function of the market and supply and demand—the supply of experienced start-up lawyers has been overwhelmed by the demand of new companies and entrepreneurs for their services.

Second, the economic incentives of working with start-ups through stock ownership have dwarfed those of working with larger companies purely for fees. Even traditional large law firms are beginning to move away from purely fee-based compensation.

The changed environment has placed greater pressure on Silicon Valley law firms. Younger attorneys have skills that make them very desirable to young, fast-growing Internet companies. It's harder for law firms to retain attorneys, since start-ups can offer greater financial incentives through stock options and can be perceived as more fun, too. Attorney turnover rates at many large Silicon Valley law firms have increased tremendously in recent years. So have turnover rates at other types of service firms serving Silicon Valley, including headhunting firms, consulting firms, and investment banks.

Silicon Valley firms have reacted by dramatically raising salaries and benefits for younger attorneys, and in some cases letting them invest in their start-up clients. Even then, it's still difficult to persuade many younger business attorneys to stay. Silicon Valley law firms often feel like shopkeepers in San Francisco in 1849, trying to persuade their hired help to stay rather than run off to the gold fields.

The rapid attorney turnover places an even greater premium on those experienced start-up lawyers who remain. Clients become obsessed with persuading these lawyers to take them on as clients. Unsolicited gifts, phone calls, e-mails, and unscheduled visits are common. In the face of all this demand for their services, lawyers are learning how to say no, a very unnatural act for many of them.

The prosperity and amount of work in Silicon Valley and other technology centers have attracted the attention of larger law firms in other areas, which are opening offices in Silicon Valley in unprecedented numbers. Even John Sterling's firm (Shearman & Sterling) has opened a Menlo Park office. Generally these out-of-town firms are not targeting start-up work—they do not have the skill sets to select or service technology companies at this stage. Rather, they are seeking to service the increasing number of larger companies in Silicon Valley, doing big case and patent litigation, as well as employment law, large financing, and merger and acquisition work, which they have done for their other large clients. Since they have vast experience in this type of work and there is growing demand for help in these areas, these larger law firms are in general doing very well.

The lower technology requirements for starting a business and the unprecedented availability of venture and angel capital have encouraged some Silicon Valley lawyers to start their own businesses. Often the lawyers most interested in doing so are the younger ones.

I already mentioned my experience with companies such as Garage.com and Financial Engines. At VLG we recently had as a third-year associate a very talented young man whose father had owned a chain of gas stations and auto repair shops. The associate came up with the idea for a business-to-business company that would connect auto repair shops, auto parts suppliers, and insurance companies in one central Internet marketplace. Since no one appeared to be doing anything similar, he took a leave of absence from VLG, started the company as its initial CEO, raised $10 million from well-respected venture capital firms, and started building it. A year later the company, Carstation.com, is the leader in its field, has just raised $32 million in second-round financing from investors including Goldman Sachs, has more than 100 employees, and looks to be a huge success. The former VLG associate remains one of the largest shareholders in the company. From a beginning lawyer's viewpoint it sure beats staying at the office until midnight working on a big merger or financing!

Silicon Valley business lawyers often have unique access to all the pieces necessary to start a company around an idea. They have credibility with and access to a variety of funding sources. They know how to structure financings and corporate partnerships. They have experience with a large number of similar companies and can help with proper sequencing. So it's not surprising that more and more lawyers are becoming entrepreneurs themselves.

WILL THE INTERNET BOOM TIMES CONTINUE?

Silicon Valley business lawyers owe much of their current success to the rising tide of venture capital and the stock market, so it's natural to ask whether this tide will continue to rise and lift all boats. Although no one can say for sure, I'm betting that the economist turned entrepreneur Michael Rothschild has the correct historical perspective.

In December 1995, when the web was in its infancy, I was struck by a cover article in *Time* magazine that talked about some very interesting discoveries that had been made by British scientists. They had been studying fossils from the Burgess Shale in the Canadian Rockies, which had been collected by the Smithsonian. The problem was that no one could visualize what the animals that made the fossils looked like. When enough samples had been collected to allow their forms to be reconstructed, the scientists were amazed.

The animals were some of the strangest looking creatures imaginable: walking X's joined together by tube-like bodies, predators with teeth directly over their stomachs. *Time* thought them strange-looking enough to commission an artist to draw a rendering of them for the cover of its December 4, 1995, issue.

The fossils dated from a period 543 million years ago called the Cambrian Era. For the four billion years preceding the Cambrian Era (once the oceans had cooled and the atmosphere had stabilized), life on Earth had evolved slowly from single-celled organisms to simple plants. Then in a brief ten-million-year stretch (the so-called Cambrian Explosion), almost all the animals, plants, and species we know today were created in a frenzy of evolution. Some of the early results were the bizarre animals whose fossils the British scientists had studied.

What happened? The scientists believe that the simple organisms, through trial and error and genetic mutations, had finally developed genetic tool kits, the primitive precursors of DNA and RNA, that allowed them to pass on superior characteristics (teeth, fins, etc.) to their offspring. It was evolution's Big Bang, in *Time*'s words.

The development of new life forms during the Cambrian Era followed a path that is now well understood. At first organisms suddenly had the ability to evolve and had very little competition. Many bizarre life forms resulted, each in its own isolated area of the ocean floor. But as these life forms grew and expanded, they started to infringe on each other's territory. A process of "survival of the fittest" and consolidation began. The bizarre creatures were quickly eliminated by more competitive species. At the end of the 10 million years (a blink of an eye in geologic terms), things had pretty much worked themselves out, and evolution went back to its more incremental pace, which we see today.

About the same time the *Time* article came out, Netscape went public and the Internet craze penetrated the mass consciousness. One of the observers was Michael Rothschild, who had written a very informative book called *Bionomics* on the parallels between economics and biology. He had seen the same *Time* article I had. But he made a connection that I hadn't.

In a column in *Upside* magazine that was published in February 1996, Rothschild analogized what had happened in the Cambrian Explosion to what was then starting to happen in the Internet world. The development of the world wide web was equivalent to the development of DNA and RNA in his view. The result would be an explosion of new companies and business models, just as there had been an explosion of new life forms on land and in the ocean during the beginning of the Cambrian Era.

I believe that we are in the early stages of this Internet Explosion now. It's as if in 1994 there was a wide open ocean floor, and companies started to rush in to stake out territories and defend them. In the early stages companies with bizarre business models were created. Some companies were convinced that they could build a lasting business by selling below their (or anyone else's) cost. Other companies sought market share by giving away free computers or Internet access. Some of these companies may survive, but most will not.

Already there are signs that the next phase may be beginning. Companies are starting to infringe upon each other's territory, just as happened on the sea floor. Amazon.com is now selling toys, while eToys is starting to sell books. Companies with weaker business models are starting to be acquired or having more difficulty gaining access to capital. Only the fittest will survive in this classic Darwinian struggle. In the meantime there are the clever animals that stay out of the way and will be the survivors.

My guess is that the Internet Explosion will be played out in the next ten to fifteen years, not the next ten million. Then we will return to a period of incremental business evolution and development once everything and everybody are connected.

If I'm right, the role of the Silicon Valley lawyer will evolve over the next decade into a more traditional role. The entrepreneurial phase will recede, and lawyers will again tend to work for more mature companies doing more of the things most people think of lawyers as doing. But it will be a fun and enormously profitable decade, one in which lawyers will be at the center of much of the founding of the new economy. The skills they have will be in increasing demand all over the world.

17

Shepherding the Faithful

The Influence of Executive Search Firms

THOMAS J. FRIEL

If the story of Silicon Valley is the story of company creation and all that follows, what are the critical elements of company creation, and how do they interact? Answering that question is the fundamental purpose of this book, and all the contributors to it have their own perspectives to offer. There is general agreement that technology companies are formed by combining technology, money, and people in some hopefully winning recipe. Each of these main components and some others are critical, and each, at various times and in various cycles, has been in abundant or limited supply. But for at least the last twenty years, representing my active career in executive search in Silicon Valley, only one component, the people, has been in critically short supply, with no sign of relief as the millennium turns over.

The "jobs" business is a big business. In a recent report the investment banking firm of Thomas Weisel Partners estimated the size of the worldwide labor market, defining it as "all activities that revolve around finding employees," at $300 billion, of which roughly $200 billion is in the United States. This number is much larger than most previous estimates, because it includes estimates for staffing companies, temporary help agencies, and Internet recruiting or "e-cruiting," as well as traditional executive search firms, both retained and contingency. In Silicon Valley it is clearly a multibillion-dollar business, and it is growing rapidly. In fact, here, more than anywhere else, the need to find talent at every level has reached crisis proportions, with thousands upon thousands of unfilled high-skill positions and as many as two hundred open CEO positions.

Making the crisis more acute is the fact that committing to live and work in Silicon Valley is not like taking a job anywhere else. It is more like converting to a new faith and adopting its core set of beliefs and values. Faith? A factor in science and technology? It seems like a pretty long reach. But consider the definition of faith in the *American Heritage Dictionary*: "a confident belief in the truth, value, or trustworthiness of a person, idea, or thing" and "a belief that does not rest on logical proof or material evidence." In the Valley, the belief is that technological innovation and wealth creation are the reasons one lives and works, not merely the hoped for or incidental results of a career. These goals are pursued with zeal and conscientious devotion, and financial rewards, hopefully huge ones, are the expected outcome.

In using religion and faith as an analogy, I realize I risk offending some. That is not my intent, nor is it my intent to minimize or denigrate any faith. Although some here may pursue innovation and its financial rewards with a religious zeal that excludes all other beliefs, it is equally possible to adhere to the secular "faith" of Silicon Valley and at the same time live a life of deep commitment to almost any religion or none at all. In a peculiar way, and contrary to what exists in most other parts of the country and the world, traditional discrimination hardly exists in Silicon Valley. What one does or believes outside the company matters little and rarely comes up in recruiting, hiring, or daily life at the office. Here we have a very odd environment; at the same time that it is one of the most discriminatory meritocracies based on talent and performance, bordering on brutal at times, for the most part it discriminates on virtually nothing else.

If we accept that Silicon Valley has its own secular "religion," then it must have its saints and angels, its prophets and teachers, and their faithful disciples and converts. One might conceive of the prophet as Vannevar Bush, whose experiences as an educator at MIT, an inventor, leader of the Manhattan Project, and liaison with government and corporations were the catalysts for a broad vision of the technology business that made Silicon Valley possible. Bush's careful observations led him to conclude that for true technological advances to be made, risk-taking inventors needed access to resources such as venture capital and top research universities. Bush pioneered partnerships between research institutions and businesses, seeking to gain advances while not becoming encumbered by slow-paced corporate decision-making, politics, and bureaucratic nonsense. He created a structure that enabled the engineer or scientist to retain control while deriving the greatest benefit from external resources.

If Vannevar Bush was the prophet, then his student Fred Terman could be called the teacher of the new religion. Bush shared with Terman his ideas about the future of regional economies—that these economies would be based on the interrelationships of academics, entrepreneurs, and venture capital. During Terman's long career at Stanford University, he put into place the structure of university–business–venture capital collaboration that was the foundation for Silicon Valley, and he inspired the region's early technological pioneers, including Bill Hewlett and David Packard.

Terman embodied in his own life many of the tenets of the new "religion." During his entire career, he worked seven days a week and wasn't interested in vacations. "Why bother when your work is more fun?" was his reply, according to a source at the Stanford News Service. He did not consider this attitude singular, and others in the area today still believe it normal. Silicon Valley is populated by the faithful who stay until the job is done, and for whom a regular day is measured by accomplishment, not the clock. This insatiable passion for discovery and the useful application of technology can seem almost insane to those outside the area.

Similarly, Terman's emphasis on collegiality and collaboration among professionals gave birth to strong networks that have continued since the 1930s. These networks promoted the sharing of knowledge among professionals, regardless of company affiliation, allowing individuals loyal to a higher purpose rather than a corporation to work together to solve problems. Although conventional corporations still view such behavior as traitorous, descendents of Terman find it normal. The free exchange of ideas has sped up the pace of development for almost every company in Silicon Valley. This continuous interaction also makes changing jobs easier for Valley professionals, creating a win/win situation for company and employee. It enables individuals to pursue projects of greatest interest and to leave situations that have become unrewarding or companies that they no longer perceive to be at the leading edge.

This environment also fostered the forgiveness of failure as defined by traditional corporations "back East." Those who have failed—or did not succeed with their last project—are not "tainted goods" in the employment market, and my colleagues and I regularly place "failed" senior executives who would be rejected by more traditional companies elsewhere. Company founders and venture investors, who have experienced setbacks, know innovation is only possible when risks are taken. Development of technology and its rapid commercialization is only possible in an environment where people can freely experiment and create.

Terman and his disciples also fostered an atmosphere of entrepreneurialism through individual and collaborative interaction. "There wasn't enough faculty to go around," says Edward Ginzton, former chairman and CEO of Varian and a graduate student of Terman's, "so he encouraged us to create our own seminars, to teach each other. To be working for yourself, by yourself, along with Fred Terman, arguing with him about problems, helping him write his books. . . . It was just an exciting period to be a member of his graduate courses, an unforgettable experience" (Tajnai 1985). The excitement of collaborative interaction persists, as attested to, for example, by the popularity of "hot groups," in which ideas are shared and mobility encouraged. "Hot groups" have been a part of Silicon Valley businesses since before the phrase was coined, and local company leadership has come to realize that it must understand, support, and be an integral part of these mini–think tanks or the consequences for the company may be serious.

The saints and angels of the Silicon Valley religion were those who had the money to invest in fledgling technology companies. One of the earliest was the federal government. Terman had developed many contacts during his leadership of a wartime defense project and, after the war, these individuals helped him bring federal monies to research efforts in Silicon Valley. Luckily, venture capital funding via private limited partnerships replaced the government in the early 1970s, well in advance of the end of the Vietnam and Cold wars, rampant inflation, and military cutbacks. Silicon Valley enterprises as a result were able to focus on nonmilitary applications and grow their businesses dramatically.

Of course, these early venture capitalists were part of an inner circle. Most had been entrepreneurs or had previously held senior positions with local technology companies. They possessed intimate knowledge of technology and business acumen, giving them a unique perspective and ability to evaluate investment opportunities. They lived the religion by helping others grow. Recently, "angels," individuals who finance enterprises, have become a more prominent source of venture funds. Ironically, Garage.com, a company formed to formalize angel investing, recently invoked the religion metaphor for venture investing by naming its password-protected site featuring funded companies "heaven."

Regardless of their experience or functional expertise, successful venture capitalists take a strong role in building a management team, often calling upon executive search consultants, and in recent years even recruiting recruiters to their partnerships. Bill Unger at Mayfield, David Beirne at Benchmark, Tim Haley at IVP, Rick Devine at ICG, and April King at Sequoia are prime examples.

In fact, recently the lines of distinction between the venture capital firms and search firms have started to blur even more. As several of the major venture firms have formalized their recruiting efforts, several of the major executive search firms, including Heidrick & Struggles, have announced the formation of venture capital subsidiaries to invest in their clients. The attempts by all in the game to add more value across the "technology/money/people triangle" will certainly continue.

And where do my colleagues, the executive search consultants—or headhunters—fit in? They are the shepherds, finding those who embrace the faith and bringing them in contact with others like them, and participating in the identification and conversion of new members of the flock.

THE SHEPHERDS

The care executive search consultants give to recruiting the right people to fill Silicon Valley's top positions is essential to the religion's perpetuation. The individuals executive search consultants identify and attract to opportunities at local companies need to fit in. They must either already share the faith and embrace the religion, or see it and "convert." Though the faithful here cannot imagine anyone hesitating to join them, recruiting to local companies has never been an easy task. Many from outside Silicon Valley have only worked in traditional corporate cultures with political bureaucracies and, when told of the realities of working in the area, are skeptical. But experiencing is believing, and after working in Silicon Valley many become converts, and like many converts, more zealous in their faith. Without the faithful and the converts, Silicon Valley's growth would slow and the culture would be irrevocably altered.

Executive search in Silicon Valley is a tremendous responsibility as well as a rewarding career. Once viewed as a lowly occupation, executive search consulting is today recognized as integral to the continuation of the area's unique character. Executive search consultants' abilities to reach and attract the professionals who fit in and will prosper in such an environment are sought by those who understand the vital importance of the legacy of Bush, Terman, and the first disciples. More and more, and earlier and earlier, companies are turning to search professionals to help build management teams at every level. This has led to some notable high-profile successes and some failures, as well as a proliferation of new entrants to the profession.

Although executive recruiting, personnel agencies, and other related businesses have existed in the area since the 1950s, the real explosion began in the early 1980s, as demand for managerial talent exploded to rapidly outpace supply. By the mid-1980s, the major players in the profession, Heidrick & Struggles, Korn Ferry, SpencerStuart, and Russell Reynolds, were all represented by offices in Menlo Park or Palo Alto. Search firms of all sizes and types, from boutiques to international firms, contingency and retainer, followed, smelling another gold rush. But the gold—people—wasn't always in "them thar hills." The special needs of Valley firms made executive search as difficult as prospecting for gold had once been.

With companies being created at "cyber" rates, bringing in talent from outside Silicon Valley is more necessary now than ever. Executive search consultants and their research departments identify and qualify those best suited for careers in area companies. These shepherds have become an integral part of the unique local ecology by attracting those best qualified to fill the positions.

The challenge for the executive search consultant is to find people who can embrace the Valley's principles of mutual respect and trust for all involved in the work. This is the cornerstone of Silicon Valley's corporate culture, with its distinct employer/employee relationship. Paul Mackun, in "Silicon Valley and

Route 128: Two Faces of the American Technopolis," states that "Hewlett-Packard pioneered the formation of a distinctive Silicon Valley management style, treating workers as family members. Numerous workers and companies have sought to duplicate Hewlett-Packard's management style," and Hewlett-Packard alumni have started and run many of the Valley's successful companies.[1]

Silicon Valley companies have also long been regarded as innovators in employee benefits, both formal and informal. Flexibility and recognition of the value of employees figure in the selection of top management, for these are important aspects of a company's success. Yet, despite the traditional annual report rhetoric that claims "employees are our most valuable asset," many executives who have not experienced Silicon Valley's environment find this type of business culture foreign. Some easily adjust to the Silicon Valley business culture, viewing it as an opportunity to grow professionally. Others cannot clear this hurdle and have tried to impose their own managerial style, usually with disastrous results.

The first high-profile executive searches in Silicon Valley occurred in 1983 with the CEO appointments of John Sculley at Apple Computer and Jim Morgan at Atari. Both were consumer goods executives with established reputations at Eastern companies, Sculley at Pepsico and Morgan at Phillip Morris. Although Sculley's time at Apple resulted in more notoriety, at the time there was actually more focus on Morgan's appointment at Atari. But as the two took charge of these important local companies, key differences in their styles emerged. Sculley, a pure product of the Eastern establishment, embraced the Silicon Valley "faith" in every way—dress, attitude, and relationships—and quickly became a "convert." Morgan, however, never seemed comfortable with the informality of Silicon Valley and quickly returned to the East. This pattern has repeated itself through the years. Transplanted executives have either quickly adjusted, or resisted and never fit in. Not all who have "converted" found success immediately, and some never did. But virtually all who came here and tried to operate with Eastern establishment formality ultimately failed.

The same experience has characterized companies that came to Silicon Valley from the East to invest or acquire and tried to operate under their usual business rules. Not a single noteworthy success can be found, and the failures include some of the world's best companies: DEC, IBM, Xerox, Burroughs, Motorola, Kodak, Schlumberger, Olivetti, British Telecom, General Motors, Ford, Exxon, and GE, as well as many others.

The early successes of Sculley at Apple, as well as others like Bob Jaunich at Osborne Computer, Tom Kalinske at Sega, and Jim Barksdale at Netscape, helped set the stage for a series of cross-industry searches for professional CEOs to replace technologically oriented founders. Without notable exception, the CEOs that were successful were those that quickly adopted the "religion." High-level placements in recent years, however, have for the most part involved moving industry veterans, most of whom were already steeped in the Silicon Valley faith. Prime examples in recent years include Rick Belluzzo, of Hewlett-Packard, joining Silicon Graphics and later Microsoft; John W. Thompson leaving IBM to head Symantec; and, most recently, Carly Fiorina moving from Lucent to Hewlett-Packard.

HOW EXECUTIVE SEARCH WORKS

How do executive search consultants identify and recruit those who will further the Silicon Valley faith? The process of conducting an executive search, although often shrouded in secrecy, is generally pretty straightforward, often beginning with a competitive presentation by several firms to a client search committee. This competition, or "shoot-out" in the parlance of the profession, results in a firm being selected on an exclusive basis to represent the client and conduct the search assignment. A fee is determined, generally equal to one-third of the first year target compensation for the position. This fee is invoiced in increments over the months the project is conducted and reconciled at the end of the assignment. Increasingly, equity is a component of the fee in searches for senior officers for pre-IPO companies and for CEOs for private and public companies. The use of equity aligns the incentives of the company, the search firm, and the candidate.

The balance of the project takes 90 to 180 days, in most cases, and consists of three main phases. The first of these phases, the research and preparation phase, involves writing a position description, interviewing client company executives, and creating a search plan and list of individuals to be contacted. The second phase, the outreach, qualification, and presentation phase, involves actually contacting targeted individuals, determining their interest, interviewing them to assess their qualifications, and introducing a "short list" of typically three to five qualified, interested candidates to the client for their review, interview, and assessment. The third phase, the referencing, negotiation, and closing, involves the selection of the finalist from the short list and the process of negotiating an appropriate position description, compensation package, and other related matters. Also at this stage, references are checked and due diligence is typically done by client, by candidate, and by the executive search firm.

It is in this last phase that the battle is won or lost and the most value created. Playing the role of psychiatrist, lawyer, arbitrator, devil's advocate, compensation expert, family counselor, relocation expert, investment banker, coach, and friend, the recruiter gradually and carefully nudges both candidate and client toward what they both must ultimately view as a win-win situation. For CEO searches with very complicated compensation and equity packages, outside experts must often be consulted. The last 24 hours of a CEO search often leaves everyone exhausted, much like lawyers and investment bankers pricing an IPO. This end game results in exhilaration if success is achieved, or despair if the deal falls apart at the last minute and a restart is required.

While the steps of the executive search process are generally consistent from search to search and from firm to firm, often the results are not. As in any industry, stars have emerged based on the reputations of their firms and the individual search consultants' ability to obtain and successfully complete the highest profile assignments. Among the large international firms, Heidrick & Struggles, Korn Ferry, and SpencerStuart lead the pack in such assignments, followed by the smaller, specialized boutiques Ramsey-Beirne and Christian & Timbers. The key partners in these firms and others who stay on top in this business have built their reputations on getting the best candidates into the search and getting them closed.

So how does this work differ in Silicon Valley from elsewhere in the country? The main challenge faced by executive search firms in the Valley is to bring to our clients executives who have already adopted the "faith" or who are ready to convert, while at the same time dealing with a limited supply of candidates and overwhelming demand.

In the first place, the number of open positions here is unprecedented, and cutting through the clutter to get the attention of qualified candidates is becoming extremely difficult. Many of the CEOs and other senior officers I know have told me they are only taking calls now from recruiters they know personally, and some have stopped responding completely.

Second, the unvested, stock option, "in the money" wealth that most local executives are holding is astronomical by historic standards. This is requiring clients to raise option awards to enormous levels and, in some cases, to guarantee some of the future assumed appreciation, to provide buyouts (to compensate for expected wealth forgone by moving), to offer signing bonuses ranging from tens of thousands to millions of dollars, and to agree to things that would have never been discussed even three years ago. Compensation now sometimes includes second homes, airplanes, favored investment opportunities, and other perks. A prime example of a recent high-profile recruitment would be the $100 million or so package needed to recruit former Andersen Consulting CEO George Shaheen to Webvan.

Finally, these high-profile CEO, COO, and CFO jobs are hard and risky, as some very recent "flameouts" have proven. As a result, the emphasis on "golden," or probably more accurately "platinum," parachutes has made negotiating employment contracts at the senior management level a more difficult and expensive proposition than ever before. Obviously the faith of Silicon Valley has never been accompanied by a vow of poverty.

The era of superstar CEOs with compensation packages previously only associated with movie stars and top athletes is certainly upon us. In fact, it is clearly only a matter of time before agents like Michael Ovitz and Lee Steinberg or the fictional Jerry McGuire begin representing CEOs as well as sports and media superstars. For the moment, however, that role still falls to my professional colleagues as we continued to "shepherd" the proven and emerging talent toward the companies so desperate for their vision and leadership.

The changes in Silicon Valley are reflected not only in executive search firms like mine, but also in the role of other players in the employment and staffing market. Perhaps nowhere else in the world have these companies grown as fast and made as much impact as they have here. These companies, unlike the executive search firms, attempt to fill the needs of growing companies for staff at all levels. It is in the middle and lower ranks at local companies that some of the less positive aspects of Silicon Valley's employment market are most in evidence.

Several prominent studies have recently claimed that there is a widening chasm that can be traced to a shift by high-technology companies to hiring temporary workers. Since the mid-1980s, employment in temporary agencies in the Valley has risen at twice the overall growth rate and now accounts for 27 percent to 40 percent of the total workforce. Greater reliance on temps is a trend in many sectors of the economy, but it represents an especially strong shift in culture in the technology industries, particularly at companies like Intel and Hewlett-Packard, which historically prided themselves on generous, almost paternalistic, employment practices. Reducing their commitments to lifetime employment while still attempting to maintain the loyalty of their workforces has caused great strain at these companies in particular.

Other negative effects are the competition foreign contract or temporary workers provide for local talent, the increased turnover and staffing costs faced by most local employers, and a host of infrastructure and public policy issues created by the influx of temporary talent. Many Valley observers also worry about the loss of loyalty to the company that stability historically provided to employer and employee alike.

PLACEMENT AGENCIES
AND CONTINGENCY SEARCH FIRMS

Although retained executive search is generally the approach of choice for senior officer positions, at the lower and middle management levels the predominant approach is contingent search, the same basic method used for administrative and clerical hires. Companies seeking individuals for these positions (and they are currently doing so by the thousands) place a "job order" or sign a contact with a contingency search firm or placement agency, often on a nonexclusive basis. If a firm supplies a candidate who is hired and remains employed a specified length of time, it receives a fee, generally 20 percent to 30 percent of the employee's yearly compensation. The advantages of this process are speed and access to the contacts of multiple firms. The disadvantages can include the limited ability or willingness of the contingency firms to spend the time and effort to conduct a thorough outreach to employed candidates not seeking a new position. Among the more prominent staffing and placement firms in Silicon Valley are Robert Half International, Adecca, Manpower, and Management Recruiters. Although these firms have different methodologies and pricing policies than executive search firms, they all have their roles to play in the continuing evolution of the Valley.

E-CRUITING AND THE INTERNET

Of particular significance over the past few years has been the impact of the Internet on recruiting. Monster Board, now a subsidiary of the search firm TMP Worldwide, was probably the first major effort to post positions on the web and use the Internet to replace traditional employment advertising and job fairs. It has been followed by Career Builder, HotJobs, Headhunter.net, Career Mosaic, and others, several of which are now public companies themselves.

According to Thomas Weisel Partners, the business of e-cruiting will reach $2 to $5 billion by 2003. Longer term, they have forecasted that it will capture one-half of the total U.S. search and recruitment market and has the potential to become a $40 billion market in the next ten years. They indicate that the current "job boards" will soon be replaced by transaction-oriented search and selection businesses and, ultimately, by full-service companies with established brands that will provide a variety of services to create long-term "employment cycle solutions" for clients and candidate alike.

The major search firms, notably Heidrick & Struggles and Korn Ferry, have entered the Internet search market as well, investing heavily in their own Internet recruiting subsidiaries. The need to invest in technology to support both their Internet and traditional search methodologies led both these leading firms to IPOs in 1999.

Among the challenges facing staffing and recruiting firms is the recruiting of talent from around the world. Immigrants may soon outnumber natives. This diversity has provided companies with links to global markets. Nationals of other countries have become point people for overseas expansion. To be successful, these overseas operations must be staffed by the faithful, just as in Silicon Valley. There is even beginning to be a small reverse flow of talent to other parts of the world. Silicon Valley, however, still remains the promised land.

THE FUTURE OF EXECUTIVE SEARCH

Finding people for businesses has itself become a big business as we enter the year 2000, and the number of companies in Silicon Valley actively seeking new CEOs and other senior officers moves into the hundreds.

This has caused, over the past two to three years, an unprecedented seller's market for talent. Now more than ever, we could probably alter Bill Clinton's famous campaign slogan to "it's the people, stupid!" Demand for executives, and in fact for talent at all levels, has gotten so frantic that companies are trying many new approaches and offering compensation, benefits, and equity packages that sometimes defy tradition. Cars, country clubs, airplanes, bounties for employees, child care, and more certainly enrich lives and bank accounts, but in the end the tenets of the faith remain largely unaffected. As I said earlier, this religion has always had at its core a "vow of wealth," not of poverty.

For those who practice the craft of executive search, the pressures and the rewards have never been higher. But that can be said for everyone associated with Silicon Valley. Will the future be like the past? In my view, yes and even more so. For those who accept the faith and buy in to the dream, there is no better place and no better time than right here, right now.

18

Guiding the Innovators

Why Accountants Are Valued

JAMES D. ATWELL

Why do Silicon Valley's high-technology companies present such complex accounting challenges? The difficulties are more readily summed up than surmounted: many are young firms, headed by founders with little experience of securities laws and regulations, with few tangible assets, highly uncertain revenue streams, no profits, and many stock options outstanding. They engage in complex transactions with other firms, and often invent new business models. Generally accepted accounting principles did not evolve from the needs and practices of such firms.

Silicon Valley's research-rich environment spawns many businesses, such as Internet search engines and technology companies, that break not just new technical ground but new accounting and legal ground as well. Valley companies thus make accountants an integral part of their development team. Accountants and lawyers collaborate closely, and venture capitalists funding high-tech start-ups rely on these teams of professional advisers to structure financial and legal matters in accordance with SEC regulations, and to avoid missteps that could delay or derail their desired exit, the initial public offering (IPO).

In the past fifteen years or so, the number of missteps that fast-growing, high-tech companies can make has multiplied. New software, software/hardware combinations, and intellectual property issues have taken Valley companies into uncharted financial and legal territory, where complex transactions can have unexpected consequences for a company's profit and loss statement

(P&L). The creative business practices that innovative young companies put in place to sell products, attract financing, and motivate employees and strategic partners create further complications. Providing guidance to these innovators makes being an accountant in the Valley a unique challenge.

THROUGH THE EYES OF VALLEY ENTREPRENEURS

The most sought-after accountants on this high-tech turf are those dedicated to start-ups, or the emerging company sector. They have worked with specific industries and markets from the start and use that understanding to help with company positioning and to interpret and apply both published and unwritten rules and standards.

"One of the key elements that played a major role in my success was the 'partnership' that I established in 1979 with accountants Bob Stavers and Nick Moore of PricewaterhouseCoopers. They, along with John Cardoza of Cooley Godward, my corporate counsel, were an integral part of my management team," says Bob Welch, a Silicon Valley entrepreneur for 30 years, who in April 1999 sold Telegra, a test equipment company he co-founded, to Hewlett-Packard. "I learned that it was important to get them involved early in my business decision process, whether it be evaluating an acquisition, new equity financing, revenue recognition issues, or preparing our company for a public offering."

Welch has vivid recollections of key moments with his advisory team, from the time Bob Stavers picked up the phone to get timely SEC comment clearance on a lingering S1 filing for Zitel, necessary before making a public offering, to when Stavers guided valuation negotiations when Welch's start-up OEMTek was sold in 1986 to Corvus Systems. There's something about the thrill of making a sale on a tax-free stock exchange for a gain of about 1,250 times the original investment that stays with you.

"I consider it a mistake for entrepreneurs to treat their accounting firm solely as an auditor, not a partner," Welch observes. "When you include legal and accounting advisers in significant business decisions, they are in a much better position to help management position the company for profitable growth and success."

Michael Kourey of Polycom agrees. The senior vice president of finance and administration, CFO, and board member of the leader in enterprise collaboration and DSL-based integrated access products says,

> I believe the role of the independent accountant is different in the technology community than it is in the broader business community. This is particularly the case in Silicon Valley, arguably the center of the technology universe. In addition to their traditional roles as auditors and tax advisers, outside accountants in Silicon Valley are some of the experts we bring in to structure our deals and their strategic parameters, and help our management teams come up with an architecture that's going to make sense on every level.

"Right now," Kourey adds,

> being in Silicon Valley is like being in Florence during the Renaissance. Enormous changes, such as the macro shift from the circuit switch network to the IP network, and having broadband deployed from the enterprise all the way to the consumer's home office and living room, have created tremendous opportunities. Venture capital is readily available and deals are flowing, from the formation of start-up companies to the strategic alliances between companies at arm's length to the outright merger of equals and acquisition. With all of that happening, there are significant accounting ramifications for which you need experts ready to jump in and assist quickly.

Good accountants here help structure business models and transactions to radically reduce the risks that are inherent in being a public technology company. And, in an environment as dynamic as Silicon Valley, the risks can be significant.

THE ROLE OF THE SILICON VALLEY ACCOUNTANT

Accountants in Silicon Valley must stay on top of rapidly changing guidelines that affect high-tech start-ups. High-tech companies that have distributed equity widely, and that operate in rapidly changing environments, tend to adopt a "we'll do whatever it takes" attitude that has attracted increased attention from the SEC and Financial Accounting Standards Board (FASB). Often, the announcement of a position on a new issue or problem in a speech may serve as the only notice that the issue will be under scrutiny and that ignoring it could be costly. Moreover, these organizations are often playing catch-up. Because of the rapid pace of innovation in the Valley, official rules and regulations are often a step behind the latest business models. "A lot of the changes and the interpretations that can have significant impact on companies come in the form of speeches from the SEC, for example during an annual joint meeting of the American Institute of Certified Public Accountants and the SEC," says Larry DeBower, a partner with PricewaterhouseCoopers in San Jose. "There is far less of the traditional exposure process that takes place so people can think about the changes and prepare for them. At the same time, the extent to which interpretations and guidance are provided by the SEC has increased significantly."

The Silicon Valley accountant in particular must focus on complex and evolving rules and regulations governing high-tech company practices in three areas: equity, revenue recognition, and acquisitions.

Equity as Incentive

Unlike other companies, high-tech start-ups tend to raise capital for their ventures through preferred stock financings. For years, Boston was the only other high-tech community in the world that faced the kinds of equity questions associated with Silicon Valley. Today, venture capital and its associated accounting issues are expanding to other areas, such as Seattle and Austin. Silicon Valley, however, remains the primary location in which these problems must be resolved. Venture capital–fueled start-ups dominate the Valley, and young technology companies, unable to offer large cash salaries or even guarantee that they will exist in two to four years, routinely attract and retain talented executives and staff by issuing stock options and warrants.

Equity is also an important way for Valley start-ups, which tend to outsource critical parts of their products or services, to keep their strategic partners close. "The bright lines between companies are blurring as companies work more closely together on innovative products and services than they ever did in the past," says DeBower. "Accounting for that is becoming more and more difficult, and that's why the rules, particularly those governing revenue recognition and equity arrangements, are changing."

A critical part of the Silicon Valley accountant's job is to advise companies on the lines that they must not cross in order to conform to written acceptable standards on equity financing. The SEC and FASB have been concerned, for example, about companies being overly aggressive in pricing stock options attractively for employees and management. Normally, when a company goes public, accounting rules specify that the exercise price of an option is equal to the fair value of the underlying stock; there is then no impact on the company's expenses, or therefore its income statement. But, if a company issues an option *below* fair value, the difference between the fair value and the exercise price is a form of compensation and is charged against the company's P&L for the vesting period, typically four years. The SEC staff have recently stated that they consider the estimated offering price to be the fair value of the company's common stock one year prior to the offering, unless there is objective evidence to refute this presumption. That presents a challenge, considering how difficult it can be for a privately held company even to determine, let alone to prove, its fair value if it wishes to dispute the SEC's assessment.

Overall, the rules and regulations on equity instruments have become more precise about the impact of various equity instruments, such as warrants, preferred stock, or options, on a company's P&L. The two biggest changes in this area are rules that 1) provide specific guidance on when charges must be taken related to equity transactions; and 2) specify the level of evidence necessary to support the privately held company's estimate of its fair value.

Spotlight on Recognizing Revenue

Even when there are explicit rules governing a subject, the Silicon Valley accountant must stay alert to the high-tech industry's tendency to outgrow the rules before new ones are issued. The SEC and FASB have issued more and more rules of late on revenue recognition for all industries, but software companies have had precise, if difficult-to-implement, revenue recognition rules since 1991. These rules were prompted by the software industry's history of restatements of previously issued financial statements, often surrounded by litigation.

The needs of Silicon Valley companies continue to evolve in the area of revenue recognition. Valley pioneers, spurred on by short product lives and a long list of customer expectations, tend to enter into long-term arrangements that involve much more than the straightforward purchase of products or services. Such bundled, or multiple-element, arrangements may include a combination of several products, software updates, technical support, installation, or training. Under the software revenue recognition rules as changed substantially in 1997, these multiple elements require high-tech companies to defer revenue if their value cannot be unbundled and proven, which leads to lower earnings.

A new task force made up of leading corporate executives and accountants has been formed to interpret the software rules. Considering the number of new dot.com companies valued on revenue rather than earnings, it's safe to predict that problems surrounding revenue recognition will continue, and the guidance provided by accountants will continue to evolve. In the case of more.com, for example, PricewaterhouseCoopers helped the company structure their contracts so they could recognize revenue while adhering to Generally Accepted Accounting Principles (GAAP).

Acquisition Accounting

Many types of companies face issues related to acquisition accounting. But in the Valley's brand of high-tech industry, in which companies in small sectors grow quickly, expand, and compete with numerous other entrants in the sector, consolidation through acquisitions is especially frequent. Silicon Valley accountants must be well versed in acquisition accounting matters, such as how companies account for purchased R&D in acquisitions for which purchase accounting is used, and the numerous rules and interpretations that must be considered when using pooling of interest accounting.

In 1997 Polycom faced some difficult issues when it acquired a company that had made a technology breakthrough. "We were concerned," explains Michael Kourey, "that if we did not protect escrow due to a particular outstanding legal issue after the acquisition closing, we could be unnecessarily exposed. Jim [Atwell] identified the best strategy to secure a portion of the escrow amount post-closing until the resolution of the legal issue. This provided us with long-term protection and still allowed us to meet all of the pooling rule requirements."

HANDLING A HYBRID

Because the application of the rules differs somewhat among industry segments such as semiconductors, computers/hardware, software, communications, life sciences, and the Internet, when an innovation comes along that doesn't fit neatly into one of the established categories, only accountants familiar with high-tech industries can correctly determine which guidelines to follow. In such a situation, the accountant is a trusted business adviser, best brought into the early stages of business planning.

"We often know what it is we want to accomplish," says Geoff Tate, the CEO of Rambus, a company that designs and licenses technology for semiconductor chips. "Then, we look to our professional advisers to tell us what the options are and help us figure out the best option that aligns with our company objectives."

Rambus became a client at PricewaterhouseCoopers's San Jose office as a start-up, about six years before its 1997 public offering. So, when its CEO wanted to create a business model that gave his company a highly predictable revenue stream, we understood what the issues were and how to help. Tate recalls,

> In the early days, when investors heard we were licensing, they'd think of MIPS, a company that developed microprocessors in 1989 and that in 1990 was positioning itself to compete with Intel in the workstation space. The company was doing a combination of licensing and building computers. It wasn't quite the same business model as ours, because we provide the patents and knowledge so that *others* can build integrated circuits, but MIPS had a licensing component. Unfortunately, the MIPS model didn't achieve what the accountants wanted it to achieve, to match the revenue with the spending required to generate the revenue. It gave licensing intellectual property a bad name for a long time, because the way the company did revenue recognition caused huge peaks and valleys in profits.

Since there were no revenue recognition guidelines specifically for an intellectual property–licensing company, Rambus had to find the closest analogy and apply its guidelines. Even though it looked like a semiconductor company, the way Rambus recognized revenue was more like a software company. The company worked for years to deliver on its commitments under contract.

"Together we developed our policy of recognizing income not when the money comes in from a licensee, but over the period of time during which we support that license," explains Rambus CFO Gary Harmon. "That was very important in terms of smoothing out our revenue, [and] also taking into account that we are not successful until that licensee goes into production. At that time it was a unique business model. And, because it was such a conservative way of booking revenue, we thought surely we'd have no questions from the SEC."

When the company filed for its IPO, however, it was assigned to the Semiconductor Unit of the SEC. The SEC examiner was accustomed to dealing with companies that made things and was less familiar with the current interpretations of the software revenue recognition rules. Time passed as the examiner consulted with examiners from the SEC's Software Unit. A team from Rambus, including the CFO and vice president of engineering, along with a team from PricewaterhouseCoopers spent time explaining the Rambus business and business model to the SEC examiner.

Two weeks before the company's IPO, Harmon and Tate continued on their road show to ensure that their company's story was fresh in the minds of the institutional investors. While driving between presentations, they'd call us for the latest on the SEC comments. Two days before the scheduled offering, the possibility still loomed that the company could lose the position regarding its revenue recognition policy, and be required to restate its financials and reprint and recirculate its prospectus. The delay could have taken the shine off its offering and perhaps caused it to miss an important market window.

"We got the SEC approval while we were driving around on the last day of the last part of our road show," recalls Tate. "It was a nail biter." In the end, Rambus went public as scheduled and its stock price doubled on the first day of trading.

"An accountant coming from a background of working with steel making or auto industry clients isn't likely to understand the subtleties of the particular accounting issues high-tech companies face," Harmon notes. He concludes, "High-tech companies don't want to get a detailed 'GAAP explanation' of things. We want to do things, and need to know how to do them properly within the accounting rules."

BREAKING NEW GROUND

In some cases, that means going where no Valley accountant has ever gone before.

In the fall of 1994, Walter Kortschak, a partner with the venture capital firm of Summit Partners; Jeff Saper, a partner with the law firm Wilson Sonsini Goodrich & Rosati; and I engineered what is widely viewed as the first leveraged buyout recapitalization in the Valley. Chong-Moon Lee, the founder and CEO of Diamond Multimedia, the leader in providing high-end video and graphic accelerator boards to the PC industry, had grown his business to more $200 million in revenues and was ready to move to the next phase of growth. The company was outgrowing many of the controls and systems it had in place, and it was important to make some changes.

"After twelve years of struggle, I was able to build up a company named the seventeenth fastest growing private company in the U.S. by *Inc.* magazine, and the eighth fastest growing private company in Silicon Valley in 1993," recalls Lee.

By 1994, *IDG Report* named our company number one in market share and revenue in high-end, multimedia graphic accelerator boards to the PC industry. It was an exciting and unusual situation. Diamond Multimedia had $203 million in revenue, no debt, no investors, no loans, and $27 million cash sitting in a bank account. The company had close to 10 percent net profit after tax and $1 million revenue per employee, with just 0.03 percent uncollectable accounts. We were in such good shape, we were ready for an IPO in every respect. However, from my point of view as sole owner and a major shareholder, I needed to consider the IPO's lock-up period that would preclude me from selling my shares of stock for two years. I needed to capture some of my company's value in cash, and Jim Atwell came up with a creative solution: a brand new style of LBO [leveraged buyout] plus IPO model. This was the first transaction of its kind to be implemented in the industry. In the LBO/recapitalization process, I sold my shares to the company and arranged for heavy bank loans to the company, using my stock as collateral. Summit and TA Associates simultaneously invested in the company.

As Kortschak says, "Our objective was to provide a significant amount of liquidity to Chong-Moon Lee, but also allow for a structure that eventually would give us the opportunity to issue stock options to employees and management that were attractively priced." Because the company was heavily leveraged with bank debt, the fair value of the common stock before the IPO was approximately seven cents. To support our position, we brought in a third party for an independent valuation prior to the public offering. Four months later the company went public at a significantly higher share price.

"We invented the structure and worked as a team breaking new legal and accounting ground," says Kortschak.

UNWRITTEN RULES, REAL CONSEQUENCES

In some areas there are no published rules, but significant consequences for taking an overly aggressive position. For example, in 1999 the SEC pushed back on In-Process R&D (IPR&D) in response to some companies' aggressiveness in this area. IPR&D refers to obtaining a piece of technology that is still in the development stage in a merger or acquisition, and then writing off the portion of the purchase price related to that technology. It seemed a reasonable solution, until some companies assigned as much as 50–80 percent of an acquisition's price to the undeveloped asset, which they then wrote off. When several dozen companies had to restate their published earnings in light of this inappropriate allocation of costs, behavior began to change. It is now common to find companies attributing between 10 and 20 percent of purchase price to IPR&D. Companies that team up with an experienced accountant in sensitive areas like this are less likely to have to restate earnings, which can be a blow to management credibility.

Sometimes traditional accounting standards no longer accommodate the way an industry functions. Then behavior can change in unexpected ways. For example, stock options, once used only to retain and reward executives, became a vital tool for emerging businesses to reward employees throughout the organization. The companies would award options at low prices, which would rise significantly if the company succeeded in making a public offering. Despite vehement Silicon Valley company protests, the FASB maintained that offering stock at a price that did not reflect a company's true value was compensation, and GAAP requires that the difference between the price at which the stock was issued and the post-IPO sale price result in a non-cash charge to the company's P&L for the vesting period.

Five years ago, most companies attempted to arrive at a value for options granted to employees so that there would be no P&L charge. Because the IPO price was significantly higher than the option price, the SEC would question the price put on the options by the company. Such a delay caused some companies, such as HMT Technology Corporation, a provider of the information-storing media known as thin-film disks inside hard disk drives, to take what they perceived to be a lower IPO price.

Today, to avoid having their offerings delayed, some companies are being as conservative as possible in valuing their stock, and taking maximum P&L charges as a result. Wall Street has become accustomed to discounting this non-cash charge when valuing companies.

WHEN RULES NEED MENDING

Unfortunately, sometimes accounting rules aren't in the best interests of businesses, especially high-tech ones. For example, two high-tech companies recently merged, and rather than use purchase accounting rules, which would have required them to subtract the purchase price from their P&L over time, they instead used pooling of interests, essentially combining company assets. This useful pooling method saved the combined company millions of dollars on its market capitalization. By the time this book is published, however, pooling of interests may be a memory. It is likely to be eliminated to conform to global accounting standards. Which raises the question: "Should companies be conforming to the FASB, or vice versa?"

The battlefront for accounting challenges like these is Silicon Valley, where innovative companies tend to encounter new issues first. The actions taken by Valley companies have consequences well beyond our region's borders.

"Often accounting firms are torn between accounting purity and accounting practicality," says Mark Heesen, president and formerly chief lobbyist of the National Venture Capital Association.

There is a constant dichotomy between the accounting community in general and Silicon Valley accountants as to where they're going to stand on issues. We tend to hear the accounting purists saying "We cannot get in bed with the high-tech community on issues like stock option accounting," and the more practical accountants saying, "You purists are not reflective of the new economy. You have to change your thoughts about accounting policy because the world is different than it was one hundred years ago." The reality is, accounting firms have a lot of balls in the air. They need to please the SEC, which could make life difficult for them, their partners worldwide, and the high-tech community.

Some issues, however, demand a united front. The accounting community and the high-tech venture capital community came together unconditionally in the area of securities litigation. Both worked for the passage of the 1995 federal law that made it more difficult for plaintiffs to sue high-tech company executives and their accounting firms simply because the price of the company's shares dropped a certain percentage. Another unifying issue was the campaign for the defeat of Proposition 211 in California, an attempt to circumvent federal law and allow such lawsuits to take place under California state law.

A MODEL FOR SERVING EMERGING BUSINESSES

The typical entrepreneurial team in Silicon Valley needs plenty of financial and accounting advice. Founders tend to have little or no training or experience in financial management or the public markets. And venture capitalists do not have the time to teach them. The number of portfolio companies per venture capitalist has climbed as the average age and experience level of first-time entrepreneurs falls. Some wryly joke that today's Internet start-up executives fresh out of college require adult supervision. As a result, accounting firms are working closely with start-ups to fill functional gaps, sometimes serving to help find CFOs, in addition to helping to navigate accounting rules and regulatory standards.

To be effective, accountants in a high-tech start-up environment need to understand the venture investing process and the critical development stages of these emerging companies. In the 1980s, PricewaterhouseCoopers, then a

Big Six accounting firm, helped to create the Bell-Mason Diagnostic, a tool used to systematically assess the stages of a company's growth and compare its experiences to an ideal model in order to identify and correct flaws early on. Subsequently, the firm licensed the Bell-Mason Diagnostic.

When venture capital was tight in 1991, PricewaterhouseCoopers formed what later became its Emerging Company Services (ECS) group in San Jose to assist Valley entrepreneurs through the various stages of the start-up and funding process. Nick Moore, the managing partner of the San Jose office, who later became the chairman of PricewaterhouseCoopers, brought in Brian Goncher, an MBA with start-up planning, funding, and operational experience. They shared a vision of supplementing Moore's team of accountants with a financial consulting practice made up of experienced, non-CPA financial professionals to form a group dedicated to helping start-ups get organized, connected, and funded.

Polycom's Michael Kourey recalls the help his company received when it wasn't much more than an idea. "I remember in the very early days Brian Goncher literally worked 48 hours straight with us on the original business plan and performed any other financial planning work that we needed to get done."

Because of the Valley's large number of entrepreneurs and venture capitalists, the region was an ideal environment for the ECS group, which I was given the opportunity to oversee. It took about three years to get a return on our time investment from start-ups that went on to succeed and need our auditing, consulting, tax, and other services. By the time Goncher left to found Frontier Ventures and become the venture capitalist he'd always wanted to be, he had provided strategic advice and financial consulting services to more than 250 technology companies in Silicon Valley, including Grand Junction Networks, iBAND communications, Network Appliance, ZeitNet, and Portola Communications.

Today, the Emerging Company Services group still prefers to grow its own clients, and prefers not to rely on the "beauty contest" some professional service firms participate in to woo a young company the day after it receives funding. Instead, the five-person team keeps a high profile in the local network, speaking at workshops for emerging businesses and sponsoring and chatting in forums for the exchange of entrepreneurial experiences and the discussion of technology trends, such as Round Zero.

"Start-up capital is not hard to get in the Valley these days. The challenge is finding the right people," says Nirav Tolia, a founder of Round Zero and Epinions, an Internet start-up that provides consumers with information to make informed buying decisions. Tolia remarks,

> As entrepreneurs, when we create partnerships with our service providers, we need to view them not only from a functional standpoint, but as additional resources. PricewaterhouseCoopers has been a bit of a trailblazer in this holistic approach to working with companies. Competition in the Valley demands that. We're not just relying on our accountants to advise us on our audit work, but on opportunities they see for us. And, because they have the knowledge not just from an accounting angle, but from a Valley angle, that advice is well regarded.

About ten times a week, PricewaterhouseCoopers's ECS team responds at no charge to unsolicited e-mail asking for comments on executive summaries. They refer promising entrepreneurs, such as the founders of Chipshot.com and Hotlinks, to venture capitalists, lawyers, and others in the network and offer advice for a small price. When Cook Express CEO Darby Williams was looking for strategic partners, the ECS group helped him narrow the company's list of 30 ideal partners to personal contacts at 10 of the companies. It certainly hasn't hurt PricewaterhouseCoopers to get promising Internet companies, like Yahoo!, e-Bay, and New York–based iVillage, in its pipeline. In the 1999 calendar year, PricewaterhouseCoopers handled 45 percent of the IPOs in Silicon Valley. In 1999, the firm has attempted to replicate this practice in ten other markets throughout the world.

What lies ahead? The Internet start-ups, which are typically industry-specific commerce companies, will raise new issues for accounting. Because today's Internet companies are being evaluated on their revenue streams, revenue recognition issues are hot. At press time, barter transactions are the topic of interest. The Emerging Issues Task Force has recently taken the position that, for example, a sports company receiving a 30-second commercial broadcast during the Superbowl, which normally costs $2 million, in exchange for running the television network's logo on its web site must meet specified criteria, including historical sales of advertising in similar volumes and placement on its web site to the same class of customer, in order to be able to record this transaction as revenue. If these criteria are not met, no revenue would be recorded. On the other hand, the sports company would see this as having a $2 million advertising hit both in revenue and in expense on its books. The recognition of revenue from this transaction not only makes them look more successful, it reflects the enormous coup they have achieved.

And, although Internet and technology companies are not exclusive to Silicon Valley, their issues will likely be taken on here first. Silicon Valley is in many respects a small town—but with the professional services network in place, the Valley can take on big ideas.

19

Free Advice

Consulting the Silicon Valley Way

REGIS MCKENNA

"**Y**ou're an advisor, not a consultant," said my consultant friend, leaning back in his chair after lunch at one of Silicon Valley's restaurants. "Consultants don't share their knowledge for free."

"The Valley is full of free consulting," I replied. "That's what makes it tick."

While "free advice" is a common practice in all areas of our lives, from business to love, health care to money, Silicon Valley is unique in the abundance of expertise passed on from generation to generation and given freely over lunches and dinners. It is tradition for those who have been successful to pass on their knowledge and experience to the new wave of innovators. Those from more established companies reinvest not only their money—private venture capital, or money invested by angels in Silicon Valley companies, may equal the amount invested by top venture funds—but also their experience and knowledge in the newer enterprises. In a manner of speaking, entrepreneurship and innovation are inherited in this community. This inheritance is one of the fundamental reasons that Silicon Valley is almost impossible to duplicate anywhere else in the world. An open knowledge architecture, passed on from innovative generation to innovative generation, is at the heart of this dynamic community. And, by and large, knowledge is free to those who know how to network.

In this environment of abundant free advice, what is the place of the professional consultant, whose job is to provide advice for a fee? Silicon Valley's evolving views toward consulting services and free advice can be traced to its unique, technology-driven engineering culture, which has evolved over more than 50 years. Consulting as a respected profession is a recent phenomenon in Silicon Valley. Historically, there has been an aversion to professional consultants, and for years, being a consultant translated as "being between jobs." That has all changed, however. Much of the transformation is due to the emergence of large companies, increased competition, the speed of change, the complexity of business issues, and the scarcity of experienced talent, as well as the convergence of information technology, telecommunications, and strategy. Many of these factors have emerged only in the last decade. Outsourcing of all sorts of corporate functions and needs is now generally accepted, as specialization and competition intensify.

The nature and character of consulting have also changed. It is no longer a profession that primarily conducts studies and criticizes management for doing a poor job of implementing theoretical strategies. Today, Silicon Valley's savvy consultants have joined the network and probably give away as much advice as they charge for. Certainly, most have learned the value of participating in the social architecture of open knowledge, and the value of equity ownership.

A CULTURE OF SELF-RELIANCE

Until recently, professional consulting had little place in Silicon Valley. The Valley's engineers developed a pragmatic culture of self-reliance that left little room for professional advice. It might be valuable to look briefly at the roots of this culture. Many have recognized the role former Stanford professor Frederick Terman played in the formation of Hewlett-Packard and the early technology environment. I make a distinction, however, between the technologies Terman sponsored and the beginning of the culture of independence, egalitarian management, and networking and the introduction of venture capital. The latter culture was spawned in the late 1950s by the rebellious actions of eight young engineers employed by Bill Shockley, inventor of the transistor. In 1957, eight of his Palo Alto company's—and the nation's—most gifted researchers had had enough of William Shockley's mercurial personality. They joined forces, leaving Shockley Transistor to form Fairchild Semiconductor (see Chapter 8). In the decades to follow, the "Traitorous Eight," as Shockley dubbed them, went on to form and lead many of Silicon Valley's most successful firms. Among the group were Bob Noyce, who would co-invent the integrated circuit and found Intel with Gordon Moore, and Gene Kleiner, who with Tom Perkins (who ran Hewlett-Packard's computer operations) would found the prestigious venture capital firm Kleiner Perkins Caufield & Byers. The relationships and experience these men, and others like them, developed over the years defined the way much of business is still done in the Valley. Since the "Traitorous Eight" did not have the financial resources to fund a new company, they reached out to Art Rock for venture capital and established a corporate alliance with Fairchild to back the new enterprise. Rock eventually relocated from New York to San Francisco, becoming a venture capital legend by choosing to fund Intel and Apple.

The rebellion at Shockley shaped the culture and future of Silicon Valley more than any other single event. The "Traitorous Eight" left their secure employment and founded a new company based on an egalitarian form of management, where ideas and performance counted more than seniority or titles. To finance their new business, they sought out venture capital and a strategic alliance. This radical style of management (and it was radical at the time) was a direct reaction to Shockley's command-and-control management style. The model has been duplicated by the hundreds of companies that spun out of Fairchild over the next twenty years and thousands of entrepreneurs since. The "Traitorous Eight"—rebellious, smart, independent, and confident of their abilities—set the pattern for things to come.

Virtually no infrastructure existed to support the area's business needs in the 1950s and 1960s. The leading banks, law and accounting firms, ad agencies, and other professional services were located 50 miles north in San Francisco, or 500 miles south in Los Angeles. That might not seem far, but from a cultural standpoint, San Francisco and Los Angeles were as distant from Silicon Valley as Boston or New York. Self-reliance was thus an essential part of building new industries. With little or no infrastructure or supporting services to speak of, managers had to improvise and *make* rather than *buy*. Companies designed and built their own power supplies, process and test equipment, and just about everything else. In addition, many of these start-ups operated on the belief that the markets would evolve if their technology would be adopted.

I began my high-tech career in the early 1960s at General MicroElectronics, a small semiconductor start-up. The founders spun the business out of Fairchild and brought with them a rudimentary knowledge of metal-oxide semiconductor (MOS) technology. The GMe engineers developed the technology and the company became the first to commercialize MOS technology, producing chips of higher density and lower power than those commonly available. Worth no more than a few million dollars, the company made everything from silicon ingots to packaged chips. They built much of their own photolithography and processing systems, and they packaged and tested the devices—all under one roof. They built or modified the test equipment because no one at the time had systems capable of testing these complex chips. In short, GMe was vertically integrated. Fairchild made their own test equipment as well, eventually spinning out a division to market these systems to the rising semiconductor industry. Applied Materials, founded in 1967 by a number of industry veterans, began by supplying components to these in-house do-it-yourself operations and has grown to become a world leader in technology, with more than $5 billion in revenues.

Much of today's multibillion-dollar semiconductor equipment industry began as do-it-yourself operations within the semiconductor companies. GMe had a Systems Division where they produced the first commercial calculator using MOS devices, the Victor Comptometer 3900. A visitor to the company could start at one end of the plant and watch raw, molten silicon formed into ingots and sliced into wafers, then walk to the other end of the building and see the final product, calculators, coming off the assembly line.

For these companies, each phase of technical growth posed new problems of hiring and training skilled people, managing cash flow and inventory, learning to market and sell new things, and building equipment and facilities both here in the Valley and in other parts of the world. Fairchild was the first Valley company to build production facilities in Japan, and National Semiconductor was first in Scotland. In the 1960s, competition for talented people resulted in a broad distribution of stock or stock options to almost all employees. Options provided a means to attract people from the larger, established firms while keeping salary costs low. Sharing the wealth was a natural evolution of the egalitarian culture. It's little wonder that the management of these companies felt capable of addressing most, if not all, their needs on their own.

Most young company founders at the time were well-educated and skilled engineers accustomed to solving problems for themselves. Many had moved from the East Coast and gained their knowledge at places like MIT, Bell Labs, Texas Instruments, and General Electric. Leaving the more conservative environment of the East Coast, they moved west, much like the early pioneers who moved away from traditional family and business ties. On their own, the entrepreneurs developed an attitude of independence and self-confidence. As the technology evolved and businesses grew, they met each new challenge with the conviction that it could be addressed like any other engineering problem. Confidence, personal drive, or dynamic leadership often overcame all obstacles.

On the Silicon Frontier, new friendships were formed around shared experiences. When, in its own pioneering tradition, Fairchild began creating its own spin-offs, strong personal relationships endured. Lasting friendships engendered spontaneous collaborations and job-search networks. Gifted engineers moved from one exciting job to the next, finding new product-development opportunities and different management styles (and new stock options) with each move. As workers moved from job to job, a colleague from one firm might become a competitor, a customer, or even a boss at another. Friends traded the wisdom they had gained through experience. Because the Valley was small and most people worked in the semiconductor industry or at electronics businesses, it was easy to pick up the phone or meet at a bar and get advice from a friend. Early in the Valley's development, it was well understood that competitiveness should not get in the way of the concentration of technology expertise benefiting all.

Until the early 1990s, technology marketing was seen as sales. Technology firms marketed their products to engineers and corporate buyers. The founders of Valley firms always met with customers because all sales were business-to-business or business-to-government activity. There was no mystery to this type of sales and marketing. Engineers with no formal management training found themselves meeting with customers and making presentations to distributors, sales organizations, bankers, lawyers, and military brass. This was their MBA in management—figuring out business practices as they went along. Business skills were "invented" as needed. Of all the entrepreneurs I have met over the years, from Dave Packard and Bob Noyce to Scott McNealy and Steve Jobs, I have never met one that did not exude confidence in his business skills and abilities.

TECHNOLOGY DRIVES CHANGE

In this atmosphere of self-reliance, consulting firms from outside the region didn't understand the Valley as well as firms within the Valley understood themselves. Not surprisingly, then, the first consulting services to gain a foothold here came from within the Valley. Until the late 1980s, most of the Valley's companies were small technology-oriented businesses developing and marketing their products to other technical firms. Small consulting firms emerged to address the needs of these start-ups. Some of these consulting firms became part of the network, acquiring business by reference from venture capitalists, accounting and law firms, and members of the highly mobile workforce. Many of these consulting firms' principals became owners of equity in their client companies, receiving options or equity for services or investing in their clients' firms. Because these small consulting firms were close to the start-ups and the active venture network, their counsel was more pragmatic, more creative, and more focused on building alliances than the advice of the bigger firms would have been.

That kind of advice was better suited to the Silicon Valley of the 1980s, however, than to the booming region of the 1990s. In recent years Silicon Valley has grown to thousands of companies, and dozens of multibillion-dollar companies have emerged as well. As these companies grew, they found they needed an array of services and expertise often not available in the local firms. Larger firms can afford to outsource various activities to consultants because they have developed internal organizations that can support and interface with a larger set of outsiders. Their boards of directors are more willing than those of entrepreneurial companies to reach outside the company for expertise and assistance when major problems arise. These large companies have attracted big consulting firms to the area over the past decade, and by now virtually all of the large national and international professional service firms have opened offices in Northern California.

For most of Silicon Valley's new companies, speed is essential. The market simply doesn't allow for the old "trial and error" management of the past. Skills, resources, and knowledge are needed to get products to market faster than a potential competitor, and whoever can help is enlisted. Objectives, goals, financial perspective, competitive positioning, organizational concerns, alliance building—all must be integrated into a firm's strategy. Professional consulting firms can be essential in helping to provide the expertise that will give new companies a competitive edge.

Furthermore, companies today cannot hope to succeed without integrating information technology and the world wide web into their strategic planning. The microprocessor, personal computer, and web have inspired a revolution in how businesses design products and services, how they interact with markets and customers, and how they organize, communicate, and compete. With the burgeoning growth of the personal computer and Internet, dozens of companies have developed into multibillion-dollar enterprises, selling to other businesses as well as consumers. Systems integrators, or consultants who specialize in computer and network applications, have long been asked to address IT solutions and solve technical problems. But in recent years IT and telecommunications have become strategic tools, essential for adaptation, speed, cost management, innovation, growth, and competitiveness. Every company, big or small, must understand the value of these tools in order to succeed.

The world wide web and information technology have had a major impact on the consulting industry, as well as on the businesses it serves. Consulting firms must thoroughly understand the role of IT and communications strategies in order to help their clients address present and future markets. Thus, many consulting firms have become more pragmatic by developing or merging to offer implementation capabilities. Many firms have also added people with technology expertise and experience so they can address not only general business issues, but industry issues as well. I call it "in vitro consulting." To bring in the top talent, consulting firms compete with their clients for the best people. They therefore have to offer competitive employment packages.

The demand for people and the rapid growth of the e-business market and available capital have radically changed the business model of consulting firms. An October 1999 *Upside* article by Susan Fisher summarizes the dramatic changes in professional consulting brought about by the Internet. Fisher writes:

The U.S. Internet consulting services market, including business strategy consulting, is expected to bring in $710 million this year, according to Framingham, Mass.–based research firm International Data Corp. (IDC). The market will swell to $4.38 billion in 2003, IDC projects. The stakes are actually much higher, though, considering that many firms use strategy consulting as the front door into the multibillion-dollar market for designing Web sites, developing applications and tying the new technology into legacy systems.

The race is on to fill a yawning marketplace gap with consultants who can provide "technically enlightened strategy," says analyst Stan Lepeak of Meta Group Inc., Stamford, Conn. "The people who understand the Web are in the boutiques. But they don't have enough vertical industry experience to provide real strategy," Lepeak says. "The people who provide high-end strategy don't understand the technology well enough yet."

Knowing that the corporate world will give much more than a penny for their thoughts on how to leverage the Web, an assortment of companies with varying backgrounds and expertise are charging into the e-business advice arena. They're filling gaps in their skills and knowledge by reorganizing their firms, making acquisitions, arranging partnerships and attracting talent.

The result is a complex, competitive market divided by business heritage and approach. On one front, there's rivalry between the newer Web-focused firms—the so-called boutiques—and the older, traditional business consultants and system integrators. On another, there's competition between the firms that deliver only business advice and others that view strategy consulting as one component of a broader set of offerings, including implementation.

CONSULTING THE SILICON VALLEY WAY

Despite the new pressures on businesses and the growing expertise of consulting firms, a strong "do-it-yourself" bias remains in the Valley. By and large, traditional Silicon Valley executives still do not like consultants. Perhaps that is an overstatement. Some consultants have integrated their activities into the network of assets available to entrepreneurs. But those who have are not necessarily classified as professional consultants. Nonetheless, they offer perhaps even more value than those who profess expertise in the science of management do.

One example is Larry Sonsini, a partner in the law firm of Wilson Sonsini Goodrich & Rosati. Larry has come to be identified with high-tech start-ups, IPOs, and advice to the venture capital community. Few in this community think of Larry as a lawyer. He is sought out for his business acumen as much as, if not more than, for his legal advice. He has achieved this status by reaching beyond his legal knowledge, assisting with industry issues, and providing services to start-ups in exchange for equity, thereby taking risks along with investors. He is a member of the board of directors of numerous successful high-tech companies. Through his experience of helping to launch so many new and eventually successful companies, he has gained unique insights about what it takes to succeed. More important, Larry has a sense that he is a part of a vital community that must be sustained. If it is sustained, we all win. One might argue that Larry is not a consultant, but I would say he is just the type of consultant that has helped Silicon Valley to achieve its success. His expertise displaces the professional consultant's advice, and it is free, dispensed to those who are his clients or within his network. Larry's business card may read "Attorney at Law," but his role as business advisor comes first. This model is duplicated many times throughout the Valley. Venture capitalists, university professors, retired executives, attorneys, accountants, communications professionals, and others with distinctive experience and skills provide guidance, network access, and advice. Certainly some do it for money, but most do it for equity and the value of the relationship.

Sandy Kurtzig, founder of ASK Computer, once remarked to me that she saw no need to hire a consulting firm. "If I need business advice, I call my friend Larry Sonsini. If I need technology or operations help, I call Andy Grove [then President of Intel], and if I need marketing advice, I call you." Over the years Silicon Valley industries have diversified, but many of the same people have stayed involved. Fairchild veterans watched as the semiconductor, electronic instruments, and aerospace industries were joined by companies making every type of computer, as well as biomedical firms, genetic engineering companies, materials manufacturers, and software developers and publishers. The list of successful executives who became venture capitalists is long. Former Hewlett-Packard executive Tom Perkins; former vice president of marketing and sales at Fairchild and National, Don Valentine; former Intel executives Bill Davidow and John Doerr; former Stanford Research Institute president Bill Miller; and former Spectra Physics president Sam Colella are among the many who advise the new entrepreneurs. These are but a few of the hundreds of individuals—some of whom are active venture capitalists—who advise new and established businesses in Silicon Valley. Their years of experience are invaluable, particularly to new companies. They can spot likely winners or diagnose problems, help connect companies across industries, recommend and create alliances, identify new management prospects, raise money—in effect, become experienced members of the management team. Every successful entrepreneurial company in Silicon Valley owes its success to a network of such "advisors" who are investors–service providers, friends, or friends of friends. Stanford Professor Bill Miller (former CEO of Stanford Research Institute), for example, has been investing in and advising young companies in the Valley for 30 years. Miller says, "I give away my advice in order to stay in the deal flow."

Today Silicon Valley encompasses more than 25,000 companies and perhaps 50 or more different industries. It has moved well beyond its original geographic boundaries (fifteen years ago, I wrote that Silicon Valley had become "a state of mind"). As the number of firms increases and the borders expand, the insider network culture of shared ideas and support remains critical for regional growth. Free advice is still given all the time in the Valley. The practice is deeply embedded in the infrastructure of Silicon Valley's network. The best advice doesn't come from outside the network—it flows from a culture born of the free exchange of ideas, mutual support, and networking. Consulting services in Silicon Valley have a growth market at their fingertips. But their enduring success will depend on understanding and participating in the Valley's legacy of free advice.

Afterword: Sustaining the Edge

CHONG-MOON LEE, WILLIAM F. MILLER,

MARGUERITE GONG HANCOCK,

AND HENRY S. ROWEN

Players in the Valley and interested observers worldwide face a set of pressing questions: How long will Silicon Valley's leading role last? Will its habitat prove flexible enough to promote innovation and entrepreneurship into the next generation of leading technologies? Will the performance of its firms be undermined by too much wealth generated in too a short time? Will other regions forge ahead, as Silicon Valley did relative to Route 128 in the 1990s? These questions about the region's long-term health can be thought of in terms of internal and external challenges—and opportunities.

Internal challenges and opportunities. As illustrated in this book, Silicon Valley's success has led to an increasing concentration of networks of people and firms. This concentration has been critical to the Valley's rise, but it may also be affecting its long-term viability. The region today is experiencing population overload, growing traffic congestion, and skyrocketing property prices—all consequences of growth and success. The cost of this congestion is more than the time spent in traffic jams. For a community in which face-to-face interactions are essential to its functioning, anything that impedes such meetings is damaging. And although existing owners benefit, stratospheric home prices have made recruiting from outside the region markedly more difficult. And they cause many, especially lower-skilled workers, to have to move beyond the edges of the Valley and spend enormous amounts of time commuting.

Some business activities are also being crowded out of the region. As the Valley becomes home to more firms' headquarters, and to more market strategists and designers of technology and business models, manufacturing is increasingly being done elsewhere, often under contract. Some observers question the viability of this split structure, arguing that design should not be remote from manufacturing because there are too many interactions between the two activities. The market will be the test of this proposition, and so far its judgment is that physical separation is viable.

Other challenges arise from the ever-increasing wealth to be attained in the Valley. An example is the increasingly common practice of creating companies with the intention of selling them to larger ones. This amounts to creating a firm just to do product development. In itself, there is nothing wrong with this model; the value created is paid for by the acquiring firms. But this is a different kind of entrepreneurship from that involved in building firms. If we accept the view that large firms tend to lose their vitality over time, it is important for the long-term health of the Valley that there be many small firms striving to become large ones.

The Valley's success has also raised disturbing questions about social equity. Some very large fortunes have been created here and many thousands of workers have become millionaires. A significant portion of the Valley's population lags behind, however, facing the well-known "digital divide." A good deal of local philanthropic attention is focused on improving primary and secondary public schools, many of which, as in most of America, lag behind. This poor performance implies a loss in human capital and reinforces a class-ridden social structure that most Americans intensely dislike. Furthermore, it is unhealthy for a society that lives on the quality of its people. The resources, and especially the entrepreneurial skills, that are here might be able make a considerable dent in this and other social problems.

In response to these challenges, community organizations such as Joint Venture: Silicon Valley have stepped forward to offer a collaborative team of industry, government, and community leaders for fact finding, policy initiatives, and community activities. One Joint Venture initiative, Smart Valley, fulfilled its mandate to "create a 21st century electronic community" by wiring elementary schools to the Internet, providing guidelines for best practices in telecommuting, and prototyping on-line building permit applications to local governments. In addition, private philanthropy has risen dramatically, fueling, for example, a sixfold increase in the number of charitable funds established and a ninefold increase in dollar donations to the Silicon Valley Community Foundation between 1993 and 1999. In the social sphere, as in Silicon Valley's business environment, entrepreneurial collaborations among people and firms may be the strongest tool for meeting the region's internal challenges.

External challenges and opportunities. A second set of challenges—and opportunities—comes from outside the Valley. A striking feature of the world today is the rapid spread of entrepreneurship, Silicon Valley style. New centers are emerging within the United States, but even more striking is increased activity outside the United States. Many governments around the world have noticed that their countries are behind in the great industrial revolution surrounding the Internet and are trying to make up for lost time. Dramatic changes inspired by American institutions (often specifically those of Silicon Valley) are taking place in popular attitudes, business practices, and government policies. Japan, for example, in the last three years has made sweeping changes in laws and regulations concerning securities, venture capital, bankruptcy, and university-business connections, all designed to remove obstacles to entrepreneurship. Similar changes, and debates about changes, are under way in Korea, India, France, and Germany, among other countries.

This is not to suggest that the Silicon Valley model is a case of one size fits all. Each region draws from its own history and builds on different strengths. We can see a divergence in the successful strategies of Hsinchu, Taiwan, Israel, and Bangalore, India, for building a viable high-tech region. The successes of these regions seem likely to reinforce their specific strengths. Not only are new regions emerging, but linkages among them are growing, and this will have profound implications for the world information technology industry, for other sectors in which technologies are advancing rapidly (such as biotechnology), and for these countries' economies.

What does this prospect imply for Silicon Valley? That there will be losers as well as winners among firms hardly needs to be said, but the main question concerns the net impact. Our view is that this is a positive sum game, and that many opportunities will be created because of complementarities between the Silicon Valley system and those of other regions. As long as this region retains its strengths, firms and regions from around the world will find it essential to multiply their networks of connections with the Valley.

We close by returning to a theme from Craig Johnson's chapter (Chapter 16), where he draws an analogy between the Internet revolution and the explosion of new life forms in the Cambrian geological era. He writes that most of those life forms were eliminated through competition in the following ten million years; Johnson expects the Internet explosion to be played out in the next ten to fifteen years, followed by a return to more incremental business evolution.

Whether that provocative forecast is right—or whether new technologies bring another explosive era of change—it promises to be an exciting era for Silicon Valley as it enters the twenty-first century. And our answer to the question of whether the Valley can sustain its spectacular record of successful leadership in the tumultuous Internet era and beyond is yes. Despite very real challenges, Silicon Valley will be able to adapt to—and perhaps, yet again lead—the next wave of technology. As demonstrated in this book, the habitat here is robust and flexible, an enduring source of strength that gives the Valley its leading edge.

NOTES

1. The explicit focus of this book is on Silicon Valley's information technology industries. However, the Valley is also a major biotechnology center. As one measure, at the end of 1998 the market capitalization of Silicon Valley's biotech firms was the largest in the U.S. The University of California at San Francisco has been the source of at least 46 biotech companies (*New York Times*).

2. William F. Miller, one of the co-editors, has used the "habitat" terminology and framework for many years. See "The Habitat for Entreneurship," Silicon Valley Networks Project Discussion Paper, Asia/Pacific Research Center, Stanford University, forthcoming. Others have also contributed to this concept of Silicon Valley as an "ecosystem"; see, for example, Bahrami and Evans 2000.

3. Although the focus of this book is on start-ups, we do not intend to diminish the importance of Valley start-ups that have grown into large, established firms. Not only do they innovate, but they also thrive on a symbiotic relationship with start-ups, spinning out small ventures as well as "spinning in" new firms. Cisco is a leading example: it has bought about 50 firms since 1993, thereby strategically adding technology and talent in what a company insider dubbed, "A&D," Acquisition and Development.

4. Biotechnology clusters are subject to somewhat different influences. Their firms are more closely linked to star scientists, who are usually found in great universities. Secrets and patents also play a larger role than in the IT industry (Zucker, Darby, and Armstrong 1998; Zucker, Darby, and Brewer 1997), so there is less circulation of ideas. The Bay Area not only has two major biology research universities (Stanford and UCSF), it has venture capital and legal establishments that specialize in this sector.

5. Ronald Gilson discusses the importance of a distinctive California rule for covenants not to compete for facilitating the Valley's labor mobility in "Why Silicon Valley? California's Peculiar Legal Infrastructure," Silicon Valley Networks Project Discussion Paper, Asia/Pacific Research Center, Stanford University, forthcoming.

6. Important partners with Stanford and Berkeley, the region's other educational institutions, including San Jose State University, Santa Clara University, Foothill College, and De Anza College provide the largest source of engineers, businesspeople, and technicians.

7. We thank James Lavin for contributions on key properties of the Valley's labor market. See Lavin's "Recruit, Retrain, Reward, Retain, Relocate: Silicon Valley's High Tech Labor Mar-

ket," Silicon Valley Networks Project Discussion Paper, Asia/Pacific Research Center, Stanford University, forthcoming.

8. For a view that the coaching function of VCs has been exaggerated, see Zider 1998.

CHAPTER 2, BROWN AND DUGUID

1. The hybrid character of localization may be true of more than industrial organization. See Duguid and Silva Lopes 1999.

2. Formal components of benchmarking can also involve selling your competitors the very tools you use yourself to stay ahead. Hewlett-Packard, for instance, created an important market by selling its high-quality testing tools, although these inevitably gave its competitors the means to improve their products.

3. Networks of practice are similar to the "occupational communities" discussed by van Maanen and Barley (1984). Part of our point in changing the terminology is to direct attention from the "community" aspect of such groups to the centrality of practice in these networks.

4. Constant also shows how such associations can stop the flow of knowledge. Professional antibodies, like corporate antibodies, may emerge when new ideas threaten.

5. We are grateful to Martin Kenney for this point.

6. In the rapidly changing world of modern, high-tech innovation, building a structure for creative abrasion may be much more of a challenge than unleashing the spontaneity of creative destruction, yet the former tends to get far less attention.

7. "The whole idea of a firm with definite boundaries cannot be maintained intact," Kenneth Arrow (1983, 147) noted, while contemplating flows of knowledge and information.

CHAPTER 6, LEE

1. Dan Gillmor, "Andy Grove Chairman, Intel Corp," *San Jose Mercury News*, January 22, 2000.

2. Presentation in Strategy and Entrepreneurship in Information Technology Program, Stanford Graduate School of Business, September 1999.

3. Author's personal notes, September 1999.

4. Kathleen Eisenhardt et al., "Exploiting Uncertainty: High Performers Change the Dynamics of Competition," Andersen Consulting and Stanford University, 1997.

5. Intraspect Software press release, January 28, 1998.

6. "Turn On, Type In and Drop Out," 1997, 51–52.

7. Don Listwin, Presentation at the Asia Pacific IT Summit, Stanford University, November 1999.

8. Scott Thurm, "Joining the Fold: Under the Cisco System Mergers Usually Work; That Defies the Odds," *Wall Street Journal*, March 1, 2000, 1, 12.

9. S. Tessler, A. Barr, and A. Morgan, unpublished interview notes, August 1999.

10. Thurm, "Joining the Fold," 1.

11. Kirkpatrick 1997.

CHAPTER 8, LÉCUYER

1. For heroic accounts of Robert Noyce, see Wolfe 1983, 346–373, and Malone 1985, 73–113.

2. Gordon Moore, interview by Ross Bassett and author, February 18, 1997; Jean Hoerni, interview by author, February 4, 1996; Sheldon Roberts, interview by author, July 6, 1996; Jay Last, interview by author, April 1, 1996.

3. Eugene Kleiner, interview by author, May 21, 1996; Julius Blank, interview by author, June 20, 1996; Victor Grinich, interview by author, February 7, 1996.

4. Roberts, interview by author, July 6, 1996.

5. Moore, interview by Allen Chen, July 9, 1992, Intel Museum.

6. In the mesa process, two layers of dopants were diffused beneath the surface of a silicon slice or wafer. A patch of wax was then applied to the top of the wafer. The final step was to etch away some of the upper surface, except under the patch. This left a small platform, or "mesa," over a wider bottom layer—hence the structure's name.

7. Hoerni, interview by author, February 4, 1996.

8. Noyce, interview by Herb Kleiman, November 18, 1965, Herb Kleiman collection, M827, Stanford Archives and Special Collections; Hoerni, interview by author, February 4, 1996; Roberts, interview by author, July 6, 1996.

9. Grinich, interview by author, February 7, 1996; Hoerni, interview by author, February 4, 1996; Moore, interview by Allen Chen, July 9, 1992, Intel Museum.

10. William Shockley, notebook, entry for June 5, 1957, box B4, William Shockley Papers, SC222 95-153, Stanford Archives and Special Collections.

11. Kleiner to Hayden, Stone & Company, June 14, 1957, courtesy of Jay Last.

12. Kleiner, interview by author, May 21, 1996; Hayden, Stone & Company, "Fairchild Camera and Instrument Corporation," (New York: Hayden, Stone & Co., 1958), 3, courtesy of Jay Last; Anthony Perkins, interview with Arthur Rock, *The Red Herring* (March 1994), 54–59.

13. Last to parents, July 7, 1957, courtesy of Jay Last; Last, interview by author, April 1, 1996; Roberts, interview by author, July 6, 1996.

14. Noyce, interview by Herb Kleiman, November 18, 1965, Herb Kleiman collection, M827, Stanford Archives and Special Collections; Wilson 1985, 31–34; Perkins, interview with Rock, 54; Hayden, Stone & Company, "Fairchild Camera and Instrument," February 1958.

15. Fairchild Camera and Instrument, "Prospectus," January 25, 1960, courtesy of Eugene Kleiner; Fairchild Camera and Instrument, "Annual Report," 1957, collection of the author; Richard Hodgson, interview by Rob Walker, September 19, 1995, Silicon Genesis, M471, Stanford Archives and Special Collections.

16. Fairchild Camera and Instrument, "Annual Report," 1957; Nelson Stone, interview by author, April 21, 1995; Hodgson, interview by Rob Walker, September 19, 1995, Silicon Genesis, M471, Stanford Archives and Special Collections.

17. "Contract Among the California Group, Parkhurst (Hayden Stone), Fairchild Controls, and Fairchild Camera and Instrument," September 23, 1957, box B4, William Shockley Papers, SC222 95-153, Stanford Archives and Special Collections.

18. "New Palo Alto Company Plans to Produce Transistors," *Palo Alto Daily Times*, October 17, 1957, collection of the author; Grinich, interview by author, February 7, 1996; Thomas

Bay, interview by author, July 2, 1996. For the military's interest in silicon, see Misa 1985, 254–87.

19. Noyce, interview by Herb Kleiman, November 18, 1965, Herb Kleiman collection, M827, Stanford Archives and Special Collections.

20. Hester 1961, 18–19; Kleiner, interview by author, May 21 and June 5, 1996; Bay, interview by author, July 2, 1996.

21. "Meeting Review: Eat Later," *IRE Grid*, May 1960, 32–33; "Fairchild Devices in B-70 Bomber," *Leadwire*, December 1960, 3, courtesy of Jay Last; Bay, interview by author, July 2, 1996; Grinich, interview by author, April 23, 1996.

22. Last, "Meeting Reports, etc., 10/57–3/59," entries for January 2, February 7, February 24, and March 30, 1958; Bay, interview by author, July 2, 1996.

23. Last, "Meeting Reports, etc., 10/57–3/59," entries for January 2, February 3, February 10, February 17, and March 2, 1958; "Fairchild Devices in B-70 Bomber," *Leadwire*, December 1960, 3, courtesy of Jay Last.

24. Moore 1998, 53–62; Last, interview by author, April 1, 1996.

25. Kleiner, interview by author, May 21, 1996; Last, interview by author, April 1, 1996; Moore, interview by Allen Chen, January 6, 1993, Intel Museum.

26. Moore and Noyce, "Method for Fabricating Transistors," U.S. Patent 3,108,359, filed June 30, 1959, granted October 29, 1963; Moore 1998, 56; Moore, interview by Bassett and author, February 18, 1997.

27. Fairchild Semiconductor, "Fairchild Silicon Transistors," 1958, courtesy of Sheldon Roberts; Last, "Meeting Reports, etc., 10/57–3/59," entry for January 2, 1958, courtesy of Jay Last.

28. Moore, interview by Bassett and author, February 18, 1997; Kleiner, interview by author, May 21 and June 5, 1996, and June 16, 1998.

29. Last to Vic Jones, September 20, 1957, courtesy of Jay Last; Kleiner, interview by author, May 21 and June 5, 1996, and June 16, 1998.

30. Kleiner, interview by author, May 21, 1996.

31. Last, "Meetings Reports, etc., 10/57–3/59," entry for August 25, 1958, courtesy of Jay Last.

32. Bay, interview by author, July 2, 1996; oral communication from Bay, March 16, 1999; Bay, interview by George Rotsky, circa 1988, George Rotsky collection, M851, Archives and Special Collections, Stanford University; oral communication from Hodgson, October 10, 1998.

33. An overwhelming share of Fairchild's sales in 1958 and 1959 were in the military sector: 92 percent of the firm's sales in the summer of 1958 were renegotiable, a percentage that grew to 99 percent between September 1958 and August 1959. For data on Fairchild's sales, see Fairchild Camera and Instrument, "Prospectus," January 25, 1960, courtesy of Eugene Kleiner.

34. Moore 1998, 57; Jay Farley, "Reliability Assurance at Fairchild Semiconductor Corporation," November 11, 1959, in Fairchild Semiconductor, "Product Catalog," 1962, courtesy of Jay Last; Hoerni, interview by author, February 4, 1996; oral communication from Jay Last, June 1, 1998.

35. Roberts, interview by author, July 6, 1996; Last, "Meeting Reports, etc.," entry for May 7, 1958, courtesy of Jay Last; Atalla et al. 1959, 749–783.

36. Hoerni, interview by author, February 4, 1996; Hoerni, "Semiconductor Device," U.S. Patent 3,064,167, filed May 1, 1959, granted November 13, 1962; Hoerni, "Method of Manufacturing Semiconductor Devices," U.S. Patent 3,025,589, filed May 1, 1959, granted March 20, 1962.

37. Hoerni, interview by author, February 4, 1996.

38. Ibid.

39. Ibid.; Grinich, interview by author, February 7 and April 23, 1996; oral communication from Last, February 24 and 25, 1999.

40. Oral communication from Moore, June 2, 1998.

41. Harry Sello, interview by Rob Walker, April 8, 1995, Silicon Genesis, M741, Stanford Archives and Special Collections; Hester 1961, 18–19; L. N. Duryea, "Fairchild Investigation," May 28, 1959, box B4, William Shockley Papers, SC 222 95-153, folder "Fairchild Info 3 July 1959," Stanford Archives and Special Collections.

42. Hoerni, interview by author, February 4, 1996; Progress Reports, Physics Section, February 1, 1960; March 1, 1960, box 5, folder 1; April 1, 1960, box 5, folder 1; October 1, 1960, box 5, folder 3, all in Fairchild Semiconductor Papers, 88-095, Stanford Archives and Special Collections; Hoerni, "Planar Silicon Transistors and Diodes," paper presented at the 1960 Electron Devices Meeting, Washington, D.C., October 1960, Bruce Deal Papers, 88-033, Stanford Archives and Special Collections.

43. Noyce, interview, no date, Intel Museum. For a discussion of reliability concerns in the development of the integrated circuit, see Kleinman 1966.

44. Noyce, interview, no date, Intel Museum; Grinich, interview by author, May 14, 1996.

45. The integrated circuit was invented independently by Jack Kilby of Texas Instruments. Noyce, "Semiconductor Device-and-Lead Structure," U.S. Patent 2,981,877, filed July 30, 1959; Reid 1984, 76–78; Wolff 1976, 45–53; Moore 1998, 59–60.

46. Last, interview by author, April 1, 1996; Progress Reports, Micrologic Section, August 1, 1960, box 5, folder 3; October 1, 1960, box 5, folder 4; December 1, 1960, box 5, folder 7, all in Fairchild Semiconductor Papers, 88-095, Stanford Archives and Special Collections; Progress Reports, Device Development Section, May 1, 1961, box 6, folder 4; June 1, 1961, box 6, folder 5, in Fairchild Semiconductor Papers, 88-095, Stanford Archives and Special Collections.

47. H. S. Scheffler, "The Minuteman High Reliability Component Parts Program: History and Legacy," Rockwell International Report C81-451/201, July 31, 1981, National Air and Space Museum.

48. Ibid.

49. Kleiner, interview by author, June 5, 1996.

50. "Autonetics Contracts: Now Total 8 Million," *Leadwire*, December 1960, courtesy of Jay Last.

51. "Minuteman Avionics Reliability Increases," *Aviation Week*, December 12, 1960, 99–103 and 105; "FSC Signs Two Autonetics Contracts; Will Receive $1,511,210 for Reliability Program," *Leadwire*, June 1960, courtesy of Jay Last.

52. Bay, interview by author, July 2, 1996.

53. Bay, interview by author, March 18, 1997.

54. *Leadwire*, October 1959–May 1960, courtesy of Jay Last.

55. R. Painter et al., "Across-Board Competency New Transistor Field Need," *Electronic News*, July 25, 1960, 1 and 4, and "Transistor Entry Tightens," August 1, 1960, 1 and 4.

56. Kleiner, interview by author, May 21 and June 5, 1996; Roberts, interview by author, July 6, 1996; Hoerni, interview by author, February 4, 1996; Perkins, interview with Rock, 54–59.

57. Don Hoefler, "Silicon Valley, USA," *Electronics News*, January 11, 1970, 1, 4–5; Last, interview by author, April 1, 1996; Roberts, interview by author, July 6, 1996; Hoerni, interview by author, February 4, 1996.

58. Moore, interview by Bassett and author, February 18, 1997.

CHAPTER 9, ROWEN

1. This chapter draws heavily on the work of Professor Timothy Bresnahan of Stanford University and his co-authors. At this writing, Professor Bresnahan is on leave as chief economist of the Anti-Trust Division of the Justice Department. He bears no responsibility for this interpretation of his work.

2. As Assistant Director of the Bureau of the Budget, the organization responsible for overseeing all federal government spending activities, in the mid-1960s, I observed close up the independence of congressional committees and the consequent limits to having a coherent, top-down program for science and technology. I concluded that this fragmentation is a major strength of the American system.

3. A fourth role, often prominent in other countries, is relatively unimportant in the United States. It is protection against foreign competitors and promotion of exports. However, an example of the former in the United States is government preference for American supercomputers over Japanese ones. An example of the latter is pressure on the Japanese government to give U.S. semiconductor makers a given share of the Japanese market. Neither policy loomed large in the overall computer market.

4. Ronald J. Gilson remarks, "Silicon Valley's Idiosyncratic Legal Infrastructure," at Silicon Valley: Center of Innovation Conference, Stanford University, June 3, 1999.

5. The electric dynamo and its applications entailed striking lags. Michael Faraday invented the electric motor in 1821 and the dynamo in 1831. For several decades its main application was the electric telegraph (which itself required further inventions for long-distance use). Still more decades passed before inventions needed for practical dynamos for lighting, heating, and electric motors came. By 1889 only 3 percent of U.S. homes had electric lighting, and electric motors in manufacturing amounted to only 5 percent of factory mechanical drives. Three decades later, the market penetration of the latter had only reached about 50 percent. The changes required in the design of factories were profound and required contributions of many kinds of specialists (David 1990).

CHAPTER 10, GIBBONS

A large number of people have provided me with a great deal of assistance in developing and refining this paper. That group includes particularly: Bill Hewlett, for suggesting the topic and giving generously of his time in discussing its development; Charles Krenz, for collecting the initial data on Stanford start-ups and for his assistance in analyzing it; Tom Mitchell, for updating that data and analysis; and several people who contributed significantly to the process of reducing many disparate conversations and points of view to a limited number of central ideas and themes. Those people include: Gordon Moore, Bert Sutherland, Larry Thielen, Bill Edwards, Pitch Johnson, John Linvill, and Don Valentine. A number of other people provided important insights but wished to remain anonymous for a variety of reasons.

I am indebted in a different way to Fred Terman, for providing important opportunities and contacts in Silicon Valley during my early years on the Stanford faculty. The spirit of innovation and interaction that he fostered is responsible in a general way for much of the contribution that the university has made to Silicon Valley.

The Stanford Alumni Association gave me the opportunity to present this material in many venues over a period of more than a decade. Invitations to speak at professional and community meetings followed, based on the interest that people around the world have in the general subject of what makes Silicon Valley work. The questions that were asked by a large variety of people attending those talks highlighted many points that were unclear or poorly presented, and led to significant improvements in the development. I am thus indebted to scores of people whom I do not know and can therefore only acknowledge in a general way. The paper is much better than it would have been without their gently constructive criticism, though I have surely not made as many modifications and corrections as might be desirable.

Finally I want to thank Harry Rowen and Bill Miller for encouraging me to turn an "after dinner" talk into a chapter of this book without attempting to change it into a properly researched paper. I hope that the general limitations of the work will not detract too much from the insights that I have received from highly regarded practitioners in the art of entrepreneurship.

1. In the computing industry alone, the number of new companies has increased from 7 in 1959 to 87 in 1975 to 294 in 1990, for a compound annual growth rate of 13% (Saxenian 1994).

2. Personal communication.

3. Some of the data for this chapter was collected and analyzed by Charles H. Krenz as a project in the Stanford Graduate School of Business in 1988.

4. Personal communication.

5. See, for example, http://www.garage.com or www.svangels.com.

6. We define a professional venture capitalist as a managing partner in a firm that has raised its investment resources from a set of limited partners who are not personally involved in making the investment decisions.

7. Personal communication.

8. Gordon Moore, personal communication.

9. Personal communication.

10. William Spencer, personal communication.

11. Douglas Jackson, personal communication.

CHAPTER 11, CASTILLA ET AL.

1. For a detailed historical account, as well as a comprehensive inventory of current knowledge, see Wasserman and Faust 1994.

2. MAGE was developed as a device to be used in molecular modeling. It produces three-dimensional illustrations that are presented as interactive computer displays. Transformations of these displays are immediate. Images can be rotated in real time, parts of displays can be turned on or off, points or nodes can be identified by picking them, and changes between different arrangements of objects can be animated. For more information on MAGE, see Freeman, Webster, and Kirke 1998, or visit http://www.faseb.org/protein/kinemages/kinpage.html to learn about and download the MAGE program. One of the difficulties of presenting network diagrams in printed form is that the dynamic capabilities of the program generating the pictures cannot be displayed; only static cross-sections can be presented.

3. For their indispensable help in developing methods and compiling data to construct this visualization, we are grateful to Dimitris Assimakopoulos (Hull University Business School, United Kingdom) and Sean Everton (Stanford University).

4. There are 372 people (or nodes) and more than 1,500 lines, out of a possible 69,006 ($[n \times (n-1)]/2$). Each person in the network is connected to four others, on average.

5. Centrality can be measured in several ways, each of which is associated with a different substantive interpretation. A person's "degree centrality" is simply the number of other people to whom the given person is tied. Degree is typically used as a measure of an actor's involvement in a network (Freeman 1979). In this sense, a person tied to two other people is said to be twice as involved as a person with only one link. In contrast, "betweenness centrality" is usually interpreted as a measure of an actor's power. A person gains power over any two other actors when she lies on the shortest path between the two in a given network of relations. In a network of N actors, an actor obtains the highest possible "betweenness" score when all $N-1$ other actors are tied only to that person. In this case the focal person would lie on all the shortest paths in the network and would be called a "star." The relative betweenness of a point is a ratio that measures the extent to which a point in a network approaches the betweenness score of a star (Freeman 1979). A person's relative betweenness can vary from a minimum of 0, when it lies on no shortest paths, to a maximum of 1, when the person is in fact a star. We calculated the degree and the relative betweenness of each person on the semiconductor industry genealogy chart.

6. A separate analysis with the companies as nodes, connected if they shared a founder, indicates that Fairchild Semiconductor and Amelco (founded in 1961 by Hoerni, Kleiner, Last, and Roberts) were the most central companies in the semiconductor network. Full results of the network analysis using the program UCINET 5 are available upon request.

7. At the present time, the Honors Cooperative Program has been integrated into the regular engineering curriculum.

8. Faculty interview.

9. Personal interview.

10. See Paul Hirsch's 1972 discussion of the importance of "boundary spanning units" or "contact men" in locating talents and marketing new products for organizations in cultural industries. We argue here that members of research centers and programs who have worked both in industry and at universities broker and facilitate the interaction between the university and industry to the benefit of both.

11. There are some omissions, such as Tom Flowers, Bud Moose, and Ray Lyon, who started early SBICs and were leaders of the old Western Association of Small Business Investment Companies (WASBIC). These people were not included since they primarily did real estate deals. WASBIC was the predecessor of today's Western Association of Venture Capital (WAVC). The information is current from 1958 up to December 1983, to the best of Asset Management Company's knowledge. West Coast offices of venture firms based elsewhere are not included as West Coast firms unless they joined the Western Association of Venture Capital (WAVC). Only those individuals whose principal occupation has been venture capital are coded in the genealogy chart, together with some investment bankers who were included when direct venture capital investment was a significant part of their business. We have done additional research to verify and complete some of the information contained in the chart whenever possible. In addition, we have sought to identify other firms and connections.

12. Our findings are tentative; data collection and analysis are still in progress.

13. This is out of the possible 8,256 lines ([n × (n-1)]/2).

14. Figure 11.2 represents people rather than firms. But the comparable network graph for semiconductor firms, although not as densely connected as that for people, is quite different from Figure 11.4, and does not break down into clear components.

15. This is out of the possible 60,378 ties ([n × (n-1)]/2).

16. Among the central actors who followed this pattern are David G. Arscott, who started Arscott, Norton & Associates in 1978 and worked for the previous ten years in Citicorp Venture Capital Ltd.; Dean C. Campbell, who also worked for Citicorp Venture for a year early in the 1980s and then for Institutional Venture Partners; Walter Baumgartner, who worked for Bank of America Capital Corporation from 1975 to 1979, and in 1979 moved to Capital Management Services, Inc; and Lawrence G. Mohn Jr., who worked for Bank of America Capital Corporation from 1975 to 1980 and left to work for Hambrecht & Quist. Kirkwood Bowman, the venture capitalist with the highest degree centrality in the whole network (connected to 32 people in the industry—five times the average nodal degree) also worked for Bank of America Capital Corporation from 1975 to 1979, then worked for WestVen until 1981, when he started working for Hambrecht & Quist.

Fuller results of the network analysis are available upon request. Our cautionary note in the section above on the semiconductor industry genealogy analysis, on the different meanings of centrality in networks with differently defined ties, also applies here.

17. Because this study is only illustrative, we have left in the data for California firms not located in Silicon Valley. Our preliminary analysis suggests that confining ourselves to Silicon Valley firms would not significantly change the results.

18. An interesting complementary analysis would be to study the network of industrial firms that are related by virtue of having had the same law firms, accounting firms, and investment underwriters on their IPOs. Such firms are tied to one another in the sense that they talk to the same partners in other institutional sectors, and thus might be expected to receive simi-

lar or related advice, information, and perhaps personnel flow into the firms or their boards of directors. One interesting issue would be to see whether such linked firms were more likely to pursue similar strategies than pairs of firms not linked. For a related argument, that board overlaps lead to similar anti-takeover strategies, see Davis 1991.

19. Full results of the network analysis are available upon request.

CHAPTER 12, SAXENIAN

1. For an account of the postwar growth of the Silicon Valley economy, see Saxenian 1994. For more data on immigrants in Silicon Valley, see Saxenian 1999.

2. Interview, Lester Lee, July 1, 1997.

3. Ironically, many distinctive features of the Silicon Valley business model were created during the 1960s and 1970s by engineers who saw themselves as outsiders to the mainstream business establishment centered on the East Coast. The origins of the region's original industry associations like the American Electronics Association were an attempt to create a presence in a corporate world that Silicon Valley's emerging producers felt excluded from. In the early days, these organizations provided role models and support for entrepreneurship similar to those now being provided within immigrant communities. See Saxenian 1994.

4. This list includes only professional associations whose focus is technology industry. It does not include the numerous Chinese and Indian political, social, and cultural organizations in the region; nor does it include ethnic business or trade associations for nontechnology industries.

5. This parallels Granovetter's (1995b) notion of balancing coupling and decoupling in the case of overseas Chinese entrepreneurs.

6. The following discussion is based on interviews with K. Y. Han and Jimmy Lee.

7. In 1996, 82 companies in the Hsinchu Science Park (or 40 percent of the total) were started by returnees from the United States, primarily from Silicon Valley, and there were some 2,563 returnees working in the park alone. Many other returnees work in PC businesses located closer to Taipei.

8. Institute for Information Industry, Market Intelligence Center (III-MIC), Taipei, 1997.

9. Interview, Ken Hao, April 15, 1997. See also Miller 1997.

10. Interview, Ken Tai, May 16, 1997.

11. Interview, Radha Basu, October 1, 1997.

12. Similarly, when Texas Instruments set up the first earth station in Bangalore, it entailed a long-winded process that included breaking or removing 25 government regulations.

PART III, INTRODUCTION

1. Calculations based on data from *San Jose Business Journal Book of Lists,* 1989 and 1999.

2. The geographic scope of the region shown here includes all of Santa Clara County and extends into adjacent zip codes in Alameda, San Mateo, and Santa Cruz counties. This is consistent with Joint Venture: Silicon Valley's 2000 Index (see Joint Venture: Silicon Valley 2000,

36, for full details). Technology companies listed include top firms by either annual revenues or market capitalization value. Service providers in other categories are compiled using a combination of criteria, including number of employees and annual value and number of venture deals. Special thanks to Sheila Rowen for graphics assistance and to Sumit Bhansali for research assistance.

CHAPTER 13, HELLMANN

I would like to thank Laura Comay and Henry Rowen for many helpful comments. Special thanks go to Anne Devine, especially for saving me from my initial idea to compare venture capitalists to nannies. Financial support from the Stanford Center for Entrepreneurial Studies is gratefully acknowledged. All errors are mine.

1. Not all venture capitalists play an equally active role in supporting their companies, and some of the venture capitalists that have a close relationship with the firms they finance may do more harm than good. Nonetheless, the distinct feature of venture capital overall is that investors do play a much larger role than just providing financial capital.

2. Note also that not all start-up companies are financed by venture capital. Indeed, most start-ups are probably first financed by a combination of family and friends and so-called "angel" investors, who are wealthy individuals investing their own money. Although there are no reliable estimates on the amount of money invested by angel investors, it is believed that the amount they invest is at least twice as large as the amount invested by venture capitalists, and possibly even five to ten times as large. See also Benjamin and Sandles (1998).

3. This is particularly important when considering European data. The European Venture Capital Association (EVCA) estimated a total of 14.5 billion ECU (approximately $13.5 billion) in investments in 1998, but the EVCA definition of venture capital is much broader than the U.S. definition.

4. The data in this section come mainly from reports by Venture Economics and Venture One, firms that track data on the venture capital industry. For a more detailed overview of the venture capital industry, see Fenn, Liang, and Prowse (1995).

5. Although there is some variation in the structure of deals that venture capitalists strike with entrepreneurs, the overall framework of start-up financing is remarkably similar across different companies. There are many legal details to these contracts, so rather than focusing on that, I will focus on the essential economic elements that drive the legal structure.

6. A closer look at venture capital contracts reveals that venture capitalists rarely hold straight equity, but typically hold equity that has some preferential status, such as convertible preferred equity. The main differences are that these instruments allow venture capitalists to hold a disproportionately large fraction of voting rights, and it gives the venture capitalist some additional protection in case of bad performance.

7. The one issue where there obviously can never be perfect alignment is the pricing of equity, that is, the division of surplus between the entrepreneur and the venture capitalists. Compared to public stock, there are relatively few objective methods of valuing venture capital stock. This is not surprising, given that venture capitalists invest in situations that are inherently un-

certain, where there is little relevant historic data, and where the ultimate value of the company depends on unproven (indeed unprovable) assumptions and expectations. Nonetheless, valuations follow an economic logic. With the recent rise of venture capital, for example, the demand for investments increased dramatically, and as a consequence company valuations also rose significantly.

8. The basic equity contract obviously exposes the founders directly to the risk of their own company. The contract with the venture capitalists may often include additional benchmarks. Moreover, incentives are provided not only for the founders, but also for many of the newly hired executives and employees. Indeed, the generous offering of stock and stock options has become a trademark feature of Silicon Valley financing. Although stock options are sometimes portrayed as a cheap way for companies to attract and motivate good employees, this is obviously not literally true, since the value of these stock options can be very large. The point of these stock options is that they are a form of deferred compensation, and they tie the pay to the performance of the firm, thus providing particularly good incentives.

9. Data are for 1997 and express the percentage share of capital commitments to independent private funds.

10. Finally, the government also plays a role in financing venture capital funds. Several local and state governments have experimented with setting up venture capital funds. The most significant program, however, is a federal program administered by the Small Business Administration (SBA), called the Small Business Investment Corporation (SBIC) program. Many of the early venture capital funds in the 1960s and 1970s participated in the SBIC program, which offered matching funds at favorable terms. When the venture capital market took off during the 1980s, the SBIC program became increasingly less important. This was because of the regulatory restrictions associated with SBICs, because of some shortcomings in the structure of the program, and because of the uncertainty about the SBA, which the Reagan administration wanted to get rid of. By the late 1990s many of the obvious flaws of the SBIC program had been fixed, and the demand for the program improved slightly.

11. Note also that the first major initiative of the European Venture Capital Association was to promote the creation of a new pan-European stock market. These efforts led to the creation of the EASDAQ, which essentially imitates the NASDAQ. In the United States the NASDAQ, rather than the New York Stock Exchange, is believed to have been instrumental to the development of the U.S. venture capital industry. The reason is that the NASDAQ made it easier for young, growth-oriented companies that may have a great economic future, but no profits and an unimpressive balance sheet, to be listed.

12. One of the notable features of Silicon Valley is that established corporations themselves have come to rely on the supply of acquisition candidates for their own strategy. Consider the example of Symantec, a leading software house for the PC (see Blackburn et al. 1996). Few of the products sold by Symantec were actually developed by Symantec itself. Instead the company developed methodologies and business practices to assimilate entrepreneurial start-ups. Symantec therefore relied much less on internal research to come up with new technologies and products, and instead focused on developing marketing expertise in helping new products to achieve deeper market penetration. The point to note about Symantec's strategy is thus that it heavily relied on external entrepreneurs and venture capitalists to bring to it the next generation of

products. Another well-known example of a company that relied heavily on this is Cisco, which grew in large part because of its many strategic acquisitions of start-ups.

13. Indeed, one of the noticeable findings in the Symantec case study is that the founders did not stay very long after the acquisition, precisely because they had lost their role as leaders of an independent company.

14. The SBIC program became somewhat discredited because of evidence of some fraudulent behavior in the late 1970s. It is unclear how widespread this fraudulent behavior ever was. More importantly, fraud appears to have been a problem only during a very limited period of the program's history.

15. Nor are these two regions the only ones to have venture capital. Especially in the late 1990s a number of other locations emerged as centers of venture capital activity, such as the Seattle area, the Washington, D.C. area, and the area around Austin, Texas (see "Venture Capitalists" 1997).

16. Venture capitalists have additional ways of involving their successful executives in their business. One way is through "entrepreneur in residence" programs, in which the venture capital firm provides office space and a modest salary for a few selected executives, involving them informally in their activities while the executives get some "sabbatical" time to think about their next career move.

17. See also Kawasaki (1999) and Zider (1998) for a critical discussion of these issues.

CHAPTER 17, FRIEL

1. Mackun n.d. The irony of Hewlett-Packard, which should not be lost on any Valley veteran, was that the company in 1999 for the first time went outside to recruit a CEO, bringing in a product of the establishment, who since her arrival has been exhorting her colleagues to "go back to the garage."

CHAPTER 18, ATWELL

The author gratefully acknowledges the editorial contributions in this article of Janice K. Mandel, writer/interviewer.

REFERENCES

Alexander, Kobi. 2000. Quoted in the *Financial Times*, Jan. 10.

Angel, David. 2000. "High-Technology Agglomeration and the Labor Market: The Case of Silicon Valley." In *Understanding Silicon Valley: The Anatomy of an Entrepreneurial Region*, ed. Martin Kenney. Stanford, Calif.: Stanford University Press.

Arrow, Kenneth J. 1983. *Information and Economic Behavior*. In *Collected Papers*, K. Arrow, 136–52. Cambridge, Mass.: Harvard University Press.

Asher, Norman, and Leland Strom. 1977. *The Role of the Department of Defense in the Development of Integrated Circuits*. Washington: Institute for Defense Analysis.

Asian Americans for Community Involvement (AACI). 1993. *Qualified, But . . . A Report on Glass Ceiling Issues Facing Asian Americans in Silicon Valley*. San Jose, Calif.: Asian Americans for Community Involvement.

Atalla, M., E. Tannenbaum, and E. Scheibner. 1959. "Stabilization of Silicon Surfaces by Thermally Grown Oxides." *Bell System Technical Journal* 38:749–83.

Autler, Gerald. 1999. "Global Networks in High Technology: The Silicon Valley–Israel Connection." Master's thesis, Department of City and Regional Planning, University of California at Berkeley.

Bahrami, Homa, and Stuart Evans. 2000. "Flexible Recycling and High Technology Entrepreneurship." In *Understanding Silicon Valley: The Anatomy of an Entrepreneurial Region*, ed. Martin Kenney. Stanford, Calif.: Stanford University Press.

Bardhan, Ashok Deo, and David K. Howe. 1998. "Transnational Social Networks and Globalization: The Geography of California's Exports." Berkeley, Calif.: Fisher Center for Real Estate and Urban Economics, University of California at Berkeley, Working Paper No. 98-262, Feb.

Benjamin, G., and E. Sandles. 1998. "Angel Investors: Culling the Waters for Private Equity." *Journal of Private Equity* 1, no. 3 (spring): 41–59.

Black, Bernard S., and Ronald J. Gilson. 1997. "Venture Capital and the Structure of Capital Markets: Banks Versus Stock Markets." *Journal of Financial Economics* 47:243–77.

Blackburn, J., T. Hellmann, S. Kozinski, and M. Murphy. 1996. "Symantec Corporation: Acquiring Entrepreneurial Companies." Case Study S-SM-27, Stanford University Graduate School of Business.

Bresnahan, Timothy F. 1999. "Computing." In *U.S. Industry in 2000: Studies in Comparative Performance*, ed. D. C. Mowery. Washington, D.C.: National Academy Press.

Bresnahan, Timothy F., and Shane Greenstein. 1997. "Technical Progress in Computing and in Uses of Computers." *Brookings Papers on Economic Activity: Microeconomics.* Washington, D.C.: The Brookings Institution.

Bresnahan, Timothy F., and Manuel Trajtenberg. 1995. "General Purpose Technologies: 'Engines of Growth.'" *Journal of Econometrics* 65:83, 108.

Bridges, James. 1957. "Progress in Reliability of Military Electronics Equipment during 1956." *IRE Transactions for Reliability and Quality Control* 11:1–7.

Brown, John Seely, and Paul Duguid. 1991. "Organizational Learning and Communities of Practice: Towards a Unified View of Working, Learning, and Innovation." *Organization Science* 2, no. 1:40–58.

———. 2000. *The Social Life of Information.* Boston, Mass.: Harvard Business School Press.

Bygrave, W., and J. Timmons. 1992. *Venture Capital at the Crossroads.* Cambridge, Mass: Harvard Business School Press.

Cairncross, Frances. 1997. *The Death of Distance: How the Communications Revolution Will Change Our Lives.* Boston, Mass.: Harvard Business School Press.

Callon, Scott. 1995. *Divided Sun: MITI and the Breakdown of Japanese High Tech Industrial Policy, 1975–1993.* Stanford, Calif.: Stanford University Press.

Castells, Manuel. 1996. *The Rise of the Network Society.* Oxford: Blackwell.

———. 1997. *The Power of Identity.* Boston, Mass.: Blackwell Publishers.

Castells, Manuel, and Peter Hall. 1994. *Technopoles of the World: The Making of Twenty-First-Century Industrial Complexes.* London: Routledge.

Ceruzzi, Paul. 1989. *Beyond the Limits: Flight Enters the Computer Age.* Cambridge, Mass.: MIT Press.

———. 1998. *A History of Modern Computing.* Cambridge, Mass.: MIT Press.

Chang, Shirley L. 1992. "Causes of Brain Drain and Solutions: The Taiwan Experience." *Studies in Comparative International Development* 27, no. 1 (spring): 27–43.

Christensen, Clayton M. 1997. *The Innovator's Dilemma: When New Technologies Cause Great Firms to Fail.* Boston, Mass.: Harvard Business School Press.

Clark, Jim. 1999. *Netscape Time.* New York: St. Martin's Press.

Cohen, Stephen S., and Gary Fields. 1999. "Social Capital and Capital Gains in Silicon Valley." *California Management Review* 41, no. 2:108–30.

Collaborative Economics. 1999. *Innovative Regions: The Importance of Place and Networks in the Innovative Economy.* Pittsburgh, Penn.: The Heinz Endowments.

Constant, Edward W. 1987. "The Social Locus of Technological Practice: Community, System, or Organization." In *The Social Construction of Technological Systems: New Directions in the Sociology and History of Technology,* eds. W. Bijker, T. Hughes, and T. Pinch, 223–42. Cambridge, Mass: MIT Press.

———. 1989. "Science in Society: Petroleum Engineers and the Oil Fraternity in Texas, 1925–1965." *Social Studies of Science* 19:439–72.

David, Paul A., 1990. "The Dynamo and the Computer: An Historical Perspective on the Modern Productivity Paradox." *American Economic Review: Papers and Proceedings,* May.

Davis, Gerald. 1991. "Agents without Principles? The Spread of the Poison Pill through the Intercorporate Network." *Administrative Science Quarterly* 36:583–613.

Degrasse, Robert. 1987. "The Military and Semiconductors." In *The Militarization of High Technology,* ed. John Tirman, 77–104. Cambridge, Mass.: Ballinger Publishing Co.

DeVol, Ross C. 1999. *America's High-Tech Economy.* Santa Monica, Calif.: Milken Institute.

Downes, Larry, and Chunka Mui. 1998. *Unleashing the Killer Ap: Digital Strategies for Market Dominance.* Cambridge, Mass.: Harvard Business School Press.

Duguid, Paul, and Teresa da Silva Lopes. 1999. "Ambiguous Company: Institutions and Organizations in the Port Wine Trade, 1814–1834." *Scandinavian Economic History Review* (special issue on Institutional Theory and Business History, eds. Mary Rose and Sverre Knutson) 47, no. 1:83–102.

Economist. 1999. "Know Thyself." Oct. 30–Nov. 5, 76.

Evans, Peter B. 1995. *Embedded Autonomy: States and Industrial Transformation.* Princeton: Princeton University Press.

Fenn, G., N. Liang, and S. Prowse. 1995. "The Economics of Private Equity Markets." Staff Study #168, Board of Governors of the Federal Reserve System.

Fernandez, Roberto, Emilio J. Castilla, and Paul Moore. 2000. "Social Capital at Work: Networks and Employment in a Phone Center." *American Journal of Sociology* 105 (Mar.): 1288–1356.

Fernandez, Roberto, and Nancy Weinberg. 1997. "Sifting and Sorting: Personal Contacts and Hiring in a Retail Bank." *American Sociological Review* 62:883–902.

Financial Times. 1999. Dec. 12.

Fishbein, Samuel. 1995. *Flight Management Systems: The Evolution of Avionics and Navigation Technology.* Westport, Conn.: Praeger.

Fisher, Susan E. 1999. "E-business Strategy Boom." *Upside* 11, no. 1 (Oct.): 52–56.

Florida, Richard L., and Martin Kenney. 1987. "Venture Capital and High-Technology Entrepreneurship." *Journal of Business Venturing* 3:301–19.

Fortune, Jan. 10, 2000.

Freeman, John. 1990. "Ecological Analysis of Semiconductor Firm Mortality." In *Organizational Evolution: New Directions,* ed. J. V. Singh. Thousand Oaks, Calif.: Sage Publications.

Freeman, Linton C. 1979. "Centrality in Social Networks: Conceptual Clarification." *Social Networks* 1:215–39.

Freeman, Linton C., Cynthia M. Webster, and Deirdre M. Kirke. 1998. "Exploring Social Structure Using Dynamic Three-Dimensional Color Images." *Social Networks* 20:108–18.

Funding a Revolution: Government Support for Computing Research. 1999. Washington, D.C.: National Academy Press.

Galanter, Marc, and Thomas Palay. 1991. *Tournament of Lawyers: The Transformation of the Big Law Firm.* Chicago: University of Chicago Press.

Garnsey, Elizabeth, and Helen Lawton Smith. 1998. "Proximity and Complexity in the Emergence of High Technology Industry: The Oxbridge Comparison." *Geoforum* 29, no. 4:433–50.

Gilder, George. 1989. *Microcosm.* New York: Basic Books.

Gilson, Ronald J. 1996. "The Fading Boundaries of the Firm: Comment." *Journal of Institutional and Theoretical Economics* 152:80–84.

Golding, Anthony. 1971. "The Semiconductor Industry in Britain and the United States: A Case Study in Innovation, Growth, and the Diffusion of Technology." D. Phil. thesis, University of Sussex.

Gompers, Paul A., and Josh Lerner. 1998. "What Drives Venture Capital Fundraising?" *Brookings Papers on Economic Activity: Microeconomics*, 149–92. Washington, D.C.: The Brookings Institution.

Gonzales-Benito, Javier, Stuart Reid, and Elizabeth Garnsey. 1997. "The Cambridge Phenomenon Comes of Age." Research Papers in Management Studies, WP 22/97. Cambridge: Judge Institute of Management Studies.

Granovetter, Mark. 1973. "The Strength of Weak Ties." *American Journal of Sociology* 78:1360–80.

———. 1985. "Economic Action and Social Structure: The Problem of Embeddedness." *American Journal of Sociology* 91:481–510.

———. 1995a. "Coase Revisited: Business Groups in the Modern Economy." *Industrial and Corporate Change* 4:93–131.

———. 1995b. "The Economic Sociology of Firms and Entrepreneurs." In *The Economic Sociology of Immigration: Essays on Networks, Ethnicity and Entrepreneurship*, ed. Alejandro Portes. New York: Russell Sage.

Granovetter, Mark, and Patrick McGuire. 1998. "The Making of an Industry: Electricity in the United States." In *The Law of Markets*, ed. Michel Callon, 147–73. Oxford: Blackwell.

Grove, Andrew S. 1996. *Only the Paranoid Survive*. New York: Currency/Doubleday.

Han, Shin-Kap. 1994. "Mimetic Isomorphism and Its Effect on the Audit Services Market." *Social Forces* 73:637–63.

Hannan, Michael T., and John Freeman. 1977. "The Population Ecology of Organizations." *American Journal of Sociology* 82:929–64.

———. 1984. "Structural Inertia and Organizational Change." *American Sociological Review* 49:149–64.

Harmon, Steve. 1999. *Zero Gravity: Riding Venture Capital from High-Tech Start-Up to Breakout IPO*. Princeton: Bloomberg Press.

Hayek, Freidrich. 1945. "The Use of Knowledge in Society." *American Economic Review* 35 (Sept.): 519–30.

Hellmann, T. 1997. "Venture Capital: A Challenge for Commercial Banks." *Journal of Private Equity*, fall: 49–55.

Hellmann, T., L. Lindsey, and M. Puri. 1999. "The Role of Banks in Venture Capital: Empirical Evidence." Mimeo, Stanford University Graduate School of Business.

Hellmann, T., S. Milius, and G. Risk. 1995. "Apple Computer—Strategic Investment Group." Case Study S-SM-21, Stanford University Graduate School of Business.

Hellmann, T., and M. Puri. 1999. "Venture Capital and the Professionalization of Start-Up Companies: Empirical Evidence." Mimeo, Stanford University Graduate School of Business.

Hennart, Jean-Francois. 1993. "Explaining the Swollen Middle: Why Most Transactions Are a Mix of 'Market' and 'Hierarchy.'" *Organization Science* 4, no. 4:529–47.

Herrigel, Gary. 1996. *Industrial Constructions: The Sources of German Industrial Power*. Cambridge: Cambridge University Press.

Hester, William. 1961. "Dr. E. M. Baldwin." *Solid State Journal* Mar.: 18–19.

Hirsch, Paul M. 1972. "Processing Fads and Fashions: An Organization-Set Analysis of Cultural Industry Systems." *American Journal of Sociology* 77:639–59.

Hoefler, Don C. 1971. "Silicon Valley, USA." *Electronic News*, Jan. 11.

Holbrook, Daniel. 1995. "Government Support of the Semiconductor Industry: Diverse Approaches and Information Flows." *Business and Economic History* 24:133–65.

"How to Make $400,000,000 in Just One Minute." 1996. *Fortune* May 27.

Jager, Rama Dev, and Rafael Ortiz. 1997. *In the Company of Giants*. New York: McGraw Hill.

Johnson, Jean M. 1998. *Statistical Profiles of Foreign Doctoral Recipients in Science and Engineering: Plans to Stay in the United States*. Arlington, Va.: National Science Foundation, Division of Science Resources Studies, NSF 99-304, Nov.

Joint Venture: Silicon Valley Network. 1995. "Joint Venture Way."

———. 1998a. "1998 Index of Silicon Valley."

———. 1998b. "Silicon Valley 2010."

———. 1999a. "Internet Cluster Analysis."

———. 1999b. "Workforce Study: Analysis of the Workforce Gap in Silicon Valley."

———. 2000. "2000 Index of Silicon Valley."

Kaplan, David. 1999. *The Silicon Boys and Their Valley of Dreams*. New York: William Morrow and Co.

Kawasaki, G. 1999. "Let the Hard Times Roll! Why Too Much Capital Can Kill You." *Journal of Private Equity* 2, no. 4 (summer): 70–71.

Kenney, Martin, ed. 2000. *Understanding Silicon Valley: Anatomy of an Entrepreneurial Region*. Stanford, Calif.: Stanford University Press.

Kenney, Martin, and Richard Florida. 2000. "Venture Capital in Silicon Valley: Fueling New Firm Formation." In *Understanding Silicon Valley: The Anatomy of an Entrepreneurial Region*, ed. Martin Kenney. Stanford, Calif: Stanford University Press.

Kenney, Martin, and Urs von Burg. 1999. "Technology and Path Dependence: The Divergence Between Silicon Valley and Route 120." *Industrial and Corporate Change* 8, no. 1:67–103.

———. 2000. "Institutions and Economies: Creating Silicon Valley." In *Understanding Silicon Valley: The Anatomy of an Entrepreneurial Region*, ed. Martin Kenney. Stanford, Calif.: Stanford University Press.

Kirkpatrick, David. 1997. "Meanwhile, Back at Headquarters . . ." *Fortune* 136, no. 7 (Oct. 13).

Kleinman, Herbert. 1966. "The Integrated Circuit: A Case Study of Production Innovations in the Electronics Industry." Ph.D. diss., George Washington University.

Kogut, Bruce, Gordon Walker, and Dong-Jae Kim. 1995. "Cooperation and Entry Induction as an Extension of Technology Rivalry." *Research Policy* 24:77–95.

Krugman, Paul. 1995. *Development, Geography and Economic Theory*. Ohlin Lectures, vol. 6. Cambridge, Mass.: MIT Press.

———. 1996. "What's New about the New Economic Geography?" *Oxford Review of Economic Policy* 14, no. 2.

LaPlante, Alice. 1997. "The Man Behind Cisco." *Electronic Business* (Dec.).

Larson, Andrea. 1992. "Network Dyads in Entrepreneurial Settings: A Study of the Governance of Exchange Processes." *Administrative Science Quarterly* 37:76–104.

Lave, Jean, and Etienne Wenger. 1991. *Situated Learning: Legitimate Peripheral Participation.* New York: Cambridge University Press.

Lazerson, Mark, and Gianni Lorenzoni. 1999. "The Firms That Feed Industrial Districts: A Return to the Italian Source." *Industrial and Corporate Change* 8, no. 2:235–66.

Leonard-Barton, Dorothy. 1995. *Wellsprings of Knowledge: Building and Sustaining the Sources of Innovation.* Cambridge, Mass.: Harvard Business School Press.

Leone, Anthony, Jose Vamos, Robert Keeley, and William F. Miller. *A Survey of Technology Based Companies Founded by Members of the Stanford University Community.* Office of Technology Licensing, Stanford University.

Lester, Richard. 1998. *The Productive Edge: How U.S. Industries Are Pointing the Way to a New Era of Economic Growth.* New York: Norton.

Levin, Richard. 1982. "The Semiconductor Industry." In *Government and Technical Progress: A Cross Industry Analysis*, ed. Richard Nelson, 9–100. New York: Pergamon Press.

Lewis, Michael. 2000. *The New New Thing.* New York: W. W. Norton and Co.

Light, Ivan, and Edna Bonacich. 1988. *Immigrant Entrepreneurs: Koreans in Los Angeles, 1965–1982.* Berkeley, Calif.: University of California Press.

Locke, Richard M. 1995. *Remaking the Italian Economy.* Ithaca, NY: Cornell University Press.

Lynn, Leonard H., N. Mohan Reddy, and John D. Aram. 1996. "Linking Technology and Institutions: The Innovation Community Framework." *Research Policy* 25:91–106.

McGahan, A. 1996. "Passion for Learning." Case Study 9-796-057, Harvard Business School.

McKendrick, David, Richard F. Doner, and Stephan Haggard. 2000. *From Silicon Valley to Singapore: Location and Competitive Advantage in the Hard Disk Drive Industry.* Stanford, Calif.: Stanford University Press.

Mackun, Paul. n.d. "Silicon Valley and Route 128: Two Faces of the American Technopolis." Available at Internet Valley, www.internetvalley.com/archives/mirrors/sv%26128.html.

McNally, J. O., G. H. Metson, E. A. Veazie, and M. F. Holmes. 1957. "Electron Tubes for the Transatlantic Cable System." *The Bell System Technical Journal* 36:163–88.

McPherson, J. Miller, and James Ranger-Moore. 1991. "Evolution on a Dancing Landscape: Organizations and Networks in Dynamic Blau Space." *Social Forces* 70:19–42.

Malone, Michael. 1985. *The Big Score: The Billion Dollar Story of Silicon Valley.* New York: Doubleday.

———. 1995. *The Microprocessor: A Biography.* Santa Clara, Calif.: Springer-Verlag.

Marshall, Alfred. 1890. *Principles of Economics.* London: MacMillan and Co.

———. 1916. *Principles of Economics: An Introductory Volume.* 7th ed. London: MacMillan and Co.

Meyerson, Debra, Karl E. Weick, and Roderick M. Kramer. 1996. "Swift Trust and Temporary Groups." In *Trust in Organizations: Frontiers of Theory and Research*, eds. R. Kramer and T. Tyler, 166–95. Thousand Oaks, Calif.: Sage Publications.

Miller, Matt. 1997. "Venture Forth." *Far Eastern Economic Review*, Nov. 6, 62–63.

Mintz, Beth, and Michael Schwartz. 1985. *The Power Structure of American Business.* Chicago: University of Chicago Press.

Misa, Thomas. 1985. "Military Needs, Commercial Realities, and the Development of the Transistor, 1948–1958." In *Military Enterprise and Technological Change: Perspectives on the American Experience,* ed. Merritt Roe Smith, 253–87. Cambridge, Mass.: MIT Press.

Mokyr, Joel. 1990. *The Lever of Riches.* Oxford: Oxford University Press.

Moore, Gordon. 1998. "The Role of Fairchild in Silicon Technology in the Early Days of Silicon Valley." *Proceedings of the IEEE* 86, no. 1:53.

Mounier-Kuhn, Pierre E. 1994. "Product Policies in Two French Computer Firms: SEA and Bull (1948–64)." In *Information Acumen: The Understanding and Use of Knowledge in Modern Business,* ed. Lisa Bud-Frierman, 113–35. London: Routledge.

Mowery, David C., and Nathan Rosenberg. 1993. "The US National Innovation System." In *National Systems of Innovation,* ed. Richard R. Nelson. New York: Oxford University Press.

Nohria, Nitin. 1992. "Information and Search in the Creation of New Business Ventures: The Case of the 128 Venture Group." In *Networks and Organizations: Structure, Form, and Action,* eds. N. Nohria and R. Eccles, 240–61. Boston: Harvard Business School Press.

Orr, Julian. 1996. *Talking About Machines: An Ethnography of a Modern Job.* Ithaca, N.Y.: IRL Press.

Piore, Michael J., and Charles E. Sabel. 1984. *The Second Industrial Divide: Possibility for Prosperity.* New York: Basic Books.

Podolny, Joel M. 1993. "A Status-based Model of Market Competition." *American Journal of Sociology* 98:829–72.

Podolny, Joel M., and Karen L. Page. 1998. "Network Forms of Organization." *Annual Review of Sociology* 24:57–76.

"Politics and Silicon Valley." 1999. *The Economist,* Oct. 30.

Porter, Michael. 1990. *The Competitive Advantage of Nations.* New York: The Free Press.

———. 1998. "Clusters and the New Economics of Competition." *Harvard Business Review* Nov.–Dec.: 77–90.

Portes, Alejandro, ed. 1995. *The Economic Sociology of Immigration: Essays on Networks, Ethnicity and Entrepreneurship.* New York: Russell Sage.

———. 1996. "Global Villagers: The Rise of Transnational Communities." *The American Prospect,* Mar.–Apr.

Powell, Walter W. 1996. "Interorganizational Collaboration in the Biotechnology Industry." *Journal of Institutional and Theoretical Economics* 152:197–216.

Powell, Walter W., and Peter Brantley. 1992. "Competitive Cooperation in Biotechnology: Learning throughout Networks?" In *Networks and Organizations: Structure, Form, and Action,* eds. N. Nohria and R. Eccles, 366–94. Boston: Harvard Business School Press.

Powell, Walter W., Kenneth W. Koput, and Laurel Smith-Doerr. 1996. "Interorganizational Collaboration and the Locus of Innovation: Networks of Learning in Biotechnology." *Administrative Science Quarterly* 41:116–45.

Powell, Walter, and Laurel Smith-Doerr. 1994. "Networks and Economic Life." In *The*

Handbook of Economic Sociology, eds. Neil J. Smelser and Richard Swedberg. Princeton: Princeton University Press.

Putnam, Robert D. 1993. *Making Democracy Work: Civic Traditions in Modern Italy*. Princeton, N.J.: Princeton University Press.

Reed, George. 1986. "U.S. Defense Policy, U.S. Air Force Doctrine and Strategic Nuclear Weapon Systems, 1958–1964: The Case of the Minuteman ICBM." Ph.D. diss., Duke University.

Reid, T. R. 1984. *The Chip: How Two American Companies Invented the Microchip and Launched a Revolution*. New York: Simon and Schuster.

Reinhardt, Andy. 1999. "Meet Cisco's Mr. Internet." *Business Week*, Sept. 13.

Richardson, D. C., and J. S. Richardson. 1992. "The Kinemage: A Tool for Scientific Communication." *Protein Science* 1:3–9.

Riordan, Michael, and Lillian Hoddeson. 1997. *Crystal Fire: The Invention of the Transistor and the Birth of the Information Age*. New York: W. W. Norton.

Rosenberg, Nathan. 1994. *Exploring the Black Box: Technology, Economics, and History*. New York: Cambridge University Press.

Ryle, Gilbert. 1949. *The Concept of Mind*. London: Hutchinson.

Sahlman, W. 1988. "Centex Telemanagement, Inc." Case Study 9-286-059, Harvard Business School.

———. 1990. "The Structure and Governance of Venture-Capital Organizations." *Journal of Financial Economics* 27:473–521.

Saxenian, AnnaLee. 1994. *Regional Advantage: Culture and Competition in Silicon Valley and Route 128*. Cambridge, Mass.: Harvard University Press.

———. 1996. *Regional Advantage: Culture and Competition in Silicon Valley and Route 128*. 2d ed. Cambridge, Mass.: Harvard University Press.

———. 1999. *Silicon Valley's New Immigrant Entrepreneurs*. San Francisco: Public Policy Institute of California.

———. 2000. "The Origins and Dynamics of Production Networks in Silicon Valley." In *Understanding Silicon Valley: The Anatomy of an Entrepreneurial Region*, ed. Martin Kenney. Stanford, Calif.: Stanford University Press.

Schlender, Brent. 1997. "The Adventures of Scott McNealy: Javaman." *Fortune* 136, no. 7 (Oct. 13).

Schumpeter, Joseph. 1962. Capitalism, Socialism and Democracy. New York: Harper & Row.

Seidenberg, Philip. 1997. "From Germanium to Silicon: A History of Change in the Technology of Semiconductors." In *Facets: New Perspectives on the History of Semiconductors*, eds. Andrew Goldstein and William Aspray, 36–74. New Brunswick, N.J.: IEEE Press.

Sharp, Michael. 1989. "European Countries in Science-Based Competition: The Case of Biotechnology." DRC Discussion Paper #72, SPRU, University of Sussex. Quoted in Mowery and Rosenberg 1993.

Smith, W. J. 1963. "Minuteman Guidance System—Evaluation of Achieved Reliability." *Aerospace Reliability and Maintainability Conference*. New York: AIAA.

Southwick, Karen. 1999. "Java Takes Off." *Upside Today*, Aug. 23.

Spender, J-C, and Eric H. Kessler. 1995. "Managing the Uncertainties of Innovation: Extending Thompson." *Human Relations* 48, no. 1:35–57.

Stark, David. 1996. "Recombinant Property in East European Capitalism." *American Journal of Sociology* 101:993–1027.

State of California, Department of Finance. 1996. *Santa Clara County Net Migration by Race, July 1990–July 1996.*

Stinchcombe, Arthur L. 1965. "Social Structure and Organizations." In *Handbook of Organizations*, ed. James G. March. Chicago: Rand McNally.

Stranix, Richard. 1960. "Minuteman Reliability. Guide for Future Component Manufacturing!" *Electronics Industries* Dec.: 90–104.

Sturgeon, Timothy J. 1992. "The Origins of Silicon Valley: The Development of the Electronics Industry in the San Francisco Bay Area." Master's thesis, Department of Geography, University of California at Berkeley.

————. 2000. "How Silicon Valley Came to Be." In *Understanding Silicon Valley: The Anatomy of an Entrepreneurial Region*, ed. Martin Kenney. Stanford, Calif.: Stanford University Press.

Suchman, Mark C. 1994. *On Advice of Counsel: Law Firms and Venture Capital Funds as Information Intermediaries in the Structuration of Silicon Valley.* Ph.D. diss., Stanford University Department of Sociology.

Suchman, Mark C., and Mia L. Cahill. 1996. "The Hired Gun as Facilitator: Lawyers and the Suppression of Business Disputes in Silicon Valley." *Law and Social Inquiry* 21:679–712.

Summers, Lawrence H. 2000. "The Imperative of Balanced Global Economic Growth." Remarks at the Institute for International Economics, Washington, D.C., Jan. 14. U.S. Treasury Department web page.

Tajnai, Carolyn E. 1985. "Fred Terman, the Father of Silicon Valley." Stanford Computer Forum, May.

Takahashi, Dean. 1998. "Ethnic Network Helps Immigrants Succeed." Wall Street Journal Interactive Edition, http://public.wsj.com/careers/resources/documents/19980318-takahashi.htm.

Teece, David J. 1986. "Profiting from Technological Innovation: Implications for Integration, Collaboration, Licensing, and Public Policy." *Research Policy* 15:285–305.

Timmons, Jeffry A. 1994. *New Venture Creation.* 4th ed. Homewood, Ill.: Irwin McGraw Hill.

"Turn On, Type In and Drop Out." 1997. *Forbes* 160, no. 12 (Dec. 1).

van Maanen, John, and Stephen R. Barley. 1984. "Occupational Communities: Culture and Control in Organizations." In *Research in Organizational Behavior* 6, ed. Barry M. Staw and L. L. Cummings, 287–365. Greenwich, Conn.: JAI Press.

"Venture Capitalists: A Really Big Adventure." 1997. *The Economist*, Jan. 25.

Waldinger, Roger, and Mehdi Bozorgmehr, eds. 1996. *Ethnic Los Angeles.* New York: Russell Sage.

Wasserman, Stanley, and Katherine Faust. 1994. *Social Network Analysis: Methods and Applications.* New York: Cambridge University Press.

Watts, Duncan J. 1999. *Small Worlds: The Dynamics of Networks between Order and Randomness.* Princeton: Princeton University Press.

Wenger, Etienne. 1998. *Communities of Practice.* New York: Cambridge University Press.

Wilson, John W. 1985. *The New Venturers: Inside the High-Stakes World of Venture Capital.* Menlo Park, Calif.: Addison-Wesley.

Wolfe, Tom. 1983. "The Tinkerings of Robert Noyce: How the Sun Rose on the Silicon Valley." *Esquire Magazine* (Dec.): 346–74.

Wolff, Michael. 1976. "The Genesis of the Integrated Circuit." *IEEE Spectrum* 13:45–53.

Wuerth, J. M. 1976. "The Evolution of Minuteman Guidance and Control." *Navigation: Journal of the Institute of Navigation* 23, no. 1 (spring): 64–75.

Zider, Robert. 1998. "How Venture Capital Works." *Harvard Business Review* Nov.–Dec: 131–39.

Zucker, Lynne G., Michael R. Darby, and Jeff Armstrong. 1998. "Geographically Localized Knowledge: Spillovers or Markets?" *Economic Inquiry* XXXVI (Jan.).

Zucker, Lynne G., Michael R. Darby, and Marilynn B. Brewer. 1997. "Intellectual Human Capital and the Birth of U.S. Biotechnology Enterprises." *American Economic Review* (June).

INDEX